SYMPATHETIC INK

LIVERPOOL ENGLISH TEXTS AND STUDIES, 47

For all my family, for Cassilda, and for all her family

SYMPATHETIC INK
INTERTEXTUAL RELATIONS IN NORTHERN IRISH POETRY

SHANE ALCOBIA-MURPHY

LIVERPOOL UNIVERSITY PRESS

First published 2006 by
Liverpool University Press
4 Cambridge Street
Liverpool L69 7ZU

Copyright © 2006 Shane Alcobia-Murphy

The right of Shane Alcobia-Murphy to be identified as the author
of this work has been asserted by him in accordance with the Copyright,
Design and Patents Act 1988.

British Library Cataloguing-in-Publication data
A British Library CIP record is available

ISBN 1-84631-032-6
ISBN-13 978-1-84631-032-4

Typeset by
Frances Hackeson Freelance Publishing Services, Brinscall, Lancs
Printed in Great Britain
by Biddles Ltd, King's Lynn

Contents

Abbreviations

Paul Muldoon

NW: *New Weather*. London: Faber, 1973.
M: *Mules*. London: Faber, 1977.
WBL: *Why Brownlee Left*. London: Faber, 1980.
Q: *Quoof*. London: Faber, 1983.
MB: *Meeting the British*. London: Faber, 1987.
MM: *Madoc: A Mystery*. London: Faber, 1990.
SB: *Shining Brow*. London: Faber, 1993.
PQ: *The Prince of the Quotidian*. Meath: Gallery Press, 1994.
AC: *The Annals of Chile*. London: Faber, 1994.
LT: *The Last Thesaurus*. London: Faber, 1995.
SHSM: *Six Honest Serving Men*. Meath: Gallery Press, 1995.
KS: *Kerry Slides*. Meath: Gallery Press, 1996.
NSP: *New Selected Poems 1968–1994*. London: Faber, 1996.
H: *Hay*. London: Faber, 1998.

Medbh McGuckian

FM: *The Flower Master*. Oxford: Oxford University Press, 1982.
VR: *Venus and The Rain*. Oxford: Oxford University Press, 1984.
OBB: *On Ballycastle Beach*. Oxford: Oxford University Press, 1988.
MC: *Marconi's Cottage*. Meath: Gallery Press, 1991.
CL: *Captain Lavender*. Meath: Gallery Press, 1994.
RBB: *On Ballycastle Beach*. Revised edn, Meath: Gallery Press, 1995.
S: *Shelmalier*. Meath: Gallery Press, 1998.
DB: *Drawing Ballerinas*. Meath: Gallery Press, 2001.
HTL: *Had I a Thousand Lives*. Meath: Gallery Press, 2003.

Acknowledgements

Some of the chapters in this book are based on the following articles and essays that I have published during the past ten years: 'Obliquity in the Poetry of Paul Muldoon and Medbh McGuckian', *Éire-Ireland*, 31.3–4 (Winter, 1996); '"You Took Away My Biography": The Use of Quotation in the Poetry of Medbh McGuckian', *Irish University Review*, 28.1 (Summer, 1998); 'Roaming Root of Multiple Meanings': Intertextual Relations in Medbh McGuckian's Poetry', *Metre*, 5 (Winter, 1998); '"A Dove Involving A Whole Nation": Politics in the Poetry of Medbh McGuckian', *Études Irlandaises*, (Summer, 1999); 'Writing in the Shit: Authority and the Northern Irish Poet', *Canadian Journal of Irish Studies* (Winter, 1999); '"Don't Mention the War!": The Trouble(s) in Northern Irish Poetry', in Michael Hensen (ed.), *Aesthetics of Violence*, (Passau: Verlag Karl Stutz, 2001); 'A Code of Images: Northern Irish Centos', *Irish Studies Review* 10.2 (2002). My thanks go to the editors who prepared them for publication.

There are a number of people and organisations that need to be acknowledged, as without their help this book would never have come to fruition. I wish to thank John Kerrigan for having the patience of Job and the wisdom of Solomon – I have greatly benefited from his keen insights into Northern Irish literature. Thanks are also due to the Research Institute of Irish and Scottish Studies (RIISS) and the Carnegie Trust for funding several trips to the Special Collections Department at Emory University. Many scholars have given up their time either to read or to listen to sections of this book, and I thank them for all their advice: Anthony Cond, Patrick Crotty, Steve Dornan, Fidelma Farley, Andrew Gordon, Margaret Maxwell, Liam McIlvanney, Katherine Meffen, Paul Shanks, Daniel Smith, Dan Wall and George Watson.

Introduction

Every cultural narrative – be it a poem, play, painting, film, novel, or ideological manifesto – is in some sense a reinterpretation of its own history, an attempt to retell a story of the past as it relates to the present, an act of 'understanding otherwise' the motivating subworld of symbols which informs our consciousness of the world. Narrative is where the text of the imagination interweaves with the context of history.[1]

In its terrible state o'chassis, does Northern Ireland's history interweave with or overwhelm the poetic imagination? When it comes to a 'chronic sovereignty neurosis'[2] the cultural spin doctors are always ready with their diagnoses, but what about the creative writers? The dilemma involves not only the writer's perception of how *poiesis* intersects with politics, but also his or her relation to tradition(s), literary or otherwise: does he or she embrace the community with all its intimate biases or become a solitary figure, abstracted, seeking objectivity? In *Transitions*, Richard Kearney uncovers an apparent transitional crisis at the core of modern Irish cultural narratives and explores how they mediate between the images of the past and those of the future. Of particular importance are what he terms 'postmodern' narratives, those which 'borrow freely from the idioms of both modernity and tradition, one moment endorsing a deconstruction of tradition, another reinventing the stories of the past transmitted by cultural memory.'[3] There are, broadly speaking, two competing conceptions of postmodernism: one that is anti-referential, anarchic, decentred, revelling in endless simulation, resulting from the consumerisation of the image and the destructive logic of late capitalism;[4] another which is referential and self-reflexive.[5] The latter, to which Kearney subscribes, is the more constructive for writers and artists. As Hutcheon has put it, postmodernism is 'where documentary historical actuality meets formalist self-reflexivity and parody'; it is 'an exploration of the way in which narratives and images structure how we see ourselves and how we construct our notion of self, in the present and in the past.'[6]

Writing about the plight of visual artists living in Northern Ireland who have been forced 'to define their identity in terms of their behavioural reactions to an unbearable socio-political milieu', John Hutchinson rightly claims that they have adopted a 'critical postmodernism',[7] a way of both expressing and examining questions of inheritance, tradition and identity while striking a mean between an art-for-art's sake and overblown didacticism or propaganda. Rather than accept uncritically specific emblems and iconography associated with the different traditions in Northern Ireland, the artists present their enduring legacy with an oblique gaze. For example, in one of Paul Graham's photographs – 'No. 4, Shankill Road (1985)'[8] – the date '1690', painted in orange on the road surface, can be seen adjacent to a security ramp. While the ramp has been installed to impede paramilitary operations in the area, the date signifies faith in an altogether different protector, namely the spirit of seventeenth-century Protestant resilience. The photograph does not adjudicate over the merits or legitimacy of the inscription; indeed, the viewer is left to ponder the extent to which the *graffito* is intended as a transgressive defacing of the civic surface that gives voice to a personal (or communal) dissent with the manner in which the security services operate in that area. Yet Graham's text does record an instance of how the urban space is demarcated by means of a shibboleth; the visual mnemonic forms part of the identitarian discourse operating within the community, encoding a narrative of cultural expression.

Such visual quotations are of the utmost importance in Northern Irish art, offering an ironic and often oblique viewpoint on the Troubles. This type of postmodernism offers 'a perspective on the present and the past which allows an artist to speak *to* a discourse from *within* it, but without being totally recuperated by it'.[9] In 'Your Move',[10] Jack Pakenham depicts a paramilitary meeting in session, with five figures seated around a table looking at what appears to be a cross between a street map and a board game. Using a biblical reference (the Israelite markings for the Angel of Death) and nationalist iconography (a shamrock), the terrorists distinguish between those who are legitimate targets and those who are to be spared. The irony is that the viewer cannot know which is which, as the masked figures could belong to any number of proscribed organisations, Protestant or Catholic. The painting alludes to the idea that those in Ulster carry the map of religious geography in their minds almost from birth and suggests that mapping streets according to religious or political affiliation allows a mentality to develop which treats lives as counters. Hinting that this psychology is both restrictive and self-defeating, Pakenham does not allow the figures (who have all been injured by the conflict) to see the outside world: the room's only window is bricked up. Peter O'Neill's 'Rosebud',[11] a photowork employing similar iconography – a *Monopoly*™ game board upon which (toy) knives, guns and bombs are arranged – is equally ironic. Although the title calls to mind Citizen Kane's cherished childhood memory of plenitude, the streets lined with implements of war represent targets of a (fictional) IRA terrorist campaign on the so-called mainland: the English version of *Monopoly*™ is used.

The trouble with quotations or visual references is that they are open to misinterpretation. Discussing Philip Napier's 'Ballad No. 1', a wall-mounted audio-visual installation featuring an automated accordion that repeatedly plays a single note once a button is pushed, and an image of Bobby Sands, the first prisoner to die during the 1981 hunger strike in the Maze prison, Luke Gibbons surmises that the intake and expelling of air from the accordion 'allows it to double up as an artificial lung attached to the barely photogravure image of the republican hunger-striker. [...] The blown-up photogravure effect of the image is achieved through small nails, a reminder of the aura of martyrdom which surrounded Sands' death on hunger strike in 1981.'[12] Gibbons develops his critique by contending that the artist juxtaposes the emblems – accordion; nails; photographic image used for IRA propaganda in broadsheets and murals – to suggest 'a living monument for the [1845–48] Famine and the dark shadow which it cast on the lung of the body politic'.[13] However, Gibbons misreads these icons. As Daniel Jewesbury points out, the piano accordion is associated with Loyalist marching bands rather than with traditional nationalist culture, and the face of Bobby Sands is made up of accordion buttons, not nails. Therefore, as Jewesbury concludes, it is difficult to argue that Napier is colluding with familiar nationalist rhetoric that links the hunger strike either to the Great Famine or to Christian martyrology. Rather, Napier's reliance on iconography simultaneously reiterates the iconic status of Sands and questions its legacy. The single note played continuously is multivalent in meaning: while it could connote the ways in which the dying breaths of a nationalist hunger-striker were mobilised for IRA propaganda, it could equally suggest the ways in which that death had galvanized the Loyalist opposition to Sinn Féin demands. The monotonous yet frenetic playing of a single note may also suggest a laboured, one-dimensional (if potent) rhetoric, a limited and somewhat self-enclosed discourse stemming from the prison protests. And while the exhibition visitor may equally deem the noise to be full of fury, signifying nothing, the installation requires that third party to activate the otherwise dormant noise, implicating him in its continuation.

For the Northern Irish writer, intertextuality is the equivalent of the visual quotation and the same ambiguity occurs as to the artist's intent when using it: straightforward citation of exemplar, parodic rewriting or ironic critique? There are, however, differing versions of intertextuality and it is important for the purpose of this book to make clear to which version I am referring. Both Fredric Jameson and Roland Barthes, for instance, deny the author any critical (ironic) distance: intertextuality is simply the superimposition of previous texts which noisily drown out an original voice with a cacophony of other voices.[14] While it is useful to state that, due to the linguistic medium, texts are necessarily 'woven with citations, references, echoes, cultural languages … which cut across it through and through in a vast stereophany',[15] does this really mean that the concept of the 'autonomous work of art' is obsolete? Michael Riffaterre is equally reader-centred in his critical perspective, as is evident from his belief that a text is that which contains 'a paradigm for the reader's transformative praxis',[16] yet his definition of intertextuality offers more scope to the author than that of either Barthes or Jameson:

> Intertextuality is a modality of perception, the deciphering of the text by the reader in such a way that he identifies the structures to which the text owes its quality of work of art. […] The intertext proper is the corpus of texts the reader may legitimately connect with the one before his eyes, that is, the texts brought to mind by what he is reading.[17]

Riffaterre, however, incorrectly distinguishes between intertextuality and quotation: 'it would be wrong to confuse the intertext with allusion or quotation', he says, 'for the relation between these and the text is aleatory – identification depends upon the reader's culture – while the relation of text to presupposition is obligatory since to perceive these we need only linguistic competence'.[18] Such a distinction ignores the fact that what he considers to be an intertext – namely the perception of ungrammaticalities vis-à-vis the sociolect[19] – is equally dependent on the same contingencies. Linda Hutcheon notes a further crucial inaccuracy in his differentiation between influence and intertextuality. Riffaterre's concept of influence is, she says, 'a vertical relationship of text to text, a relationship of recurrence and sameness' and intertext is 'related to text laterally through simultaneity and other-ness'.[20] Metafictional parody (or ironic intertextuality), however, disrupts the neat formalist distinction between the two. A more pertinent approach to intertextuality is one that stresses the dialogic potential of quotations inserted into texts, with or without inverted commas. For the writer, quota-tion or allusion can involve more than pretentious name-dropping:

> To quote is not merely to write glosses on previous writers; it is to interrogate the chronicity of literature and philosophy, to challenge history as determining tradition and to question conventional notions of originality and difference. Consequently, to read an explicitly (or even tacitly) quoting text is not to engage in a simple play with and of sources but to recognise and establish criteria of significance.[21]

Despite the naïveté of supposing that the mere presence of a quotation signals a determined critique of tradition and genre on the author's part, Worton and Still's essay is noteworthy for its emphasis on the strategic im-port of quotation. Emphasis is duly placed on the relational aspects of intertextuality, facilitating dialogue between source and target texts and enabling the reader to participate in the construction of meaning without fully superseding the author. As Jean Weisgerber states, '[t]he use of cryptic quotations shows that literature has become a two-sided activity – the au-thor designs the jigsaw puzzle, the reader fits its pieces together. Under-standing means re-creating: the production and the enjoyment of art have been made to coincide.'[22]

Writing this monograph, there were times when I found myself stepping back from all of the historical texts, source books and dictionaries scattered on my desk and wondering exactly what kind of activity I was being asked to participate in. At the darkest moments I strongly empathised with Rüdiger Imhof's experience in the British Library:

> I was sitting in the British Library for two weeks doing research. I was up there in the gallery overlooking the reading room downstairs. And there was this guy. Every day I watched him doing nothing but picking up books, putting them on his table, putting in little pieces of paper. He would open them occasionally and excerpt something. I was so fascinated. And on my last day, I was sitting in the cafeteria and he was sitting at the same table. And I pulled all my pluck and asked him 'Excuse me, what are you doing there?' And he said 'I'm writing a novel and I have the complete works of Sigmund Freud on my table incorporating quotations from Freud'. This about sums up what we scholars are doing. There is this lunatic including quotations in the book and we then try to pick them out. Spending years and years and years to find them.[23]

Having spent seven years in a library playing the literary sleuth – less Sherlock

Holmes or Hercule Poirot than Jacques Clouseau – I certainly share Imhof's exasperation at the curiously symbiotic relationship of writer and scholar in their respective quests for erudition and technical sophistication. Yet I would baulk at calling the writer a 'lunatic' (however much in jest); rather, I would ask why writers resort to literary allusions and investigate the effects which this activity has on their relationship with the reader. When a text exists as an amalgamation of intertexts, three basic questions must be asked: if the texts are assemblages of quotations and literary allusions, can they feasibly be described as original; is the writer being elitist, reducing the audience to a selective cabal of the *cognoscenti*; and is he or she being evasive, ventriloquising unpopular political sympathies, hiding behind other voices, 'whispering morse'?[24]

This monograph focuses on the intertextual relations in the work of two highly-regarded, though often regrettably misunderstood Northern Irish poets: Paul Muldoon and Medbh McGuckian. In contrast to the visual artists' use of iconography, literary quotations tend to be less well-known. As a result, the poets' use of quotation has been received with much bemusement and, at times, outright hostility. Though Muldoon's notoriously allusive and often ludic textual strategies have earned him an unwarranted reputation for semantic impenetrability, a close textual analysis in Chapter 1 reveals the salutary functions of his obliquity. His parodic narratives exemplify Kearney's category of a postmodernist text: they are both deconstructive and reinventive; they eschew closure and yet do not degenerate into an endless play of images. The first chapter examines how Muldoon sets up particular readings of his work, how he uses quotations to guide rather than to hinder the reading process.

Medbh McGuckian's recourse to intertextuality differs considerably from Muldoon's, both in degree and in kind. Critics are undecided both as to the merits of her oblique voice and as to whether or not it constitutes a strategic dislocation or a poetic failure on her part. In his review of the revised edition of *On Ballycastle Beach*, Ian Sansom admits not simply a dislike for her occasional 'hermeticism', but also a genuine admiration for several of the poems.[25] In contrast, Steven Blyth's review of the revised edition of *Venus and the Rain* insists that her fractured discourse inhibits all communication. 'Poems should allow the reader some imaginative elbow-room', he states, 'and martian metaphors can sometimes startle, but the detachment that frequently occurs here deflects impact and significance.'[26] The reviews, situated within a page of each other in the *PN Review*, differ in their approach to her work: whereas Sansom's, in principle, accepts obliquity as a writer's strategy but is wary of the difficulty which this spawns in the reading process, Blythe's review sees the difficulty as proof of the writer's solipsism. My own approach to McGuckian's apparent hermeticism in Chapter 2 is to examine its root cause. I demonstrate that her poetic texts are made up from quotations exhumed from other writers' work (critical prose, biographies, memoirs, plays, poems, etc.) and then rearranged to form centos, poems where a multitude of voices intersect. A McGuckian poem is not white noise; rather, it is a structure of harmonies, conversations and intertextual dialogues. Because McGuckian's secret writing avoids all acknowledgement of her sources – even her worksheets do not record them – the reader is left in ignorance as to why her texts are so fractured. I examine the merits of this and defend her against the obvious charge of plagiarism.

The second part of this monograph focuses on how the two poets' use of intertextuality allows them to engage obliquely with politics, language and tradition in Northern Ireland. Much has been written already on the Northern Irish reticence, about how the poets talk of politics 'in coded ways',[27] how they have 'generated elaborate circumlocutions or forms of doublespeak',[28] thus producing work which is 'oblique, unpresumptuous, and sometimes reticently unforthcoming'.[29] This has been thematised in the poetic texts themselves since the early seventies. Witness, for example, Paul Muldoon's 'Hedgehog', his symbol for the taciturn poet, 'giv[ing] nothing / Away, keeping itself to itself',[30] or Seamus Heaney's explicit reminder in 'Whatever You Say Say Nothing' that 'Smoke-signals are loud-mouthed compared with us'.[31] Although, as we shall see from Chapter 3, recent artworks do at times manifest similar self-reflexive anxieties concerning both artistic responsibility and the artist's place in a time of violence, nevertheless this reticence has become more complexly implicated in the formal construction of the Northern Irish poetic texts themselves. No longer resorting to overt and self-explanatory mytho-historical analogies – such as Heaney's infamously dehistoricising 'Bog poems'[32] – the poets now write *from within* other texts. In Chapter 4, therefore, I will focus upon Northern Irish centos – texts that exist as *bricolages* of quotations – and will demonstrate the subtlety with which the familiar ghosts have been deployed. I will examine the inherent difficulties of tackling political subject matter through verse and demonstrate how literary reference provides Muldoon and

McGuckian with oblique analogies for the Troubles. Comparing the approach to conflict taken by Northern Irish poets with that of visual artists, I examine their particular ways of looking at the Troubles in Chapter 5 (scopic gaze, epiphanic reveries, detached looking). In Chapter 6, I analyse how the poets' very different practices of quotation relate to their use of the Irish language and varieties of English. In each chapter in Part II, I use the work of Seamus Heaney as a foil, contrasting his direct and self-conscious approach to the Troubles with the younger poets' more oblique strategies. My decision to use Heaney in this way stems from the fact that he is not only their contemporary but, more importantly, he is also their immediate precursor. A clear subtext of this book, then, is an examination of how the younger poets differ from Heaney when they interweave the text of imagination with the context of history.

Notes

1   Richard Kearney, *Transitions: Narratives in Modern Irish Culture* (Dublin: Wolfhound Press, 1988) 10.
2   Richard Kearney, *Postnationalist Ireland: Politics, Culture, Philosophy* (London: Routledge, 1997) 178.
3   Kearney, *Transitions* 14.
4   See Richard Kearney, *Poetics of Imagining: From Husserl to Lyotard* (London: Harper Collins, 1991) 217, and Fredric Jameson, 'Postmodernism: Or, the Cultural Logic of Capitalism', *New Left Review* 146 (1986): 53–92.
5   See Linda Hutcheon, *A Poetics of Postmodernism: History, Theory, Fiction* (New York: Routledge, 1988) 52.
6   Linda Hutcheon, *The Politics of Postmodernism* (London: Routledge, 1989) 7.
7   John Hutchinson, 'Postmodernism in Ireland: Notes and Propositions', *Circa* 48 (November–December, 1989) 26.
8   Paul Graham, 'No.4, Shankill Road', *Troubled Land: The Social Landscape* (London: Grey Editions, 1987) n.p.
9   Hutcheon, *Poetics* 35.
10 Jack Pakenham, 'Your Move', in Brian McAvera, 'Jack Pakenham, Painter and Poet', *Works 75–89* (Derry: Orchard Gallery, 1990) 10.
11 Peter O'Neill, 'Rosebud', in Brian McAvera, *Art, Politics and Ireland* (Dublin: Open Air Press, n.d.) 98.
12 Luke Gibbons, *Transformations in Irish Culture* (Cork: Cork University Press, 1996) 172.
13 Gibbons, *Transformations* 174.
14 See Jameson, *Postmodernism* 77 and Barthes, *Image Music Text* (London: Fontana, 1993) 160

15 Barthes, *Image Music Text* 160.

16 Anonymous, 'Interview with Michael Riffaterre', *Diacritics* 11 (Winter, 1981) 12–16.

17 Michael Riffaterre, 'Syllepsis', *Critical Theory* 6.4 (Summer, 1980) 625, 626.

18 Michael Riffaterre, 'Syllepsis' 627.

19 See Riffaterre, 'Syllepsis' 626–27, 'Interpretation and Undecidability', *New Literary History* 12.2 (Winter, 1981) 230–33, and 'Intertextual Representations: On Mimesis as Interpretative Discourse', *Critical Inquiry* 11.1 (September, 1984) 142–43.

20 Linda Hutcheon, 'Literary Borrowing … and Stealing: Plagiarism, Sources, Influences, and Intertexts', *English Studies in Canada* 12.2 (June, 1986) 229–39.

21 Judith Still and Michael Worton, 'Introduction', in eds. Worton and Still, *Intertextuality: Theories and Practices* (Manchester: Manchester University Press, 1990) 12.

22 Jean Weisgerber, 'The Use of Quotations in Recent Literature', *Comparative Literature* 22.1 (Winter, 1970) 44.

23 Rüdiger Imhof, 'Not Only Here for the Beer: Tea with Rüdiger Imhof', interview by Rudi Heid et al, *Pulp* 4 (1999) 9.

24 Seamus Heaney, 'Whatever You Say Say Nothing', *North* (London: Faber, 1975) 59.

25 Ian Sansom, 'Savours', *PN Review* 106 (November–December, 1995) 60.

26 Steven Blyth, 'Gift Rapt', *PN Review* 106 (November–December, 1995) 59.

27 Bernard O'Donoghue, '"The Fascination of What's Difficult": Poetry and Complexity', *Stand Magazine* 34.2 (Spring, 1993) 17.

28 Joe Cleary, '"Fork-Tongued on the Border Bit": Partition and the Politics of Form in Contemporary Narratives of the Northern Irish Conflict', *South Atlantic Quarterly* 95.1 (Winter, 1996) 227.

29 Neil Corcoran, *After Yeats and Joyce: Reading Modern Irish Literature* (Oxford: Oxford University Press, 1997) 142.

30 Paul Muldoon, 'Hedgehog', *New Weather* (London: Faber, 2nd edn 1994) 27.

31 Heaney, 'Whatever You Say Say Nothing', *North* 59.

32 See Patricia Coughlan, '"Bog Queens": The Representation of Women in the Poetry of John Montague and Seamus Heaney', Toni O'Brien Johnson and David Cairns (eds), *Gender in Writing* (Milton Keynes: Open University Press, 1991) 88–89.

Part I

I

'As if he's swallowed a dictionary':
The Oblique Poetry of Paul Muldoon

Most of the time I don't get it
Once in a while I do
It seems everything's encoded
I just don't have a clue[1]

Although Paul Muldoon's poetry is renowned for its erudition, allusiveness and formal precision, it is also notorious for being enigmatic and unforthcoming. A 'Muldoonian' poem is described thus: 'confessional but reticent, lucid but ambiguous, idiomatic but classically formed, artless but supremely erudite, confident but self-effacing, approachable but unknowable'.[2] Two main strands of thought fuel the accusation that he is 'simply' a playful technician. First, some critics focus unduly on the Barthesian nature of his work whereby the author's ashes rest peacefully in a well-wrought urn and authority (in every sense) passes on to the reader: 'Far from placing writerly control as the central organizing principle of the poetry, [Muldoon] undermines expectations of a stable point of origin in language or intention.'[3] This contention goes against his own stated conviction that 'it's the poet's job to take into account, as best he or she is able, all possible readings of the poem',[4] and, I will argue, it also misrepresents the function of his literary allusions. Secondly, and more damningly, his poetry is said to suffer from a surfeit of intellect. 'The questions that gather above the young genius's head', writes Fennella Copplestone, 'are ones about content, meaning, and commitment. Self-caricature might be another, along with playing to the gallery that has come to see and love the Oirish in the clever wee man, who does his bit for Ireland by including so much of the macgibberish in his lines.'[5] His work has at times, therefore, been dismissed as 'postmodern quixotica',[6] while he himself has been described derogatively as 'a sophisticated high-gloss technician'.[7]

There is little doubt about Muldoon's wide-ranging intelligence, nor can one question his commitment to the exigencies of poetic form. However, when the two go hand-in-hand, critics have been tempted to agree with the self-condemnatory lines from *The Annals of Chile*: 'Thing is, *a Phóil*, your head's so far up your own fat butt / you've pretty much disappeared' (*AC* 163). Literary humour abounds in his oeuvre and it is often very capricious: the final poetic enjambment of 'Why Brownlee Left' (*WBL* 22) depicting the horses 'shifting their weight from foot to / Foot' is a literal translation of '*enjamber*';[8] the fifth line of the tenth stanza of 'The More a Man Has the More a Man Wants' (*Q* 44) quotes the fifth line from Shakespeare's tenth sonnet ('for thou art so possessed with murd'rous hate');[9] when the first letter from each line of 'Capercaillies' (*MM* 6–7) is taken together they form the question 'Is this a *New Yorker* poem, or what'; and the repetition within the first line of 'Lag' appropriately reproduces the link between the Siamese twins, Chang and Eng – 'We were joined at the hip. We were joined at the hip' (*H* 26). Though admiring his ingenuity, one can be forgiven for thinking it is all just alphabet soup. Indeed, *The Spirit of Dawn*, *The Last Thesaurus*, 'The Birth' (*AC* 31) and *The Noctuary of Narcissus Batt* all strain themselves to contain word-lists in alphabetical order. Instead of 'getting round', as his Bateson lecture would have us believe,[10] Muldoon, like the Last Thesaurus, seems 'rather less round than square; / He looks as if he's swallowed a dictionary' (*LT* n.p.).

Perhaps the poetry's most annoying aspect for some commentators is its smug knowingness. Witness, for example, the description of a boxing match in 'Yarrow':

> When John L. Sullivan did for Jake Kilrain
> in the seventy-fifth round, it was with such a blow
> as left them both
> utterly winded (note the caesura) …
>
> (*AC* 64)

The sign-posted pause for breath matches the line's caesura, and we ask: so what? Of course, one should not condemn out of hand such mischievous humour. Look, for example, at the following gem from *Hay*:

> A horse farts and farts
> on the wind-tormented scarp.
> A virtuoso.
>
> (*H* 72)

With the obvious double-meaning of 'wind-tormented', this haiku seems at first glance wholly unremarkable; yet it does have a winning subtlety since 'virtuoso' means 'lover of f[ine] arts'. Similarly, when making hay with clichés he usually rises above the asinine:

> while I continued to put the little bit of carte
> before the laughing jackass's
> 'Au foin? Au foin? Au foin? Au foin?'
>
> (*H* 119)

Yet does this sort of verse really challenge the reader and, more crucially, does it fulfil the terms of Muldoon's own poetic manifesto? 'The point of poetry is to be acutely *dis*comforting, to prod and provoke, to poke us in the eye, to punch us in the nose, to knock us off our feet, to take our breath away.'[11]

By illustrating what appears to be an irritating surfeit of intellect, I am merely playing devil's advocate as Muldoon's poetry truly rises above art for art's sake. Many synopses of his technical versatility simply emphasise the surface effects of his poetry – the inclusion of outrageous rhymes, literal clichés, the avoidance of a determinate tense, his self-referential wordplay, his anecdotal, misdirecting narratives – without noting the ironic distancing and defamiliarisation which lie behind such strategies. Indeed, such formal complexity has been regarded as the enviable technical ingenuity of a poet at the height of his powers. Heralded as a practitioner of the 'New Narrative' by the editors of *The Penguin Book of Contemporary British Poetry*, his work has come to be seen as deploying reflexive, fragmentary fictions suited to postmodernity. Rather than narcissistic introspection, his best poems are self-reflexive metafictions, fictions 'about fictional systems, processes of mediation and representation in the text and elsewhere'.[12] While it is true that Muldoon does not voice straightforward political convictions – as a poet he quite justifiably 'insists on the freedom not to espouse directly any political situation'[13] – nevertheless his work is neither apolitical nor 'macgibberish'. His literary allusions are not a vain display of learning rather they act as guides, allowing the reader to follow his engagement with such weighty issues as the role of a writer in a time of violence.

In this chapter I want to argue that, by and large, Muldoon's literary and historical allusions facilitate an economy of effect and a shorthand for the poet, allowing him to give both a context and point of access to the reader. The overt nature of these allusions – the frequent use of italics, quotation marks, historical personae, dates, placenames – guides the reader toward specific readings of his poems. When asked about his faith in referentiality, Muldoon stated that 'what a poem is aiming towards, ideally, is a sense that there's no argument with it. It does *not* mean whatever you want it to mean.'[14] Rather than opening up his poems to limitless readings, he subscribes to the notion of limited connotation: 'I'm one of those old fogies who was brought up on New Criticism and practical criticism; I believe that one of the writer's jobs is to reduce the number of possible readings of a text.'[15] Summing this up neatly in his Bateson lecture, he 'argues for the primacy of unknowing yet insists on almost total knowingness on the part of poet as first reader'.[16] In this regard, he cites Robert Frost as his exemplar, admiring, as he says in a later interview, 'his mischievous, sly, multi-layered quality under the surface'.[17] As Rachel Buxton convincingly argues, the appeal of Frost's work for Muldoon lies in the playfulness and its resistance to 'single fixed readings'.[18] However, this is only half the story. While Muldoon resists predetermination on a thematic level, in his form he often seeks fixity. In an extract from Muldoon's elegy for Mary Farl Powers (cited by Buxton), one can see how Muldoon's structure of quotations directs the reader's reception of the poem, making him understand the speaker's grief by alluding not only to Lucky's 'think', his infamous disquisition on Western metaphysics (reduced here to the despairing inarticulacy of '*quaquaqua*'), but also to the moment when the dumb speak in *Finnegans Wake* ('quoiquoiquoiquoiquoiquoiquoiq!'):

> The fact that you were determined to cut yourself off in your prime
> because it was *pre*-determined has my eyes abrim:
> I crouch with Belaqua
> and Lucky and Pozzo in the Acacacac-
> ademy of Anthropopopometry, trying to make sense of the
> 'quaquaqua'
> of that potato-mouth; that mouth as prim
> and proper as it's full of self-opprobrium,
> with its '*quaquaqua*', with its 'Quoiquoiquoiquoiquoiquoiquoiq'.

Thematically, the speaker's anguish in the face of Powers's acceptance of her pre-ordained fate is evident; yet, paradoxically, in a text which adopts a rigid rhyme scheme, Muldoon deliberately leads the reader to view this passage as the poem's emotional centre, placed as it is at its mid-point.

In his rationale for poetic composition, therefore, there is a discernible tension between imaginative free play and the ordered manipulation of the reader's textual experience, and this often constitutes one of the thematic concerns of his poetry. For example, in 'The Bangle (Slight Return)', the extraordinarily rich poem that concludes *Hay*, we find

> The waiter's eyebrow-ring
> glittering as he drew himself up
>
> to recommend the *Caprice des Dieux*, his *nu sculon herigean*
> counterpointed by the jitter and jaunt and jar
> of their harness, their own improvised *ceintures*
>
> *de ficelle* ...
>
> (*H* 114)

In what way are the *ceintures de ficelle* 'improvised', given that the rhyme scheme and metre determine their appearance at this juncture? To what extent are the gods (or the poet) entirely capricious?[19] Set against caprice is the invocation of Caedmon's Hymn, a paeon to God's settled purpose and design: '*Nu we sculon herigean* / *heofonrices Weard* / *Meotodes meahte* / *ond his modgepanc*'. ('Now we must praise / the kingdom of heaven's guardian / The might of the Creator / and his purpose.') To what extent is the poet in control of the meaning in his poetic texts? Are his conscious intentions fully subsumed by the unconscious promptings of the muse? The sequence contains one portrait of the artist that conveys the fine line between such disparate dispositions:

> Downhill all the way as the packet pitched and rolled
> and made heavy weather
> of a groundswell that seemed as likely to overturn as uphold
> the established order, such order as we decipher
> while we sit and play, or are played by, our toccatas,
> stately at the clavichord
>
> (*H* 128)

Does he play, or is he played? While the poem repeatedly emphasizes happenstance and serendipity, its rigidly set form as a series of sonnets with a fixed rhyme scheme and structure that echoes 'Yarrow'[20] suggests utter predetermination and control on the poet's part. That the sequence references other poems in the collection ('The Mud Room', 'Hay', 'Long Finish', 'Errata', 'Symposium', 'They that wash on Thursday'), and also acts as a self-correcting text ('"For "errata", Virgil smiled, 'read "corrigenda"''' [*H* 140]), reinforce this view. It is certainly true, as the poet contends, that 'there's many a slip / twixt what one supposedly determines / and the al-al-al-al-aleatory' (*H* 124), and that mistakes and chance verbal associations can be

enabling and poetically revealing for artist and reader alike. However, never
has chance seemed so contrived.

'Something Else', an extended sonnet from his fifth collection, *Meeting
the British*, is typical of his impish, prismatic style. Its narrative thread flows
with both rhyme and reason from the contemplation of a dinner companion's
lobster, to thoughts of different kinds of dye, to the infamous anecdote of
how the nineteenth-century author Gérard de Nerval used to take his pet
lobster for a walk on a leash, to his tragic suicide on 26 January 1855 in the
rue de la Vieille-Lanterne, all of which makes the speaker 'think of something else, then something else again' (*MB* 33). The reader follows the narrative through a process of analogic association, gleaning a scenario of ill-
fated or misplaced desire through, first, the recurrence of the colour red
and, secondly, through the poet's subtly constructed web of intertextual
allusions. The cited texts upon which the speaker muses, Nerval's dark,
melancholic 'El Desdichado' and his evanescent, non-linear romance *Sylvie*,
both hint indirectly at his own precarious relationship with the unnamed
and silent companion. The form of Muldoon's text is here central to its
meaning: its *mise-en-page* and the clever enjambment between the second
quatrain and first tercet both mimetically represent time inexorably passing; the disrupted traditional sonnet rhyme scheme and the supplementary
final line indicate a latent wish to deny both the passing of time (the deaths
of the lobster, Nerval, the relationship) and writing's *différance*, its 'fugitive
inks' complementing the equally chimerical objects of desire. Muldoon's
choice here of Nerval as a literary exemplar, one who sought to '*dérouter le
lecteur*', is symptomatic of his penchant for narrative indirection and signals
his abiding concern for the reader's activity. In contrast to Heaney's lobster
from 'Away from it All', a symbol of the poet out of his element and strug-
gling to survive, 'out of water, / fortified and bewildered',[21] Muldoon's lobster stands for a work which can survive in both the aesthetic and the public
realms (and it is the author who firmly guides the crustacean, not the other
way round).

Muldoon's associational logic may suggest arbitrariness as the paratactic
arrangement of his narratives and structures of imagery disrupt hierarchies.
In his sonnet 'The Marriage of Strongbow and Aoife', the reader wonders
which narrative is more important, that of the marriage between Strongbow
and Aoife MacMurrough, a union leading to the Norman conquest of
Ireland, or the tense stand-off between the speaker and his dinner-guest,

Mary (*MB* 11). Yet herein lies Muldoon's oblique approach to political concerns: by personalizing the distant, historical account, and by granting the intimate encounter the enormity of historical significance, he intensi- fies the sense of betrayal inherent within both accounts ('It's as if someone had slipped / a double-edged knife between my ribs'). Similarly, in 'Long Finish', a ten-stanza poem using a Provençal form with two repetends, Muldoon incorporates an anecdote detailing the senseless death of a man 'who'll shortly divine / the precise whereabouts of a landmine / on the road between Beragh and Sixmilecross' (*H* 79). While with Heaney such a death would feature prominently in a text, giving rise to a moral on stoic forti- tude in the midst of the Troubles (as in 'Keeping Going' from *The Spirit Level*), with Muldoon it becomes an affective detail amongst other narra- tives which tell of the fine line between 'longing and loss'.

In 'The Mud Room' the reader is stopped short when he comes across the almost casual description of the latest controlled explosion in Belfast:

> and the dull glow
> of pine-ash, the hubcap from a Ford Sierra
> blown up in – yes, sirree –
> a controlled explosion in Belfast, the Kaliber six-pack,
> the stack of twenty copies of *The Annals of Chile* ($21 hardback).
> (*H* 7)

What is shocking is the use of parataxis – the non-hierarchical list – and the seemingly inappropriate tone in which the event is narrated. Yet such tech- niques convey the way in which violence is perceived from a safe distance, and how repetition can induce apathy. However, the religious context in which the detail is narrated complicates this point: 'when we paused to draw breath, as the Children of Israel / might draw breath on the Sabbath'. Do the Passover rituals mentioned in the poem, and the contemplation of the Haggadah, reinforce apathy or do they make the poet (and reader) meditate on violence?

When Heaney approaches the same theme in 'Known World'[22] he does so more directly. A visit to Macedonia prompts him to contemplate 'That old sense of a tragedy going on / Uncomprehended', and his first impulse is to invoke an artistic allusion, referring to conflict in aesthetic terms: 'A pity I didn't know then (for Caj's sake) / Hygo Simberg's allegory of Finland'. He translates Simberg's image of the wounded angel into more familiar terms: 'A first communion angel with big white wings'. Yet even when he has transformed the unknown into the known, he self-reflexively meditates

on his right to interpret Simberg's allegory: 'who's to know / How to read
sorrow rightly, or at all?'. At the time he felt 'involved at the moment and
closer than usual and yet half-culpably secure'.[23] Having raised the issue of
his self-doubt, however, he invokes a further allusion:

> The open door, the jambs, the worn saddle
> And actual granite of the doorstep slab.
> Now enters another angel, fit as ever,
> Past each house with a doorstep daubed 'Serb house'.

Referring here to the Passover (Exodus, 2:12), he links that genocide to the
contemporary circumstances in the Balkans. Explaining why the houses
were 'daubed "Serb house"', Karl Miller, in conversation with Heaney, states:
'This was a message which was painted on thresholds in order to dissuade
those who would otherwise enter the house and kill everyone inside.'[24]

Muldoon's approach, then, is less direct but no less effective or politi-
cally/ethically engaged. Obliquity is not necessarily equivalent to disen-
gagement. As Bernard O'Donoghue astutely observes, 'In a fraught world,
the voice that shouts loudest is not necessarily the most creditable. There's a
mock innocence in [Muldoon's] poems, a disturbing way of reporting violence – horribly literal, half-humorous – that works as a shock tactic. It
works as a way of conveying how shocking the violence is.'[25] In what follows, I want to examine the ways in which Muldoon uses literary and historical allusions as a way of referring to violence without ever becoming
moralistic or directly stating his own beliefs. As the poet says in 'They that
Wash on Thursday':

> So I learned first hand
> to deal in the off-, the under-, the sleight-of-hand,
> writing now in that great, open hand
> yet never quite showing my hand.
>
> (*H* 83)

This chapter adopts Linda Hutcheon's approach to intertextual relations
since, in contrast to other models, it focuses on their dialogic nature and
strategic importance to the author. Postmodern intertextuality 'directly con-
fronts the past of literature – and of historiography, for it too derives from
other texts (documents). It uses and abuses those intertextual echoes,
inscribing their powerful allusions and then subverting that power through
irony.'[26] When the literary or historical quotations and allusions self-reflexively manifest their status as intertexts in a poem, the reader, by actively
searching out the poem's links with its sources, can produce a new reading

of both the present and the past texts. Hutcheon's conception of postmodernism – a 'postmodernism of complicity and critique, of reflexivity and historicity'[27] – counters a common understanding of it as an 'unprincipled neo-pragmatist relativism'.[28] Although the popular understanding of postmodernism suggests an unending play between interreflecting mirrors, implying infinite simulation,[29] Muldoon offers a related, but significantly different, image to describe his poetic practice, one in accordance with Hutcheon's emphasis on ironic perspective: 'I've become very interested in structures that can be fixed like mirrors at angles to each other – it relates to narrative form – so that new images can emerge from the setting up of the poems in relation to each other: further ironies are possible, further mischief is possible'.[30] His narratives are neither self-focused nor infinite as such; rather, they distort the real, alienating the viewers' perceptions, making them see things in a different light. When asked 'Is there a risk of the poems becoming rather hermetic? And of turning a book of poems into a hall of mirrors?', Muldoon's reply was instructive: 'Well, "hermetic". That depends whether you feel lost or enlarged in a hall of mirrors.'[31] Far from making his poetry hermetic (thus closed to uninitiated readers), intertextuality opens the poetic text: while quotations allow Muldoon to offer a critique (and appreciation) of exemplary writers, the manner in which he quotes enables the reader to determine the nature of this critique.

A typical example is 'A Tennyson Triptych, 1974'[32] which incorporates several quotations from Tennyson's oeuvre:

> Though his voice was that of a parakeet
> crying out in a hurricane
> there was no mistaking the refrain
> of The Charge of the Light Brigade:
>
> no mistaking, once the engineer
> cut through the 'huzzin' an' maäzin'
> of Thomas Edison's
> wax cylinder, that smack of Lincolnshire.

This first section appears to balance admonition with admiration: though implicitly criticising Tennyson for a lack of originality by comparing his poetry to the squawking of a parakeet – a term applied to persons in reference to the imitative faculty of the birds – Muldoon appears to praise the uniqueness of his 'The Charge of the Light Brigade'. Yet the praise is barbed, since it is well known that, despite protestations to the contrary, Tennyson borrowed the metre from Dryden. Similarly, by selecting a quotation from

'Northern Farmer. Old Style' – 'huzzin' and maäzin" – Muldoon offers praise for the use of dialect, 'that smack of Lincolnshire', but qualifies it by imitating the infamously sonorous arch-rhymed quatrains of *In Memoriam A.H.H.* In this way, Muldoon's poem offers a more subtle critique than Tom Paulin's (admittedly funny) prose piece which was published alongside it: 'Tennyson has always weighed on me as the original National Heritage Poet – all that is bogus, empty, self-parodic, dishonest, false and dead-as-doornails in the culture epitomized by his verse. His cadences remind me of cheap firetongs, flat clangy tin-trays furred with velvet, the boring sonorities of Gielgud's voice'. The humour of Muldoon's poem resides not in over-the-top commentary, but in his re-contexualisation of Tennyson's themes and imagery. Muldoon plays along with the Laureate's discomfort at technological progress in 'Northern Farmer. Old Style' by having the gas stove pilot light 'flare / with "a little flash, a mystic hint"' and by having the 'Ansaphone' record '"The woods decay, the woods decay and fall ..."'. Both quotations in their original context refer to death and immortality: the former occurs in *In Memoriam A.H.H.* (XLIV), a lamentation for Arthur Hallam, while the latter is taken from 'Tithonus', a poem which tells of Tithonus's grief at being granted immortality but not eternal youth. The latter especially is an excellent example of Muldoon's wit: he not only gives the theme of immortality a twentieth-century twist by preserving the woman's voice on the Ansaphone, he also ends the poem as he began by referring to Tennyson's own intertextual borrowing – in this instance from Book 6 of Wordsworth's *Prelude* ('The immeasurable height / Of woods decaying, never to be decayed, / The stationary blasts of waterfalls').

Muldoon believes that 'at some level all poetry is in dialogue with something else'[34] and his most sustained exchange has been with Seamus Heaney. Muldoon is himself convinced that Heaney is the pre-eminent contemporary Irish poet: 'A country can only entertain one writer at a time, and Seamus is the man, quite rightly'.[35] However, such admiration does not carry over into an imitation of Heaney's poetics nor an acceptance of his politics. On many occasions the younger poet has taken it upon himself to criticise stances taken by the older poet. In one interview, Heaney's representative status comes under fire: 'There's no tribe in Ireland for which I would feel comfortable as spokesman. I wonder who would, who does, who is? I think Seamus flirted – I think "flirted" is the word – with the idea for a while.'[36] Similarly, Muldoon comments in a later review on the negative effect this has had on Heaney:

> Throughout this sequence Seamus Heaney is resolutely questing and questioning, constantly refining and redefining. He is, for example, now more likely to question the received opinions and stock responses of Irish Catholicism and Irish Nationalism, though the drift of the most intensely lyrical passage of 'Station Island' would seem to suggest that the fatalism of both have marked him indelibly.[37]

The most well-known parody of Heaney occurs in 'The More a Man Has the More a Man Wants' (*Q* 40–64):

> Gallogly lies down in the sheugh
> to munch
> through a Beauty of
> Bath. He repeats himself, *Bath*,
> under his garlic-breath.
> *Sheugh*, he says. *Sheugh*.
> He is finding that first 'sh'
> increasingly difficult to manage.
> (*Q* 49)

These lines mimic Heaney's pietistic attitude towards place-names in 'Broagh':[38] while asserting a welcome inclusivity between Protestants and Catholics, Heaney's essentialistic viewpoint glosses over its own exclusivity ('that last / *gh* the strangers found / difficult to manage'). Similarly, the older poet's 'Widgeon',[39] dedicated to Muldoon, informs the latter's 'The Lass of Aughrim' (*MB* 15). Heaney's poem metaphorically transforms the bird's voice-box into 'a flute stop / in the broken windpipe' from which the poet can actualise 'his own small widgeon cries'. Muldoon's text parodies this supposedly natural composition, picturing an Indian boy striking up a tune – 'The Lass of Aughrim' – on '"what was the tibia / of a priest / from a long-abandoned Mission"'. The humorous revision occurs in two key areas: first, Muldoon hints at the ideological and cultural background behind all writing, foregrounding the Indian boy's colonial heritage by having him play a tune which is incongruous only if the role of the Irish missionaries is not recognised; and, secondly, the Orphic power which Heaney's poem claims for art is comically sent up by having the boy try 'to charm / the fish from the water'.

The most involved intertextual dialogue between the two writers is carried on over several texts. In *The Place of Writing*, Heaney praises Muldoon as '[o]ne of the most resourceful in changing the demands and pointing to a new agenda for Irish poetry', this new direction signalling a contrast with Heaney's own poetic practice since Muldoon is said 'to deride the notion that poetry might have a desirable, never mind a demonstrable, relation to the life of a nation'.[40] This is on a par with an earlier review in which he claimed that Muldoon's poetry displayed 'the imagination's confidence and pleasure in re-ordering the facts of place and time, of history and myth', and that '[w]hat he has to say is constantly in disguise, and what is disguised is some conviction like this: the imagination is arbitrary and contrary, it delights in its own fictions and has a right to them'.[41] The oblique posture that Heaney detects in Muldoon's verse is explained in his Ellmann lecture when he comments on Muldoon's inclusion of the discussion about poetry between F. R. Higgins and Louis MacNeice in his *Faber Book of Contemporary Irish Poetry*. Muldoon is said to reject Higgins's 'hazy romantic notions about the poet's bardic relation to territory and inheritance',[42] a wry acknowledgement of the divergence between Heaney and the younger poet. What is most significant is a curious passage in which Heaney comments that Muldoon is rewarded by the Muse for not consciously writing on behalf of his community:

> She has certainly been generous on this score to Paul Muldoon … whose swerves away from any form of poker-faced solidarity with the political programs of the Northern Catholic minority (from which he hails) have kept him so much on his poetic toes that he has practically achieved the poetic equivalent of walking on air.[43]

Muldoon refers to this passage in his rebuttal of Heaney. The first theme which the younger poet picks up on is that of 'walking on air', a feature which he feels suits Heaney's verse far more than his own. In 'The Key' (*MM* 3–4), he includes a brief verse dialogue with Foley, a sound engineer,[44] concentrating on a Heaneyesque tension between two kinds of poetry: one which defends 'that same old patch of turf' and another that is content 'to ventriloquize the surf' (*MM* 4), a theme already implicit in the Higgins/MacNeice dialogue. The 'old patch of turf' hints at Heaney's pre-occupation with digging the bog, as well as his reverence for place-names (hence identifying him with Higgins), whereas ventriloquising the surf is more in line with Muldoon's interests, as detailed to John Haffenden. The inference of a dialogue with Heaney remains inconclusive until we come to *The Prince of the Quotidian*:

> The mail brings 'literature' from Louisiana
> on various plantation tours
> and a Christmas poem from Doctor Heaney:
> the great physician of the earth
> is waxing metaphysical, has taken to 'walking on air';
> as Goethe termed it, *Surf und Turf.*
>
>   (*PQ* 14)

By including a phrase from the Ellmann lecture,[45] he is both throwing the description back on to Heaney and registering a change in the older poet's poetic practice; it also suggests that 'The Key' was ironically referring to Heaney's new metaphysical thematics, his focus on the transcendental in *Seeing Things* which received extensive coverage in academic circles.[46] The reference to Goethe can be properly explained if compared with another earth/air duality which crops up in a choral interlude, *Shining Brow*, based on Goethe's 'Hymn to Nature': 'We mount the winding stair. / With every step, we melt / back into earth and air' (*SB* 32). Whether Heaney really has adopted the Yeatsian mantle is open to debate, but there is little to suggest that Muldoon's 'dialogue' with Heaney has been anything other than 'friendly',[47] and the phrase 'walking on air' celebrates Heaney's new style. Muldoon's intertextual references are not included merely for display but are a means of 'speaking through other people, other voices'.[48] Discussing 'the idea of poetry as ventriloquism', Neil Corcoran declares that Muldoon 'finds his voice, "unexpectedly", by initially sounding out through – impersonating – Seamus Heaney'.[49] This not only overstates the case but also mistakes impersonation for ventriloquism. Muldoon does not impersonate other writers such as Heaney; he speaks through them, using their words for ironic (or other) purposes.

Muldoon's use of intertextuality can be very poignant, allowing the poet to approach a sensitive topic obliquely without recourse to blunt declaration. One particularly moving example is to be found in *The Prince of the Quotidian*: 'A man with a belly like a poisoned / pup careened towards us, much the worse for drink' (*PQ* 11). At this juncture, the reference is obscure and the reader has little idea to whom the poet refers. However, Muldoon returns to the image later in the collection:

> That man with the belly like a poisoned pup was once a strange child with a taste for verse: now everything turns on a pub;
> 'The Lion's Head', 'McKenna's', 'The White Horse'.
>
> (*PQ* 25)

The intertextual reference – 'a strange child with a taste for verse' – is a direct quotation from Derek Mahon's 'Courtyards in Delft'.[50] The line contrasts the former glories of a poet with his medical problems, namely his crippling alcoholism.[51] It is apt that Muldoon uses a quotation to refer to Mahon since he is celebrating the latter's past poetic genius while lamenting his incapacitating disease. Peter McDonald asks why in 'Alien Nation'[52]

Mahon repeats Muldoon's list of pubs.[53] The answer is that Mahon, now recovered, is (implicitly) acknowledging the younger poet's professional tribute and personal concern:

> I know you and you know me, you wretched buggers,
> and I've no problem calling you my brothers
> for I too have been homeless and in detox
> with baaad niggas 'n' crack hoes on the rocks
> and may be there again, for all I know –
> who, once a strange child with a taste for vorse,
> would lurch at 3.00 a.m. through drifting snow
> to the Lion's Head, McKenna's, the White Horse …

Mistaking obliquity for elitism, many critics suspect that Muldoon's use of intertextuality lacks any purpose whatsoever. The 'vitreous surface of quotation, allusion and catalogue'[54] of 'Madoc – A Mystery' (*MM* 15–261) has raised the hackles of critics. It is all 'a waste of intelligence,' asserts one reviewer, 'a rattle of bright beads in a tin'.[55] John Banville sums up the case for the prosecution:

> I cannot help feeling that this time he has gone too far – so far, at least, that I can hardly make him out at all, off there in the distance, dancing by himself. Yes, art *should* be resistant, poetry *should* hold back something of its essential self. The trouble is 'Madoc' demands that the reader works in ways that seem inappropriate to the occasion: one pictures details of Ph.D students already setting to, tracking down the references, preparing the glosses, grinding keys.[56]

It must be admitted that Banville does have a point: the sheer scale and range of intertextual references, allusions and quotations contained within the poem far exceeds anything which the poet has previously or subsequently produced, and any reader who does not have access to the relevant scholarly resources may become hopelessly lost trying to follow its multiple narratives. To understand the epic poem, one certainly requires 'a thorough grounding in the classics, a knowledge of western philosophy, a grasp of American history and a fondness for obscurity to boot'.[57] The danger in relying so heavily on intertextuality is that its obliquity will alienate those critics and general readers who are either unable or unwilling to trace the references. There is, of course, no argument against this: the reading experience of 'Madoc – A Mystery' can be excruciatingly hard work. The same, however, could be said of many acknowledged literary masterpieces including T. S. Eliot's *The Waste Land* and Ezra Pound's *Cantos*. The real question is whether or not Muldoon's use of intertextuality is, as his detractors claim, arbitrary nonsense. I will spend the rest of this chapter demonstrating that although the poem is, at times, 'a lexical romp', it is by no means 'some kind of intellectual bingo'.[58]

To understand why Banville is incorrect to claim that 'Madoc – A Mystery' makes the reader work 'in ways that seem inappropriate to the occasion', one should look no further than the poem's self-conscious presentation of its textuality. The text is engaged with the acts of writing and reading; like Bouvard and Pécuchet, the narrator performs the constant task of reading and copying other texts, so much so that the poem seems to be a tapestry of quotations, stressing its own materiality, contextuality and intertextual provenance. Extracts of poetry intermix with personal correspondence, missives, communiqués; there is a gloss, a code, a motto, ogam script, a Mohawk Prayer Book, a preface and a map. Language comes under close scrutiny with definitions of 'Pantisocracy' and 'Aspheterism' being supplied along with the (often spurious) etymological derivation of such words as 'penguin', 'Monadnock' and 'semantics'. Neologisms[59] are juxtaposed with such rareties as 'furbelow' and 'arquebus'; slang and dialect are placed side by side with the language of Romantic lyricism;[60] the words from numerous different languages jostle for the reader's attention. The poet stresses the materiality of the written script: letters are capitalised to register surprise and italicised for emphasis;[61] words are elongated to convey a tone of speech and broken up to suggest code.[62] Poor spelling and irregular capitalisation are included not simply for the sake of authenticity but to foreground the text's status as quotation:[63] 'I set out early and proceeded on through a Countrey as rugged as usial. At 12 miles decended the mountain to a leavel pine Countrey' (*MM* 171). The poem includes clichés concerning writing – 'another twist in the plot' (*MM* 16), 'was totally written off' (*MM* 18) – as well as quotations which talk of putting pen to paper – 'a fine morning we commenced wrighting &c.' (*MM* 203). Muldoon even foregrounds the processes of poetic composition with its choosing of vocabulary and rhyme, in a passage that self-reflexively comments on the end result: 'Pike, pickerel. Hog, hoggerel. / Cock, cockerel. Dog, doggerel' (*MM* 178).

The narrative inscribes its own structural flaws into the text. The narrator is unreliable and appears to be making it up as he goes along: 'Inside the pearwood box – hold on a minute – / is an exact replica / of the valise' (*MM* 188). At times, he is forced to admit the sheer implausibility of his own tale with ironic asides: nearly half-way into the poem he concedes that things have fallen 'a little too patly into the scheme / of things' (*MM* 106). At one point he even admits that his narration has unaccountably gone awry: 'An even more distressing thought ... How might Coleridge have stolen a pirogue, when there was none to steal?' (*MM* 218). Towards the end, all semblance of omniscience has faded: referring to South, he says that 'As to where he goes? It's a matter of pure conjecture' (*MM* 233). The convoluted narrative structure can be likened to the treadmill described in '[Vico]':

> A hand-wringing, small, grey squirrel
> plods
> along a wicker
>
> treadmill that's attached
> by an elaborate
> system of levers ...
>
>   (*MM* 108)

This, in turn, is attached to another treadmill 'in which there plods / a hand-wringing, small, grey squirrel' (*MM* 109). Parallelism is a key trope and is symbolised by Thomas Jefferson's 'newly-modified polygraph', a writing apparatus with two or more pens attached to a perpendicular and horizontal ruler enabling documents to be duplicated instantaneously:

> In modern times the word is generally associated with the 'lie detector machine' invented in 1915 by the psychologist William Moulton Marston and further developed as the 'Keeler polygraph' by the American criminologist Leonarde Keeler in 1931. The word *polygraph*, however, had been applied first by Cotteneuve in 1763 to a multiple-pen machine and by Joseph Booth in 1784 to a technique he referred to as 'Polygraphic Art, or the Copying or Multiplying of Pictures in Oil Colours, by a Chymical or Mechanical Process'.[64]

There are four interlinked aspects of the 'polygraph' which are of particular relevance to the structure of Muldoon's poem and his use of intertextuality: the above definition suggests both the production of multiple texts and the interrogation of veracity; two other definitions link the polygraph to secret writing and to a prolific, highly allusive author.[65] The fact that 'the snaggle-toothed gopher' is associated with the working of this machine (*MM* 163, 234) is important, as it demonstrates these differing functions in action:

> [Jefferson]
>
> Has today received (1) a live gopher (2) a magpie (3) a piece of chequered skin or hide and (4) a cipher that reads ... 'A-R-T-I-C-H-O-K-E-S'.
>
>   (*MM* 134)

This extract relates to the articles sent back to Jefferson by the Lewis and

Clark expedition. However, the truthfulness of Muldoon's account is put into question if we refer back both to the actual invoice forwarded by the explorers at Fort Mandan to the President[66] and to subsequent letters by Jefferson: instead of a gopher there appears 'a living burrowing squirrel of the praries',[67] which alternatively is referred to as the black-tailed prairie dog, *Cynomys ludovicianus,* and a 'barking squirrel'.[68] Writing to Henry Dearborn, Jefferson compares the 'little burrowing dog' to 'what we call woodchucks, or ground hoggs',[69] while to Charles Willson Peale he confides that it is 'a species of Marmotte'.[70] Muldoon equally fails the polygraph test with his cipher letter: while it is true, as Richard Dillon relates, that 'One of the first things he [Lewis] did to prepare for the journey was to work out with the President a cipher, based on one evolved by mathematician Robert Patterson, with the key word "artichokes"',[71] nevertheless in his study of the documents of the Lewis and Clark expedition, Donald Jackson has found that, apart from a sample message used before the expedition itself, '[a]pparently no occasion for Lewis to use this form of communication arose during the expedition'.[72] This falsification of historical circumstance recurs repeatedly in the poem, suggesting that its events, allusions and quoted extracts parallel their verifiable historical counterparts but do not match them exactly, a circumstance symbolised by the replica of the valise whose contents are at first stated as being 'identical' to the original, but later qualified by the phrase 'All except for ...' (*MM* 188).

Narrative red herrings are not simply a source of fun. Commenting on the dynamics of his poem, Muldoon himself has admitted that, although 'Madoc – A Mystery' is intended as 'a rollicking yarn', this should not discount the fact that '[s]erious things can be happening along the way'.[73] He reiterated this in an interview with Blake Morrison: 'It's true that I am interested in having fun in poetry. But I don't believe that seriousness and solemnity come as sort of a package deal: one way to deal with the most disturbing things in the world is to laugh.'[74] In fact, Muldoon uses historical data self-reflexively in a manner akin to historiographical metafiction. According to Linda Hutcheon, such a text 'shows fiction to be historically conditioned and history to be discursively structured'[75] and foregrounds 'the politics of human agency'.[76] 'Madoc – A Mystery' continually alerts the reader to a disjunction between official history and fictional re-creation, not only by including obvious disruptive elements – the inclusion of inverted commas around 'Smith' in '[Paine]' (*MM* 131) is enough to suggest that this is not a faithful account of the duel between Hamilton and Aaron Burr – but also by tonal modulations and the withholding of information. 'Exactly a week later' not only encourages the reader to search for the actual date of the duel (11 July 1804),[77] it also maintains a chronological connection between the historical and fictional narratives ('[Watt]', which precedes '[Paine]', has to do with the pantisocratics), thus confusing fact and fiction. The ironic title of the section, the metaphorical description ('blood-trump', 'milty spleen') and the use of cliché ('whisked away') all make the reader aware of the subjectivity of Muldoon's account. An even more obvious example is '[Kant]' (*MM* 125):

> April, 1804. It stands to, well, 'it stands to reason'
> that Wilkinson, who's 'in the pay of' Spain,
>
> should 'sow the seeds of treason'
> in the 'fertile mind' of Aaron Burr,
>
> of whom Alexander Hamilton holds 'a despicable
> opinion'.
> The tedium, de dum, of it all. The slurry-slur.
>   (*MM* 125)

The inverted commas highlight the clichéd nature of this account, while the narrator's interjection – 'The tedium, de dum, of it all' – comments both on this strand of the narrative and the mode of its expression. Although it refers to a meeting which actually took place between Aaron Burr and General Wilkinson at Richmond Hill, Burr's country home on the northern fringes of New York City, the tone of this piece should alert the reader to its pseudo-objective status. In fact, the date given, 'April, 1804', is inaccurate[78] – the slurry slur, indeed, does not stand to reason.

Without ironic narrative interjections or obvious textual clues it becomes more difficult to spot fact from fiction. Only by following Muldoon's path through historical sources and literary references can we avoid false trails. The reader may well decide that it is not worth the effort of trawling through historical and biographical sources, and that is his prerogative. However, in light of the poem's intense focus on unresolved issues of historical importance, a scholarly approach to the text is not inappropriate. 'Madoc – A Mystery' requires a different kind of reading to any of Muldoon's other long poems. Although '7, Middagh Street' (*MB* 36–60), his most allusive and intertextual poem prior to his pantisocratic epic, has also prompted scholars to produce well-researched papers, ably tracking down the allusions to Auden, Yeats, MacNeice, Shakespeare, Masefield, etc.,[79] and although it takes an equally cavalier attitude to biographical exactitude, it does not require the same degree of care on the reader's part. Fact and fiction intermingle without interfering with the poem's thematics. For example, in the section entitled 'Carson' (*MB* 52–54), the narrator borrows liberally from Virginia Spencer Carr's biography of Carson McCullers in order to describe how George Davis came upon 7 Middagh Street:

> In itself, this old, three-storey brownstone
> is unremarkable, and yet so vivid was the reverie
> in which it appeared to George one night
> that when he drove
> next morning to Brooklyn Heights
> he found it true.
>
> (*MB* 52)

The general outline of this is historically correct, but one detail is changed for reasons best known to the poet:

> A few days later, Davis startled Carson with an account of a strange dream. In his sleep he had vizualized an old, Victorian brownstone large enough for him and any of his friends with whom he might wish to share it. It was for rent, and exactly what he had been looking for. The dream had been so vivid that the next morning Davis impulsively took a subway to Brooklyn Heights to the neighborhood he already knew well and where he felt intuitively he would actually find such a house.[80]

The fact that Davis did not in fact drive to Brooklyn Heights is insignificant. In contrast, 'Madoc – A Mystery''s falsifications are important since the primary aim of a historiographical metafiction is to enable the reader 'to acknowledge not only the inevitable textuality of our knowledge of the past, but also both the value and the limitation of the inescapably discursive form of that knowledge'.[81]

One example concerns the infamous cipher letter sent by Aaron Burr to General Wilkinson via Samuel Swartwout. The narrative details themselves foreground the materiality and deceptive nature of writing:

> July 29th, 1806. Aaron Burr entrusts a certain Samuel Swartwout with a letter for General Wilkinson. This letter is written in three ciphers; one hieroglyphic, another based on a specific edition of *Entick's Pocket Dictionary*, the third an alphabet cipher devised by Wilkinson and 'Captain Smith'.
>
> (*MM* 194)

Although these facts concerning the different codes are accurate,[82] the reappearance of the Hitchcockian 'MacGuffin' wearing his inverted commas as always signals a fictive presence.[83] The date proves controversial: Muldoon's time frame for the writing and delivery of the cipher letter is in line with early historical opinion[84] rather than more recent accounts by critics such as Milton Lomask, who contend that 'Swartwout was to carry one copy of the ciphered letter overland by way of the Ohio and Mississippi Valleys. Dr Bollmann was to take a duplicate by sea to New Orleans. Swartwout left Philadelphia on 24 July, [Dr Justus Erich] Bollmann about a week later.'[85] Muldoon also does not alert the reader to a third, important figure, Jonathan Dayton who, according to Mary-Jo Kline, was the author of both letters. This claim is supported by Brunson, who fills in the missing narrative details:

> Former United States Senator Jonathan Dayton, deeply involved in Burr's plan, wrote a letter of introduction for his nephew, Peter V. Ogden, to Colonel Thomas H. Cushing, Commander of the Second United States Regiment of Infantry and second in command to Wilkinson. The same author was to introduce Swartwout also, since Ogden was to accompany Swartwout on much of his journey. Ogden, who left Philadelphia several days after Swartwout did, caught up with him in Pittsburgh. There he gave Swartwout 'a sealed paper', along 'with a message said to be from Colo. Burr.' The message instructed Swartwout to 'Distroy [sic] the ciphered letter and to deliver the sealed paper in lieu of it'. What Burr's ciphered letter contained may never be known since the ciphered letter that Swartwout actually delivered to Wilkinson was probably written by Jonathan Dayton.[86]

The date and quotation from the cipher letter included in '[Marconi]' are equally problematic. Muldoon pointedly singles out the contentious issues which have puzzled historians over the years. While Brunson records that 'Oct. 4, 1806: Swartwout found Wilkinson at Natchitoches, visiting in the quarters of Colonel Thomas H. Cushing', Mary-Jo Kline states that '[a]ccording to Swartwout, he arrived at Natchitoches on 4 Oct.; by Wilkinson's recollection, the New Yorker did not reach his camp until "about the 8th"'.[88] The phrase '"Our object, my dear friend" reflects only one version of Burr's letter:

> Time was to show that Wilkinson modified this letter upon occasion to suit his own purposes. In the copy he sent Jefferson the name of Burr appears in the first line, which is not the case in the version he himself afterwards quoted. Wilkinson also omitted the acknowledgement of a letter from him to Burr, dated May 13, which showed that the two men were in previous communication. He sought to give the impression that he had received a fresh proposal. Such was not the implication of the instructions to him in the body of the letter, but here the ingenious General made a significant alteration. Burr had said: 'Our object, my dear friend,

is brought to a point so long desired.' In the version now submitted his sentence reads: 'The project is brought to the point so long desired.'[89]

The poem's historical inaccuracies and narrative implausibilities are not lapses on Muldoon's part; this is chaos by design. The poem's 'dis-closive form' and intriguing subtitle ('A Mystery') indicate that it is a form of anti-detective story. In accordance with this genre, the poem 'substitutes for the detective as central and ordering character the decentering and chaotic admission of mystery, of nonsolution'.[90] The poem contemplates several mysteries, all of which remain unsolved: has Sara Coleridge been abducted, and if so why and by whom?; do the Welsh Indians exist, and if so where do they reside?; who wrote the Roanoke Rood? More interestingly, the text also involves what Stefano Tani calls 'intertextual detection':

> By now the detective is the reader who has to make sense out of an unfinished fiction that has been distorted or cut short by a playful and perverse 'criminal', the writer. Thus, detective, criminal, and detection are no longer within the fiction, but outside it. The detective is no longer a character but a function assigned to the reader as the criminal is no longer a murderer but the writer who 'kills' (distorts and cuts) the text and thus compels the reader to become a 'detective'.[91]

In 'Madoc – A Mystery', the codes, cipher letters, cryptograms and excerpts from poems, letters, memoirs and travelogues are all clues which both aid and frustrate the eager scholarly detective. Why, for example, is the fifty-fourth section entitled '[Luther]' (*MM* 75)? The text is a dream recorded by Southey (7 November 1804) ten days after its occurrence:[92]

> *I was haunted by evil spirits, of whose presence, though unseen, I was unaware. At length an arm appeared through a half-opened door, or rather a long hand. I ran up and caught it. I pulled at it with desperate effort, dragged a sort of shapeless body into the room and trampled upon it, crying out the while for horror.*
>
> (MM 75)

Chronologically out of place in 'Madoc', the extract is also heavily edited, stripped of its context (the fact of it being a nightmare is only revealed in the following poem '[Scaliger]'),[93] and in its present form reminiscent of the haunting of Lockwood in *Wuthering Heights*. Southey's comment concerning the dream, omitted by Muldoon, is instructive: 'This is a valuable dream, for an old monk would have believed all to have been verily what it appeared, and I now perfectly understand by experience what their contests with the devil were' (Dowden 367). This, of course, is the joke behind the section's title as Luther reputedly threw his inkpot at the Devil.

A more involved example of how Muldoon uses intertextual references
in the poem can be seen in '[Benjamin]' (*MM* 223), a poem which contains
the following lines about Lord Byron:

> As he sprawls there, a group of boys
> begin to jeer, '*Diavolo*'.
> That night, he writes to Southey to propose
> he either retract the 'Satanic' canard
> or give him satisfaction. (This missive's intercepted by
> Kinnaird.)

The context for '[Benjamin]' has been prepared for us by a proleptic reference in '[Pythagoras]' (*MM* 19): '"Until we discovered his gloss / in sympathetic ink: / C[*oleridge*] RO[*bert Southey The S*]ATAN[*ic School*]"'. The lack
of any defining details or context renders the sympathic gloss redundant
and makes the reader search for further clues relating to the Satanic School.
The name crops up twice: first in '[Neurath]' (*MM* 210), and then in
'[Ricoeur]' (*MM* 245). The reader is helped by a date and a cited textual
reference: 'March 1st, 1809. In *English Bards and Scotch Reviewers*'. However, although it is somewhat true that Byron 'launches a fierce / attack on
the "ballad-monger" Southey and Tom Moore' in the 1809 text, Muldoon's
interpretation, by juxtaposing the two different poets within the same contextual framework, elides the distinct sources of satire, runs contrary to
scholarly opinion and misleads the reader as to the provenance of 'The
Satanic School'. Although Byron's attack on Southey was in full earnest
(owing in part to his aversion to the Lake School of poets),[94] it was hardly
'fierce' in 1809 and did not result in a rift between them.[95] Muldoon hints
at possible rancour due to Byron's remark about the Fricker sisters being
'milliners of Bath'[96] (*MM* 42), and Byron's own animosity toward Southey
is highlighed by including stanzas 226 and 227 of *Vision of Judgement*[97]
which rail against the latter's acceptance of the Poet Laureateship (1813).
However, Muldoon omits the more direct allusion to the Satanic School in
the preface to that work:

> In this preface it has pleased the Laureate to draw the picture of a supposed 'Satanic School',
> the which he doth recommend to the notice of the legislature, thereby adding to his other
> laurels the ambition of those of an informer. If there exists anywhere, excepting in his
> imagination, such a school, is he not sufficiently armed against it by his own intense vanity?
> … I say nothing for the cowardice of such a proceeding; its meanness speaks for itself; but I
> wish to touch upon the *motive*, which is neither more nor less, than that Mr. S. has been
> laughed at a little in some recent publications, as he was of yore on the 'Anti-jacobin' by his
> recent patrons. Hence all this 'skimble scamble stuff' about 'Satanic', and so forth.[98]

This preface points towards the true source of 'The Satanic School', namely Southey's preface to his *Vision of Judgement* and not, as Muldoon has it, the satirical attack in Byron's *English Bards*. He also omits Byron's letter to John Murray (24 November 1818)[99] as well as the appendix to *The Two Foscari* (11 December 1821),[100] both of which relate to the rumours which Southey was alleged to have spread concerning Byron's life in Switzerland with Claire Clairmont, Mary Godwin and Shelley.[101]

In line with historiographic metafiction's emphasis on the textual nature of history, '[Benjamin]' (*MM* 223) highlights the selection, editing, dating and presentation of historical documents and texts. The narrator states that Byron is jeered at 'Later that afternoon, or the next', and that he writes the letter 'That night'. The ambiguity reflects a real editorial problem due to the existence of two notes: the first is dated 6 February 1822, the postscript of which reads 'I have just got Southey's pretended reply – to which I am surprized that you do not allude – what remains to be done <had I not better> is to call him out – the question is – would he come? for if he would not – the whole thing would appear ridiculous – if I were to take a long and expensive journey to no purpose. – You must be my Second';[102] the second is dated 7 February 1822, and states 'Sir – My friend the Honourable Douglas Kinnaird will deliver to you a message from me, to which an answer is requested.'[103] In its new context it questions the omniscience of the narrator and helps problematise the presentation of the entire Byron–Southey dispute.[104] Muldoon's chronological presentation of this literary conflict is similarly put in question when the narrator states in '[Neurath]' that 'Southey henceforth dubs them "The Satanic School"' (*MM* 210): the text is dated 1 March 1809, yet the first mention of 'The Satanic School' does not occur until 11 April 1822 in the preface to Southey's *Vision of Judgement*.[105] This preface is included in 'Madoc' (*MM* 245) but without a proper citation or date and is, in fact, out of sequence as it occurs after the report of Burr's death (14 September 1836). The quotation itself does not bear any marks to indicate that it has been amended or edited, yet a total of 19 sentences have been cut from various parts of the preface.[106] Although in this case Muldoon's editing does not affect the sense of the preface, it does suggest that the reader should be vigilant when reading the poem's quoted documents.

More humorous examples of misdirection occur in '[Malthus]' (*MM* 142) and '[Smith]' (*MM* 145), both of which relate Southey's concern over the price, production and reception of *Madoc*. On closer inspection, the first text is composed of two extracts from separate letters: the first sentence comes from a letter to Charles Williams Wynn, dated 6 April 1805, while the remainder is taken from one dated 25 June 1805 to the same person.[107] By editing the first so heavily, Muldoon hides Southey's grave anxiety at the lack of profit from the sale of his poem: '… and I vehemently suspect that in consequence, the sale will be just sufficient for the publisher not to lose anything, and for me not to gain anything' (322). '[Smith]' is made up of three extracts from three different letters: the opening two sentences come from the same letter dated 25 June 1805 to Wynn; the following two sentences are taken from a letter to Grosvenor Bedford, dated 6 December 1805; and the remainder comes from a letter to Thomas Southey, dated 7 December 1805.[108] The text stresses how positive the sales of *Madoc* have been. The reality, however, can be seen in a subsequent letter to Grosvenor Charles Bedford (23 October 1809):

> My business affairs are bad at this time, but they will soon be better. I am working very hard for Longman. I write – write – write – to what end? The public did not buy. I'll no doubt wipe my backside with *Thalaba, Madoc*, and *Kehama* … I borrow and borrow from Longman.[109]

The sale of Southey's text was, in fact, very slow: in its first year it only yielded £3 17s 1d, while his total profit from it was £25,[110] and in 1808 he wrote to Wynn saying 'The small edition of "Madoc" has not yet paid the expenses'.[111] One can but hope that Muldoon's 'Madoc' has fared better than Southey's.

Muldoon's careful marshalling of source material does not produce easily understood poetry; the cited historical documents, dates and biographical minutiae are all intrusive, demanding attention from the reader. One could be forgiven for thinking that behind the scholarly facade lies only a smug intelligence. However, his work is not hermetic in the negative sense (impenetrable); rather, he takes on the attributes of Hermes, the inventor of alphabets and the messenger of the gods.[112] Unlike those authors whose meaning remains obscure because they provide too little information, Muldoon's poetry is accessible because he provides so many intertextual references which guide the willing reader, limiting the possible readings rather than multiplying them. Muldoon is aware of the difficulties his work presents but quite correctly states that '[o]ne has to learn to read these poems, just as one has to learn to read a three-line, little imagist poem, just as the writer had to learn to write it'.[113]

Notes

1 Paul Muldoon has recently become part of a garage band, *Rackett*, at Princeton. The quoted lyrics, written by Muldoon, are from one of their songs 'Most of the Time (I Don't Get It)'.

2 Anonymous entry in the online 'Literary Encyclopedia': *http://www.litencyc.com/php/speople.php?rec=true&UID=3249*, consulted 17 April 2005.

3 Clair Wills, *Improprieties: Politics and Sexuality in Northern Irish Poetry* (Clarendon Press, 1993) 203. Wills, of course, does *not* treat Muldoon as a 'playful technician', but undue emphasis on the Barthesian quality of his work tends to underemphasise authorial control and intentionality.

4 Paul Muldoon, 'Getting Round: Notes Towards an *Ars Poetics*', *Essays in Criticism* 48 (April 1998) 121.

5 Fennella Copplestone, 'Paul Muldoon and the Exploding Sestina', *PN Review* Vol. 106 (1995) 35.

6 Eamonn Grennan, 'Introduction: Contemporary Irish Poetry', *Colby Quarterly* 28.4 (December, 1992) 189.

7 John Mole, 'The Reflecting Glass', *Encounter* 62.3 (March, 1984) 49.

8 Dillon Johnston, *Irish Poetry After Joyce* (Notre Dame: University of Notre Dame Press, 1985) 265.

9 Tim Kendall, *Paul Muldoon* (Brigend: Seren, 1996) 108.

10 Muldoon, 'Getting Round' 107–28.

11 Paul Muldoon, 'The Point of Poetry', *Princeton University Library Chronicle* 49.3 (Spring, 1998) 516.

12 Wench Ommunddsen, *Metafictions?: Reflexivity in Contemporary Texts* (Melbourne: Melbourne University Press, 1993) 18.

13 Muldoon, 'Getting Round' 127.

14 Paul Muldoon, interview by Edward Brunner et al., *Crab Orchard Review* 1.2 (1996) 20.

15 Paul Muldoon, 'An Interview with Paul Muldoon', interview by Lynn Keller, *Contemporary Poetry* 35.1 (Spring, 1994) 13. See also Paul Muldoon, 'An Interview with Paul Muldoon', interview by Clair Wills et al., *Oxford Poetry* 3.1 (Winter, 1986–87) 15; 'The Invention of the I: A Conversation with Paul Muldoon', interview by Earl G. Ingersoll and Stan Sanvel Rubin, *Michigan Quarterly Review* 37.1 (1998) 67; interview by Jean W. Ross, *Contemporary Authors Database* 9 September 1988: from the internet.

16 Muldoon, 'Getting Round' 127.

17 Paul Muldoon in John Brown, *In the Chair: Interviews with Poets from the North of Ireland* (Clare: Salmon, 2002) 188.

18 Rachel Buxton, '"Structure and Serendipity": The Influence of Robert Frost on Paul Muldoon', *Critical Ireland: New Essays in Literature and Culture* (Dublin: Four Courts Press, 2001) 20.

19 When in an uncollected poem entitled 'Caprice des Dieux', *Times Literary Supplement* 11 May 1984, Muldoon described Irish poets in terms of a selection of cheeses, he admitted that 'For myself? A little *Caprice des Dieux*' (516).

20 Clair Wills sheds light on this in her monograph on Muldoon: 'Formally the shape of the poem is absolutely predetermined – each of the thirty sonnets uses six of the ninety rhyme

words from 'Yarrow' (rhyming *ababcdcdefgefg*), in the order in which they first occur in the earlier poem – which gets you to sonnet 15, and then the whole pattern is repeated in reverse' (*Reading Paul Muldoon*, [Newcastle-upon-Tyne: Bloodaxe, 1998] 209).

21 Seamus Heaney, 'Away from it All', *Station Island* (London: Faber, 1984) 17.

22 Seamus Heaney, 'Known World', *Electric Light* (London: Faber, 2001) 19–23.

23 Seamus Heaney, *Seamus Heaney in Conversation with Karl Miller* (London: BTL, 2000) 28.

24 Karl Miller in *Seamus Heaney in Conversation with Karl Miller*, 27.

25 Bernard O'Donoghue cited in Robert Potts, 'The Poet at Play', *Guardian*, 12 May 2001: Saturday Review, 6.

26 Linda Hutcheon, *A Poetics of Postmodernism: History, Theory, Fiction* (New York: Routledge, 1988) 118.

27 Linda Hutcheon, *The Politics of Postmodernism* (London: Routledge, 1989) 11.

28 For an overview of this misconception, see Thomas Docherty, *Alterities: Criticism, History, Representation* (Oxford: Clarendon Press, 1996) 196.

29 Richard Kearney, *The Wake of Imagination: Ideas of Creativity in Western Culture* (London: Hutchinson, 1988) 5.

30 Paul Muldoon, interview by John Haffenden in *Viewpoints: Poets in Conversation* (London: Faber, 1981) 136.

31 Paul Muldoon, interview by Wills et al., 14.

32 Paul Muldoon, 'A Tennyson Triptych, 1974', *Times Literary Supplement* 2 October 1992, 9.

33 Tom Paulin, Untitled, *Times Literary Supplement* 2 October 1992, 8.

34 Paul Muldoon, personal interview, Yeats Summer School, 11 August 1996.

35 Paul Muldoon, 'Q. & A. with Paul Muldoon', interview by Kevin Barry, *Irish Literary Supplement* 6.2 (Fall, 1987) 36. See also Muldoon, interview by Keller: 'I think Seamus Heaney is a great poet. Great inspiration, actually, and a challenge, I think, in the best sense, to many poets, including myself, because Seamus *has* managed to keep going, and to keep producing poems of consistently high standard. That's quite an achievement' (26).

36 Muldoon, interview by Barry, 36.

37 Paul Muldoon, 'Sweeney Peregraine', *London Review of Books* 1 November 1984, 20.

38 Seamus Heaney, 'Broagh', *Wintering Out* (London: Faber, 1972) 27.

39 Seamus Heaney, 'Widgeon', *Station Island* (London: Faber, 1984) 48.

40 Seamus Heaney, *The Place of Writing* (Atlanta: Scholars' Press, 1989) 39 and 41, respectively.

41 Seamus Heaney, *Preoccupations: Selected Prose 1968–1978* (London: Faber, 1980) 213.

42 Heaney, *The Place of Writing* 42.

43 Heaney, *The Place of Writing* 52.

44 The name itself is humorous as a Foley artist is someone who works on a Foley stage, adding sound effects and editing the sound track for a film's post-production.

45 Muldoon is also referring to 'The Sharpening Stone', *The New Yorker* 23 October 1995, 62–63 repr. in *The Spirit Level* (London: Faber, 1996) 59–61 which Heaney sent to Muldoon as 'a Christmas poem'.

46 Neil Corcoran, in '"A Languorous Cutting Edge": Muldoon versus Heaney?', *Princeton University Library Chronicle* 59.3 (Spring, 1998), adds that Muldoon's poem also refers to Edna Longley's 'polarizing' of the two poets when she says that '[w]hat is physical in Heaney

becomes metaphysically problematic in Muldoon' (564).

47 Muldoon, personal interview, Yeats Summer School, 11 August 1996.

48 Muldoon in interview by Haffenden, 134.

49 Corcoran, 'Muldoon versus Heaney?' 570 and 571, respectively.

50 Derek Mahon, 'Courtyards in Delft', *Selected Poems* 1990 (London: Penguin, 1993) 120–21.

51 Seán Dunne refers to it in his review, 'A Poet's Box of Puzzles', *Irish Times* 20 August 1994 and it is later repeated by Tim Kendall in *Paul Muldoon* (Brigend: Seren, 1996) 193.

52 Derek Mahon, 'Alien Nation', *The Hudson Letter* (Meath: Gallery Press, 1995) 61–62.

53 Peter McDonald, *Mistaken Identities: Poetry and Northern Ireland* (Oxford: Clarendon Press, 1997) 157.

54 Jane Stabler, 'Alive in the Midst of Questions: A Survey of the Poetry of Paul Muldoon', *Verse* 8.2 (Summer, 1991) 60.

55 Michelle Stone and B. Hoche, '[Madoc]: [A Mystery]', *Graph* 9 (Winter, 1990) 32.

56 John Banville, 'Slouching toward Bethlehem', *New York Review of Books* 38.10 (May, 1991) 39.

57 Peter Finch, Review of *Madoc – A Mystery, Poetry Wales* 27.1 (June, 1991) 64.

58 Eve Patten, 'Clever, Comic, Liberating', *Fortnight* 291 (January, 1991) 26–27.

59 For example, 'retinagraph' (*MM* 18), 'Signifump' (*MM* 58), 'Lasaber' (*MM* 261).

60 Slang: 'take a dump' (*MM* 17), 'a whatsit' (*MM* 18), 'smithereens' (MM 257). Dialect: 'Mon is the mezjur of all thungs' (*MM* 26). Romantic lyricism: 'birch-bower' (*MM* 40), 'fluted cypresses' (*MM* 18).

61 For example: 'MADOC' (*MM* 49), 'EVANS' (*MM* 191); 'This includes the *other* Prince of Wales' (*MM* 95), 'He's a *South*' (*MM* 147).

62 See especially *MM* 130, 134 and 244.

63 Berand DeVoto, in *The Journals of Lewis and Clark* (London: Eyre and Spottiswoode, 1954) states that the spellings of the original Lewis and Clark journals are a part of their charm (vii). Charles G. Clark, in *The Men of the Lewis and Clark Expedition: A Biographical Roster of the Fifty One Members and a Composite Diary of Their Activities from All Known Sources* (California: Arthur H. Clarke, 1970) comments on the Captain's 'charming disregard for the accuracy of spelling' (24). Donald Jackson, in *Letters of the Lewis and Clark Expedition with Related Documents 1783–1854*, 2nd edn. (Urbana: University of Illinois Press, 1978) is more harsh, commenting on 'Clark's ingenious phonetic atrocities' (217).

64 Silvio A. Bedini, *Thomas Jefferson and His Copying Machines* (Charlottesville: University Press of Virginia, 1984) 46. See also Dumas Malone, *Jefferson and His Time, Jefferson the President: Second Term 1805–1809*, Vol. 5 (Boston: Little Brown and Co., 1974) 26.

65 See Bedini, *Thomas Jefferson*: 'it appeared in literature to describe a prolific writer and one who aped the dress and manner of another individual, and finally it was applied to a form of secret writing' (48).

66 See DeVoto, *The Journals of Lewis and Clark* 493–94 and Jackson, *Letters of the Lewis and Clark Expedition* 234–36.

67 Jackson, *Letters of the Lewis and Clark Expedition* 236.

68 DeVoto 26.

69 Jackson, *Letters of the Lewis and Clark Expedition* 254.

70 Jackson, *Letters of the Lewis and Clark Expedition* 261.

71 Richard Dillon, *Merriwether Lewis: A Biography* (New York: Coward-McCann, 1965) 36.

72 Jackson, *Letters of the Lewis and Clark Expedition* 10.
73 Paul Muldoon, 'Lunch with Pancho Villa', interview by Kevin Smith, *Rhinoceros* 4 (1990) 84.
74 Paul Muldoon, 'Way Down upon the Old Susquehanna,' interview by Blake Morrison, *Independent on Sunday* 28 October 1990, 37.
75 Linda Hutcheon, '"The Pastime of Time Past": Fiction, History, and Historiographic Metafiction,' *Genre* 20.3–4 (Fall–Winter, 1987) 299.
76 Linda Hutcheon, *Irony's Edge: The Theory and Politics of Irony* (London: Routledge, 1994) 11–12.
77 See Mary-Jo Kline, (ed.), *Political Correspondence and Public Papers of Aaron Burr*, Vol. ii (Princeton: Princeton University Press, 1983) 808 and Milton Lomask, *Aaron Burr: The Conspiracy Years of Exile 1805–1836* (New York: Farrar, 1982) 28.
78 See Thomas Perkins Abernethy, *The Burr Conspiracy* (New York: Oxford University Press, 1954) 15 and Lomask, *Aaron Burr* 27.
79 See especially Jonathan Allison, 'Questioning Yeats: Paul Muldoon's '7, Middagh Street', in Deborah Fleming (ed.), *Learning the Trade: Essays on W. B. Yeats and Contemporary Poetry*, (West Cornwall, Connecticut: Locust Hill Press, 1993) 3–20; Richard Brown, 'Bog Poems and Book Poems: Doubleness, Self-Translation and Pun in Seamus Heaney and Paul Muldoon', in Neil Corcoran (ed.), *The Chosen Ground: Essays on the Contemporary Poetry of Northern Ireland* (Dufour: Seren, 1992) 163–64; Mark Ford, 'Out of the Blue', *London Review of Books* 9.22 (December, 1987) 20–21; Edna Longley, 'The Aesthetic and the Territorial', in ed. Elmer Andrews (ed.), *Contemporary Irish Poetry: A Collection of Critical Essays* (London: Macmillan, 1992) 64–67; and Paul Scott Stanfield. 'Another Side of Paul Muldoon', *North Dakota Quarterly* 57.1 (Winter, 1989) 129–43.
80 Virginia Spencer Carr, *The Lonely Hunter: A Biography of Carson McCullers* (New York: Doubleday, 1975) 116.
81 Hutcheon, *Poetics* 127.
82 See Lomask, *Aaron Burr* 115–19 and Kline, *Political Correspondence* 984.
83 In '[More]' (*MM* 74) the MacGuffin changed his name to 'Smith'.
84 See Abernethy, *The Burr Conspiracy* 59 and Malone, *Jefferson the President: Second Term 1805–1809*, Vol. 5 263.
85 Lomask, *Aaron Burr* 119.
86 B. R. Brunson, *The Adventures of Samuel Swartout in the Age of Jefferson and Jackson* (Lewiston: Edwin Mellen Press, 1989) 7–8.
87 Brunson, *The Adventures of Samuel Swartout* 8.
88 Kline, *Political Correspondence* 974.
89 Malone, *Jefferson the President: Second Term 1805–1809*, Vol. 5 264.
90 Stefano Tani, *The Doomed Detective: The Contribution of the Detective Novel to Postmodern American and Italian Fiction* (Carbondale: Southern Illinois University Press, 1984) 40. See also William V. Spanos, *Repetitions: The Postmodern Occasion in Literature and Culture* (Baton Rouge: Louisiana State University Press, 1987) 24–25.
91 Tani, *The Doomed Detective* 113.
92 See Edward Dowden (ed.), *The Correspondence of Robert Southey with Caroline Bowles to which is Added: Correspondence with Shelley, and Southey's Dreams* (Dublin: Hodges Figgis, 1881) 366–67.

93 This, of course, relates to Scaliger's *Concerning Bad Dreams*, published in 1539.

94 See Charles M. Fuess, *Lord Byron as a Satirist in Verse* (New York: Columbia University Press, 1912) 60.

95 See Kenneth Curry, *Southey* (London: Routledge and Kegan Paul, 1975) 68–69. Rowlan E. Prothero in *The Works of Lord Byron* (London: John Murray, 1898) notes that 'The satire did not prevent the two men from meeting at Holland House (Sunday, September 26, 1813) on friendly terms' (Appendix I, 377).

96 See *Don Juan*, Canto III, Stanza 93 and Byron's letter to John Murray (11 September 1822), in Leslie A. Marchand, (ed.), *'In the Wind's Eye': Byron's Letters and Journals 21– 1822* Vol. IX (London: John Murray, 1979): ' I hear he says his wife was not a milliner at Bath. — Ask Luttrell — I have heard Nugent his friend say twenty times — that he knew both his & Coleridge's Sara at Bath — before they were married & that they were Milliners — or Dress-maker's apprentices. — There is no harm if they were that I know — nor did I mean it as any' (207).

97 Byron, *The Complete Poetical Works*, eds Jerome J. McGann and Barry Weller (Oxford: Clarendon Press, 1991) Vol. VI, 342–43.

98 Byron, *Complete Poetical Works* Vol. VI, 309–10.

99 See Prothero, *The Works of Lord Byron* 271–72.

100 See Prothero, *The Works of Lord Byron* 387–89 and Robert Southey, *Essays Moral and Political*, Vol. II (Austin, Texas: University of Texas Press, 1957) 187–90.

101 See Fuess 188. For a refutation by Southey concerning Byron's allegations, see his Letter to *The Courier* (5 January 1822) in Southey *Essays*, Vol. II 191–96, Prothero 389–92. They also refer to the Satanic School.

102 Byron, *'In the Wind's Eye': Byron's Letters and Journals 1821–1822*, ed. Leslie A. Marchand, Vol. Ix (London: John Murray, 1979) 101.

103 Byron, *Letters and Journals* 102.

104 For a comprehensive overview of the conflict between the two poets, see Prothero, Appendix I, 377–99 and Robert Southey, 'Two Letters Concerning Lord Byron', *Essays* Vol. II (London: John Murray, 1832) 183–205.

105 See C. L. Cline, *Byron, Shelley and Their Pisan Circle* (London: John Murray, 1952) 83 and William Haller, *The Early Life of Robert Southey, 1774–1803* (New York: Columbia University Press, 1917) 295.

106 The opening three sentences of the preface have been omitted, as well as one from between the quoted second and third sentences; nine sentences are then omitted and seven are taken from the conclusion. Compare '[Ricoeur]' with Robert Southey *Essays*, Vol. II 183–87.

107 Charles Cuthbert Southey (ed.), *The Life and Correspondence of Robert Southey*, Vol. 2 (London: Longman et al., 1849–50) 322–24 and 329–30.

108 See Southey, *Life and Correspondence of Robert Southey*, Vol. 2 329, 356, 357. Both poems disrupt the chronology of 'Madoc', the date of '[Schiller]' is 5 May 1805, while '[Hamilton]' is only 7 September.

109 Kenneth Curry, ed., *New Letters of Robert Southey* Vol. I (New York: Columbia University Press, 1965) 519–20.

110 See Lionel Madden (ed.), *Robert Southey: The Critical Heritage* (London: Routledge and Kegan Paul, 1972) 7, 24 and a letter from Southey to W. Williams Wynn, 28 September

       1807 in Curry, *New Letters of Robert Southey* 457.
111 Robert Southey, *Selections from the Letters of Robert Southey*, Vol. ii, ed. John Wood Warter,
       (London: Longman et al., 1846) 81.
112 See Dillon Johnston, 'The Go-between of Recent Irish Poetry', in Michael Kenneally (ed.),
       Cultural Contexts and Literary Idioms in Contemporary Irish Literature (Gerrards Cross: Colin
       Smythe, 1988) 174.
113 Muldoon, interview by Julian Stannard, *Thumbscrew* 4 (Spring, 1996) 7.

2

Medbh McGuckian:
A Threader of Double-Stranded Words

The poetry of Medbh McGuckian has by no means received universal critical acclaim and many of her reviewers have been notoriously acerbic and
personal in their attacks. Patrick Williams classifies her work as 'colourful
guff': 'McGuckian's concoctions of endless poeticism are non-visionary, and
the funny, sealed little worlds where harmless cranks parley with themselves
in gobbledegook won't impinge on the real world of loot and dragons.'[1]
Such criticism of her work's supposedly vexatious obliquity is not unusual:
she is labelled fey and mannered,[2] whimsical,[3] at best intricate and enigmatic, at worst inaccessible and subjective.[4] Gerald Dawe complains that
much of her imagery is 'imprecise to a fault and, like candy floss, rather
bland a second time round';[5] Mary O'Donnell believes that her 'literary
"autism"'[6] is an Art for Art's sake; and Andrew Elliott is tempted to view her
poetry as 'the powerfully rehabilitated feminine icon co-opted by the morality of monetarism into a meaningless "folly-studded" aesthetic'.[7] Behind
the indignation of these critics lie three essential objections: first, that her
work is deliberately obfuscatory; secondly, that she has imperfectly absorbed
the influence of both literary peers and precursors;[8] and thirdly, that her
poems lack coherent subject matter.[9] All three are reductive misreadings of
McGuckian's oeuvre. This chapter offers a corrective account by redirecting
critical atttention towards her peculiar method of composition, focusing
especially on her hitherto unnoticed strategies of quotation.

There is some truth, however, in the accusation that her work 'hoards
knowledge that belongs exclusively to the poet's private life'.[10] Indeed,
McGuckian admits as much in her interview with Kathleen McCracken
when, describing her poems, she states 'I'm not sure they don't remain private, at least until some scholar totally identifies with me. When I read one,
I know who it is for, what I felt, what they felt. [...] But there's usually one
special person the poem is a private message to.'[11] Three examples spring

readily to mind: 'Spy Fever'[12] is written specifically to commemorate the birthday of a poet at Princeton, its title deriving from a letter sent by him;[13] 'The Sun Trap' (*FM* 24) is based on early love-letters sent to her, from which she quotes liberally;[14] and the content of 'Dear Rain' (*MC* 22–23) is due in part to correspondence with Paul Durcan.[15] A degree of privacy especially pertains to those literary pastiches of hers which employ intertextual allusions as in-jokes. For example, McGuckian informs me that 'Ales Stenar'[16] ostensibly refers to 'a sort of Stonehenge near Lund. There is a man there called Lars who has translated Heaney and Muldoon and they had also written about the stones.'[17] The published version not only shields 'Lars' from the public with the abbreviated dedication 'To L. H. S.', it also obliquely refers to the group of Irish poets who attended the poets' convention held at Ales Stenar in 1990. The first draft, included among her papers at Emory University, is written on the back of the 'Programme of Events' and is described as 'a pastiche of Seamus Heaney'.[18] Lines such as 'I felt the thickness of this line / Like the proximity of dawn' and 'A torness rooted in the curve of what's there' are excellent examples of well-intentioned imitation: reminiscent of Heaney, they are inflected humorously by McGuckian's own inimitable use of simile. Once the in-joke is known, then the opening lines 'In a moment that was coming to think of itself / As post-everything' is transformed from being an expression of heartfelt existential angst to a clever dig at the vacuous pretentiousness of certain conferences, with the 'six poets' who 'contradicted each other, / searching the soul of the sea / for the death of grace' being the target of her displeasure.

Even if the primary addressee is named, a poem's personal message may not be immediately accessible and the poem-as-communiqué may remain oblique. 'Unused Water' (*CL* 28), dedicated to Joan McBreen,[19] is one such poem. Though evocative and imagistic, the opening verse's relation to McBreen is uncertain: 'Lost earrings, / a dash of acrid green / in the wrong time of the year'. The title, the poet explains, is suggestive of the amniotic fluid which, although present, is not of use to McBreen who has just undergone a hysterectomy.[20] The 'lost earrings' refer both to the actual earrings left behind during a visit, and to the non-functioning ovaries. In a surgical context, 'acrid' is an apt description of the earrings' colour, counteracting the normally fertile connotations of 'green'. Without being privy to the poet's intentions, a reader would miss this primary level of signification. However, this is not to say that the reader's response is unduly curtailed: by being receptive to the colour symbolism (green, darkness) and the contrast between water and dryness, he would still be able to focus on the main theme of an apparent loss and ultimate regaining of fertility.

This argument becomes clearer if one looks at 'Lines for Thanksgiving' (*CL* 13), the opening poem of her fifth collection. McGuckian revealed in an interview that the primary intention when writing the text was to refer both to her summer residence, Marconi's Cottage (Ballycastle), and to Gallery Press, the publishing house which took control of her work once Oxford University Press turned down her fourth collection (entitled *Marconi's Cottage*). The poem 'is a goodbye to *Marconi's Cottage*. It is all about *Marconi's Cottage*. It was written for Peter [Fallon], and it just describes the cottage, and thanking him for giving me the book – it was like the book was the house itself'.[21] Perhaps the somewhat acrimonious circumstances surrounding her change of publisher determined that the autobiographical details be alluded to obliquely, thus necessitating a stratagem not entirely unfamiliar in her poetry: 'Every poem I've written is about something that's happened to me … but I have coded it.'[22] During the summer of 1991, negotiations became fraught between McGuckian and her commissioning editor at Oxford University Press, Jacqueline Simms. Oxford University Press (OUP) were unwilling to bring out her new collection, but had offered to publish a *Selected Poems* which would incorporate some of the new poems. Peter Fallon, the editor of Gallery Press, indicated a desire to publish her forthcoming work, but also wished to bring out revised editions of her first three collections. OUP then felt compelled to set restrictive conditions for the proposed publication of her *Selected Poems*: first, she would have to guarantee that her first three books would not be reprinted by another publisher during the lifetime of the *Selected Poems*; secondly, a clause would have to be included in the OUP contract that would rule out the publication of any rival *Selected Poems*; and thirdly, she would have to make it clear to Gallery Press that she has accepted the terms as set out by OUP.[23] These prerequisites were unacceptable to McGuckian, so the publication was cancelled and rights for her existing collections were subsequently reassigned to her.

The reader of 'Lines for Thanksgiving' would be hard-pressed to find such a narrative, but two details are highly suggestive: firstly, the title refers to, and gives thanks for, her first appearance as a Gallery Press poet (*Marconi's Cottage* was published on Thanksgiving Day, 28 November 1991); and secondly, while the religious connotation of 'monstrance' in the third stanza is perfectly apt, it also has the more obscure meaning of *monstrance du droit*, 'a writ issuing out of Chancery, for restoring a person to lands or tenements legally belonging to him, though found in possession of another lately deceased' (*Oxford English Dictionary*), thus alluding to the restoration of copyright to McGuckian for her first three collections. As with 'Unused Water', the poem is necessarily oblique since its sensitive context is to be shielded from the wider public. However, the text's meaning is not confined to the poet's primary intention. Indeed, her blunt statement of intent does scant justice to the multivalent strands of imagery running through the poem's corpus and it is evident from its sinuous narrative progression that the primary impulse has receded into the background:

> Two floors, their invisible staircase
> crouching muscularly,
> an old wall, unusually high,
> interwoven like the materials for a nest,
> the airtight sensation of slates:
> all as gracefully apart
> as a calvary from a crib
> or the woman born in my sleep
> from the stranger me that is satisfied
> by any street with the solemn name of a saint.

Talking to the poet about the labyrinthine complexity of her similes, Cecile Gray makes the astute observation that '[i]t's as if you take the image and push it to its uttermost. It's as if, maybe, the image goes beyond the initial experience and begins to weave itself out in more than one direction at once ...'[24] The ambiguity surrounding the uncertain terms of comparison in this opening stanza is productive, throwing up surprising juxtapositions and forcing the reader to explore multiple avenues of thought. What, one might ask, is 'interwoven like the materials for a nest' – the 'old wall', the 'Two floors', or both? The images themselves (floors, staircase, wall, slates) may suggest an actual building, yet one is equally aware that the poet is referring to something other than that which is physically manifest. In what way can an *invisible* staircase crouch 'muscularly'? Much of the uncertainty is due to McGuckian's propitious use of imagery whereby the physical, textual and spiritual are so closely intertwined. An overly literal reading fails to account for the tension established between the acute sense of enclosure ('crouching', 'airtight') and the evocation of a temporal space between 'calvary' and 'crib'. This tension is compounded by the distance implied between the two antithetical sides of the poet's consciousness: 'the woman born in my sleep'

/ 'the stranger me'. The house in the first instance becomes synonymous with the poet's lifeline, the distance between the two 'floors' being a metaphorical description of McGuckian's awareness of her own mortality; in the second instance, the two-storey house is emblematic of the split between her conscious and dream selves. But what is the reader to make of the religious register of her language (thanksgiving, calvary, crib, gracefully, saint, eternally, monstrance)? Within the context of *Captain Lavender*, one could tentatively suggest that it is occasioned by the impending death of her father, and that she is investigating the consolations of her Catholic upbringing. However, one could equally surmise that the poet herself is adopting the role of a priest,[25] the house figuring as her poem/prayer. Indeed, speaking to Catherine Byron, the poet explained that, in general, the house 'is probably the poem itself [...] or a symbol for the world of the poem'.[26]

McGuckian's poetry is oblique for a more fundamental reason than her use of either literary pastiche or encoded missives: she occludes her idiosyncratic relationship to literary exemplars. In interviews she states that 'the poetic process is a vatic one' whereby the poet becomes 'possessed';[27] passively subjugating her will to the 'creative force', she regards her profession as having 'a priest-like function, it's one of just being a window, and you are nothing – you yourself are something that is seen through'.[28] Although this may well be the ideal, the method of composition is decidedly more architectonic:

> I never write just blindly, I never sit down without an apparatus, I always have a collection of words – it's like a bird building a nest – I gather materials over the two weeks, or whatever. And I keep a notebook or a diary for the words which are happening to me and occurring to me. I never sit down without those because otherwise you would just go mad, trying to think of words.[29]

Where does she find these words and are the sources significant? Are the fragments randomly listed? Although she never records her sources and rarely acknowledges her borrowings in her published work, a detailed analysis of her word lists and early drafts in her notebooks[30] and unbound work-sheets[31] confirms that the 'collections of words' result from her reading of diverse texts. One reviewer, Catriona O'Reilly, came unwittingly close to this conclusion: 'McGuckian's intense, improvisatory movement', she states, 'owes much to Marina Tsvetaeva, and there is in general a considerable debt to her sources, in particular to Mandelstam and the Celan of *Mohn und Gedächtnis*. Such influences contribute to the work's slightly dislocated quality, many poems reading like translations from the Russian.'[32] What O'Reilly did not realise is that McGuckian's poems borrow wholesale from the translations themselves; the authors (and translators) are her muses. The 'collection of words' is meticulously recorded from biographies, memoirs, critical essays, etc., and are subsequently arranged into poetic texts. Realising this, the next stage is to trace the sources and to see if they open up any new readings.

Two worksheets, comprising 85 phrases written in columnar form, act as the basis for 'Lines for Thanksgiving'[33] since 26 of the phrases are used to make up the poem. One of the foreshortened phrases – 'a past that had almost sunk into the ground, lying by the water's edge like an idler taking the air' – eventually brought to mind the intertext which McGuckian was using, namely Proust's *Swann's Way*.[34] Comparing the two – Proust on the left, McGuckian on the right – one can gauge the extent to which the poem is a bricolage of quotations taken from the first volume of *In Search of Lost Time*:

two floors joined by a slender staircase (50)	
a line invisibly ruled (219)	Two floors, their invisible staircase
the apse, crouched muscularly (77)	crouching muscularly,
an old wall, rough-hewn and unusually high (72)	an old wall, unusually high,
interwoven like the materials for a nest (60)	interwoven like the materials for a nest,
the airtight compartment of separate afternoons (161)	the airtight sensation of slates:
the actual sensation of change (100)	all as gracefully apart
how poor the light is on the slates (7)	as a calvary from a crib
the slender columns … drew so gracefully apart (7)	or the woman born in my sleep
a calvary or a crib (57)	from the stranger me that is satisfied
a woman would be born during my sleep (3)	by any street with the solemn name of a saint.
streets with the solemn names of saints (56)	
seemed to me fuller […] than any other (173)	The moon there, fuller than any other,
slipped into every fold in the sky (73)	slips through my fingers into every fold
stirred-up colours (53)	of the sky, in turn, stirring up satin
as a mother might run her hand through her boy's hair (14)	like a mother repeating its double journey
eternally repeating its double journey (202)	and the same message, as if it were
the same message (52)	still impossible to speak
impossible to speak from one town to another (223)	from one town to the next.
the fire keeping in all night (6)	
the extra gas jet (35)	The fire keeping in all night
several 'thicknesses' of art (46)	is an extra gas jet, its several
unequal in length like the rays of a monstrance (182)	thicknesses of unequal length
if I had just won a victory it was over her (43)	like the rays of a monstrance.
everything that was not myself (188)	If I had just won a victory
by the water's edge (201)	it was over everything that was not
	myself, by the water's edge.

The opening five lines are made up from eight modified quotations from *Swann's Way*, juxtaposed to depict a single, enclosed and homely space. Describing this location in animistic fashion – dormant yet alive, it is 'crouching muscularly' – McGuckian is influenced by a Proustian manner of perception. Thus, the architecture's solidity is illusory, its identity subject to change and not as 'airtight' as it first appears. Describing the body's confusion upon awakening and its attempt to deduce its location, Proust's narrator states: 'Its memory, the composite of its ribs, its knees, its shoulder-blades, offered it a series of rooms in which it had at one time or another slept, while the unseen walls, shifting and adapting themselves to the shape of each successive room that it remembered, whirled round it in the dark' (4–5). The awakening body carries within it, and calls to mind, the memories of all the rooms it has ever slept in. For McGuckian, the poet (and the body of the poem) carries within the texts which she has read. Fragments from Proust's narrative are 'interwoven like the materials for a nest', thereby confirming what she had said in interview about using the 'collection of words': it is 'like a bird building a nest'. Crucially, the citation is taken from a passage describing the making of the narrator's aunt's tea: 'The leaves, having lost or altered their original appearance, resembled the most disparate things, the transparent wing of a fly, the blank side of a label, the petal of a rose, which had all been piled together, pounded or interwoven like the materials for a nest' (60). Like these leaves, the quotations are transformed and seem disparate when transplanted from the original text, yet they re-form to create something new and unified. The intertext is here more significant, however, as the tea's perfume is what triggers the narrator's remembrance of things past and allows him to recover time past:

> Thus would I often lie until morning, dreaming of the old days at Combray, of my melancholy and wakeful evenings there, of other days besides, the memory of which had been more recently restored to me by the taste – by what would have been called at Combray the 'perfume' – of a cup of tea, and, by association of memories, of a story which, many years after I had left the little place, had been told me of a love affair in which Swann had been involved before I was born, with a precision of detail which it is often easier to obtain for the lives of people who have been dead for centuries than for those of our own most intimate friends, an accuracy which it seems as impossible to attain *as it seemed impossible to speak from one town to another*, before we knew of the contrivance by which that impossibility had been overcome.
>
> (223, emphasis added)

Where Proust is referring to the way in which the narrator is able to recall the events prior to his birth, McGuckian is talking about quite a different form of speaking between 'one town to another', yet she too is moving backwards in time (from 'calvary to crib'). Her opening line cites an idea formed by Proust's narrator that 'all Combray had consisted of but two floors joined by a slender staircase'. McGuckian is not simply concerned here with location: the phrases taken to make up her poem all come from the chapter entitled 'Combray', and so for her it is the text which is being considered architectonically. Her poem, then, can be considered as a self-reflexive meditation on art, the inspiration behind it and the way it incorporates a dialogue between the author and her precursor.

McGuckian's reading of Proust is succeeded by a reading of the fragments she has assembled from his text. Repeating that 'double-journey' – a journey undertaken both by Proust's narrator and the poet – when constructing her text, she feels as if a new self has been created. In *Swann's Way*, the 'woman born in my sleep' is a dream self: in one respect, she is 'the girl of my dream' (3), an erotic Other; yet she is also inherently himself, a product of his own subconscious. For McGuckian, the use of another author's words seems to create a rift between the supposedly self-identical lyrical 'I' whereby the poet speaks directly in her work, and the 'I' who is not McGuckian but a 'woman born in my sleep'. To use Rimbaud's words, '*Je est un autre*'. The 'I' is neither McGuckian nor Proust. Everything in the text is in tension and occupies a liminal position: the staircase between two floors; 'everything that was not / myself, by the water's edge'. This self-division is productive and welcomed by the poet; the two selves are kept 'gracefully apart'. The 'woman born in my sleep' is, ironically, less troubling or alienated than 'the stranger me that is satisfied / by any street with the solemn name of a Saint'. This concurs with the experience of Proust's narrator, for whom the real world of Combray, with its 'streets with the solemn names of saints', was 'a trifle depressing' (56). Writing from within someone else's text, inscribing 'several thicknesses' into her own art, McGuckian allows her own three stanzas to play host to Proust's 'Combray'. The text is like a monstrance, a receptacle used for the exhibition of relics or the transparent vessel in which the host is exposed. Like Proust's work, 'Lines for Thanksgiving' occupies the space between two kinds of art: the mimetic and the autotelic, 'an art made by imitating things outside itself, and an art that is an internally coherent making'.[35]

Quite often McGuckian's poems address the very issue of intertextuality and can be read, on one level, as a commentary on the relations set up between poet and literary exemplar. 'Reading in a Library' (*HTL* 33) is one such text, referring in its title to the time of writing, itself a time of *reading*. The poem was originally included in an interim collection entitled *An Invalid in War* (2001) and was sent to me with the inscription 'For the indefatigable sleuth!' It was subsequently recollected in *Had I a Thousand Lives* (2003). After some literary detective work and cross-referencing it was possible to determine that the poem pays homage to the influence of Elias Canetti and the eloquence of his prose memoirs, making use, as it does, of seventeen fragments from *The Torch in My Ear*.[36]

waking me up with my name (152)	You wake me up with the name
the name which I had been carrying (178)	I carry inside me like a first
our first language (223)	language. It becomes needles
the needles he held in his lips (64)	on your lips, slightly grey, a waste
slightly grey words (89); a waste of light (109)	of light I swallow like a syrup.
swallowed them like syrup (271)	
a tree that forked [...] at the level of her eyes (260)	A tree forks at the level
its dark dipthong (119); he raised his right hand	of your eyes, it spreads my dark
halfway, opening it upward like a cup (78)	diphthong upward like a cup,
I placed myself expectantly under his opened	I place myself expectantly
hand each time (83)	under your open hand.
you talk with your hands (190)	You talk with your hands
he zigzagged softly from person to person (201)	like two people, you zigzag
the names rubbed together, that was	softly from person to person,
their goal (301)	rubbing my names together
	as if that were your goal,
pushing my thoughts into the space	not pushing my thoughts into
under the bed (103)	the space beneath the bed.
her brimming body (64)	I bring a sentence to your body,
I was filled with him as with a bible (159)	brimming like an island, I sit
	filled with that, as with a bible.

Having made use of this second volume of Canetti's autobiography for the composition of 'The Dead Are More Alive' (*DB* 12–3; see Chapter 5), McGuckian draws on it again to construct a self-reflexive poem addressed to the Austrian polymath, giving thanks for his guiding inspiration, but also implicitly asserting her own authority. Canetti's words, (or rather, the translator's words), are refreshing and invigorating; inherently poetic, the words are like a 'first language' which she carries inside of her. Yet what they inspire is already foreknown and intrinsic to her own self as a poet; they awaken that which already lies dormant in her. The three negative images which follow – the 'needles on your lips', the 'slightly grey' words, the 'waste of light' – imply a degree of criticism. Perhaps in their original context they lack a certain poetic valency for the poet and are something which she must simply 'swallow'. Yet for all that, she pictures herself as grateful and expectant in the following stanza, with Canetti as the benevolent master. His nurturing influence allows her voice to develop; the 'dark dipthong' is brought upwards into the light and given the freedom to grow. The original context for the image of the forked tree is illuminating as it is an instance of a reaffirmation of love and the occasion for the return of words. In a fit of jealous pique, Veza, a young woman with whom the young Canetti was very much in love, hid her love letters to him: 'She [...] looked for a tree that forked approximately at the level of her eyes and had a hollow space; she stuck the large package of letters inside' (260). The letters may have been written by Veza, but they are inspiring to Canetti and ownership soon reverts back to him. Perhaps McGuckian is here both acknowledging the original provenance of her words and asserting her ownership of them in their new context. The fact that the tree 'forks' marks a key developmental stage: while the image reaffirms the idea of growth implicit in the poem's opening stanza (the first language is in its early developmental stage, 'carried' like a foetus), it suggests that the 'first language' has now taken a new direction. Canetti's influence on McGuckian is not, therefore, overpowering or inhibiting and does not push her 'thoughts into / the space beneath the bed'. Indeed, the poem's conclusion asserts her own activity: rather than remaining a receptacle into which words are placed, the poet brings 'a sentence to your body, / brimming like an island'. This suggests an offering on her part, having formed an original, coherent text from his inspiring words. 'Body' invokes the immediate physical presence of the precursor and the act referred to is the intimate presentation of a love-token to the master. Yet it also connotes a 'corpus' of work, and her poem adds to his own composition, and is not 'supplementary' in the negative sense. But what exactly is said to be 'brimming like an island'? If it is 'your body', then one can say that McGuckian's reuse of his words is an act of communication, ending their splendid isolation. If it is the 'I' who is 'brimming like an island', then the phrase connotes both the distinctness and separateness of McGuckian's work from that of her literary exemplar.

The quotations transplanted from source texts carry an intentional meaning for McGuckian and are not arbitrary. Speaking to Blakeman, she reveals:

'I like to find a word living in a context and then pull it out of its context. It's like they are growing in a garden and I pull them out of the garden and put them into *my* garden, and yet I hope they take with them some of their original soil, wherever I got them … .'[37] This activity of transplantation results in a wonderfully poetic (yet seemingly decontextualised and oblique) use of language. The relation between the quoting and quoted texts is paramount; indeed, as Marjorie Garber argues (paraphrasing Walter Benjamin), '[t]o quote a text is to break into it, to 'tear' something out of it, to become a 'thought fragment' and thus a focus for critical attention'.[38] However, there are times when McGuckian uses a source text more sparingly, for narrative purposes only. One such example is 'The Katydid', a poem included in the Oxford edition of *The Flower Master* yet excluded from the revised Gallery Press edition.[39] The opening stanza contains very specific deictic elements:

> The Little Orchid saw from Pewter Lane
> The Forbidden City beyond the Jade Canal,
> Its roofs of yellow tile, the hawks around
> The Gate of Western Flowering.

A note attached to the text alerts the reader to its context: 'The Empress Dowager tried and failed to abolish foot-binding in nineteenth-century China.' From Marina Warner's *The Dragon Empress*[40] we learn that the Empress Dowager, Tz'u-hsi, who effectively ruled over China as Regent (from 1862–73, 1875–89 and 1898–1908) after her husband's death on 22 August 1861, was born Lan Kuei (Little Orchid) in 1835. As an adolescent, she came to live in that part of Peking known as Pewter Lane from where she could see 'the imperial yellow tiles of the Forbidden City'.[41] Having been established as an imperial concubine of third class (*Kuei Jen*), her subsequent rise to power was spectacular and calculated: 'she concentrated titles, wealth and power on her immediate relations, manipulated the succession to create her sister's son emperor, and so contrived the eclipse of the direct Aisin Gioro line by the *Yehe Nara*' (Warner, 14). This 'eclipse' is referred to obliquely in the second stanza wherein McGuckian suggests that Tz'u-hsi's initial empowerment is due to her sexual attractiveness (and prowess):

> On soft clogs she crawled to the Emperor's side,
> A total eclipse with her apple-head,
> Her water-chestnut eyes, the charm of the katydid,
> The white tiger, the fragrant bamboo.

Warner tells of how, when chosen to spend the night with the Emperor, '[e]tiquette required that Tz'u-hsi should crawl up from the foot towards the emperor' (Warner, 42). The exotic images of the final line refer to sexual positions outlined by Chinese handbooks of erotic lore: '"The White Tiger Leaps" (woman taken from behind) ... "Approaching the Fragrant Bamboo" (both standing)' (Warner, 42–43).

Tz'u-hsi was, according to Warner, criminally avaricious, a flaw damaging to both her international and her domestic policy-making. Her love of wealth and theatrics proved devastating to the country's finances: the household alone cost £6,500,000 per annum to run, she embezzled vast sums from the admiralty towards the reconstruction of her summer palace, and 'the panoply of the court remained unrestrained even in the face of the imminent bankruptcy of China' (Warner, 149). This is why the third stanza alludes to her private activities as opposed to her public duties: 'Now she sails her marble picnic boat / In the garden of Acquatic Grasses'. While within the poem's narrative such a detail marks her rise to power, it also hints at a regal insouciance in the face of rebellion within her own territory, trade wars and imperial incursion. As Warner reveals, 'the two-tiered paddle steamer, a folly of solid marble where Tz'u-hsi picknicked' (168) was built with money embezzled from the navy, thus weakening the country's defences.

In the past, intertextual dialogue with precursors has been deemed problematic for an Irish woman poet. The dilemma, as it has been presented, was due to the lack of *Irish* female precursors. This has apparently foreclosed access to traditions which are readily available to male contemporaries. Eavan Boland,[42] for example, has consistently bemoaned the remorselessly determined and determining forces acting on Irish women poets: place is a 'brute, choiceless fact';[43] Irish history is 'a given; we are all constructed by that construct';[44] and their status (as objects) has been been preordained.[45] However, her idea of what constitutes an 'Irish poem' or 'the national tradition' remains singularly prescriptive[46] and neglects the poets of the Irish Literary Revival, not all of whom reinforced the notion of the passive female, or felt duty-bound to discuss the national question.[47] From an essay entitled 'The Timely Clapper', it is clear that, contrary to Boland, McGuckian's poetic craft has suffered little from any perceived absence of Irish female precursors. In it, she expresses a willingness to stray beyond the parochial for literary influences and hopes that, in the coming years, 'academics would

ask me to review books about Rilke as well as women's rhapsodies about
him. Interview Muldoon and Ní Dhomhnaill on their symbiosis as well as
ourselves alone. Show curiosity as to what Eavan or Nuala might get out of
Brodsky or Walcott in a poetry conversation, for the map's sake.'[48] Her
diary for 1968–69,[49] for example, is replete with quotations from writers as
diverse as Christina Rossetti, Conrad Aiken and Laura Riding-Jackson. For
a proper appreciation of McGuckian's work, it is imperative that one investigate the manner in which she interacts in her poetry with those writers
whom she admires.

'Grainne's Sleep Song' (*OBB* 18) appears relatively straightforward: beginning with a speaker whose irritability is conveyed by pathetic fallacy –
the day is 'hostile', the house 'hadn't enough sleep either' – its second half
describes the emergence of a more creative self who leaves the 'uncompleted
story' behind and carves verses from 'Where Claribel low lieth'. The dramatic shift in emotional register is linked to a simultaneous change in relations between the speaker and her lover. 'Drudgery', pursuing kisses and
demands regarding her clothing each imply the speaker's embittered dissatisfaction at her lover's imperious attitude, but 'affectionate' indicates a gradual
assuagement, culminating in the carving of 'both our initials in full'. Yet, as
Michel Riffaterre contends, the literary text is 'a sequence of embeddings
with each significant word summarizing the syntagm situated elsewhere',[50]
and one detail of 'Grainne's Sleep Song' stands apart as an 'ungrammaticality'
vis-à-vis its 'idiolectic norm':[51] the 'pre-war squirrel jacket'. Both the jacket's
style and the vague temporal deixis ('pre-war') intimate a context other
than that of the 1980s, one which becomes clearer when the poem is compared with Olga Ivinskaya's *A Captive of Time*,[52] a memoir of her relationship with Boris Pasternak:

He would come into my room at six in the morning, still
sleepy of course – which meant that the boulevard, the
houses, the streetlights hadn't enough sleep either ... (22)
I decided he must just the moment before have torn himself
away from a passionate embrace, which had left him
dishevelled and on fire. I fancied I heard the sound of rapturous
kisses still pursuing him as he walked on the stage ... (7)
Very agitated, I began to pull on the dark-blue crepe de chine
dress with large white polka dots which had been brought   The house
from home and handed in for me at the prison. It had been   Hadn't had enough sleep either, and
a favourite of BL's. Seeing me in it, he had often said: 'Olia –   In drudgery still heard the sound of kisses
that's how you should look, that's how you came to   Pursuing her. But 'That's how you should look',
me in my dream.' (102)   You said, as I put on my pre-war squirrel

A fine, driving October snow began to fall. I put on my   Jacket. 'Not always in sports shoes.' (*BB* 18)
pre-war squirrel coat. It was cold in the room. Pasternak
bent over my hand and asked what books of his I had (9).
Aliosha Nedogonov, modest and likeable, always in sports shoes ... (5)

Selecting anecdotes and modifying tropes, McGuckian's reading of *A Captive of Time* parallels her own life with that of Ivinskaya. Since the biography documents an adulterous affair, it is understandable why the poet does not advertise its presence by means of footnotes or quotation marks. However, the poem's speaker differs significantly from her Russian counterpart: whereas the former is beleaguered and put upon, the latter, though initially jealous, enjoys a mutually gratifying relationship. 'That's how you should look' is not imperious, but quietly suggestive; 'the streetlights hadn't enough sleep' does not connote peevishness, but youthful passion. Her quotations not only encode details of a clandestine love affair, but also allow her to empathise with both Ivinskaya and Pasternak as literary figures. Yet while the speaker claims the latter's writings as her own ('Without Love'), it is noteworthy how she does not dwell on the hardships undergone by Russian writers:

We had a small room leading out onto a verandah which served   Like a porch in winter,
as a dining-room in summer and a porch in winter. (41)   Blue, cold and affectionate, I stepped
He [the cat] would leap into the room through the fortochka,   With you for a moment out of my
blue, cold, and affectionate. Boris was enchanted by him, as he   Uncompleted story, something sterile
was by anything beautiful. (43)   I contracted fourteen years ago on the beach,
His first piece of prose to be published ... was the opening   Entitled 'Wild Without Love'. And stopping
part of a never-completed story entitled 'Without Love' ... . (xx)   In the entrance of strange houses, sudden
after we had once tramped the streets for ages, stopping in the   Downpours, I began to read, instead of
entrances to the courtyards of strange houses to bicker for a   Letters never answered, well, salads
while or make things up again ... (24)   And love-walks. (BB 18)
His own changing state of mind is mirrored in nature and merges And love-walks. (BB 18)
with it – in this case during the kind of incomparably luxuriant
Russian summer, constantly refreshed by sudden downpours and thunderstorms ... . (xxi)
As soon as my pregnancy was confirmed, I began to receive white bread,
purée instead of kasha, and salads ... (101)

Unaware that McGuckian is quoting from *A Captive of Time*, the reader may well surmise that the 'letters never answered' denote the speaker's frosty indifference, and that the 'salads and love-walks' attest to the resumption of cordial relations with her lover. Although this is not a misreading, it overlooks a crucial subtext: love can flourish in spite of political oppression. In *A Captive of Time*, the unanswered letters allude to Ivinskaya's period of incarceration at a forced labour camp (October 1949–April 1953), during which she had little contact with Pasternak; the 'salads' refer to the enforced change in her diet once it had been established that she was pregnant while imprisoned in the Lubianka.[53] When the speaker says that she began to read of the latter instead of the former, she is consciously focusing on the positive aspects of the story. Indeed, although the concluding act of carving 'initials in full' refers to Ivinskaya's first horrifying interrogation,[54] she transforms it into an act of blissful union: 'Both our initials in full'.

Discovering a structured embedding of quotations in a McGuckian poem brings new contextual frames to light and helps revise the often tenuous arguments presented by academics interpeting her work. Knowledge of the particular biography or memoir the poet was using at the time of writing would have saved Patricia Boyle Haberstroh from making unwarranted assumptions like those contained in her recent *Women Creating Women*. Analysing 'Little House, Big House' (*OBB* 33), Haberstroh contextualises the poem within the literary/socio-political paradigm of the Anglo-Irish Big House tradition: 'Alluding to the big houses inhabited by English settlers and the small homes of the Irish cottagers, the speaker imagines a different kind of house.'[55] Since the poem is bereft of footnotes, dates, or historical personae, this is a questionable critical reflex. It is noteworthy that she does not discuss the poem's only cited placename, Tarusa – a town whose Eastern European location weakens the plausibility of her narrowly focused argument.

> Since our blood
> Is always older than we will ever be,
> I should like to lie in Tarusa under matted winter grass,
> Where the strawberries are redder than anywhere else.

Knowing that Tarusa was the town in which Marina Tsvetaeva's family had their summer residence, Meva Maron was able to take the reference as evidence of a possible intertext: 'But Tarusa and all the strawberries at the end of "Little House, Big House", which caught my eye because I used the same quote in a more satirical poem presumably about the same time … does more than let you say, "Aha, Tsvetaeva! I've solved the crossword".'[56] However, her letter to the *Honest Ulsterman* is yet another example of (unintentional) misdirection since McGuckian's reference is far more indirect than Maron suspects. Although 'Tarusa' and the 'strawberries' are mentioned in Tsvetaeva's *A Captive Spirit*, McGuckian in fact appropriates her final lines from Ivinskaya's autobiography. Discussing the tragic suicide of Tsvetaeva on 31

August 1941, Ivinskaya laments the fact that, contrary to the Russian poet's wishes, Tsvetaeva was buried in an unmarked grave in Yelabuga:

> In May 1934, while she was still in Paris, Marina had written: '*I should like to lie in* the khlyst [Russian religious sect. Tsvetaeva's family spent their summers in *Tarusa* before the Revolution] cemetery at Tarusa, under an elder bush, in one of those graves with a silver dove on it, *where the wild strawberries are larger and* redder *than anywhere else* in those parts'.
>
> (191, emphasis added)

The poem is, in effect, a meditation upon Tsvetaeva's death ('So different from an ordinary going-away'). That McGuckian is not simply quoting Tsvetaeva, but Ivinskaya's account is confirmed by further unattributed quotations.

In the second stanza's final line, McGuckian states that she deepens shadows with her 'autumn brown raincoat'. Connotations of death and decay are confirmed when we learn that, during her final days, Tsvetaeva was 'dressed very badly – in a long dark dress, an old brown autumn raincoat, and a beret of a dirty-blue colour she had knitted herself'.[57] Similarly, in the previous lines, McGuckian asks: 'Why should I take / My apron off for a wineless dinner?' The growing apathy and despair to which these lines allude are made all the more moving when we realise that before her death, Tsvetaeva 'did not even take off the apron with the large pocket in which she had been doing her housework that morning ...' (190). McGuckian's 'wineless dinner' is a clever allusion to 'For My Poems',[58] and gives one possible reason for the Russian poet's fateful decision to take her own life. The poem begins by declaring 'For my poems, stored deep like wines of precious vintage, / I know a time will come'; during her depressing days spent in the wooden house on Zhdanov Street, it was evident that she was no longer able to compose.

'Little House, Big House' self-reflexively gestures towards the imaginary communication between McGuckian and Tsvetaeva: the impulsive telephone conversation – 'That I could hardly keep my hand / From phoning you, impromptu' – indicates that a connection between authors (across space and time) is being made. In the original context, the line refers to Pasternak's letter to Ivinskaya's mother, dated 2 January 1953, expressing his warm affection: 'I could hardly refrain from phoning you right away – I am still trying to keep myself in hand now, because I am not supposed to get worked up' (129). That McGuckian regarded Tsvetaeva's suicide with compassion (and even respect) is confirmed in a personal interview[59] when she contrasts

Tsvetaeva's conduct with that of Mayakovsky: 'I suppose her's [suicide] was more understandable, her's was more choreographic. He had written one poem against it, and then he did it, I found it disappointing – whereas I felt that her reasons were not cowardice but real despair, and that I could admire her.' Her ability to identify with the poet is not belied by their different social or political circumstances, as shown by her comments in a review of Tsvetaeva's prose:

> But I understand something of her obsessive maternal instinct towards both husband and son, a reaction of sorts to those bereavements; her absolute need for the emotional involvement in her subject matter; her abject loyalties; and the social, psychic break between her prolonged adolescence with its security and material comfort, its privileged education, and the nightmare of her maturity, its wars, deprivation, and exile: 'caught up in the middle of her life by a brutal era' (to quote Joseph Brodsky).[60]

Interestingly, the poem's title, which Haberstroh so decisively misreads, points towards an alternative reading as it contains a veiled reference to the love affair between Boris Pasternak and Olga Ivinskaya. She describes how he kept a country house (*dacha*) at Peredelkino, a village situated 20 kilometres from Moscow, and how he lived there with his second wife, Zinaida Nikolayevna, in what is called 'the big house' as opposed to Ivinskaya's 'little house' nearby:

> I think Zinaida Nikolayevna understood very well that by making a good home for BL, she strengthened her position as his legal wife and the mistress of *the 'big' house* – which made it easier for her to reconcile herself to the open existence of *the 'little' house* (that is, mine), and she knew that any ill-considered attempt to put pressure on BL would have meant disaster for her.
>
> But it was not quite as simple as that. In his last years, the study with his favourite books and his desk had its due place in his heart, but he often said to me: 'I am going off to work. I have to be worthy of you. My place of work is over there.'
>
> (187, emphasis added)

Several narratives conjoin, the thematics of which differ according to our own identification of the speaker and addressee. For instance, when, in the fourth stanza, McGuckian says 'And the house like me / Was tangled with the emotion of cut flowers', the emotion in question alternates between despair (Tsvetaeva) and frustration (Ivinskaya), depending on which historical figure she is empathising with at the time. It is also important to note the implicit link between Pasternak and Tsvetaeva which the poem makes. Ivinskaya reports in her memoirs that '[d]uring my years with BL I heard him speak over and over again about his sense of responsibility for

Marina's return to Russia, for her feeling that she was utterly abandoned, and for her death. Till the end of his life he never ceased to mourn her' (171). This guilt was occasioned by his reluctance to allow Tsvetaeva to stay at 'the big house' when she turned to him for help towards the end of her life, a refusal which he later deemed a contributing factor to her decision to commit suicide: 'Years later BL told me that he had not invited Marina to stay – the thing he would really have liked to do – partly because of his own indecisiveness and partly because of the domestic situation at the Peredelkino house' (180).

Without knowing the poem's source, one of the main difficulties critics face is in identifying the referents behind its multiple spatio-temporal deictics and indefinite interpersonal contexts. The stamps in 'Little House, Big House', for example, have 'squirrels on them' (*BB* 33): at once indicative of a particular time and place,[61] they are also unspecific since it is difficult to know which postal services have issued stamps of this description. Yet Docherty and Haberstroh, though obviously correct in pointing out that multiple readings arise from McGuckian's pronouns, are both widely off the mark in their rationalisation of this technique; indeed, it is reductive to claim that the poet is presenting a 'blank phenomenology',[62] an unidentifiable voice, as if each poem lacked specificity. 'Visiting Rainer Maria' (*MC* 10–11) is a particularly good example. While its title directs attention to an imagined meeting with Rainer Maria Rilke,[63] the 'he' of the poem's first stanza does not simply refer to the Swiss-German poet:

Their encounter was brief: Mandelstam was just leaving
the Crimea and they were just arriving. (64)
'Your little paw, like a baby's, all black from the charcoal,
your blue smock – it's all memorable to me, I haven't
forgotten anything'. (78)
It tells one something of their life together that the first sentence
would have been equally suitable for the last letter in 1938. (77)
The second is an everyday interior scene – a poem
made of a kitchen conversation. (89)

He said he was just leaving
As I was just arriving, in my blue
Smock, yesterday, without meaning to.
Though this first sentence would
Have been equally suitable
For the last, for a poem made
From a kitchen conversation.
(*MC* 10)

The pronouns are singular, yet their referents are plural. Borrowing extensively from Clarence Brown's biography of Mandelstam,[64] the poet juxtaposes several pairings within the one stanza: the first two lines refer to Mandelstam's meeting with Tsvetaeva in the Crimea; the next four are quotations from letters to and from his wife; and the conclusion describes a poem written for Arbenina, with whom he is said to have had an affair (89).

While the 'I' of McGuckian's poem adds herself to the list of Mandelstam's admirers, it emerges that she is also taking Mandelstam's role: his 'blue smock' is now worn by the Northern Irish poet. That this is a marriage of true minds becomes clearer as the poem progresses:

'the air is always sort of steamy, the way it is in a room'. (94)

'I always remember the lower shelf as chaotic: the books were not standing upright side by side but lay like ruins.' (21)
His childhood comes to life with great vividness. The sense impressions give pleasure: snow-cold, blindingly white bed linen. (21–22)
Mandelstam was very taciturn, smoked a lot, and had the habit of using his shoulder as an ashtray and throwing ashes all over his suit. (48)
a demented young Turk who kept scrubbing the floor with a tooth brush. (82)

The air was the way it always
Is in a room; books lay in ruins
On the snow-cold bed. He must have been
Scrubbing the floor with his toothbrush,
Using his shoulder as an ashtray
(*MC* 10)

For the second stanza, McGuckian has selected two distinct types of phrases from Brown, linked by the dichotomy between tidiness and unkemptness: on the one hand, they allude to Mandelstam's childhood and adolesence, particularly to items of decor (books, bed) and his unclean appearance; on the other, they refer to his stay at Batum, to its steamy air and the Turk scrubbing the floor. The function of her quotations is purely descriptive, outlining scenes specific to Mandelstam. Yet by the third stanza, the speaker has become part of the audience listening to Mandelstam:

The shape, dictated by the curved outer wall and the eccentricities of the corridor, consisted mostly of angles, none of the walls being perpendicular to any other. (86)
'Suddenly he touched my sleeve softly and with his eyes pointed toward the face of Osip Emilevich. I have never seen a human face so transformed by inspiration and self-forgetfulness.' (88)
'Those are the special blocks of shops near the sea. Whole streets of them, extinguished, in darkness, with shutters locked tight by heavy iron padlocks.' (95)
Peter's city, 'the most intentional city in the world', in Dostoevsky's phrase, for what is new and Western. (223)

So was my shape dictated by
The curved outer wall, the eccentricities
Of the corridor, all sorts of untils.
And I thought to myself, if he touches
My sleeve even softly, whole streets
Of shops near the sea will be extinguished
In the most intentional darkness
(*MC* 10)

Curiously, the speaker is more acted upon than acting: the room in Batum imposes its shape upon her; she wishes to be 'touched' by Mandelstam, to have the same sublime reaction as Blok upon hearing the great poet speak (88). Yet her desire to lose herself completely in his poetry remains unfulfilled: 'if he touches … [i]f he mentions …'. The 'partings of quite a different / Cast', though alluding to Mandelstam's 'Tristia' (No. 104) and his period spent as internal exile,[65] also calls attention to a possible divergence by McGuckian from his poetics: her poetry radically differs from Acmeism, and does not 'renounce the moon' (152). However, this does not deflect her adoration for him, as is evident from the speaker's adopted subject position:

'Yesterday, without meaning to, I thought to myself "I must find it"   I said, I must find it,
– using the feminine form of must.' (78)   Using the feminine form of must … .

'I run, leaving behind Mandelstam, the train, and the sentence.   … I have been
End of the platform. A post. I also turn to a post. The cars go   Not his, not his, not his, his …
past: not his, not his, not his … his.' (63)   (*MC* 11)

These extracts from the fifth and sixth stanzas refer, respectively, to Mandelstam's desperate loneliness at his separation from Nadhezda and to the tearful parting from Tsvetaeva. McGuckian appropriates the depth of emotion expressed by these lines; they express her love for the Russian poet. The poem's conclusion appears to contradict this harmony:

The 'it' of my translation means 'silence'; the   The it of his translation may mean silence,
'she' of his meant 'Aphrodite'. (166)   But the she of mine means Aphrodite.
                                                                                        (*MC* 11)

Clair Wills, though rightly pointing out that these lines refer to the disagreements which have emerged over how to translate the first line of Mandlestam's 'Silentium',[66] does not take the reading any further. Sarah Broom, on the other hand, vigorously argues that McGuckian is reprimanding Mandelstam, claiming that 'Mandelstam's Aphrodite … has none of the essence of the real feminine'.[67] Both readings suffer from a partial knowledge of the lines' source. They actually refer to a disagreement between Clarence Brown and Richard McKane: the 'it' of the former's translation means 'silence', the 'she' of the latter's means 'Aphrodite'.[68] McGuckian's poem re-enacts this problem of attribution: while the 'his' of McGuckian's poem seems to refer to Mandelstam, it in fact refers to Brown. Broom's reading is clearly insufficient, as Mandelstam did not translate his work into English. The problem does not even arise in Russian. As Brown states, 'the problem, if it is a problem, lies more in the translation than in the original, it being one of the penalties of speaking English that one *must* resolve an ambiguity of which the Russian reader may hardly be aware. In English the Russian *ona* is either 'it' or 'she'; it cannot, as in Russian, be *both* it and she' (166). The speaker is forced to choose because she speaks English; in the end, she sides with McKane.

McGuckian has been honest about her method of composition. Talking to Rebecca Wilson, she states that 'I just take an assortment of words, though not exactly at random, and I fuse them. It's like embroidery. It's very feminine,

I guess. They are very intricate, my poems, a weaving of patterns of ins and outs and contradictions, one thing playing off another.'[69] However, the 'embroidery' is so intricate, it is little wonder that her quotations have thus far gone unremarked. An initial reading of 'The Man with Two Women' (*MC* 14–15), for example, discloses a narrative with two clear movements: the first half is the speaker's retrospective narration of her maudlin state of mind during 'a hope-lessly / ill-advised summer', with political menace lurking in the background ('Irish clouds ... still in their / Army uniforms'); the second half reverses the prevailing gloom with its sensual, quasi-erotic account of her encounter with an unnamed lover. Yet like both 'Grainne's Sleep Song' and 'Little House, Big House', the poem is complicated by the fact that its words are taken from a monograph detailing a ménage-à-trois, namely Ann and Samuel Charters' *I Love: The Story of Vladimir Mayakovsky and Lili Brik.*[70] Indeed, the unusual verse-form provides a teasing visual clue to the identity of its biographical subject as it mimics Mayakovsky's characteristically jagged lineation:

> I'd been walking
>   on a very old street
> Leading to the sea,
>   to a gritty beach
> With huge stones,
>   where I would sit
> In a stylish sundress,
>   laced boots and pearls,
> Re-reading five, ten times,
>   the simplest letters
> From people who lived there
>   and emigrated.
>   (*MC* 14)

The embroidery is intricate but cannot compensate for the stanza's stylistic inadequacies, particularly its unspectacular use of adjectives. Exactly why McGuckian deploys quotations here is at first unclear as she avoids a coher-ent rewriting of or commentary on the biography. The opening four lines describing the speaker's walk to the sea is made up from two quotations, the first voiced by Yury Annenkov:

> In confusion Mayakovsky left Paris for a few days in March and went alone to Nice on a gambling trip. While there, he met a friend from Russia, the painter Yury Annenkov.
> '*I'd been walking on a very old street leading to the sea*, and I noticed a familiar profile. I opened my mouth to say hello as Mayakovsky said to me, "Have you a thousand francs?" He explained he was coming back from Monte Carlo and he'd lost everything gambling'.
> (319–20, emphasis added)

There is no contextual link here with the following intertext: 'Away from the distractions of Moscow, he [Mayakovsky] threw himself into the composition of "The Cloud in Trousers". Kuokkala was a country resort in the sparse pine woods on the shores of the Gulf of Finland, with *a gritty beach that had huge stones* protruding irregularly from the water' (43, emphasis added). While the first extract refers to his stay in Nice, the second describes a sojourn in Finland, at the summerhouse of the literary critic Kornei Chukovsky. The real purpose behind the quotations becomes evident when we realise that the poem's speaker is taking Lili Brik's place. Indeed, for McGuckian, falling in love with the muse is not uncommon: 'When I'm with a person that's written the book, I'm almost in love with the person during the course of that book.' The poem documents her *coup de foudre* whilst reading the biography. The 'I' is double, though without the source text one would not realise that 'where I would sit / In a stylish sundress, / laced boots and pearls' refers to two women, McGuckian and Lili Brik. The first half of the image comes from a description of the Briks' apartment on Zhukovsky Street (Petrograd) at the time of Mayakovsky's first meetings with Lili: 'On the walls were Japanese fans and a large oil painting by Boris Grigoryev, a portait of Lili lying on the grass *in a dress and laced boots* in front of a flaming sunset, which Mayakovsky had titled "Lili Spilled Out"' (51, emphasis added). McGuckian ties in this extract with another representation of Lili Brik (a photograph by Alexander Rodchenko), also in their apartment:

> He [Mayakovsky] is in his shirt-sleeves, staring across to her with a tight half-smile, as if he were waiting for her to respond to something he's said. Lili, *in a stylish sundress and pearls*, is staring down at her plate, her thin body tense, as if she were warding him off. Their love had become a series of uncomfortable evasions.
>
> (301–2, emphasis added)

The juxtaposition of clothing imagery is not arbitrary: the extracts link together the commencement and decline of the intense love affair, a prolepsis neatly prefiguring the end of the speaker's short-lived tryst in McGuckian's own narrative. The poem's retrospective air corresponds to the subtext embedded in the first stanza: Mayakovsky's tragic suicide. Two quotations voice the speaker's desire to regress into the past and salvage something of his legacy. The first is voiced by Rita Rait directly after hearing about Mayakovsky's suicide on 14 April 1930: '"I go upstairs, *rereading five, ten times*. 'Lili, love me'. Oh, God. Lili isn't there. Osya isn't there. Has any-

thing happened to them?"' (355, emphasis added). The second is spoken
by Mayakovsky's associate, Lunacharsky: "'Not all of us are like Marx, who
said that poets experience a great need for kindness. Not all of us understand this, and not all of us understood that Mayakovsky was in need of
great kindness, that often he needed nothing as much as a kind word, perhaps even *the simplest* of words; it would have reached the heart of this
double, it would have balanced the deep sadness inside him"' (362, emphasis added).

Discussing how her alteration and arrangement of quotations refract the
original sentiments, McGuckian states that '[t]he words are given to me ...
and the authors, and the translators, especially if they're dead, they are very
aware of me using them and that they want it, they want me to make the
same words live again in a new way and do things with it that carries me
and marks my reading of the book and marks my learning process with
them'.[72] Quotations are intended to register her appreciation of the text and
it is not coincidental that many self-reflexively centre around the act of
reading:

He swept on to the first section of the poem, exposing the emotional pressures that were gnawing at him as if there in the doorway he'd suddenly pulled off his shirt. (53)	... and suddenly, In the doorway, pulling off his shirt.
'I was interested in many women but I never promised the poem to anyone, and my conscience is clear if I dedicate the poem to you'. (55)	Though I never promised my long kiss To anyone,
Suddenly, everyone felt – like a cold draft passing through the convolutions of the brain – that this moment was to be remembered ... and he turned his yard-wide shoulders, as if harnessed ... (334)	he turned his yard-wide Shoulders as if harnessed ...
	(*MC* 15)

In 'The Man with Two Women', the lover's divestment of clothing is purely
sensual, a prelude to sexual consummation of mutual desire; in the source
text it is used as a simile to describe Mayakovsky's heartfelt recitation of
'The Cloud with Trousers', how he exposed 'the emotional pressures that
were gnawing at him' (53). McGuckian unites both meanings, hinting at
her own reaction on reading about her muse. Indeed, his poem becomes 'a
kiss', and the act of turning his 'yard-wide shoulders' becomes almost erotic,
though in the original context it denotes Mayakovsky's 'helplessness, loneliness, heartache' (334) upon reciting his own poem about an exhausted
horse he had seen lying on a Moscow street.

The arrangement within a single text of her eclectic assemblage of raw
materials can be likened to a 'patchwork', the function of which is akin to,

but significantly different from, that which is described in the second verse of Michael Longley's poem of the same name:

> I pull over us old clothes, remnants,
> Stitching together shirts and nightshirts
> Into such a dazzle as will burn away
> Newspapers, letters, previous templates …[73]

Recycling text is not useful in itself. However, if the 'previous templates' are not burned away but held together and made either ironic or parodic, the reader can be made aware of the intricate workings and purposeful intent of the new text. The stitching together of textual fragments is not an uncritical act; rather, as one reviewer (in a different context) put it, McGuckian 'is not sewing things up, but taking them apart, and the finery which she decks out her poems initially disguises the real point of her needlework – which is to unstitch, expose, impale'.[74] Although the craft under discussion in her early poetic manifesto 'The Seed-Picture' (*FM* 23) uses seeds rather than thread, it is still a 'womanly or domestic' craft according to the poet,[75] and the image used to convey confinement is notably that of embroidery:

> Was it such self-indulgence to enclose her
> In the border of a grandmother's sampler,
> Bonding all the seeds in one continuous skin,
> The sky resolved to a cloud the length of a man?

The 'sampler' not only connotes a beginner's exercise, but also the pattern or archetype from which a copy may be taken, suggesting the continuation of tradition. Yet such an occupation is restrictive, enclosing the woman 'in one continuous skin', and is dictated (ominously) by 'the length of a man'. The danger is made even more apparent at the poem's close, when the speaker states that

> The single pearl barley
> That sleeps around her dullness
> Till it catches light, makes women
> Feel their age, and sigh for liberation.

The final two lines contain an ironic awareness of marginality: though symbolising confinement, the portrait, like a latter-day version of Browning's 'My Last Duchess', disturbs patriarchy, since the woman's image, silent and enclosed within a frame, is implicitly given a voice.

One must be wary when ascribing such a marginal position to McGuckian considering that she has been published by the Oxford University Press for nine years and currently has contracts with Wake Forest (USA) and Gallery Press (Republic of Ireland). The fact that she has been the recipient of the Eric Gregory Award (1980), the Rooney Prize (1982), a Northern Ireland Bursary (1982), an Alice Hunt Barlett Award (1983), the Cheltenham Festival of Literature Award (1989) and the American Ireland Fund Literary Award (1998) also weakens the case for marginal status. However, it is true that, in contrast to Muldoon's overt use of citation, McGuckian feels impelled to adopt a more covert form of ironic intertextuality in order symbolically to undermine the (male) English canon: 'I have to live under this mountain and try to belong to it without becoming narrow or jealous, to be eternally grateful to Milton without being deluged into silence, to continue what women have begun without succumbing to the inevitable real or ritual self-immolation.'[76] The gathering together of seeds (vocabulary) and subsequent attachment 'by the spine to a perfect bedding' (i.e. her book of poems) constitute a 'deterritorialization', a 'writing in the interstices of masculine culture, moving between use of the dominant language or form of expression and specific versions of experience based on marginality'.[77] In a third-year university essay entitled 'The Idea of an Anglo-Irish Tradition', Maeve T. P. McCaughan (as she was then known) wrote about the tension between the anxiety of influence and the need for enabling precursors. Focusing on the poetry of W. B. Yeats, she stated that '[i]t was because he was capable of this supreme detachment that Yeats transcended the pronunciation of his poetic predecessors to become a major influence in English and world literature. And yet it was only *through* their pronunciation that he eventually *found* his medium.'[78] Her method of working 'through their pronunciation' is, however, very different from that of Yeats as she has to struggle against a male-orientated canon. Her thoughts on this matter are revealed in a tribute to Eavan Boland where she quotes approvingly from Gilbert and Gubar's *Madwoman in the Attic*:

> The female poet's basic problem is an anxiety of authorship; a radical fear that she cannot create, that because she can never become a 'precursor', the act of writing will isolate or destroy her. [...] Her battle is not against her (male) precursor's reading of the world but against his reading of *her*. In order to define herself as an author she must redefine the terms of her socialization. [...] Frequently, moreover, she can begin such a struggle only by actively seeking a female precursor.[79]

McGuckian's redefinition of 'the terms of her socialization' takes the form of embedded quotations, the thematics of which emphasise her struggle against patriarchy.

Gilbert and Gubar's seminal study of the way in which women are depicted in patriarchal Western culture contends: 'the text's author is a father,
a progenitor, an aesthetic patriarch whose pen is an instrument of generative power like his penis' (6). Male sexuality is, therefore, 'the essence of
literary power' (4); female sexuality, by contrast, is defined as passive, subordinate and devoid of this generative power. What, then, 'does it mean to
be a woman writer in a culture whose fundamental definitions of literary
authority are … both covertly and overtly patriarchal?' (45–6). The woman
is inscribed in literary texts as either an 'angel in the house' or as a 'monster-
woman', one who 'embodies intransigent female autonomy' (28). One of
the key examples cited early on by Gilbert and Gubar is that of the fairy tale
Snow White, in which the 'vexing polarities of angel and monster, sweet
dumb Snow White and fierce mad Queen' are depicted. Their monograph
investigates how such imagery influences 'the ways in which women attempt the pen' (46) and argues that, when writing, the nineteenth-century
female author must combat such a restrictive and self-defeating socio-sexual
differentiation by redefining the way in which she herself is read. While
contemporary women are able to 'attempt the pen with energy and authority', they are only able to do so 'because their eighteenth- and nineteenth-
century foremothers struggled in isolation […] to overcome the anxiety of
authorship that was endemic to their literary subculture' (51).

McGuckian's response is to pay homage to her literary foremothers, and
to Gilbert and Gubar, by constructing a poem from within *The Madwoman
in the Attic*. She uses intertextual allusions in 'Journal Intime' (*MC* 26) to
inscribe within her own text the psychodrama of female literary authorship:

In the dreams of men (76)	In the dreams of men the pattern
By moonlight the pattern of the wallpaper (90)	Of the wallpaper by moonlight
'the colour of masculinity' (70)	Is the death-devoted colour of masculinity.
artfully placed mirrors (228)	And in artfully-placed mirrors,
a single grieving shape (218)	A single, grieving shape, to the
though weak-eyed (215)	Weak-eyed, echoes and re-echoes,
whose histories echo and re-echo each other (229)	More than sister, more than wife.
more than sister … a 'more than' wife (228)	

The opening sentence portrays evocatively the female writer's imprisoning
gendered subject position. The 'dreams' suggest a male fantasy of female
enclosive domesticity; socialised as a passive, submissive and subservient
angel of the house, the woman's own dreams are delimited by 'the death-
devoted colour of masculinity'. The outlet for the woman's writing is

restricted to the private self-communication of a 'Journal Intime'. The woman as 'angel' is selfless and, as Gilbert and Gubar argue, she is not just 'a memento of otherness', she is also a '*memento mori*'. The angel-woman, the 'spiritual messenger, an interpreter of mysteries to wondering and *devoted* men, […] becomes, finally, a messenger of the mystical otherness of *death*' (24, emphasis added). The three quotations used by McGuckian inscribe and conjoin three important contexts. Referring to the way in which the Queen internalises the strictures uttered by her looking-glass in *Snow White*, Gilbert and Gubar cite Simone de Beauvoir's contention that women 'still dream through the dreams of men' (76). The woman, therefore, lacks all agency and her social (and literary) role is defined by men. This is reiterated by the second quotation which refers to Charlotte Gilman Perkins' *The Yellow Wallpaper* (1890), a story that recounts in the first person the experiences of a woman suffering from post-partum depression. Having been forbidden by her husband to write until she has fully recovered,[80] she is confined to a room which she thinks of as 'a one-time nursery' and becomes, in turn, intrigued and horrified by its yellow wallpaper. She begins to discern the figure of a woman (her alter ego) moving behind its outside pattern: 'At night in any kind of light, in twilight, candle light, lamplight, and worst of all by moonlight, it becomes bars! The outside pattern I mean, and the woman behind it as plain as can be.'[81] In the story, the woman reads her self as a text; she begins to read, in Annette Kolodny's words, 'her own psyche writ large'.[82] This, in effect, is what McGuckian is doing in the poem: she is discovering the symbolisation of the woman writer's untenable reality and is attempting to escape such male codification. The third quotation intimates one attempt at escape by citing Mrs. Gaskell's remark regarding the Brontë sisters' desire '"to throw the colour of masculinity into their writing"' (70).

Such an attempt at 'putting on' (or acquiring) male power is central to the concerns of the four-line sentence that concludes the opening stanza. The lines are almost impossible to paraphrase as they can be read in a number of differing ways. What 'the Weak-eyed' might see in the 'artfully-placed mirrors' is a 'grieving shape', someone who is 'more than sister, more than wife'. Is the female author caught within the binary oppositions set out by patriarchy, defined within the 'artfully-placed mirrors'? Is the female author here equated with 'the Weak-eyed', or does she actively construct a self in her art which only the 'Weak-eyed' could construe as 'a single, grieving shape'? As such, is this subversive 'self' free from the codification which defines her only in relation to the male ('more than sister, more than wife')? The five textual fragments sampled from *Madwoman in the Attic* provide a clue as to McGuckian's intent. They refer to the battle waged by two female authors – George Eliot and Mary Shelley – with 'Milton's bogey', namely the misogynistic portrayal of women in literature, and the way in which this (pre)determines the subordinate nature of the female writer. Gilbert and Gubar delineate the female writers' anxieties towards this bogey: in Milton's account of woman, she is secondary to man, an Other whose 'otherness leads inexorably to her demonic anger, her sin, her fall, and her exclusion from that garden of the gods which is also, for her, the garden of poetry' (191). What the female writer sees in literary texts – when art acts as a mirror put up to nature – is a monster, akin to Gilman Perkins' woman in the wallpaper or the Queen's self reflected in the looking-glass. The first quotation refers to *Frankenstein*'s obsession with incest, whereby the likenesses between each character are 'like the solipsistic relationships among artfully placed mirrors' (228). Although it is a standard Gothic trope, in Shelley's text it is said to be a 'metaphor for the solipsistic fever of self-awareness' (229). The text establishes a number of characters whose histories 'echo and re-echo' each other (229) because it is a self-reflexive psychodrama, one in which the author is attempting to discern her own position within the Miltonic schema. Eliot's *Middlemarch* can be viewed in the same way since Dorothea is depicted as wishing to make herself the equal of Casaubon by being ministered to by this 'weak-eyed' husband (215). While the powers of the Miltonic father-figure 'are not quite absolute' (215), nevertheless Dorothea is said to transform, ultimately, into 'the archetypal wretched woman Blake characterized as Milton's wailing six-fold Emanation, his three wives and three daughters gathered into *a single grieving shape*' (218, emphasis added). McGuckian's text, then, registers the way in which two foremothers struggled to wield the pen and delivers a judgement on their efforts: while the 'weak-eyed' may have regarded them as marginal Others, and although the characters within their texts may have been marginalised and subject to the strictures of patriarchy, nevertheless to the contemporary reader the authors themselves can hardly be described diminutively as 'single, grieving shape[s]'.

'Journal Intime' can itself be regarded as an 'artfully placed mirror'. First, the text itself is mirror-like in that the opening tropes and quotations are repeated in its conclusion:

	It is so
she looked outward, if only upon the snow (37)	Unthinkable she should look outward
a one-time nursery (89)	From the depressed, pink light of her
to dilate upon (221)	One-time nursery, if only to dilate
the same two faces (229)	Upon the same two faces, if only, upon the snow.
A child's first and most satisfying house (88)	In a child's first (and most satisfying)
'a name repeated in all kinds of characters' (276)	House, where everyone is repeated
	In everyone else, the door that is so light
	To her, so dark to us, is wise enough
his voice resides now in her own mirror,	To dream through. Her voice fills the mouth
her own mind (38)	Of her own mirror, as if she were a failure:
	As if, what is lifelike, could be true.

McGuckian references the two texts cited in the opening stanza: *Snow White* and *The Yellow Wallpaper*. For Gilbert and Gubar, the prospect of being 'caught and trapped in a mirror rather than a window [...] is to be driven inward, obsessively studying self-images as if seeking a viable self' (37). McGuckian's poem, of course, is one such mirror into which she herself is looking and working out her own psychodrama, and that of her foremothers. The reference, though, refers to the first Queen, who dies when giving birth to Snow White, and who is said to have been freer than the 'evil' Queen in that she 'looked outward, if only upon the snow' (37). The poem, however, decidedly states that this is 'so / Unthinkable'; the woman's gaze is forced to remain within the 'one-time nursery' (referring to the unnamed protagonist's place of confinement in *The Yellow Wallpaper*). This location is contrasted with the carefree environment of the womb, the 'child's first house': repetition here has to do with the passing on of biological traits; it is only when the child becomes socialised that she becomes subject to patriarchal codification. Yet while the fairy tale suggests that the second Queen 'has internalised the King's rules' because 'his voice resides now in her mirror, in her mind', McGuckian's poem argues against this. Her literary foremothers, she implies, have deconstructed the workings of patriarchy in their texts. Thus, the female author's voice is said to fill 'the mouth / Of her won mirror'. Within the patriarchal code this would mean that she was indeed 'a failure' as she has not allowed herself to become a subordinate figure deprived of authorship, but not for a contemporary author like McGuckian.

The poem is also an 'artfully placed mirror' owing to its method of construction. For Gilbert and Gubar – citing Adrienne Rich – one of the key strategies in the feminist revisionary struggle is '"the act of looking back, of seeing with fresh eyes, of entering an old text from a new critical direction"'

(49), and this is precisely what the Northern Irish poet does. Constructing a palimpsest – a literary psychohistory – she incorporates the tropes and ideas of her foremothers in order to read into, and out from, their psycho-dramas. Crucially, she does so by using their one of their own strategies whereby 'revolutionary messages are concealed behind stylistic facades' (74). The embedded citations, unacknowledged and devoid of quotation marks, replay the concealments and evasions of her predecessors.[83] Indeed, reading about the strategies employed by her precursors affirms her own right to lift the pen.

In her work, McGuckian celebrates the art of key female literary precursors. One striking example is 'Garbo at the Gaumont',[84] a poem based on Tatyana Tolstoy's moving biography of her father, *Tolstoy Remembered.*[85] McGuckian's text characteristically calls attention to this act of quotation:

> … As the eyelid protects
> The eye, in a house that love has borrowed,
> Never to be refurnished, none can tell
> Exactly what room was used for what,
> Until the day after the day after tomorrow.

McGuckian's 'love' for the muse (Tatyana Tolstoy) borrows from the 'house' (text) in order to bring the precursor to life. By inserting a quotation relating to the room in which Leo Tolstoy wrote *War and Peace*, McGuckian has, in fact, metaphorically refurbished the Tolstoy residence at Yasnaya Polyana: 'We imagined we were exploring the rooms my father had described in his novel', writes Tatyana Tolstoy, 'and we argued passionately over *exactly which room had been used for what*, as though the Rostovs had been actual people who really lived there once' (144, emphasis added). The poem ends with a quotation intimating the reciprocation of the poet's love: '" *The day after the day after tomorrow* I shall come into the nursery and kiss you … My fine and sprightly wife, my darling wife"' (195–96, emphasis added). Although the conclusion may well be voiced by Leo Tolstoy, it is not his love that the poet requires; indeed, much of the poem questions his beliefs.

Clarifying the poem's title, Tatyana Albertini's epigraphical essay makes a pointed reference to the hardship which both she and her mother had to endure owing to Leo Tolstoy's conscientious objection to materialism:

> I only once saw her perplexed. There was a film of *Anna Karenina*, the one starring Greta Garbo, showing at one of the big Paris cinemas. My mother, a cousin, and I decided to go and

see it. But when we arrived at the Gaumont-Palace box-office we had to give up the notion, since the prices were way above our means, and we were forced to trudge sadly home again. When we got back, my mother said with a sweet and disappointed little smile: 'I wonder what papa would have said if he'd seen that. Or the sight of me sweeping the floor, doing my shopping, and not knowing if I'll have enough left to pay the rent.'[86]

The title not only points to Leo Tolstoy's presence in the poem through its allusion to *Anna Karenina*, but it also indirectly contrasts Karenina's suicide with Tatyana Tolstoy's indefatigableness and it suggests a belated rebellion against the father figure. Similarly, the first stanza questions his unenlightened chauvinism toward women:

Influenced by her hatred of everything that smacked of war,
I never gave my son 'military' toys. (250)
It became immediately clear to him then why Ilya had so abruptly
acquired the manner of a great virtuoso: our carpenter, Prokhor, was
in the room putting up the inner windows for the winter. (178)
More than once, for example, I have felt his powerful hands gripping
my shoulders as he forced me round so that I shouldn't see
the new moon from the right. (161)
It is a whole world, an enchanting childhood world, filled with an
almost wild gaiety sometimes, that has vanished with him. Never
again a child taking its first steps, no more laughter, games,
lit-up trees at Christmas. (221)
Alas, I was to prove that I was indeed an authentic member of my sex. Like a true
woman I have left my book unfinished to this day … (164)

The carpenter that made my son
His military toys is putting up
Winter's inner windows. His hands
So powerfully grip this newest moon,
My shoulder is forced round from right
To right, till the room that was like
A garden where he took his first
Steps, and lit up trees, wishes
Not to go on the move, to leave
Its book unread, unfinished,
Like a true woman.

The poem shares with Tatyana Tolstoy's reminiscences a wry intelligence that undermines the apparent capitulation to patriarchy. Towards the end of the first stanza, for example, McGuckian notes the debilitating effects that child-care has upon the writing of poetry: in the new context, it is the son, and not the father, who forcibly turns the woman around. However, the 'book' has not remained 'unread' and, despite the distractions of caring for children, she has succeeded in writing her poem. The patronising essentialism of 'Like a true woman' rings hollow when related to *Tolstoy Remembered*. Attempting to overcome her father's prejudices about women writers, Tatyana Tolstoy tricks him into believing that an article she had written, summarising the principles of the American economist Henry George, had in fact been produced by a certain 'P. Polilov'. Taken in by the ruse, her father stubbornly maintains that a woman cannot produce a sustained, book-length version of the article:

As the conversation came to an end my father began to chuckle and said: 'But how sad about poor Polilov! And I'd formed such a clear picture of him too: he wore a dark blue jacket, really very dapper, in early middle age …' Then stroking my hair he added: 'Well, if you don't finish your book, then we shall be able to say you are a true woman'. (164)

Although she may have never finished that particular economic treatise, she did go on to write the biography.

Tolstoy Remembered clearly provides McGuckian with an enabling female precursor and is used again for the same purpose in 'A Small Piece of Wood' (*MC* 31–32). The relative obscurity of this poem's source material explains to some extent the ways in which she has consistently been misread and lies behind the greatest watershed in McGuckian's career to date: the enforced change of publishing house from Oxford to Gallery Press. Correspondence from both her editor at Oxford University Press, Jacqueline Simms,[87] and her assistant editor, George Miller,[88] details their unwillingness either to publish a new book of poems (*Marconi's Cottage*) or to reprint her first three collections since a *Selected Poems* was planned for November 1991. While such a course of action made economic sense,[89] it was certainly not in the poet's best interests. Crucial information explicating Simms's dissatisfaction with the new work can be found in an earlier letter which contains a detailed analysis of two poems, 'A Small Piece of Wood' (*MC* 31–32) and 'The Unplayed Rosalind' (*MC* 59–61), and illustrates the problems of not being aware of McGuckian's source texts. In the letter, her editor expresses her confusion upon reading the new poems and states that she feels out of her depth.[90] At the heart of her argument with McGuckian lies a plea for thematic coherence (linearity, narrative closure) and a reader-friendly text (commonly known literary allusions). While Simms, in her capacity as a freelance agent working for a large publishing company, is justified in wondering whether McGuckian should consider the future reader's confused reaction to the poems, her idea of which 'reader' the poet is writing for remains undefined. Her advice is sincere and cogent, but she clearly misunderstands the poetry. As is clear from her letter, Simms regards the poems as containing irrelevant verses and suggests that they work only by free association. Yet the apparent arbitrariness results from McGuckian's carefully interpolated narratives which function simultaneously on a number of thematic levels. Part of the blame must lie with McGuckian, as Simms clearly asks for confirmation about the poem's references. For example, she asks what 'Choorka' means. It is clear from a subsequent letter that no further clarification has been given, and therefore Simms continued to greet the poem with an unsympathetic response.[91]

The 'Choorka' reference is, in fact, closely 'implicated' in the poem as a whole, but recognising this is dependent on being familiar with the poet's source material. Simms's assumption that '[n]otes would kill your poems dead' is only valid for certain kinds of footnotes (long-winded, overly elaborate), and her claim that bibliographical citation or acknowledgement of indebtedness would 'let you off the hook' is unfounded since they would, in fact, allow critics to assess the aesthetic merits of her scholarly quotations. Bearing this in mind, one should compare the attitude adopted by Simms with the reader's report from Wake Forest which stated that 'the "detective work" of positivist, fact-seeking interpretation won't help'; what is required, the report goes on to suggest, is 'an intuitive, perhaps unconscious, whole-hearted *engagement*, one that nevertheless places unusual demands on one's intellectual and academic resources, with an extraordinary poetic imagination'.[92] This report takes on the mantle of critical nemesis, redressing the faults of an earlier assessment commissioned by Oxford University Press. While the latter is questionable in its essentialist thinking and unwarranted prognosis (that McGuckian had reached 'an impasse of "almost schizophrenic alienation"'), the rebuttal overcompensates for the positivist approach. Although it would be foolish to assert that a sustained positivistic methodology could ever produce a definitive account of a McGuckian poem – as if such a thing were possible – nevertheless any research which enlightens her readership as to the meaning or significance of obscure references, and which pinpoints specific areas of ambiguity, ought to be welcomed. 'Detective work' and intuitive response can complement each other and it is demonstrably unwise to disavow the possibility of conscious argument within McGuckian's poetry.

The rare inclusion of a footnote affords the reader a glimpse of the familiar ghosts that glide in between the interstices of this text: '"Choorka", one of Tolstoy's pet names for his daughter, is translated to give the poem its title' (*MC* 110). The footnote focuses the reader's attention wholly on the speaker's adoption of Tatyana's soubriquet, thereby establishing a salient parallel between two father–daughter relationships. In its original context, 'Choorka' acts as a testament to the enduring love of Tatyana Tolstoy for an inspiring paternal figure:

He used to call me 'Choorka' [a small piece of wood], and I loved that nickname because he always used it when he was in a good mood and wanted to tease me or be nice to me. The extraordinarily strong feeling of love and veneration I felt for my father never faded. From what I remember, and also what I have been told, he too always felt a particular affection for me.[93]

McGuckian's insertion of the same word into an alternative context still maintains the theme of filial devotion (to her own father), but its status as intertext enables her to extend this metaphorically to incorporate literary paternity. Indeed, her rewriting often centres thematically on the very notion of 'power' and reconfigures the allocated gender positions of the original text:

> Every apple is a feather-room
> For seed's infectious star, and every man
> Who calls a woman 'Choorka',
> For a hundred and eight ruled pages.
>   (*MC* 32)

The 'apple' calls to mind the poem's earlier images of learning (the 'lesson-filled inkwell', 'Pictures in children's books') since the first letter of the English alphabet is traditionally represented in elementary textbooks as an 'apple' to enable the child to discover the function of the abstract signifier, 'A'. In the final stanza, however, while the 'apple' is likened to 'a feather-room', suggesting incubation and materials for flight, its effect is decidedly ambiguous: 'infectious star' can indeed suggest an enthusiasm which spurs the child on to growth (from seed to star, progressing upwards), but 'infectious' hints at a more pernicious influence. The 'star' no longer implies that destiny is due to nature, but, rather, to nurture. The ambiguity continues into the final two lines. Whereas the original context in *Tolstoy Remembered* insists upon an unqualified affection for the father, in its translated form 'Choorka' ('a small piece of wood') suggests the demeaning ways in which this love was often reciprocated. In her one 'hundred and eight ruled pages',[94] McGuckian attempts to counter the effects of patriarchal 'rule' by gender-swapping and symbolically bestowing the mantle of the male literary figure (Leo Tolstoy) on to the female (Tatyana Tolstoy). This she has done in the very first stanza:

> On the secret shelves of weather,
> With its few rhymes, in a pause
> Of blood, I closed the top
> Of my lesson-filled inkwell,
> A she-thing called a poetess,
> Yeoman of the Month.
>   (*MC* 31)

McGuckian puts immense strain on words. By means of telegraphic-like compression, the temporal and biological aspects of 'a pause of blood' suggests at once female menstruation, kinship (father–daughter), and the interiorisation of natural forces. Indeed, the speaker manages to domesticate nature ('secret shelves of weather') and, suggesting a similitude with art ('With its few rhymes'), goes on to interiorise and textualise nature until it becomes enclosed in her 'lesson-filled inkwell'. Most striking, however, is the ambiguous gender of the speaker, at once a 'poetess' and a 'Yeoman'. In the original context (autumn, 1872), the action of closing an inkwell is Tatyana's attempt to shield her written thoughts from the prying eyes of her father: 'I didn't want anyone – even the nearest and dearest to me – penetrating my inner world. I had locked myself away in my own solitude and I didn't want to share my thoughts and feelings, however insignificant, with anyone at all.'[95] McGuckian admits her own related desire for secrecy in a remarkable conversation with Nuala Ní Dhomhnaill: 'I began to write poetry so that nobody could read it. Nobody. Even the ones who read it would not understand it, and certainly no other poet would understand it.'[96] Although in 'A Small Piece of Wood', McGuckian publicly reveals this need, thus paradoxically contradicting the desire for privacy, her concealed use of Tolstoy's biography masks the real narrative – the usurpation of the (literary) father.

The frequent intersections of McGuckian's poem with Tatyana Tolstoy's biography creates a doubled speaking self, but the gender of the figure who rides out to hunt is the androgynous poetess/Yeoman of the Month. The passage in the biography from which the above images emerge reveals the simultaneous birth of the writer and the symbolic (though also painfully literal) fall of her father; thus the poet overcomes the anxiety of influence:

I remember her as always gay and alert, her hands never without some
piece of work, dressed invariably, winter and summer alike,
in a pale frock protected by a perpetually spotless apron. (30)
[B]oots with raspberry tops. (24)

I was born at Yasnaya Polyana on October 4th 1864.
Several days beforehand my father had been thrown in a
riding accident. Still a young man then, he loved hunting,
especially for foxes and hares in the autumn. So on September
26th 1864 he took his pack of borzois and rode out to hunt on a
young and spirited mare named Mashka. (17)
Papa was against expensive toys, so while we were little mamma
used to run up playthings for us herself. She had made us a golliwog
that we quite doted on. He was made of black cambric with white
linen eyes, black lambswool hair, and lips cut out of a piece
of some red material. (21)

In pale frock and raspberry
Boots, my waist the circumference
Of no more than two oranges,
I rode out to hunt, with my
White linen eyes and my lips
Cut out of a piece of red material.
(MC31)

That this stanza refers to the emergence of Tatyana Tolstoy and Medbh McGuckian as writers is confirmed by a letter to the poet Fet dated 23 January 1865, in which Leo Tolstoy writes that '[a]fter my horse had thrown me, breaking my arm, my first thought when I regained consciousness was that I was a writer. Yes, I really am a writer, but a solitary writer, a silent writer' (149). McGuckian appropriates the experience from the father and transfers its significance to the daughter by employing the conventional metaphor of procreation for poetic composition: the 'Yeoman' is clearly pregnant.

McGuckian's poems are palimpsests, a means of 'writing in the interstices of texts, boring thru the white between the lines, scribbling on the margins'.[97] Delineating the strategic values of a palimpsest, DuPlessis writes,

> By putting known phrases from 'great poems' (i.e., already written, disseminated and absorbed poems) into a structure speaking differently, series of reverberating questions are set in motion that begin to dissolve or erode a former world view; or one has evoked in all the oscillating bliss, two opposite and alternative world views simultaneously. So at all times the critique and distancing are filled with yearning and complicity.[98]

Rather than 'disseminated and absorbed poems', McGuckian brings her analysis to bear mainly upon biographies, collections of prose essays and literary correspondence. This is appropriately termed 'her borrowing, "translating" method' by Clair Wills,[99] who does not realise just how pervasive this threading of 'double-stranded words' (*BB* 57) was in McGuckian's work.[100] In a palimpsest there is 'foreground and background, new statement and obscured original which can be discovered with the force of a revelation or something left overwritten in undecidable layering'.[101] This doubleness is important as McGuckian's quotations function as 'grafts', engendering 'a new textual configuration qualitatively different from the simple sum of two units'.[102] McGuckian frequently employs a trope signifying doubleness to self-reflexively comment on the parallels she sets up by using quotations. 'A Small Piece of Wood', for example, uses an image from *Tolstoy Remembered* for just such a purpose:

After Kazan I saw something very strange: the Volga had
grown even wider, and *on our left* the water was sharply
divided into two completely distinct strips of colour, *as
though someone had unrolled two ribbons side by side,*
one blue and the other yellow. This was the place where
the Kama flows into the Volga, and although there was no
physical barrier between the two currents they flowed on for
a great distance *without mingling*, so that you could still
distinguish the one from the other by their colour. (109)

On my left two rivers flowed
Together without mingling,
As though someone had unrolled
Two different ribbons side by side
(*MC* 31)

Of course, unlike the two rivers, the different narrative levels of McGuckian's palimpsests do intersect and, although not essential for an enjoyment of the poem, awareness of how she engages with her sources is important: 'I think that if someone had all the clues then it would be more of an enjoyable crossword puzzle, but for someone who didn't they would just enjoy the sounds of the words on their own and the allusions wouldn't be as deep for them but they would still have a surplus attractiveness.'[103]

Basing her conclusions on a single example of McGuckian's appropriative praxis, Clair Wills unduly dismisses the idea that one should look for an interpretation of an author's work in McGuckian's poetry. But McGuckian's quotations are not simply 'reconfigurations' of words;[104] not only do we have 'the manipulation of the borrowed text', but also 'a return effect from the new version to the original version which it contaminates and puts in perspective'.[105] One notable example is 'Gigot Sleeves' (*MC* 35–36). Borrowing from Winifred Gérin's[106] compelling biography of Emily Brontë, McGuckian's intention is to present us with a picture of the nineteenth-century poet-novelist as 'a revolutionary who dies on hunger strike':[107]

> And everything is emaciated – the desk
> On her knees, the square of carpet, the black
> Horsehair sofa, and the five-foot-seven by sixteen
>
> Inches, of a pair of months, stopped.
>
> (*MC* 36)

The poem's conclusion refers to Gérin's description of Brontë's illness: 'its relentless progress, the *emaciation*, the fever, the shortness of breath, the pain in the side, all confirmed the family's terrors of worse to come' (248, emphasis added). Her death was, according to Dr Wheelhouse, due to 'Consumption – *2 months'* duration' (259, emphasis added) and the dimensions of her coffin are recorded as '5 feet 7 inches by 16 inches' (259). McGuckian alters the diagnosis, implying that Brontë's condition was self-induced, a protest at her restricted life.

Much of the poem's description of her living conditions – in the second, third and ninth stanzas – are taken from one paragraph:

> And she [Emily Brontë] saw to it that her privacy was guarded from all possible encroachment. *The narrow slip-room over the front hall*, once the nursery and former playroom for all the children, was now indisputably hers. How it looked during the twelve years of her unchallenged tenancy can be judged from the rough sketches with which she filled the corners of her diary-papers. It represents a Spartan enough scene. Across the window was her *camp bed*, in the left-hand wall-angle was a chest of drawers, in the centre a *square of carpet*, a low chair on

which she sat with *her writing-desk on her knees* faced the window and the view beyond, and
there was an oil lamp for the dark hours. It was a simple setting but the view from the
window was all the luxury she required. *The absence of a fireplace* or any mode of heating in
the room explains the necessity for the shawl in which she is wrapped in her sketches; it may
also explain the hold consumption took on a constitution too long exposed to winter colds.

(66, emphasis added)

McGuckian, to use Maura Dooley's words, 'reel[s] in / life with someone
else's bait'.[108] Taking five excerpts from the above passage, she quotes them
in the second, third and tenth stanzas of her poem, insisting at all times on
the cramped nature of Emily Brontë's surroundings. Even the one seemingly incongruous detail, 'the black horsehair sofa', is taken from a passage
to do with the writer's increasing frailty.[109] By stressing the phrase 'a pair of
months', McGuckian echoes Gérin's realisation that Brontë's contracting
tuberculosis was far from inevitable during her long illness.

In 'Gigot Sleeves', McGuckian is open to the criticism that Tim Kendall
leveled at Paul Muldoon's '7, Middagh Street'.[110] In both instances, the
literary allusions place a heavy burden upon the reader. To be intelligible,
Muldoon's poem requires knowledge of Humphrey Carpenter's *W.H. Auden:
A Biography*. Similarly, the reader who does not recognize McGuckian's debt
to Gérin will not pick up on the homage paid to Brontë. Yet however oblique her strategy may be, McGuckian's treatment of her subject remains
very different from that of the biographer. The poet's economic appropriation of text enables her not only to explore certain root causes of Emily
Brontë's demise (the austere living conditions at Haworth parsonage, the
stubborn neglect of her health), but also to depict them formally. Indeed,
the dimensions of her coffin are juxtaposed with the size of Emily's living
space: while William Wood, the village carpenter, says that 'he had never in
all his experience made so narrow a shell for an adult' (259), McGuckian
implies that the coffin differed little from the room in which she wrote.
Emily Brontë's emaciation parallels that of the house ('the / Narrow sliproom',
'the square of carpet'); the gradual disappearance of both writer and building is figured literally in the enjambment at the poem's close whereby one
swiftly moves from 'five foot seven by sixteen' to 'Inches of a pair of months'
to 'stopped'. Never has closure seemed so final.

Many of McGuckian's borrowings from Gérin deliberately set up a particular image of Emily Brontë, one which counters preconceived notions of
her as a sheltered recluse, and offers instead the portrayal of a lively, engag-
ing woman: 'The double-cherry performs a dance behind / Triple gauze,

she takes out the bulldogs, / Masters a pistol ...' (*MC* 35). Emphasising her subject's vibrant creativity, Gérin refers to one incident when, on Oak Apple Day, the Brontë children decided to re-enact Charles II's escape from Worcester, and Emily adopted the role of the King, hiding from the multitude in the tree-tops:

> Outside Mr. Brontë's parlour window grew *a double-cherry*, quite his favourite tree in the garden, and in default of an oak in that sparse ground the cherry tree was fixed on for the exile's hiding place. The tree was in full blossom and afforded luxurious shelter for a hunted monarch.
>
> (17, emphasis added)

With the slow decline of her father's eyesight, Emily learned the skills necessary to defend the houshold should the need ever arise: 'Her willingness to learn may be assumed considering her imaginative girlhood among "the fighting gentry" of Gondal. Indeed to *master a pistol* might be a more congenial task than learning French grammar' (147, emphasis added).

> For a gown-length, she chooses
> A book-muslin patterned with lilac
> Thunder and lightning. Her skirts
>
> Are splashed with purple suns, the sleeves
> Set in as they used to be fifteen years
> Ago ...
> ... ...
> Her petticoats have neither curve nor wave
> In them ...
>
> (*MC* 35)

McGuckian's meticulous description of Emily Brontë's clothing – the skirts splashed with 'purple suns' – appears more appropriate to the post-hippy generation of the early 1970s[111] than to Victorian England. Yet this is part of the 'rediscovery' of Brontë which the poet fosters, and is based on ample biographical evidence. In her biography, Gérin quotes an excerpt from *The Life of Charlotte Brontë*, in which Mrs. Gaskell recounts that when Brontë was staying at the Hotel de Hollande, 1 Rue de la Putterie, she '"had taken a fancy to the fashion, ugly and preposterous even during its reign, of *gigot sleeves*, and persisted in wearing them long after they were 'gone out'. *Her petticoats, too, had not a curve or a wave in them*, but hung straight and long, clinging to her lank figure"' (131, emphasis added). Reinforcing her portrayal of an unconventional Emily Brontë, Gérin describes a shopping expedition:

> Ellen Nussey told Mary Duclaux years later about such a shopping expedition to Bradford at which she was present with Charlotte when Emily bought herself *a gown length*: she chose a

white stuff *patterned with lilac thunder and lightning*, to the scarcely-concealed horror of her more sober companions. And she looked well in it; a tall, lithe creature, with a grace half-queenly, half-untamed in her sudden supple movements, wearing with picturesque negligence her ample *purple-splashed* garments; her face clear and pale; her very dark and plenteous brown hair fastened up behind with a Spanish comb; her large grey-hazel eyes now full of indolent, indulgent humour, now glimmering with hidden meanings, now quickened into a flame by a flash of indignation, 'a red ray piercing the dew'.

                                                        (171–72, emphasis added)

That McGuckian's Emily Brontë – the tragic, 'half-untamed', solitary figure – is reminiscent of a Romantic, Byronic hero reflects a biographical assumption of Byron's profound influence on the Yorkshire writer.[112] In personal correspondence McGuckian reveals that 'I was re-reading Byron and found again 'a spreading here, a condensation there' which I used in "Gigot Sleeves". I suggest she [Emily Brontë] was more Byron than he.'[113] Her characterization of Brontë also reflects Gérin's view that 'Emily Brontë was no plagiarist; few novelists were so original as she. What she took from Byron she took because the seed lay in her' (46). Gérin's emphasis on Brontë's originality may also lie behind McGuckian's allusion in the eighth stanza of 'Gigot Sleeves' to Edward J. Trelawny's *Recollections*:

> The funeral pyre was now ready; I applied the fire, and the materials being dry and resinous the pine-wood burnt furiously, and drove us back. It was hot enough before, there was no breath of air, and the loose sand scorched our feet. As soon as the flames began to clear, and allowed us to approach, *we threw frankincense and salt into the furnace*, and *poured a flask of wine and oil over the body*.[114]

Within the framework of the poem, the reference functions proleptically, prefiguring the death of the female poet, but within the wider context of McGuckian's obvious concern with the anxiety of influence, the ritual burning of the dead poet's body could suggest her attempt at poetic originality, free from any precursor's influence. Yet this reading begs the question: while Brontë may have fully internalised and personalised the influence of Byron, has McGuckian's creativity, as 'poetic biographer', suffered while reading the lives of others? Like Joyce's Shem the Penman, is she sham or shaman, plagiarist or Pelagian:[115] 'Who can say how many pseudostylic shamiana, how few or how many of the most venerated public impostures, how very many piously forged palimpsests slipped in the first place by this morbid process from [her] pelagiarist pen?'[116] To what extent does McGuckian's 'intimate' reading constitute a significant reworking of the original?

McGuckian's unacknowledged borrowings in almost every poem over the course of eleven collections are certainly greater than those of Graham Swift, whose textual (and structural) similarities to Faulkner's *As I Lay Dying* caused such a furore following his Booker Prize win for *Last Orders*.[117] Yet they are also significantly fewer than those of the 'pathological plagiarist' who plagued Neal Bowers, as documented in his *Words for the Taking*.[118] Her appropriation of source material may usefully be compared to that of two Irish contemporary writers. The playwright Brian Friel borrowed extensively, but without acknowledgement, from George Steiner's *After Babel* when writing his masterpiece *Translations*, but he was never once accused of plagiarism.[119] More recently, Nuala Ní Dhomhnaill's practice of selecting excerpts from folklore without due acknowledgement has been questioned by both Proncias O'Drisceoil and Gabriel Rosenstock.[120] However, the 'unease' which both critics felt was not put down to suspicions of plagiarism. In light of McGuckian's use of biographical material in relation to female writers, it is tempting to bring Laura J. Rosenthal's thesis to bear on the twentieth century and claim that plagiarism can be seen as 'a problem of social subjectivity – and thus a problem of gender'.[121] Rosenthal argues that originality became 'a strategy for (self-)ownership one hundred years earlier in response to reconceptualizations of property that emphasized individual ownership but limited who could inhabit the position of owner'.[122] Yet McGuckian does not occupy a comparably marginal position and has access to various literary traditions.[123] Nor is it feasible to invoke Harold Bloom's psychological model of intrapoetic relationships which contends that, to overcome the anxiety of influence and 'clear an imaginative space for themselves',[124] 'strong' poets always begin by misreading their precursors; in contrast, McGuckian seeks to revivify them. As she stated in a letter: 'A work of art is good only if it has sprung from necessity. In this nature of its origin lies its judgement. There is no other.'[125]

In the course of preparing this book, I published a couple of articles on McGuckian's poetry which prompted a flurry of correspondence from her. She was unhappy with the fact that I was looking for, and uncovering, the sources behind her work. Apologising for her initial anger, and in an effort to describe her own method of poetic composition, she wrote a poem entitled 'Mantilla'[126] and dedicated it to me. The first verse reads as follows (source added on the left):[127]

> My resurrective verses shed people
> and reinforced each summer:

seeing his time as my own time (2)   I saw their time as my own time,
                                                      I said, this day will penetrate
using a thorn to remove a thorn (61)   those other days, using a thorn
the harness of the mind (41)   to remove a thorn in the harness
                                                      of my mind where anyone's touch
                                                      stemmed my dreams.

McGuckian self-consciously describes the action of writing a poem with
the aid of a source text, the immediate purpose of which, in this instance, is
purely therapeutic. She stated in the letter: 'I had to write something in the
usual way as soon as I – as I shouldn't??? – could in case I never would again.
But I was very aware in this of doing so, and trying not to be anyone but
myself, and also of your dedication to your thankless task of studying *me*.'
The perceived (and wholly unintentional) criticism in my articles had caused
the poet great fear, anxiety and anger, yet she learned, through meditation,
to make peace with it. 'The sadness of anxiety', says the Buddhist monk
Thich Nhat Han, 'can be used as a means of liberation from torment and
suffering, like using a thorn to remove a thorn.' For her, the poems are
'resurrective', bringing her familiar ghosts back to life – their time is also
her time. While 'shed' has the connotation of separation, it also means to
send forth as an emanation, an activity usually applied to 'the origination of
created beings from God'. Both usages are relevant since those whom her
poetry brings back to life are the precursor poets rather than their biographers who supply the actual words:

> They are only looking at the person's body and physical mind and events and doings – I am
> for their seed and their undying immortal *flame*. So I recreate ... or God – Through me. I
> hope to restore to life, and make empty words full. In the text the phrases are not poetry –
> linked properly in the DNA of the poem – they ought to be. They are intended to be.[128]

However, although she distances herself from the work of the source text,
she still uses the author's words. Therefore, the question which must be
asked is whether or not McGuckian's verse really does have an 'imaginative
signature', her own unique 'poetic DNA pattern'.[129] The genetic make-up
of her poems has an inherent doubleness, forming what Michael Davidson
has termed a *palimtext*. Foregrounding its intertextual and inter-discursive
aspects, Davidson suggests that a palimtext is 'a writing-in-process' which
'retains vestiges of prior writings out of which it emerges', and, more importantly, 'it is the still-visible record of responses to those early texts'.[130]
This relationship between the source text and poem is complex, as is evident in the third stanza of 'Mantilla':

My sound world was a vassal state,
a tightly bonded lattice of water
sealed with cunning to rear
the bridge of breathing.

While 'vassal state' suggests subordination, this is not meant to imply a
weakness in the poet; instead, it represents the openness to inspiration, a
willingness to welcome the approach of the Muse through the words of a
biography or other source. Like the 'staircase' of 'Lines for Thanksgiving',
the connective 'bridge of breathing' is the vital element.[131] McGuckian's
poetic praxis constitutes a rewriting, 'a repetition that distorts and mis-
quotes, that destroys in order to transform'.[132] Dovetailing quotations within
her own work offers a belated tribute to an admired author and registers her
own continuing engagement with their oeuvre and life. This does not constitute plagiarism. Indeed, I concur with Thomas Mallon's eloquent disquisition on plagiarism in his wide-ranging *Stolen Words*: reworking T. S. Eliot's
dictum that immature poet's imitate and mature poets steal,[133] he maintains that 'the writer need not blush about stealing if he makes what he
takes completely his, if he alchemizes it into something that is, finally, thoroughly new'.[134] McGuckian's palimpsests are original and, even though they
are oblique, they possess the coherence which many of her reviewers feel
they lack.

Notes

1 Patrick Williams, 'Spare that Tree!' *Honest Ulsterman* 86 (1989) 50 and 51, respectively.
2 See Michael O'Loughlin, 'Twenty-One Today', *Books Ireland* 66 (1982) 148; Alan Jenkins
  'Private and Public Languages', *Encounter* 59.5 (November, 1982) 56; Dick Davis 'Private
  Poems', *Listener* 16 December 1982, 23.
3 See John Lucas, 'Pleading for the Authenticity of the Spirit', *New Statesman* 13 August
  1982, 20; Lucas 'A Pose for the Betrayed World', *New Statesman and Society* 26 August
  1988, 38; John Drexel, 'Threaders of Double-Stranded Words: News from the North of
  Ireland', *New England Review and Bread Loaf Quarterly* 12.2 (Winter, 1989) 188.
4 See Gerard McCarthy, review of *On Ballycastle Beach*, *Irish University Review* 19.1 (Spring,
  1989) 176.
5 Gerald Dawe, 'Notion of Perfection', *Fortnight* 190 (January, 1983) 20.
6 Mary O'Donnell, 'Responsibility and Narcosis', *Poetry Ireland Review* 35 (Summer,
  1992) 111.
7 Andrew Elliott, review of *Venus and the Rain*, *Linen Hall Review* 1.3 (Autumn, 1984) 20.
8 See Martin Booth, review of *Venus and the Rain*, *British Book News* (October, 1984) 624.

9 See especially Francine Cunningham, review of *Marconi's Cottage*, *Fortnight* 310 (October, 1992) 52.

10 Peggy O'Brien, 'Reading Medbh McGuckian: Admiring What We Cannot Understand', *Colby Quarterly* 28.4 (December, 1992) 244.

11 Medbh McGuckian, 'An Attitude of Compassions', interview by Kathleen McCracken, *Irish Literary Supplement* (Fall, 1990) 20.

12 Unpublished poem, Box 19, Poems (S), McGuckian Papers, Emory University.

13 Letter from 'John [Drexel]' dated 8 June 1987 which states 'I think of you as a spy in the house of love.' Box 3 (Correspondence September 1986–February 1988), McGuckian Papers, Emory University.

14 Letter to the author, 24 December 1995.

15 Letter from Durcan dated 21 September 1987 in which he addresses McGuckian as 'Dear Rain'. See Box 3 (Correspondence September 1986–February 1988), McGuckian Papers, Emory University.

16 Medbh McGuckian, 'Ales Stenar', *Honest Ulsterman* (94): 10.

17 Personal correspondence, 22 February 1996. See, for example, Paul Muldoon, 'The Rucksack', *Honest Ulsterman* 50 (Winter, 1975): 152.

18 Box 18, McGuckian Papers, Emory University. The poem was written on the back of a publicity flyer: 'Welcome to the Poetry Days in Malmo!'.

19 It should be noted that when 'Unused Water' was first published in *Second Shift* 1.1 (Spring, 1993): 19, it did not have any dedication.

20 McGuckian, personal interview at the John Hewitt International Summer School, 28 July 1995.

21 McGuckian, personal interview at the John Hewitt International Summer School.

22 Medbh McGuckian in Catherine Byron, 'A House of One's Own: Three Contemporary Irish Women Poets', *Women's Review* 19 (May, 1987) 33.

23 See the letter from George Miller, 13 August 1991, McGuckian Papers, MSS 770, Special Collections, Emory University.

24 McGuckian, 'Medbh McGuckian: Imagery Wrought to Its Utmost', interview by Cecile Gray, in Deborah Fleming (ed.), *Learning the Trade: Essays on W. B. Yeats and Contemporary Poetry* (West Cornwall, CT: Locust Hill Press, 1993) 171.

25 McGuckian has stated that 'I always thought of the poet as a priest'. See Medbh McGuckian, 'Comhrá with Nuala Ní Dhomhnaill', interview by Laura O'Connor, *Southern Review* 31.3 (Summer, 1995) 591. See also interview by Gray 168.

26 McGuckian in Byron, 'A House of One's Own' 33.

27 Medbh McGuckian, 'Surfacing: An Interview with Medbh McGuckian', interview by Kimberly S. Bohman, *Irish Review* 16 (Autumn–Winter, 1994): 106.

28 McGuckian, interview by Gray 168.

29 McGuckian, personal interview at The John Hewitt International Summer School.

30 See Box 21, folder 33 (notebooks), McGuckian Papers, MSS 770, Emory University.

31 These had been misfiled in Box 21 folder 29, McGuckian Papers, under the heading 'Untitled Poems'.

32 Catriona O'Reilly, 'Afloat on the Sea of Language', *Irish Times* 22 November 1997, Weekend 9.

33 McGuckian Papers, MSS 770, Box 26, Folder 57.

34 Marcel Proust, *Swann's Way*, trans. C. K. Scott Moncrieff and Terence Kilmartin, revised by D. J. Enright, 1992 (London: Vintage, 2002).

35 John Fletcher and Malcolm Bradbury, 'The Introverted Novel', in Malcolm Bradbury and James McFarlane (eds), *Modernism: A Guide to European Literature, 1890–1930* (London: Penguin, 1991) 401.

36 Elias Canetti, *The Torch in My Ear*, trans. Joachim Neugroschel (London: Granta, 1982).

37 Medbh McGuckian, 'I am Listening in Black and White to What Speaks to Me in Blue', interview by Helen Blakeman, *Irish Studies* Review 11.1 (April 2003) 67.

38 Marjorie Garber, *Quotation Marks* (New York: Routledge, 2003) 2.

39 Medbh McGuckian, 'The Katydid', *The Flower Master* (Oxford: Oxford University Press, 1982) 33.

40 Marina Warner, *The Dragon Empress: Life and Times of Tz'u-his, 1835–1908, Empress Dowager of China* (London: History Book Club, 1972) 256. The note provided by McGuckian is helpful if somewhat inaccurate: Tz'u-his, belonging to the ruling Manchu clan, despised the Chinese custom of footbinding, but did not declare it illegal until 1902.

41 Warner, *Dragon Empress* 8, 12, 13. Other references are included in the text. One can initially deduce that McGuckian is referring to Warner's text as the others do not use the name 'Little Orchid'. See J. O. P. Bland and E. Backhouse, *China Under the Empress Dowager* (London: William Heinemann, 1910), Wu Yung, *The Flight of an Empress* (London: Faber, 1937) and Charlotte Haldane's *The Last Great Empress of China* (London: Constable, 1965). Of these three, only Haldane uses the name 'Orchid'.

42 See especially Eavan Boland, 'A Kind of Scar', *A Dozen Lips* (Dublin: Attic Press, 1994) 75; 'The Irish Woman Poet: Her Place in Irish Literature', in Chris Morash (ed.), *Creativity and Its Contexts* (Dublin: Liliput Press, 1995) 33; interview by Michael O'Siadhail, *Poetry Ireland Review* 27 (Autumn, 1989) 20–22.

43 See Eavan Boland, 'The Woman, the Place, the Poet', *Georgia Review* 44.1–2 (Spring–Summer, 1990) 102.

44 Boland 'The Irish Woman Poet' 37.

45 Eavan Boland, 'Gods Make Their Own Importance: The Authority of the Poet in Our Time', *PN Review* 21.4 (March–April, 1995) 12.

46 See Edna Longley, 'Irish Bards and American Audiences', *Southern Review* 31.3 (Summer, 1995) 764.

47 Eilís Ní Dhuibhne's introduction to her recent anthology reveals Boland's misconceptions. See Ní Dhuibhne, 'Introduction', *Voices on the Wind: Women Poets of the Celtic Twilight* (Dublin: New Island Books) 13. For a discussion of how Boland unduly diminishes her literary foremothers, see Gerardine Meaney, 'Myth, History and the Politics of Subjectivity: Eavan Boland and Irish Women's Writing', *Women: A Cultural Review* 4.2 (Autumn, 1993) 144.

48 Medbh McGuckian, 'The Timely Clapper', *Krino* 14 (1993) 45.

49 This is due to be published by La Salle University, Philadelphia, under the title of 'Rescuers and White Cloaks'. A copy was supplied to me by McGuckian.

50 Michel Riffaterre, 'Syllepsis', *Critical Theory* 6.4 (Summer, 1980) 627.

51 Riffaterre defines 'ungrammaticalities' as 'bearers of the poem's literariness, because they

connect it with a generic or thematic intertext and at the same time define the poem's originality by opposing it to this intertext'. See 'Interpretation and Undecidability', *New Literary History* 12.2 (Winter, 1981) 232–33.

52 Olga Ivinskaya, *A Captive of Time: My Years with Pasternak: The Memoirs of Olga Ivinskaya*, trans. Max Hayward (London: Fontana-Collins, 1979). Further references are included in the text.

53 See Ivinskaya, *A Captive of Time* 101.

54 'the guard on duty rushed in suddenly and said: "What are your initials? Get dressed for interrogation!" I gave him my initials. *"Initials in full,"* he said – when asked for our "initials", we were always ordered to give them "in full"' (Ivinskaya 102, emphasis added).

55 Patricia Boyle Haberstroh, *Women Creating Women: Contemporary Irish Women Poets* (New York: Syracuse University Press, 1996) 145.

56 Meva Maron, 'The Stamps Had Squirrels on Them', *Honest Ulsterman* 88 (1989) 33.

57 Ivinskaya is here quoting from the account given by Tsvetaeva's neighbours, a couple called Bredelshchikov (*A Captive of Time* 188–89). Lily Feiler in *Marina Tsvetaeva: The Double Beat of Heaven and Hell* (Durham: Duke University Press, 1994) also quotes them, but she translates the reference as 'an old fall coat' (259).

58 Marina Tsvetaeva, 'For My Poems', *Selected Poems*, trans. David McDuff (Newcastle upon Tyne: Bloodaxe, 1991) 38.

59 Medbh McGuckian, personal interview, Marine Hotel, Ballycastle, 19 August 1996.

60 Medbh McGuckian, 'How Precious Are Thy Thoughts Unto Me', *Common Knowledge* 2.1 (Spring, 1993) 135.

61 See Ivinskaya, *A Captive of Time* 313.

62 See Thomas Docherty, *Alterities: Criticism, History, Representation* (Oxford: Clarendon Press, 1996) 128, and Haberstroh, *Women* 127.

63 Clair Wills in *Improprieties: Politics and Sexuality in Northern Irish Poetry* (Oxford: Clarendon Press, 1993) brings our attention to the 'unfulfilled pact' between Pasternak and Tsvetaeva to meet with Rilke as described in Boris Pasternak, Marina Tsvetayeva and Rainer Maria Rilke, in Yevgeny Pasternak, Yelena Pasternak and Konstantin M. Azadovsky (eds), *Letters Summer 1926*, trans. Margaret Wettlin and Walter Arndt (London: Cape, 1986) 189.

64 Clarence Brown, *Mandelstam* (Cambridge: Cambridge University Press, 1973). Further references are included in text.

65 See Brown, *Mandelstam* 273–75.

66 See Wills, *Improprieties* 189.

67 Sarah Broom, 'Image and Symbol in the Poetry of Medbh McGuckian', MA thesis, Leeds University, 1995, 34. Broom has recently published an extract from this thesis. See 'McGuckian's Conversations with Rilke in *Marconi's Cottage*', *Irish University Review* 28.1 (Spring–Summer, 1998) 133–50.

68 See Brown, *Mandelstam* 166.

69 Medbh McGuckian, interview by Rebecca E. Wilson, in Gillean Somerville-Arjat and Rebecca E. Wilson (eds), *Sleeping with Monsters: Conversations with Scottish and Irish Women Poets* (Dublin: Wolfhound Press, 1990) 2.

70 Ann and Samuel Charters, *I Love: The Story of Vladimir Mayakovsky and Lili Brik* (London: André Deutsch, 1979). Further references are included in text.

71 McGuckian, personal interview, Marine Hotel, Ballycastle. See also interview by Gray 174–75.

72 McGuckian, personal interview, Marine Hotel, Ballycastle.

73 Michael Longley, 'Patchwork', *Poems 1963–1983* (London: Secker and Warburg, 1991) 188.

74 Christopher Hope, 'Meaty Flavours', *London Magazine* 22.9–10 (December 1982–January 1983) 107.

75 Personal correspondence, 28 February 1996.

76 Medbh McGuckian, '"There is No Feminine in Eternity"', *Delighting the Heart: A Notebook by Women Writers*, ed. Susan Sellers (London: The Women's Press, 1989) 177.

77 Caren Kaplan, 'Deterritorializations: The Rewriting of Home and Exile in Western Feminist Discourse', *Cultural Critique* 6 (Spring, 1987) 187.

78 Medbh McGuckian, 'The Idea of the Anglo-Irish Tradition', Box 27, McGuckian Papers, Emory University. The essay was corrected by Mr S[eamus] Heaney and was awarded an A+. Heaney's final comment was 'This is a beautifully coherent and intelligent piece of work, impressively researched, firmly outlined and passionately engaged. One of the best things I've read on the subject.'

79 Gilbert and Gubar in Medbh McGuckian, 'Birds and Their Masters', *Irish University Review* 23.1 (Spring–Summer, 1993) 33.

80 This accords with McGuckian's own experience of post-partum depression. She was 'put into a mental home' and 'told not to write poetry'. See McGuckian 'Comhrá with Nuala Ní Dhomhnaill', interview by Laura O'Connor, 595.

81 Charlotte Gilman Perkins, *The Yellow Wallpaper* (New York, 1973) 26.

82 Annette Kolodny, 'A Map of Rereading: Or, Gender and the Interpretation of Literary Texts', *New Literary History* 11.3 (Spring, 1980) 458.

83 'Journal Intime' can also be regarded as an 'artfully placed mirror' for one final reason: it is placed next to 'Brothers and Uncles' (MC 27–8), a text which echoes its concerns and which also borrows heavily from Sandra M. Gilbert and Susan Gubar, *The Madwoman in the Attic: The Woman Writer and the nineteenth-Century Literary Imagination* (2nd edn) (New Haven, CT: Yale University Press, 2000). See Shane Alcobia-Murphy and Richard Kirkland, eds., *Medbh McGuckian* (forthcoming).

84 McGuckian, 'Garbo at the Gaumont', *Oxford Poetry* 4.2 (Spring, 1988): 16.

85 Tatyana Tolstoy, *Tolstoy Remembered*, trans. Derek Coltman (London: Michael Joseph, 1977). Further references are included in text.

86 See Tatyana Albertini, 'I Often Think of My Mother', in Tolstoy, *Tolstoy Remembered* 249.

87 See letters dated 2 July, 17 July, 27 August and 12 September 1991 in Box 11, McGuckian Papers, Emory University.

88 See letters dated 1 August and 13 August 1991, McGuckian Papers, Box 11.

89 A statement of account from Oxford University Press dated 20 July 1990, showed dwindling sales for all three collections during the period 1 April 1989–31 March 1990. Since publication, *The Flower Master* had sold 887, *Venus and the Rain* 1990, and *On Ballycastle Beach* 1837. See Correspondence with OUP, McGuckian Papers, Box 11.

90 Jacqueline Simms, letter dated 26 October 1990, Box 11, McGuckian Papers.

91 Undated, but probably 16 December 1990.

92 See Guinn Batten's 'Report on New Poems by Medbh McGuckian' dated 23 June 1991,

Box 11 folder 7 McGuckian Papers.
93 Tolstoy, *Tolstoy Remembered* 35.
94 In the Gallery Press version of *Marconi's Cottage*, the poems are printed on 108 pages. In its original draft, 'A Small Piece of Wood' was hand-written on ruled paper – see Poems 'S', Box 18, McGuckian Papers, Emory University.
95 Tolstoy, *Tolstoy Remembered* 95–96. Further references are included in text.
96 McGuckian, 'Comhrá with Nuala Ní Dhomhnaill', interview by Laura O'Connor, *Southern Review* 31.3 (Summer, 1995): 590.
97 Rachel Blau DuPlessis, *The Pink Guitar: Writing as Feminist Practice* (New York: Routledge, 1990) 169.
98 DuPlessis, *The Pink Guitar* 150–51.
99 Clair Wills, 'Voices from the Nursery: Medbh McGuckian's Plantation', in Michael Kenneally (ed.), *Poetry in Contemporary Irish Literature* (Gerrards Cross: Colin Smythe, 1995) 385. See also Wills *Improprieties* 172–82.
100 Wills clearly thought that only 'The Dream Language of Fergus' (*BB* 57) used embedded quotations.
101 Rachel Blau DuPlessis, *H. D.: The Career of that Struggle* (Sussex: Harvester Press, 1986) 56.
102 André Topia, 'The Matrix and the Echo: Intertextuality in *Ulysses*', in Derek Attridge and Daniel Ferrer (eds.), *Post-Structuralist Joyce: Essays from the French* (Cambridge: Cambridge University Press, 1984) 105.
103 McGuckian, personal interview, Marine Hotel, Ballycastle.
104 Wills, *Improprieties* 178.
105 Topia, *The Matrix and the Echo* 104. See also Ziva Ben-Porat, 'The Poetics of Literary Allusion', *PLT* 1 (1976) 111–15 for a demonstration of how the alluding text and referent text interact.
106 Winifred Gérin, *Emily Brontë: A Biography* (Oxford: Oxford University Press, 1978). Further references included in text.
107 Personal correspondence, 27 February 1998.
108 Maura Dooley, 'Up on the Roof', *Kissing a Bone* (Newcastle upon Tyne: Bloodaxe, 1996) 16.
109 See Gérin, *Emily Brontë*: 'About noon Emily was visibly worse and her sisters urged her to bed. The only concession she would make was to lie down on the sofa – *the black horsehair sofa* that can still be seen today' (259, emphasis added).
110 See Tim Kendall, *Paul Muldoon* (Brigend: Seren, 1996) 125–26.
111 Hence the reference to 'fifteen years ago' – the poem was first published in 1988.
112 See Stevie Davies, *Emily Brontë* (New York: Harvester Wheatsheaf, 1988) 23.
113 McGuckian, personal correspondence, 27 July 1996.
114 Trelawny in J. E. Morpurgo, *The Last Days of Shelley and Byron* (London: The Folio Society, 1952) 88, emphasis added.
115 See Jennifer Schiffer Levine, 'Originality and Repetition in *Finnegans Wake* and *Ulysses*', *PMLA* 94.1 (January 1979) 109.
116 James Joyce, *Finnegans Wake*, first pub. 1939 (London: Faber, 1975) 181–82.
117 See Chris Blackhurst, 'A Swift Rewrite, or a Tribute?' *Independent on Sunday* 9 March 1997: 5.

118 Neal Bowers, *Words for the Taking: The Hunt for a Plagiarist* (New York: Norton, 1997).

119 See F. C. McGrath, 'Irish Babel: Brian Friel's *Translations* and George Steiner's *After Babel*, *Comparative Drama* 23.1 (1989) 31–49.

120 See Proincias O'Drisceoil, 'À La Carte Plagiarism?' *Poetry Ireland Review* 34 (1992) 121–24 and Gabriel Rosenstock, review of *Spíonáin is Róiseanna, Poetry Ireland Review* 39 (1993): 102–09. Ní Dhomhnaill's borrowings were brought to my attention by Brian O'Conchubhair, University College Galway.

121 Laura J. Rosenthal, *Playwrights and Plagiarists in Early Victorian England: Gender, Authorship, Literary Property* (Ithaca: Cornell University Press, 1996) 3.

122 Rosenthal, *Playwrights and Plagiarists* 4.

123 Eavan Boland in 'Time, Memory and Obsession', *PN Review* 18.2 (November–December, 1991) 18–24 and Ní Dhomhnaill in 'What Foremothers?' *Poetry Ireland Review* 36 (Autumn, 1992) 18–31 both argue that the female Irish poet has little access to an Irish literary tradition. However, despite the weaknesses of Anne Stevenson's rebutal in 'Inside and Outside History', *PN Review* 18.3 (January–February, 1992) 34–38, scholarship has shown the abundance of precursors for Irish contemporary women poets.

124 Harold Bloom, *The Anxiety of Influence: A Theory of Poetry* 1973 (London: Oxford University Press, 1975) 5.

125 McGuckian, letter to the author, 22 February 1999.

126 'Mantilla' was written on 23 January 1997 and included in personal correspondence, 25 January 1997. The poem was collected in *Shelmalier* (Meath: Gallery Press, 1998) 119.

127 Thich Nhat Hanh, *The Miracle of Mindfulness: A Manual on Meditation*, trans. Mobi Ho, (London: Rider, 1987). The actual source text may well be a book citing extracts from this guide to meditation.

128 McGuckian, personal correspondence, 21 January 1997.

129 See Seamus Heaney, *The Redress of Poetry*, first pub. 1990 (Oxford: Clarendon Press, 1991) 6–7. These comments were omitted in the edited version of this lecture which was published in his Oxford lectures (1995).

130 Michael Davidson, 'Palimtexts: Postmodern Poetry and the Material Text', *Genre* 20.3–4 (Fall–Winter, 1987) 310.

131 The reference is also to her meditation technique which brought about a sense of calm following on from her anxiety. 'Our breath', says Naht Han, 'is the bridge from our body to our mind, the element that reconciles our body and mind and which makes possible oneness of body and mind' (23).

132 Claudette Sartiliot, *Citation and Modernity: Derrida, Joyce, and Brecht* (Norman: University of Oklahoma Press, 1995) 76.

133 See T. S. Eliot, *The Sacred Wood* (London: Faber, 1997) 105–06.

134 Thomas Mallon, *Stolen Words: Forays into the Origins and Ravages of Plagiarism* (New York: Ticknor and Fields, 1989) 25.

Part II

3

'Something a little nearer home':
The Intersection of Art and Politics

The fragmented, multivoiced complexity of much mainstream Irish poetry is often dismissed as fatally hermetic; what is allusive is elitist and insincere, a latter-day art for art's sake. Iain Sinclair's polemical introduction to *Conductors of Chaos*, for example, makes the remarkable claim that in anthologies of Irish poetry, '[e]vent is adulterated by self-regarding tropes, false language'.[1] Especially vituperative in his description of Irish anthologists' (and, by extension, Irish poets') self-interested preoccupation with '[b]og and bomb and blarney', he dismisses their work as 'a heap of glittering similes burnished for westward transit'.[2] Although justified in voicing a general anxiety concerning the impact of commercial necessity upon artistic integrity, he is wrong in assuming that Irish-American publishers set the agenda for Irish poetry. His subsequent acerbic diatribe – that '[t]oo much contemporary verse arrives smirking on the page dressed up for the anthology audition. Pre-programmed and dead in the mouth'[3] – betrays an uncharacteristic impatience with self-reflexivity and is a gross misreading of both the intentions and effects of Irish poetry that deals with the Northern Irish situation. It would, of course, be possible to empathise with Sinclair's criticism if it were limited to the minor poets riding on the coat tails of their more gifted contemporaries. Witness, for example, Stephen Smith's 'Between Omagh and Cookstown':

> We arrive guided by policemen and film-crews.
> It's a struggle to say anything new or shocking –
>
> fact goes off at a tangent into myth,
> language stakes claims.[4]

A poem about a poet in a time of violence unable to strain the resources of language may have been thematically fresh in the 1970s, but now is simply old wine in a new bottle. Similarly, Peter McDonald's 'Flat Sonnet: The Situation' is hardly subtle:

> To speak exactly about the situation is difficult,
> and yet to speak inexactly is unpardonable,
> reshaping it at best as some half-blurred fable
> where lines undraw themselves ...[5]

Rhyming 'unpardonable' with 'fable', and later 'reply' with 'lie', McDonald's poem about the Northern Irish poet's responsive urge toward the Troubles is, true to its title, 'flat'. However, Sinclair's primary target seems to be the self-reflexiveness of Seamus Heaney's political poetry.[6] Although technically conservative in its adherence to the dictates of 'the well made poem' – in Heaney's terms 'tight-arsed'[7] – his poetry's engagement with public themes does not make it 'a scapegoat shoved out in the place of morality';[8] rather, his self-reflexive literary allusions are actually used to explore the ethics of writing in a time of violence. His poetry's striking equipoise does not ignore social pressures, but is shaped by them.

In this chapter I intend to redress Sinclair's prejudice against self-regarding poetry by examining the strategies employed by Northern Irish poets who offer what Neil Corcoran has called 'situatings, enquiries into symptoms and origins, trajectories of malaise'. I will briefly examine how poetry and politics intersect in the work of Paul Muldoon and Medbh McGuckian's most influential precursor, Seamus Heaney. I will then contrast his apprehensive use of literary allusions with Muldoon's more confident deployment of intertextuality and with McGuckian's secret embedding of quotations. In particular, I will focus on how intertextual relations allow the younger poets to refer indirectly, without resorting to the extremes of either propaganda or hermeticism, both to the Troubles in Northern Ireland as well to the wider issue of colonial inheritance. This approach runs the risk of annoying those who may think they have heard it all before:

> To judge from the critical writing, it sometimes seems as if every poem written in Northern Ireland was expressly designed as a political text, a declaration of regional affiliation, part of 'the discourse of identity'. Poems are scoured for nuances of political positioning, for their contribution to the web of argument and counter-argument, are seen to succeed or fail to the degree to which they arrive at the 'correct' gesture, the 'balanced' view.[10]

Exasperated by the cyclopic approach taken by academics, Peter Sirr castigates those critics who seemingly prefer paraphrase over poetic form. While one can sympathise with his frustration, it has to be acknowledged that the pressures on Northern Irish poets to respond in some way to the Troubles are very real. Writing in the mid-seventies, Terence Brown claimed that it is almost inevitable 'that a poet in a situation like that which has obtained in Northern Ireland since 1969 should write of the "troubles"'.[11] Andrew Waterman reiterated this four years later, stating that the Northern Irish poet 'suffers the further constraint of being expected to define exactly where he stands in relation to some or other concept of nationalism and cultural allegiance'.[12] This cultural imperative for the lyric to acknowledge political allegiance and explore the causes of sectarian conflict has not diminished.[13] There is, however, a lack of clarity surrounding the issues: what exactly do we mean by 'politics' and what is its relationship with poetry?

When discussing the presence of politics in Northern Irish poetry, commentators are often at cross-purposes, referring either to different areas of experience or to distinct types of discourse: constitutional politics, party politics, gender politics, political activity, political thinking, etc. In its broadest sense, politics is defined as 'a complex of relations between the individual and society'.[14] Requiring adequate definitions of self and other, one cannot fully comprehend politics without knowing 'how the individual relates to the larger group as well as the ideology that governs that relation and how that ideology is created and, in due course, modified and used'.[15] With this in mind, one can understand Derek Mahon's contention that '[a] good poem is a paradigm of good politics – of people talking to each other, with honest subtlety, at a profound level'.[16] Yet for many critics this definition of politics is too general and much of the problem acknowledging its intersection with poetry arises from its confusion with propaganda or sectarian ideology. Edna Longley has famously proclaimed that '[p]oetry and politics, like church and state, should be separated. And for the same reasons: mysteries distort the rational processes which ideally prevail in social relations; while ideologies confiscate the poet's special passport to *terra incognita.*'[17] While she does acknowledge that the locus of a poem 'takes the measure of many perspectives and distances',[18] she believes, like Sirr, that poetry has 'suffered too much "context"':[19] imaginative response requires a discourse uninflected by sectarian bigotry. Although she refines her argument somewhat in *The Living Stream,* explaining that '[b]y politics I meant predatory ideologies, fixed agendas and fixed expectations',[20] nevertheless her resistance to cultural materialism[21] brings her into direct conflict with Seamus Deane, whose Marxist analyses never erect any such barrier between the public and the private. 'All art', says Deane, 'is mediated; it is operative in relation to an audience.'[22] The political is internalised and comes to mean cultural inheritance; the poem becomes an ideological construct, a 'text' foregrounding agency and its own 'literarity' as opposed to an unmediated, transcendental model of literature.[23]

This problem of appropriate artistic response is not limited to poetry and has been examined in some depth by several influential commentators on Irish culture: by Brian McAvera,[24] whose catalogue essay for the *Directions Out* exhibition acts as a refutation of an earlier article by Lucy Lippard[25] concerning the lack of political art in Northern Ireland; by Mary Stinson Cosgrove,[26] whose article examines the conjunction between location and art production; and by Joan Fowler,[27] whose analysis of essays by Richard Kearney and Edna Longley[28] criticises their (mis)understanding of what constitutes political art. Both Cosgrove and Fowler take McAvera to task for his contention that Northern Irish visual artists are psychologically predisposed toward obliquity. Whereas Cosgrove believes that McAvera is being both reductive and essentialist in his overlooking of the material conditions of production,[29] Fowler claims that what remains unsaid in his text is the belief that politics in art necessarily leads to propaganda.[30] Both articles are misreadings as McAvera does not neglect, discount or underestimate the political quotient of Northern Irish art and literature; he argues convincingly that the complexity of the situation dictates a more considered artistic approach. For example, in *Art, Politics and Ireland*, McAvera contrasts propaganda, which 'requires and utilises the reinforcement of reflexive bigotries in an attempt to effect change rapidly',[31] with a political art that adopts a layered, oblique approach to socio-political realities. He also demonstrates elsewhere that Northern Irish artists replace direct polemic with what he calls 'the strategies of subtext':

> [T]he angle of approach is oblique, layered subterranean. They rarely use a straight-forward singular image; rather they juxtapose, collage, build 'boxes' – they use emblem, symbol, myth – they ransack the image-bank of art-history, of history and religion, of politics and archaeology.[32]

One striking example of their ability by indirection to find direction out is the approach taken with regard to Protestant culture and its specific uses of the past. Irish history is frequently regarded as both savage and tireless,[33] capable of mauling the historian[34] with its 'oppressive burden',[35] and the infamous Protestant 'siege mentality' is no different. It is because the so-called marching season is so contentious that Northern Irish artists have to be purposefully circumspect in their work. However, rather than uncritically lauding acts of remembrance,[36] they examine the Orange Order's (perceived) inward-looking, self-defeating nature. Rita Duffy's apocalyptic 'Legacy of the Boyne' (1989),[37] for example, literalises the Orange Order's rhetoric by depicting a nightmareish scenario whereby the dead actually rise up and participate in the celebrations. That the 12 July march has a religious aspect is indicated not only by the Moses child hidden among the reeds, but also by the main figure's facial expression: wide-eyed devotion. This may, of course, teeter towards destructive fanaticism. Although Edna Longley is justified in claiming that 'Republican iconography ... merges memory into aspiration', it may not be fully correct to maintain that Orange insignia, by contrast, wholly avoid myth-making (that '[t]hey are not icons, but *exempla* or history-lessons: a heritage-pack as survival kit').[38] In her picture, Duffy exploits the historical associations of the regalia for dramatic effect: in the centre looms the commanding presence of a huge Orangeman holding a ceremonial sword, his sash flowing like the Boyne, carrying off spectral bodies with Munch-like skulls. The present conflict is viewed as a continuation of the 1690 battle: on the left of the canvas, flowing into the sash, there is a graveyard with open tombs and, to the right, a man screams as the tip of the Orangeman's sword hovers perilously above his head.

Irish political art does not reflect sectarian attitudes but refracts an artist's emotional response to them through his or her own particular medium; although their art may borrow the iconography of the different religious and political traditions, nevertheless 'its thumbprint is iconoclastic, layered, and questioning'.[39] In Victor Sloan's *The Walk, The Platform and The Field* series at the Flowerfield Arts Centre, Portstewart (1986), the images struggle to emerge from what one critic calls 'a miasma of marks', suggesting that they are 'caught between ineluctable forces'.[40] Left alone, the photographs would be realistic depictions of the Orange marches, but the artist's scraping, marking and overpainting of his photographs establishes an almost sinister aspect, blocking out the marchers' individual personalities. John Roberts is correct when he claims that the violence done to the images 'pinpoints exactly that sense of costiveness that is the Unionist political mandate'.[41] In 'No Surrender', for example, the 'X' slashed across the banner of a feminised cavalier (possibly William of Orange) is not simply indicative of Sloan's disapproval, but also suggests both the Orange Order's selective amnesia about its own origins[43] and its exclusively Unionist political agenda.[44] Interpreting the figures surrounding the banner, McAvera expresses succinctly Sloan's theme, namely that the Orange Order's unquestioning adherence to tradition engenders stifling conformity, inhibiting indivual thought:

> The portrait is encircled by a swathe of white. The head of a small boy is *inside* the circle (the intelligence has been indoctrinated) but the body is *outside* as he has to live in the twentieth century, despite the outmoded attitudes. Both the Orange Lodge member and the small girl to the right of the banner are faceless, thus representing the average person. The only living reality is the dead historical personage.[45]

For McAvera, it is Northern Irish poetry which best embraces the non-divisive and open-ended attitude towards politics: 'The continual spark of metaphor or the magical manipulations of narrative invest the poem with a density of texture (its allusiveness like the warp and woof of the spinner) which is rarely present in the photographic image'.[46] One such poem is Seamus Heaney's 'The Marching Season',[47] a short lyric comprising four regularly stressed couplets, the thematics of which tackle similar subject matter to the visual artists:

> 'What bloody man is
> that?' 'A drum, a drum!'
>
> Prepossessed by what I
> know by heart,
>
> I wait for Banquo and
> Macbeth to come
>
> Unbowed, on cue and
> scripted from the start.

The immediate context is the Orange Order's decision in 1998 to defy an order by the Parades Commission to reroute the 4 July march down the Garvaghy Road. Listening to the Orange Order's pained insistence upon its supposedly inalienable rights[48] to march somnambulistically into Protestant folk memory at this (by now) annual Siege of Drumcree,[49] one can readily appreciate the judiciousness of A. T. Q. Stewart's claim that '[t]o the Irish, all history is applied history and the past is simply a convenient quarry which provides ammunition to use against enemies in the present'.[50] This, in effect, is what the poem says, but, like much of the work by Northern Irish visual artists, it is less declarative than suggestive, using a Shakespearean allusion as a telling analogy. The opening couplet contains two quotations from *Macbeth*: the first is spoken by King Duncan asking for news about the revolt (I.ii.1–3); the second is voiced by the Third Witch, announcing

Macbeth's imminent arrival and the beginning of his treachery (I.iii.30–31). By juxtaposing the two, Heaney not only taints the celebratory marching season with the thought of impending violence, but also casts the term 'Loyalism' in a different light: the beating of the lambeg drum, previously synonymous with Loyalism, is linked here with the impending civil disobedience by the Orange marchers at Drumcree, whose violence is directed at the security forces. The poem's speaker is powerless to avert the conflict; like the approach of Banquo and Macbeth, the trouble arising from the marching season is 'scripted from the start', a phrase which not only emphasises the theatricality of the 4 July marches, but also hammers home the point that, as A. T. Q. Stewart has claimed, 'the form and course of the conflict are determined by patterns concealed in the past, rather than by those visible in the present'.[51] The strategy of using literary allusions when referring indirectly to the Northern Irish conflict is typical of Heaney's oeuvre, but the unselfconscious manner in which he resorts to Shakespeare in 'The Marching Season' is not.

Although Edna Longley claims that the poet has been won over to Seamus Deane's way of approaching the poetry/politics dichotomy,[52] Heaney's long-standing belief that the poet is a 'diviner',[53] a medium 'expressing his own subconscious and the collective subconscious',[54] is anathema to Deane, who dismisses such a position as a 'naive reflection theory'.[55] However, while Heaney is convinced that 'the transmitting power of art' has a 'political reality' which addresses itself 'to a secret unspoken level of understanding that is intimate to a country or a language to a certain community',[56] he has not been fully at ease 'raising a baton to attune discords which the cudgels are creating'.[57] In fact, Heaney's work has consistently (if not obsessively) engaged with this problem of incorporating socio-political themes into lyric poetry. In his early prose, for example, he reflects on how difficult it is for the writer 'to encompass the perspectives of a humane reason and at the same time to grant the religious intensity of the violence its deplorable authenticity and complexity'.[58] Although he has often rephrased the terms of this debate, it is always presented as the same strict binary opposition: in *The Government of the Tongue*, he takes advantage of the title's inherent ambiguity to oppose the tongue's 'right to govern' with 'the denial of the tongue's autonomy and permission';[59] in *The Redress of Poetry*, the appeal to poetry's power as a mode of redress is tempered by an altogether different imperative, 'to redress poetry *as* poetry, to set it up as its own category, an eminence established and a pressure exercised by distinctly linguistic means'.[60] Reconciling these divergent positions necessitates a third way, a 'cunning middle voice' that is both adept and dialect.[61] Balancing local knowledge with worldly experience, the poet's ideal position is 'at a tangent' to society[62] and, as a latter-day Archimedes, his angle of approach is all-important: crucially, he must deal with local politics from a distance. Adapting a fundamental law of physics, Heaney expresses his theory as follows:

> [W]e can begin to consider how important the length of the arm of the lever is when it come to the actual business of moving a world. This takes us back to another basic school-book principle of science, the principle of moments, the principle in operation when the claw-hammer draws out the nail or the crow-bar dislodges the boulder. In each case, what is intractable when wrestled with at close quarters becomes tractable when addressed from a distance. The longer the lever, in fact, the less force is necessary to move the mass and get the work going.[63]

In an oeuvre widely noted for its 'writerly self-involvements',[64] this distance becomes the focus of the poems themselves. I want to argue that Heaney tries to achieve the required distance by using literary allusions and historical analogies, though not without much soul-searching about the limitations of this approach.

Heaney's attention, like that of other Irish poets, has been attracted eastwards to the example set by writers such as Osip Mandelstam, Czeslaw Milosz, etc. Following the path set by Joyce's elision of the differences between Dublin and Lublin, Heaney's work continually sets up analogies between Northern Ireland and Eastern Europe, but for a different purpose:

> I keep returning to them because there is something in their situation that makes them attractive to a reader whose formative experience has been largely Irish. There is an unsettled aspect to the different worlds they inhabit, and one of the challenges they face is to survive amphibiously, in the realm of 'the times' and the realm of their moral and artistic self-respect, a challenge immediately recognizable to anyone who has lived with the awful and demeaning facts of Northern Ireland's history over the last couple of decades.[67]

Envious of their 'amphibiousness', Heaney dons the mask of an East European writer. One well-known instance is 'Exposure',[68] in which the poet's 'weighing and weighing' his 'responsible *tristia*' invokes not only Ovid's *Tristia*[69] but, more crucially, the poetry of Osip Mandelstam.[70] Heaney's self-description as an 'inner émigré' recalls the Russian poet's own status as an 'internal émigré'.[71] It is undoubtedly true that the allusion allows Heaney not only to draw on 'the traditional energies of exile poetry' but to highlight 'that inner expatriation which specially belongs to Northern Catholics in an incomplete state';[72] however, the parallel is far from unproblematic since, in spite of the deep-felt sense of affiliation Heaney has with Mandelstam and the obvious warmth with which he has continued to greet the Russian poet's enduring legacy,[73] his appropriation and re-contextualisation of this specific term elides the very real differences between their two lives. It ought to be clear that the acute pressures of living amidst the harsh Russian totalitarianism of the 1930s bears only superficial resemblance to the tribal exigencies and socio-political inequalities borne by the Northern Irish writer throughout the 1970s. In light of the extreme contrast between the freedom of a Laureate 'zipping through the stratosphere at Mach-2 somewhere over the Atlantic in his space-age scriptorium'[74] and the curtailment of Mandelstam's basic human rights due to politically motivated censorship and imprisonment, how seriously can we take John Desmond's claim that '[e]xile has led Heaney into an imagined community with Eastern European writers, for whom the issue of the artist's dual commitment to history and to art has often been literally a matter of life and death'?[75] Just as Seamus Deane was wrong to maintain that Paul Muldoon is '"in exile' in Princeton' (*PQ* 36), so one can hardly compare Mandelstam's fatal disaffection towards Stalinism with Heaney's principled stance that his 'passport's green'.[76] Similar to Victor Sloan's *Borne Sulinowo*,[77] a photographic exhibition which implicitly parallels the new democratic regime in Poland with the 'demilitarisation and perhaps even the withdrawal of the British Army from the Six Counties',[78] Heaney's use of an East European analogy is one-dimensional and overly simplistic.[79]

In a poem first entitled 'Quoting',[80] Heaney remarks upon the incipient power of quotation: 'Talking about it isn't good enough / But quoting from it at least demonstrates / The virtue of an art that knows its mind'. Yet East European exemplary authors have not always been resorted to with such casual facility or self-effacing adroitness; rather, as in 'Away from it All',[81] literary allusions have assumed the guise of 'rehearsed alibis'. Much of this unease originates from Heaney's continued inability to reconcile the conflicting demands of poetic form with political discourse, and in 'Away from it All' this dilemma is signalled by Heaney's quotation from Czeslaw Milosz's *The Native Realm*:

I was stretched between contemplation
of a motionless point

and the command to participate
actively in history.[82]

Heaney is far from naïve in his reference to Milosz since not only is this affinity knowingly presented as a 'rehearsed alibi', it is also one that he struggles fully to comprehend: "'*Actively?* What do you mean?'" Whereas Heaney's preface to *The Crane Bag Book of Irish Studies*[83] enlarges upon this theme by quoting an extended and more explanatory version of the quotation, the speaker's sudden intrusion in 'Away from it All' signals interrogation and self-introspection rather than passive acceptance of the precursor's advice.

Unlike Paul Muldoon's wandering thoughts and fugitive inks in his oblique parody of this poem in 'Something Else' (*MB* 33), in which associative logic takes the poet through a myriad of meditations from an initial contemplation of a lobster to an ongoing chain of anecdote and allusion, Heaney's focus is never allowed to stray too far from the enigmatic lobster:

> And I still cannot clear my head
> of lives in their element
> on the cobbled floor of that tank
> and the hampered one, out of water,
> fortified and bewildered.[84]

Heaney presents his dilemma in familiar terms as the poem repeats a scene from 'Oysters'[85] in which the speaker's meal was a 'similarly conscience-laden, question-filled debate on politics and aesthetics'.[86] This time, however, it is unclear whether the sea-creature represents art, the artist, or (to use Muldoon's phrase) 'something else again'. Although the lobster could well stand for the material reality which cannot survive when transformed through art (Milosz's sense of 'dematerialisation'), 'out of water' it may also stand for the marginalised artist who seeks transcendence from the tribe. The poet's overriding desire for a resolution of the conflict between competing allegiances to poetry and politics remains unfulfilled.[87] Just like Baudelaire's albatross – 'Brought down to earth, his gawky, gorgeous wings impede his walking'[88] – the crustacean's newly unhampered condition is fraught with danger as he is left agonisingly vulnerable (and soon to be off the menu).

In an oeuvre widely noted for its 'writerly self-involvements',[89] exemplary authors have not always been resorted to with casual facility or self-effacing adroitness. One example is the third section of 'The Derry Glosses',

THE INTERSECTION OF ART AND POLITICS

first published in 1989. Here the poet borrows from Frances A. Yates's *The Art of Memory*[90] to describe the neglected art of mnemotechnics which (following Cicero) prioritises sight as the key sense for creating order in memory:

The imaginary architecture of the art of memory
has preserved the memory of a real, but long
vanished, building. (xiii)
... of human figures *wearing crowns or purple cloaks*,
bloodstained or smeared with paint, of human figures
dramatically engaged in some activity – doing
something. (10)
Remarkably beautiful or hideous, dressed in crowns
and purple garments, deformed or disfigured with
blood or mud, smeared with red paint ... (66)
[T]he story introduces a brief description of the
mnemonic of places and images (*loci and imagines*)
which was used by Roman rhetors. (2)
Aristotle's use of this metaphor for images from
sense impressions, which are *like the imprint of a seal on wax* ... (35)

Memory as a building or a city,
Well lighted, well laid out, appointed with
Tableaux vivants and costumed effigies:

Statues in purple cloaks, or painted red,
Ones wearing crowns, ones smeared with mud or blood.
Ancient memory primers approved such

Loci et imagines, images
Impressed on sites, like seals impressed on wax,
So that mind's eye retained the heightened meaning.[91]

Associating parts of a speech with a room in a building, mnemonics aided orators to remember their arguments in the correct order. Of particular interest to Heaney is 'the heightened meaning' which sight grants the speaker. This recalls the innovatory approach of Giulio Camillo who turned medieval memory's religious intensity in an altogether new direction: the art of memory became 'the imaginative means through which the divine microcosm can reflect the divine macrocosm, can grasp its meaning from above, from that divine grade to which his *mens* belongs'.[92] Heaney's first three stanzas appear consistent with his approach in both *Seeing Things* and *The Spirit Level* regarding ideal forms; indeed the former contains a revised version of this poem.[93] The revision is important:

So that the mind's eye could haunt itself

With fixed associations and learn to read
Its own contents in meaningful order,
Ancient textbooks recommended that

Familiar places be linked deliberately
With a code of images. You knew the portent
In each setting, you blinked and concentrated.

The conclusion is comforting – 'fixed associations', 'meaningful order', 'familiar places' – with the poet both assured in his art and eagerly expectant ('portent'). The earlier version, however, plays on the idea of "haunting", portraying an unsettled 'student of mnemonics':

> And who is this in our haunted townscape staring
> But the student of mnemonics and fresh murders,
> Incredulous, abstracted, totting, sealing?

The tercet refers to a passage in *The Art of Memory* where Yates asks: 'Who is that man moving slowly in a lonely building, stopping at intervals with an intent face? He is a rhetoric student forming a set of memory *loci*.'[94] Unlike this student, Heaney's wandering figure fails to order his thoughts. Associative logic, structured rhetoric and remembered quotations – all are of little use in the face of 'fresh murders'. As in 'The Grauballe Man',[95] the poet distrusts the memory's aestheticisation of conflict. The poet's 'stare' is 'incredulous' and not awaiting any 'portent'.

Heaney's lack of success at finding an adequate distance from which to view the Troubles leads to an increasing dissatisfaction with literary allusion. We can guage this frustration by tracing his recurrent use of a symbol for violence: the stone. In 'Exposure', he bitterly regrets the ease with which he has co-opted the biblical story of David and Goliath for his own purpose: having wasted his energies setting up the writer as a hero 'On some muddy compound, / His gift like a slingstone / Whirled for the desperate', the poet has missed 'The once-in-a-lifetime portent, / The comet's pulsing rose'.[96] In 'Sandstone Keepsake',[97] the stone becomes 'a stone from Phlegethon', but the Dantean allusion is constantly undermined by the poet's stated equivocation over its precise applicability. Because it is asked as a question – 'A stone from Phlegethon, / bloodied on the bed of hell's hot river?' – the force of Heaney's analogy between Lough Foyle and Phlegethon, a river in Dante's *Inferno* (Canto xii), remains uncertain. Heaney continues with another allusive simile: 'Evening frost and the salt water / made my hand smoke, as if I'd plucked the heart / that damned Guy de Montfort to the boiling flood'. The reference is to Guy de Montfort, the emissary to Charles d'Anjou who was condemned to hell for avenging his father's murder by killing King Edward I's cousin, Prince Henry. Although he undermines the comparison between de Montfort's heart and the 'chalky russet / solidified gourd' with a hasty interjection – 'but not really' – his subsequent qualification – 'though I remembered / his victim's heart in its casket, long venerated' – leaves the reader in doubt as to the allusion's status and political valency. 'Long venerated' is particularly ambiguous since the poet too is 'one of the venerators' at the poem's conclusion.

Anyhow, there I was with the wet red stone
in my hand, staring across at the watch-towers
from my free state of image and allusion,
swooped on, then dropped by trained binoculars:

a silhouette not worth bothering about,
out for the evening in scarf and waders
and not about to set times wrong or right,
stooping along, one of the venerators.

The recourse to colloquialism – 'but not really', 'Anyhow' – and his 'folksy, offhand manner'[98] both diminish the status of his reference to Dante. What Heaney questions is the danger inherent in his own imaginative recourse to literary tradition. The reference to 'my free state of image and allusion' is important in this respect: on the one hand, the poet assumes the right and ability to inhabit a poetic world free from political implication; on the other hand, the 'free state' alludes implicitly to the Irish Free State, suggesting a nationalist resonance in his poetry. Elmer Andrews neatly summarises the tension as follows:

> The play of words in 'free state' indicates the complexity of his response: he denies the trammelling influence of nationality and at the same time acknowledges the inevitably nationalistic vantage-point from which the 'autonomous imagination' operates. To the British soldiers with their 'trained binoculars' he is merely an innocuous shadow.[99]

The literary associations of his 'sandstone keepsake' prevent easy access to any independent poetic 'state' since they implicate the natural object in both politics and history.[100]

Finally, 'Weighing In'[101] rereads a favourite biblical allusion from John's Gospel where Christ, confronted with a crowd wishing to stone a woman caught in adultery, pauses to write in the sand and tells the crowd, 'He that is without sin among you, let him first cast a stone at her.' Alluding to this passage in *The Government of the Tongue*, Christ's act was taken to be emblematic of the poet's ability to effect change: 'in the rift between what is going to happen and whatever we would wish to happen, poetry holds attention for a space, functions not as distraction but as pure concentration, a focus where our power to concentrate is concentrated back on ourselves'.[102] In the later poetic treatment, however, Heaney becomes impatient with abstraction, wishing irreverently for direct action: 'Still, for Jesus' sake, / Do me a favour, would you, just this once? / Prophesy, give scandal, cast the stone'; tired of sitting weighing his responsible *Tristia*, he is tempted just to weigh in 'without / Any self-exculpation or self-pity'.

Paul Muldoon's response to the inevitable question of finding 'an adequate strophe to the latest reprisal' is also symbolised by a stone: 'Truth? A pebble of quartz'.[103] He is wary of what constitutes 'truth' especially in relation to the Northern Irish Troubles, and in 'The More a Man Has the More a Man Wants' (Q 40–64) he subverts the desire for both closure and revelation by having this 'lunimous stone' grasped by the disembodied hand of an unidentified corpse. Like Heaney, Muldoon approaches the Troubles obliquely using literary allusions – here he is referring to Robert Frost's 'For Once, Then, Something' – yet his poetry displays neither the same degree of suspicion that this strategy is flawed nor the disabling self-consciousness of poetry's uneasy intersection with politics. Ever since he dismissed the demand to 'get down to something true / Something a little nearer home' with the riposte that 'there's no such book, so far as I know, / As *How it Happened Here* ...' (*M* 12–13), he has maintained a consistent position with regard to poetry's ability to effect change in society. He 'disavows the notion of poetry as a moral force, offering respite or retribution' and draws the line 'at the needlessly extravagant claims made for poetry at times when it's felt to be at particular risk, including the idea that poetry may even go beyond helping us live our lives and help us save not only the day but also our souls'.[104] Although this certainly contrasts with Heaney's belief in poetry's powers of redress, it does not preclude political engagement.[105]

Muldoon approaches the Troubles indirectly, using literary and historical allusions to set up oblique analogies. This strategy has attracted much criticism, the most notorious example of which is John Carey's damning appraisal of 'Meeting the British' (*MB* 16):

> [A]nother poem one would gladly trade in for some explanation of what it is about is Muldoon's title-piece, which tells of some British generals who apparently give blankets infected with smallpox to some North American Indians. 'The first recorded case of germ warfare,' says the blurb. But where is it recorded, and what really happened, are the questions you come away from Muldoon's brief, uninformative lines, wanting to ask. His refusal to communicate is itself a political decision – a cliquish nonchalance. The poems stand around smugly, knowing that academic annotators will come running.[106]

The charge levelled at Muldoon is grave: the poem smugly refuses to communicate to all but the initiated. Yet it is untrue that the lines are 'uninformative' and the question Carey finds himself asking – 'where is it recorded, and what really happened?' – is, as we shall see, a measure of the poem's success rather than its failure. Carey's complaint focuses on the oblique allusions used by the poet, whom he censures for the poem's consequent difficulty. Carey is, of course, perfectly correct when he suggests that 'Meeting the British' encourages one to consult extra-poetic material – an encyclopaedia, books on American history, a French–English dictionary – yet he is wrong to view this obliquity in such a negative light. As we have seen in the previous chapter, obliquity for Muldoon is functional rather than whimsical and far removed from the 'cliquish nonchalance' which Carey supposes. For the poem to be fully comprehensible, annotation is certainly required, yet Carey's assumption that only the *academic* can keep up with Muldoon's obliquity betrays his own elitism.[107] In reality, as Vicki Bertram states, 'strictures about accessibility depend on what kind of audience a poet is seeking'[108] and, since the thematics of 'Meeting the British' centre around the process of historical recollection, it is appropriate that the poem encourages the act of searching through historical accounts.

The deliberate mixture of historical and fictional material in 'Meeting the British' makes the poem a prime example of what Linda Hutcheon calls 'historiographic metafiction', whereby a 'theoretical self-awareness of history and fiction as human constructs (historio*graphic meta*fiction) is made the grounds for [a] rethinking and reworking of the forms of the past'.[109] Fact and fiction become confused in a tangle of intertexts, and the poet entices us to distinguish between the two. 'Meeting the British' cites the name and rank of two historical figures: General Jeffrey Amherst and Colonel Henry Bouquet. The former commanded the British forces against the Pontiac uprising in 1763–64, while the latter was a Swiss officer in British service who arrived in America in 1756. Having recruited German-speaking soldiers for a new Royal American regiment for the British army, he rose swiftly to the rank of colonel and finally became brigadier general. These two men have not been chosen arbitrarily by Muldoon since the poem refers explicitly to a strategy adopted by the British colonisers which has remained undocumented in many textbooks of American history: the ethnic cleansing of Native Americans by germ warfare. Although Muldoon is certainly using poetic licence by having Amherst and Bouquet as witnesses to the ceremonial presentation of the 'six fishhooks / and two blankets embroidered with smallpox', the accusation of murderous intent is not misdirected. The papers of Henry Bouquet[110] include letters from General Amherst inquiring into the viability of 'inoculating' the Indians with smallpox: 'Could it not be contrived to send the *small pox* among those disaffected tribes of Indians? We must, on this occasion, use every stratagem in our power to reduce them.'[111] Similarly, Amherst's biographer, Lawrence Shaw Mayo, records a letter sent by Henry Bouquet reporting 'I will try to inoculate the — with some blankets that may fall in their hands and take care not to get the disease myself'.[112] Mayo comments that 'whether the blanket treatment was practised or not must remain a question, but the credulous may draw their own conclusions from the fact that a few months later smallpox broke out with unusual severity among the Indians of Ohio Valley'.[113] The details surrounding the actual exchange of letters between Bouquet and Amherst are themselves shrouded in controversy[114] and highlight the need to determine the historiograpical methodology and possible agendas of those who interpret a nation's history. Muldoon, while replaying a scene of colonial exploitation, calls his own representation of events into question by foregrounding the ambivalence of the poem's factual–fictional status, thereby avoiding any propagandistic overtones. Talking about the risks which the poem is taking, Muldoon states:

> It could be construed as coming close to, if not exactly going over the edge into a form of propaganda, and even giving succour to a certain anti-British sentiment. Yet it doesn't quite do that because I don't think life's as simple as the insistence on anti-British sentiment from the Northern Irish perspective.[115]

The poet foregrounds the conflation of historical accuracy and fictional truth in the opening lines of the poem: 'We met the British in the dead of winter, / The sky was lavender / and the snow lavender-blue'. The tone is ambivalent, reminiscent both of an account given by an actual witness and of a story-teller setting the scene for atmospheric effect. Similarly, while the concluding nine lines appear factual, the repetition of the lavender motif strikes a poetic note, clearly inappropriate for a straightforward rendition of the facts. The effect is far from gratuitous, however, for 'lavender' connotes more than aristocratic grandeur or sophistication acting as an index of colonial superiority. Ironically, the intent of the British officers lies hidden within the word itself, as the slang term *to lay up in lavender* means 'to put out of the way of doing harm'. The lavender was used as a masking agent, giving the smallpox germs a pleasant *bouquet*. This reading is further compounded by the poem's mention of a handkerchief for, on 24 June 1763, William Trent recorded in his journal that two Delaware Indians visited Fort Pitt and that '"out of regard to them, we gave them two Blankets and a Handkerchief out of the Small Pox Hospital. I hope it will have a desired effect.'"[116] Captain Simeon Ecuyer subsequently listed the cost of the smallpox-laden items as a military expense.[117]

It is strange that Carey should deride Muldoon's work for being 'packed to the gunwales with higher education' while praising Heaney's *The Haw Lantern* for its transparency[118] as Muldoon's inclusion of names has the benefit of guiding the reader whereas the older poet's unspecific allusions often leave his poems forbiddingly enigmatic. The final couplet of 'Terminus'[119] is especially vague: 'I was the last earl on horseback in midstream / Still parleying, in earshot of his peers'.[120] What earl is he talking about, and who were his peers? Where and when did all this take place? In fact, like Muldoon's poem, the lines describe a particular meeting with the British, namely the encounter between Hugh O'Neill, Earl of Tyrone, and the Earl of Essex. Yet this interpretation relies solely on Heaney's own explanation years after the poem's publication:

> The event occurred one day early in September 1599, after O'Neill's forces had drawn the English army up to his own territory, in the wooded countryside of Louth and Armagh. The leader of the English expedition was Queen Elizabeth's favorite courtier, the Earl of Essex, and the Queen had been ordering him into action for months before he had taken this initiative. But O'Neill was a master negotiator and a great one for putting off the moment of confrontation, so he contrived to get Essex to come for a parley with him, on the banks of the River Glyde in what is now County Louth. O'Neill was on horseback, out in midstream, with the water up to his horse's belly and his Irish-speaking soldiers behind him, speaking English to Essex, who was standing facing him on the other bank ... So for each of them, this meeting by the river was a mysterious turn, a hiatus, a frozen frame in the violent action, a moment when those on either bank could see what was happening but could not hear what was being said.[121]

Unlike Muldoon's poem, Heaney's sells the reader short by keeping the reference deliberately vague; by shielding his audience from the political subject matter, one could argue that Heaney fails to convey the poem's main theme, that 'the inheritance of a divided world is a disabling one, that it traps its inhabitants and corners them in determined positions, saps their will to act freely and creatively'.[122]

Muldoon's controlled use of literary and historical allusions reaches its peak in 'Madoc – A Mystery', enabling him to construct a subtle critique of colonialism. '[Bentham]' (*MM* 135), for example, provides a devastating attack on Thomas Jefferson's hypocrisy, yet it does so indirectly:

> October, 1804. A secret letter from Merry to Burr
> encloses these lines by Tom 'Little' Moore;

§

The patriot, fresh from Freedom's councils come,
now pleased retires to lash his slaves at home;
or woo, perhaps, some black Aspasia's charms,
and dream of freedom in his bondsmaid's arms.

The italics and citation tell the reader that four lines by the Irish poet Thomas Moore have been included in a letter sent by Anthony Merry, the En-
voy Extraordinary and Minister Plenipotentiary of His Britannic Majesty,
to Aaron Burr. Since Merry has been linked to the kidnapping of Fricker
(*MM* 58), the letter may provide an answer to her disappearance. Muldoon
provides certain clues as to the letter's authenticity: the date suggests historical accuracy; Burr, Merry and Moore are all historical, rather than fictive people; Merry and Moore are documented as having met,[123] and, in the
given context, it seems feasible that a secret letter could have been exchanged
between them in October 1804, especially in light of Thomas Jefferson's
poor behaviour which resulted in infuriating Merry and his wife.[124] However, to add to the mystery, a second version of Moore's poem appears in
'[Santayana]' (*MM* 196):

> The weary statesman for repose hath fled
> from halls of council to his negro's shed
> where blest he woos some black Aspasia's grace
> and dreams of freedom in his slave's embrace.

By providing two versions of the one poem, Muldoon enables the reader to
expose the narrative misdirection as regards the 'secret letter': the extract
from '[Santayana]' is the original, appearing in the 1806 edition of Moore's
text;[125] the revised version quoted in '[Bentham]' is first included in the
1840 edition of *Poetical Works*.[126] Clearly a letter dated 'October 1804' could
not have contained these lines.

The humour of such misdirection could well be described as whimsical
and confirm the critics' view that 'Madoc – A Mystery' is 'smirking at its
own cleverness'.[127] Yet this would be seriously to misconstrue the more serious purpose behind Muldoon's use of quotation. It is evident that Muldoon,
like Toni Morrison, believes that '[l]iving in a nation of people who *decided*
that their world would combine agendas for individual freedom *and* mecha-
nisms for devastating racial oppression presents a singular landscape for a
writer'.[128] A footnote to Moore's text which is retained in the later edition
links freedom to slavery by explaining the importance of 'Black Aspasia':
'The "black Aspasia" of the present ********* of the United States, inter

Avernales Haud ignotissimas nymphas, has given rise to much pleasantry among the anti-Democrat wits in America.'[129] The footnote alludes to certain Federalist texts which spread rumours about an alleged liaison between Thomas Jefferson and Sally Hemmings ('Black Aspasia'), one of the slaves kept at Monticello.[130] By means of a typographical echo, Muldoon implicitly refers to this footnote in an earlier section entitled '[Calvin]' (*MM* 78), in which a servant named 'Minerva' is working in Jefferson's home:

> Already scared out of her wits
> by the demoniacal
>
> chuckles from the vats,
> the involuntary creak of a mangle,
>
> she happens on a bar of lye-soap
> and the name *********.

Muldoon's reference to 'Black Aspasia' is not the only means by which he points towards Jefferson's hypocrisy of espousing freedom while still keeping slaves at his home, for 'Minerva' also has several curious intertexts. The first is Noah Webster's *Minerva*, in which a controversial letter[131] from Jefferson to Philip Mazzei appeared:

> Jefferson had unfolded to Mazzei a harsh and partisan assessment of American politics. He indicated that in place of the love of liberty and republican government that had carried Americans through the Revolution, 'an Anglican monarchical, and aristocratical party has sprung up, whose avowed object is to draw over us the substance, as they have already done the forms, of the British government'.[132]

These liberal views are made to seem ironic not only by the picture painted in Moore's ballad of Jefferson dreaming 'of freedom in his bondsmaid's arms' (*MM* 135), but also by the implied reference to William Carlos Williams's 'It is a Living Coral'.[133] Linking Minerva with Jefferson, this poem is a 'parodic catalogue of the "official" American art hanging in the Capitol'[134] and demonstrates how the artefacts, sculptures and paintings all portray a militaristic, domineering nation, thereby reflecting the obverse side of American libertarian principles – slavery and the policy of Native American removal – in which Jefferson himself is implicated. Minerva, as a representative of war and freedom, is the Statue of Freedom on top of the Capitol's dome. The detailed history and debate surrounding the design of this statue reflects the ambivalent nature of 'liberty' in America at the turn of the nineteenth century:

> The third and final version of the dome statue of Liberty addresses concerns about Indians and slavery. Freedom, according to the artist, remains the focus of the statue, whether in the official title, *Statue of Freedom*, preferred by the current (1791) Architect of the Capitol, or the more accurate title given by [Thomas] Crawford and used by Jefferson Davis, *Armed Liberty*, which accurately conflates the two ideas manifest in this combined rendering of Minerva and Liberty.[135]

Muldoon's intertextual references are neither arbitrary nor meaningless: they are carefully chosen to provide unforeseen analogies and comparisons. Take, for example, the name imprinted on the bar of lye soap: in '[Calvin]' (*MM* 78), Muldoon implies that he is referring to Jefferson; in '[Adorno]' (*MM* 234), however, the name is revealed as 'Beelzebub'. The ambiguity of this reference, when put into the context of Minerva hearing 'the involuntary creak of a mangle', allows Muldoon to forge a link between Jefferson and the poet Robert Southey. The intertext in question is a letter from Southey to Wynn dated 6 April 1805, which looks at the need to civilise Ireland:

> Dissenters will die away. Destroy the Test Act and you will kill them. They affect to appeal wholly to reason, and bewilder themselves in the miserable snare of materialism. Besides, their creed is not reasonable; it is a vile *mangle* which a Catholic may well laugh at. But Catholicism, having survived the first flood of reformation, will stand, perhaps, to the end of things. It would yield either to a general spread of knowledge (which would require a totally new order of things), or to the unrestrained attacks of infidelity, – which would be casting out devils by *Beelzebub* the Prince of Devils.[136]

From the evidence of this letter and Southey's three essays on the Catholic Question,[137] Tom Paulin is correct when he states that Southey's 'attitude to Ireland evidences a strong sense of racial superiority combined with a paternalist concern which sometimes reveals fundamental feelings of guilt – a guilt that can give way to an angry desire to completely reshape Ireland'.[138] This attitude has much in common with Jefferson's view of the Native Americans.[139] Intertextuality, therefore, allows Muldoon to juxtapose Southey's attempt to colonise America through pantisocracy with Jefferson's policy of expansionism, thereby suggesting that, in both Ireland and America, 'savagism' defined the relationship between coloniser and colonised and shaped both their identities.[140]

    In contrast to the perceived political tendencies of poetry by Seamus Heaney, Paul Muldoon and other (male) Northern Irish poets, received wisdom in the 1980s had it that the poetry of Medbh McGuckian did not address or reflect the 'Troubles'. Neil Corcoran, for example, stated matter-of-factly that her work had 'little in common with that of the Northern

Irish poets who began publishing before her. It does not address itself, even obliquely, to the social and political circumstances of the North; it does not speak about "the Troubles"'.[141] To a large extent, this typified the attitude of those early reviewers who were unable to locate the poems within a Northern Irish context; Rodney Pybus went so far as to say that 'there is little sign in the Ulsterman pamphlets except their provenance and the name of Medbh McGuckian that they have not come from Dorset or Durham'.[142] Symptomatic of this failure to discern a political angle in her poetry was her exclusion from Frank Ormsby's acclaimed anthology which set out to present poetry which (quoting Seamus Deane) attempts "'to come to grips with destructive energies, they attempt to demonstrate a way of turning them towards creativity. Their sponsorship is not simply for the sake of art; it is for the energies embodied in art which have been diminished or destroyed elsewhere."'[143] Quite simply, McGuckian's poetry did not fit in. When an underlying Northern Irish context was perceived, its importance was diminished in two distinct ways: first, critics such as Hugh Haughton, oblivious to the poetry's socio-political subtexts, emphasised McGuckian's domestic location, stating that the 'territory, for all her Ulster provenance, is enclosed space';[144] secondly, commentators like Ann Beer argued that McGuckian's overriding interest was in the psyche and therefore maintained that 'geographical locations are irrelevant, although a sense of territory and personal space is central'.[145]

Such reasoning infers a sharp divide between the 'personal' and the 'political'. Michael Kenneally's preface to *Map-Maker's Colours* best exemplifies this dialectic: arguing that her poetry 'has always tended to eschew direct concern with the larger, public world', he limits its scope to '[l]ove, sensuality, domesticity, children, the environment of house and garden'.[146] There is little indication here that her indirectness could feasibly constitute a strategy to comment upon the contentious issues of historical representation, political prisoners and paramilitary violence; the phrase 'focusing instead on' implies that these issues lie outside her professional interest. The justification for such views lies in the unspoken belief that poetic discourse is private and at a remove from the public realm.[147] Although Clair Wills's comprehensive critique of the politics of poetic form in *Improprieties* represents a timely rebuff to the simplifications of this quasi-solipsistic aesthetic stance, her corrective account of McGuckian's poetry acquires the simplifying aspects of an all-encompassing theoretical dictat. Her contention that

McGuckian's obscurity 'problematizes the communicative function of poetic language, and thereby questions the grounds for reaching consensus,
and the boundaries of the public sphere itself'[148] effectively short-circuits
any attempt to demonstrate just how directly political much of her poetry
is. Similarly, Wills's theoretical considerations cloud the practical reasons
behind McGuckian's need, as a Catholic poet living in a divided community, for obscurity.

> 'Doing the double' in lyric poetry, as in living, is a coded way, not uncommon to women, of
> peeking through lace curtains and imbedding vestiges of hope and healing into the raw
> nerves that constitute a fire sale of eggrolls, for instance, or the raw nerves that encounter the
> roadblocks of 'Peace Lines' in an ordinary walk to buy a quart of milk …[149]

These comments by Nuala Archer preface a collection of poems which she
produced jointly with McGuckian and published under the auspices of the
Chestnut Hill Press. Her analysis is noteworthy for its acknowledgement of
the socio-political themes which lie dormant within McGuckian's domestic
introspection. That such recognition has not generally been forthcoming
from critics is understandable in light of McGuckian's repeated denials that
she addresses politics in her poetry and the way in which the political referent is often encoded using personal symbols.

> I have inherited grievances, but while these *are* consciously eliminated they subconsciously
> obtrude. No one here can be an observer. Everyone has lost someone or been scarred over
> twenty years. More than half of my life – all my adult life – has taken place in this war. It's
> impossible not to see the poetry as a flower or defence mechanism, so the relationship is a
> complex one. I'm not, however, a political animal … Poetry is not a servant of politics. The
> 'Troubles' affect my life and enter my poetry that way, but I avoid them as a subject as I avoid
> taking arms against a sea. The crisis informs my work, naturally, but I can't confront it there;
> it is too complex.[150]

McGuckian's interview with McCracken is ambivalent on the question of
political engagement: although it establishes that her poetry is very often *of*
and *about* the Troubles, her denial that she can 'confront' the political crisis
through verse appears to limit their presence to that of a backdrop. This is
confirmed in a later (radio) interview with Simon Armitage when she is
called upon to explain the political implications of her quotation from Picasso
which acts as an epigraph to *Captain Lavender* ('*I have not painted the war,
but I have no doubt that the war is in these paintings I have done*'):

> It's akin to what Michael [Longley] was saying about not hitching a ride on the headlines. I've
> four books that appeared in the '80s and that was really at the height of the atrocities that

were occurring, but they really just by-passed, escaped very much from everything through words during that time. But things change. When the Arts Council was beginning to allow artists into the prisons, and I was sort of accused by my own side really, of not taking issue, and not supporting them, and of escaping, then I began to feel a bit conscience-stricken as an artist. But I'm not sure if Picasso did improve his art by looking at the war directly.[151]

Prior to the first short-lived IRA ceasefire of the nineties (August 1994–February 1996), McGuckian's reticence can, to a certain extent, be put down to an understandable fear of reprisal. When asked in a personal interview whether or not the encoding of political themes was a conscious element in her poetry, she replied 'Yes. I was, I *am* living in a time when you'd have to be conscious about it. You were very afraid of being targeted on whatever side you came from and as a Catholic poet I couldn't label myself.'[152] Yet even prior to the ceasefire McGuckian had spoken out against her exclusion from Frank Ormsby's anthology, stating categorically to a journalist that her work dealt with the Troubles: '"The clouds are terrorists," she coyly reveals, "they hide the sun … and bring rain"'.[153] Understanding exactly how she encodes such ideas provides the key to unlocking the mysteries of her perplexing narratives.

I have shown in my second chapter that a McGuckian poem is palimpsestuous, a collage of quotations gleaned from biographies, memoirs or critical essays. I now want to argue that she often uses the words of other writers – the biographers or their subjects – to set up analogies for the Troubles, detailing experiences of oppression or societal turmoil. Like Heaney, she looks towards Eastern Europe for precursors. The identity of her favourite exemplar is unveiled in a personal correspondence[154] which states, 'I suppose it is difficult living here not to use codes and … it is just as dangerous for me to be outspoken in my own voice as it was for [Osip] Mandelstam.' In a radio programme scripted by McGuckian, she relates how the two-volume biography of the Russian poet written by his widow, Nadezhda, has captivated her attention:

> All this winter I have been sustained by the contemplation of the life of the Russian poet Mandelstam. Often one book will be so powerful as to keep me going, or inspire me, for a whole season like this, or so long as it takes to read it, if one reads slowly and it rewards slow reading. The intensity of Mandelstam's biography is heightened by its being written by his widow, Nadia. Her devotion and admiration are such as might tend to give us a rose-coloured portrait of him. But she depicts him honestly, with all his possessiveness, with his stubbornness, his single infidelity.[155]

McGuckian's careful reading of the second volume, *Hope Abandoned*,[156] ultimately inspired 'The Invalid's Echo' (*MC* 12–13), the first stanza of which mentions his 'single infidelity'. The quotations (indicated on the right, emphasis added) are taken from three different extracts, two of which tell of Mandelstam's intimate relationship with Olga Vaskel and the consequent jealousy on Nadezhda's part. McGuckian neatly juxtaposes references to the affair's beginning with its conclusion, describing the way in which Mandelstam abruptly broke off all contact with Vaskel:

I took my temperature *I put the thermometer back*
in its holder without shaking it, hoping that M., who
always worried terribly about me, might look and see   It was as if he put a thermometer
what it said. But he never did. (210)   Back in its holder without shaking it,
I meekly put up with his smoking, his despotism (he   Or snatched a cigarette out of my mouth
was always *snatching cigarettes out of my mouth*). (239)   Like a secret breath, the way he put
I snatched the receiver from him and heard Olga weeping   His finger on the rest, and we were disconnected.
at the other end of the line, but *he put his finger on the rest*   (MC 12)
and we were disconnected. (212)

Woven together, the quotations impart the male figure's heartless disregard. Note how the poet modifies the first quotation for tonal consistency whilst maintaining thematic relevance: although in the original context it is Nadezhda who puts 'the thermometer back in its holder without shaking it' to test her husband's waning affection, McGuckian deems it more appropriate to attribute this action to Mandelstam himself, thus compounding his 'despotism'.

Although one cannot deny the thematic importance of marital infidelity in 'The Invalid's Echo', McGuckian has insisted that 'the main thing under it is my father's illness',[157] and this is borne out by the poem's title and some of the uses to which she puts the quotations: 'Invalid's Echo' and 'disconnected' each denotes her father's impending death. Yet when McGuckian states in the fourth stanza that 'He says a prayer for the dying over / Himself and me', the 'He' struggles to remain singular. In McGuckian's poem, this superstitious act is intended to ward off death for two people – the poet's father and Osip Mandelstam: 'As a fully grown man, already inured to the idea of death, he nevertheless 'fights shy of dying' and prepares for it by *saying a prayer for the dying over himself* (256, emphasis added). The utter futility of attempting to stave off death becomes all the more poignant with the concluding stanza's foreboding dream sequence, taken from Nadezhda's despairing final letter to her husband:

It was still cold and *I was freezing in my short jacket* (but nothing like
what you must suffer now: I know how cold you are). (620)
In my last dream I was buying food for you in

a filthy hotel restaurant. (620)
When I woke up, I said to Shura: 'Osia is dead'. I do not
know whether you are still alive, *but from the time of that
dream, I have lost track of you.* (621).
At the beginning of the sixties, in Pskov, I dreamed I heard
a truck come rattling into the courtyard, and then M.'s voice
saying: 'Get up, they've come for you this time … I am no longer here.' (618)

I will be freezing in my short jacket.
In my last dream it was after January;
I was buying food for him when
A truck I have lost track of
Came rattling into the overfulfilled courtyard.
(*MC* 13)

Appropriating Nadezhda's words, McGuckian assumes the role of grieving widow, setting up a somewhat incestuous relationship with her father.[158] However, the final image of a truck 'rattling into the overfulfilled courtyard' seems curiously out of place and does not come from Nadezhda's letter; rather, it refers to Nadezhda's ingrained fear of abduction by the Russian authorities. The emphasis on oppression is not fortuitous as it is part of an important theme running throughout the poem: the heightened sense of vulnerability due to actual or suspected surveillance.

> if I could die
> The same death in the same air
> As him, I would wish my grave
> Untended too, like everybody else's;
> Like the bulb that has not been washed
> Since the revolution, the hole
> In the ceiling that has left
> A little pile of plaster on the floor.
> (*MC* 12–13)

The fifth stanza conflates three deaths by juxtaposing different extracts from *Hope Abandoned*: first, contemplating Mandelstam's death, Nadezhda writes that '*Dying the same death* as M. in my own mind, I found myself forgetting everything else in the world – including all hope for the future' (476, emphasis added); secondly, Nadezhda considers her own demise and declares, '*I would like my grave to be untended too, like everybody else*' (509, emphasis added); and thirdly, discussing Mandelstam's poetic treatment of a pilot's death, Nadezhda writes that 'M. "coexperiences" the death of the airmen, is killed *in the same* way …' (473, emphasis added). This last example is particularly important as McGuckian uses it to foreground her own empathy with both Osip and Nadezhda Mandelstam. Ironically, by inserting the quotations McGuckian is, metaphorically, tending to their graves. The remaining lines are taken from passages stressing the poverty, hardship and spirit of unbending state repression under which Russian writers toiled. The first simile describes Marina Tsvetaeva's residence in one of the side streets off Povarskaya where Osip and Nadezhda visited her in the summer of 1922: 'As M. told me later, it had previously been a dining room, with a light in the ceiling, but *the bulb had not been washed since the Revolution* and let through no proper light at all, only a dim glow' (460, emphasis added). The following lines refer to Akhmatova's lack of privacy in her own apartment due to covert surveillance by the authorities:

> What reason was there to envy Akhmatova, who did not dare utter a word in the privacy of her own room and used to point to *the hole in the ceiling from which a little pile of plaster had fallen on the floor?* Whether or not there was actually a listening device is beside the point; the fact is that her finger pointed at the ceiling and she was afraid to open her mouth.
>
> (250, emphasis added)

That McGuckian parallels her own vulnerability[159] with that of the Russian writers is suggested by the theme's persistence in other poems. In 'Balakhana' (*BB* 39–40), for example, she cites a passage from the first volume of Mandelstam's biography, *Hope Against Hope*, referring to a similar situation: 'In the years of terror, there was not a home in the country where people did not sit trembling at night, their ears straining to catch *the murmur of passing cars or the sound of an elevator*. Even nowadays, whenever I spend the night at the Shklovski's apartment, I tremble as I hear the elevator go past' (349, emphasis added). Similarly, in 'Yeastlight' (*OBB* 55) she quotes from passages referring to the intrusive searches of Mandelstam's apartment and his subsequent arrests:

During the search of our apartment in 1934 the police agents failed to find *the poems I had sewn into cushions or stuck inside saucepans and shoes*. (271) When M. was arrested again in 1938, they simply *turned over all the mattresses* … (9) … they *shook out every book* … (7)	When I found In the very cup of the town those poems sewn Into cushions, or pushed into saucepans or shoes, I took the arm of someone I didn't know Who turned over all my mattresses And shook out every book.

While the radio broadcast's transcript alerts readers to her interest in Mandelstam's biography, it is not immediately obvious from 'The Invalid's Echo'. What is most noticeable when comparing her actual borrowings to the phrases listed in the poem's worksheets[160] are the omissions, the inclusion of which would have made the allusions easier to trace. The poem's title, for example, is a shortened version of a phrase excerpted from the biography: 'When death was already close at hand, while we were staying in Savelovo in 1937,' states Nadezhda, 'he used to take me to *the tearoom called the Invalid's Echo* to drink tea, look at the people, read the newspaper, and chat with the man who ran the place' (239, emphasis added). Similarly,

McGuckian includes in the final draft's seventh stanza a shortened version of a revealing line originally copied from the biography and included in her worksheet: 'Akhmatova once said later, remembering that time and playing the hard-bitten female. *Her affair with Punin was in full swing*' (223, emphasis added). Both references would have given the reader more definite clues as to the obscure intertext. There is a clear sense that McGuckian is both embedding a private narrative into 'The Invalid's Echo' and trying to ensure that its source will not be traced. This procedure helps her to conceal the risky parallel set up between Stalinist Russia and contemporary Northern Ireland. Discussing why she dovetails quotations from Mandelstam's biography in her poetry, McGuckian declares: 'Mandelstam's living and dying under a régime inimical to him, in a police state, is not merely a metaphor. But it can't be said till it is no longer true. I have always believed that the lives of people who lived before us were the rightful soil in which poetry grows, and that to try and get in touch with their souls was the whole point of it.'[161] McGuckian's stated intention here is to allow her esteemed precursor to 'live' again through the use of biographical material. Yet there is also a suggestion in McGuckian's letter of a parallel between her own socio-political situation and that of Mandelstam. She is compelled to use Nadezhda's words as a code since, as she states, 'it can't be said till it is no longer true'.

Although it is evident from McGuckian's fourth collection, *Captain Lavender*, that her work has begun to foreground the Troubles, its treatment as a thematic concern remains oblique. One of the most complex examples is the title poem. 'Captain Lavender' (*CL* 76) is ostensibly a nine-line lyrical meditation upon the interplay of determinism and freewill. The 'fuller moon' and 'interlocking patterns of a flier's sky' recall the shapes of the female egg and male sperm during conception, an act predetermining one's physical make-up. Subsequently, our intellectual and ethical certainties are partly preordained by education as 'We are half-taught / Our real names, from other lives'. Although conceding the importance of genetics and society's dominant ideological formations, the speaker invokes a contrastive mode, a liberatory 'air-minded bird-sense'. The poem, however, does not seek to resolve the tension between them; rather, it works on all levels (thematic, linguistic, formal, structural) to emphasise their interdependence. 'Captain Lavender' consists of multiple 'interlocking patterns': the proliferation of compound nouns uniting discrete words; the phonetic resonance from insistent internal rhymes; the consistent pattern of enjambments linking each line together within separate stanzas; and the interweaving imagery blurring the distinctions between black and white. More importantly, the poem's palimpsestuous structure is itself a perplexing nexus of anecdotal, autobiographical and intertextual narratives, revealing its viewpoint of the Troubles.

> The poem is just a little snippet of a thing but it's based on a woman called Beryl [Markham] who flew the Atlantic backwards [east-west] in the 30s – she was the only woman who had ever flown the Atlantic backwards ... and when my father was dying he had this oxygen mask on in which he looked like a pilot, a First World War pilot going off to fly – so I stuck with those two [images] and I made them into a woman flying the Atlantic backwards, which was daft, she would have died, but she made it – it's also based on a story my prisoner told me when they had these prison marriages, and they get married, not for the sake of getting married – he was best man at this prisoner's wedding where the man ... was about to get out and the woman was put in for ten years. So he was best man – so Captain Lavender is the name of the woman [who flew the Atlantic]'s best man. It's okay if it gathers in my head, but nobody else could possibly understand all that.[162]

Three narratives – Markham's autobiography describing her transatlantic flight, the death of McGuckian's father, and an anecdote from the Maze prison – come together to form a poetic exploration of survival against all the odds, even when the impending death, prefigured in our genetic make-up, finally arrives. Within these contexts, the identity of 'Captain Lavender' becomes easier to recognise: he is Death personified. Yet this identity is complicated by one further hidden reference, namely what lies behind the form of address given to the figure of 'Death':

> It's the opposite of *The Flower Master*: the lavender is the flower part and the Captain is the master, so I put it the other way around. The Flower Master was birth, and the Captain Lavender was death. But I liked the idea of 'A Letter, 1916', and Sergeant Death – Dora Sigerson, sixteen dead men – fifteen are the ones who were executed but the sixteenth one was Death himself, 'Here comes our Captain through the gate' – so it's a reference to those ... rooted in 1916.[163]

Dora Sigerson Shorter's patriotic 'Sixteen Dead Men' commemorates the heroes of the Easter Rising and welcomes Captain Death in the knowledge that 'they shall come again, breath of our breath. / They on our nation's hearth made old fire, burn'.[164] The reference opens up McGuckian's poem to a new interpretation, reconfiguring the original three stories: the nationalistic dimension of the IRA prisoner's narrative is given a more central role, with the marriage of the female poet and the dead father/pilot now constituting a retelling of two core Irish myths, namely the blood sacrifice and the betrothal to the *cailleach* (the father in this instance is feminised). While the text does carry overtones of nationalistic piety congruent with her more open approach to the Troubles in the collection as a whole, it is also a therapeutic means of overcoming the consequences of death.[165]

It is true, as Steven Matthews has argued, that some Northern Irish poets have tended towards structuring myths and ahistorical correlatives when touching upon contemporary sectarian violence.[166] In particular, as Peter McDonald has argued, they have been drawn towards ancient Greek poetry and drama, bringing to bear 'the authority of the ancient texts' on 'contemporary conditions through the medium of personal poetic voice'.[167] To what extent does this 'poetic voice' rely upon the original material? One should beware of applying the terms 'correlative' or 'analogue' to a poet's transmutation of sources since, unqualified, they suggest mere imitation or direct translation, a text whose originality is curtailed. While it may be mildly ironic that Michael Longley should exhort his audience to 'break the mythic cycles and resist, unexamined, ritualistic forms of commemoration'[168] when relying so heavily upon Homer's *The Iliad* in 'Ceasefire',[169] its aesthetic power does not reside in the intertextual relation. It seems reductive to claim, like Matthews, that '[t]he poem's virtues remain contingent upon the history towards which it forms both a response and a salutary model of possibility'.[170] Similarly, the Irish parallels in Heaney's 'Mycenae Lookout'[171] may well 'jut out like bones in the grass',[172] but its success as a poetic sequence is not wholly dependent upon the 'underlife' of the *Oresteia*.[173] When McGuckian endeavours to discuss her own emotional response to the first IRA ceasefire in 'The Disinterment',[174] she too reaches out to a Greek exemplar and, while the embedding of intertextual references provides a useful contextual frame for the poet, lyrical achievement does not inhere *per se* in the poem's palimpsestuous form.

> Deep-quivering Muse, army dissolver,
> you who have driven war away,
> dance with me, anoint
> my warlike eyes with peace.

The poem begins with a powerful asseveration that art is an antidote to war. In a moment of self-implication, the speaker acknowledges her complicity in the *status quo* but, renouncing this 'warlike' disposition, she invokes her muse to '[d]ance with me' as an 'army dissolver'. McGuckian's source is

Carlo Ferdinando Russo's examination of Aristophanian dramaturgy, *Aristophanes: An Author for the Stage*,[175] but the poem is neither a critique of Russo's work, nor an examination of Aristophanes's life or plays. The opening lines are excerpts from different plays translated by Russo (*Clouds, Lysistrata, Peace* and *Acharnians*, respectively), and are not meant to be read in light of them. The rationale behind McGuckian's quotations rests in the tension between war and peace developed throughout 'The Disinterment':

and because one must also show just
how hard it is to recover peace. (142)
'terribly disfigured in the face and filled
with *cupping-glasses*'. (143–44)
However, let us repeat, *in the text of Peace* there is
absolutely nothing to suggest that on-stage there
stands a colossal statue of peace. (142–3)
*the Strong Argument has 'hands', the Weak
Argument a 'cloak'*. (109)
'there, in the refectory, live people who when they
speak of *the sky* persuade you it is *an oven lying all
around us* and that we are the coals'. (112)

How hard it is to recover peace
from the arms-dealer by whom
she has been buried!

In the text of peace
the strong argument has hands,
the weak a cloak, but no names
are heard at all.

Our cupping-glasses are filled,
the sky is an oven lying around us.

With its strong emphasis on 'peace' (repeated five times), it is obvious that the poem borrows extensively (via Russo) from *Peace*, an Aristophanian comedy centring around 'the disinterment of the goddess Peace' (136), and that there is an implicit parallel between the IRA cessation of violence and the treaty established between Athens and Sparta in 421 BC ('the text of peace'). However, the historical analogy remains superficial as McGuckian's attention does not linger over either the contextual similarities or the dissimilarities. Her lines establish an air of trepidation: the speaker is unsure of the task ahead; the arguments are personified, though strangely disembodied; and 'no names are heard at all'. With a nod toward the Greek dramatist ('backstage'), she too places the goddess within a 'cavern', but intensifies the sense of enclosure with the internal half-rhyme of 'oven' and 'prison': 'the belatedly imprisoned / maiden Reconciliation'. The scenario is reminiscent of a Gothic novel, with its incarcerated heroines, recurring womb symbolism and eventual release metaphorically portrayed as a rebirth:

*why are you changing colour? what is
this tear that falls?*' (142)
'*come here', or rather into the sky*. (139)
the choreutai are *cloud-women*
who enter from the 'corridor' like
the *island-women* in fragment 403

Why is your thigh-smoke
changing colour, what is this
lustral tear that falls?
Come here, or rather, come into the sky:

where any movement of Peace's head

of the pseudo-Aristophanic *Islands.* (109)
'only the countrymen are *pulling on*
the ropes and no one else'. (143)

that cloud-woman, island-woman,
will introduce the aerial, invisible
faile clouds pulling on her ropes.

Not only does the poem rescue the statue of 'Peace' from the 'arms dealers', it also features an 'island-woman' that is neither an aisling-figure nor *cailleach*, but one who promotes reconciliation.

Continuing its focus upon the North's political climate and the often frustrating search for an elusive peace settlement, McGuckian's recent poetry has consequently borrowed from the prevailing sociolect. This strategy constitutes a significant change in her work: whereas quotations have previously been used to encrypt political themes into her poetry, secrecy is no longer her main priority and so they serve an altogether different purpose. The last stanza of 'An Invalid in War',[176] for example, features tropes familiar to the political discourse of the province:

a dove involving a whole nation,
however often it is sold, deceived,
can never belong to anyone else.

The 'dove' as a symbol of peace is as widely recognised as both the Unionist fear of 'a sell-out' and the nationalist aspiration for 'a whole nation'. Yet McGuckian subverts the rigid political mindset by deflecting attention away from territory and towards people: if communities cohere, the nation 'can never belong to anyone else'. The poem examines how one can achieve this breakthrough by tracing the speaker's path from deep-rooted hostility to new insight.

The first stanza expresses an attitude of mistrust (if not outright contempt) towards an unnamed male figure:

If I could buy a comb and paper kiss from him,
and gaze at it, I would have paid
too much for it.

On their own, the first one and a half lines promise a wistful love poem with a regular iambic hexameter; however, by the second line's caesura, it becomes evident that the sanguine mood is illusory, the hexameter dislocating into a tetrameter and dimeter. The second stanza heightens the sense of unease: what is 'contented as the incomplete sea', her heart or the 'birthday screaming'? While 'birthday' signals an anniversary or a new beginning, 'incomplete' connotes a lack or dissatisfaction. The confusion carries over into the fourth stanza: the 'deer' is both 'still' and 'restless'; there is a 'continual dawning', yet all around is 'afternoon light'. In fact, McGuckian repeats the birth–death duality of 'The Disinterment', with the imminent 'birth' occurring after a symbolic death:

> yet gently as when the grave opens
> and sends the redeemed soul to paradise,
> the wing strokes of the wild bird
>
> heard overhead by tame birds
> of the same kind who live securely
> prompt these to beat their married wings ...

These stanzas follow on from the speaker's reassertion of her mistrust of the male figure who neither 'awakened nor inflamed / the shut-in-ness of my breast skin'. However, 'redeemed soul' signals attrition and the speaker's suspicion is grudgingly transmuted into an acceptance of the male figure's conversion. In the context of Northern Irish politics, one could view the male figure as a former advocate of violence turning towards peaceful means. In particular, the 'married wings' could represent the coming together in 1994 of the political and paramilitary wings – Sinn Féin and the IRA – in the search for peace.

The poem is, in fact, composed of selected excerpts from Kierkegaard's *Stages on Life's Way*,[177] giving to 'An Invalid in War'[178] the added function of a metacommentary (both on Kierkegaard and on the nature of poetic composition):

> What is recollected is not inconsequential to remembering. What is recollected can be thrown away, but just like Thor's hammer, it returns, and not only that, like a dove it has a longing for the recollection, yes, *like a dove, however often it is sold, that can never belong to anyone else because it always flies home.* But no wonder, for it was recollection itself that hatched out of what was recollected, and this hatching is hidden and secret, solitary, and thus immune to any profane knowledge – in just the same way the bird will not sit on its egg if some stranger has touched it.
>
> (12, emphasis added)

Once the reference is discovered, the nature of the 'dove' changes dramatically: the conventional symbol of peace now heralds a consideration upon the nature of poetic 'recollection'. Distinguishing between the opposed activities of remembering and recollecting, Kierkegaard values the latter over the former, stating that reflection is of more consequence to the writer than memory. This is reminiscent of the Wordsworthian recollection in tranquility. He lays emphasis on the vital import of illusion and, in another passage from which McGuckian borrows, comments that

To go on living an illusion in which there is no *continual dawning*, never day-break, or to reflect oneself out of all illusion is not as difficult as to reflect oneself into an illusion, plus being able to let it work on oneself with the full force of illusion even though one is fully aware. To conjure up the past for oneself is not as difficult as to conjure away the present for the sake of recollection. This is the essential art of recollection and is reflection to the second power.

(12–13, emphasis added)

It is at this point that the intertextual relations in McGuckian's poem become both more exciting and increasingly complex. While the passage from *Stages on Life's Way* focuses upon the fictionalising process necessary to a writer's imaginative recollection, McGuckian's poem does not, on the surface at least, appear to follow this line of thought:

To go on living in an illusion in which there is *a continual dawning*. (13)	There is a continual dawning in the afternoon light, which explains why the deer became so still,
I have, therefore, chosen *the afternoon light*. (16)	but not why she was restless,
… and not only the *one about to give birth* … (19)	as one about to give birth.

Even when one recalls McGuckian's tendency to use 'birth' as a metaphor for poetic creation, the reader is at a loss to make full sense of the juxtaposition with Kierkegaard. It is only when one realises that the enigmatic 'deer' carries with it a further intertextual reference that one begins to make sense of the connection. She is, in fact, referring to Seamus Heaney's use of the deer as a symbol for a particular type of poetry: in poem after poem,[179] the hunt for the deer describes the poet's own visionary quest. McGuckian's text refers specifically to the first of Heaney's Oxford lectures, delivered on 24 October 1994, in which he defines 'redress' as "'*Hunting*. To bring back (the hounds or deer) to the proper course'".[180] Two details confirm this: first, just prior to this definition, Heaney uses the image of birds to signify the intersection between actuality and possibility in a way which is congruent with both McGuckian and Kierkegaard's musings upon the immense importance of 'poetic farsightedness' (Kierkegaard 9–10);[181] and secondly, the bird imagery of 'An Invalid in War' refers to a passage in Kierkegaard's text:

When I was a child, a little pond in a peat excavation was everything to me. The dark tree roots that poked out here and there in the murky darkness were vanished kingdoms and countries, each one a discovery as important to me as antediluvian discoveries to the natural scientist … Then I climbed up into the willow tree that leaned over the excavation, sat far out as possible, and weighed the branch down a little in order to gaze down into the darkness; then the ducks came swimming to foreign lands, climbed the small tongue of land that ran out and along with the rushes formed at a bay, where my raft lay in harbor. *But if a wild duck flew from the woods over the excavation, its cry awakened dim memories in the heads of the sedate ducks and they began to beat their wings, to fly wildly along the surface.* Then a longing awoke in

my breast also, until I once again gazed myself into contentment with my little peat excavation.
(363–64, emphasis added).

This particular passage reminds McGuckian of Heaney's own famous account of how he 'spent time in the throat of an old willow tree at the end of the farmyard'.[182] Both childhood reminiscences centre upon the importance of recollection, the main thesis of the poem.

What is also surprising about 'An Invalid in War' is the multivocality of McGuckian's allusions, enabling her to weave together seamlessly different thematic concerns. For instance, her description of the soul ascending into paradise is a shortened version of a (translated) quotation which Kierkegaard himself has taken from Oehlenschläger's *Aladdin*:

> Gently as when the grave opens and sends
> The redeemed soul to paradise,
> She opens her lovely eyelids
>
> And heavenward turns her gaze … (159)

Taking cognisance of Kierkegaard's commentary upon this text, one notices that McGuckian is criticising the prejudices inherent in his allocation of gender positions: whereas the Danish philosopher praises the Gulnare's gaze for what its says about the depth of her love – 'but just as gently as when the grave opens, the transfigured one extricates herself from the concealment of love into a beauty of soul, and in this transfiguration she belongs to the husband' (159–60) – McGuckian rejects outright the presumption that the female belongs to the male and is not influenced by the male scopic gaze: 'A single nerve in his threadbare eyes / neither awakened nor inflamed / the shut-in-ness of my breast skin'.[183]

The reference to 'wild' and 'tame' birds has, however, a more direct source, namely Søren Kierkegaard's 'The Book of Adler'[184] which discusses the ideal critical distance which an author should maintain from his readership:

> The art in all communication is to come as close as possible to actuality, to contemporaries in the role of readers, and yet at the same time to have the distance of a point of view, the reassuring, infinite distance of ideality from them. Permit me to illustrate this by an example from a later work. In the imaginary psychological construction 'Guilty/Not Guilty?' (in *Stages on Life's Way*), there is depicted a character in tension in the most extreme mortal danger of the spirit to the point of despair, and the whole thing is done as though it could have occurred yesterday. In this respect the production is placed as close as possible to actuality: the person struggling religiously in despair hovers, so to speak, right over the head of contemporaries. If the imaginary construction has made any impression, it might be like that which happens

when wing strokes of the wild bird, in being overheard by the tame birds of the same kind who live securely in the certainty of actuality, prompt these to beat their wings, because those wing strokes simultaneously are unsettling and yet have something that fascinates. But now comes what is reassuring, that the whole thing is an imaginary construction, and that an imaginary constructor stands by.

(xii, emphasis added)

The intersection of art and life which Kierkegaard describes is not simple: the aesthetic product of the writer's mind is an 'imaginary construction' and, while it is not coterminous with 'actuality', it does have an affective function. The intertext allows McGuckian to explore her own responsibility with regard to those who read her poetry. Her poem exemplifies, in one respect, the ideas expressed in Kierkegaard's metacommentary: her text is also an imaginary construction which reassuringly retains its fictionality while referring obliquely to contemporaneous events. Refracting the sentiments of stale political discourse through her poetry, McGuckian hopes to stir the minds of those who 'live securely in the certainty of actuality'.

McGuckian has become far more willing to reveal the political nature of her poetry, owing both to the relaxation of sectarian tensions during the peace process and to her work in the Maze prison. Symptomatic of this recently adopted directness are comments made in an interview with Rand Brandes: 'I have not lost the conviction that poetry must strive after the beautiful, true, and good, but the certainty that it affects politics and ought to has changed my attitude towards it and to myself.'[185] Her palimpsestuous texts may well establish an enabling critical distance for herself, setting up parallels with other writers, ventriloquising her sentiments through the words of others, but does this method constitute a poetics of the latest atrocity? Is her unacknowledged borrowing from texts simply a means of encoding her own political biases? Does the immediacy of her content negate its aesthetic qualities?

A test case is 'The Pyx Sleeper',[186] the poet's response to the death of an IRA operative on 18 February 1996. While on board a double-decker bus travelling down Wellington Street in London, the bomb which Edward O'Brien was carrying detonated prematurely, killing him instantly. The explosion was further confirmation that the first IRA ceasefire of the 1990s had come to an end. Comfortable with her fresh outlook, McGuckian was able to tell the assembled audience at the Yeats Summer School (15 August 1997) that 'The Pyx Sleeper' was dedicated to O'Brien. Instead of expressing either the expected revulsion or outright condemnation, the poem surprisingly offers compassion towards the bomber. McGuckian's comments on the matter are instructive: 'O'Brien comes in and out of this as a young patriot amazingly from the South and not from here, repudiated by his family and almost by his own battalions ... He was endangering everyone around him. I would have bathed him in protection.'[187] The poem seeks to understand his motivation even though his actions were condemned unreservedly by his own family.[188] The opening stanzas confirm her assertion that it is 'a love-poem in the manner of a nationalist poetess':

His teaching aims to be a 'frankly sensuous philosophy'. For 'only *where sensuousness begins* do all doubt and conflict cease'. (xii)
We consume *the air* and are consumed by it; we *enjoy* and are enjoyed. (40)
This *open-air of the heart*, this outspoken secret, this uttered sorrow
of the soul, is God. God is a tear of love, shed in the deepest
concealment over human misery. (122)
the individual is a *sexless*, independently complete, absolute being. (170)
But this distinction between what God is in himself or for himself than
he is for me; *what he is to me is to me all that he is*. For me, there lies
in these predicates under which he exists for me, what he is in himself,
his very nature; *he is for me what he can alone ever be for me*. (15–16)

Now where sensuousness begins
the air enjoys him, his open-air heart,
his open-eyed dream, his sexless sex.

What he is to me is to me
all that he is, he is for me
what he alone can ever be for me.

The poem's 'sensuousness' is conveyed by repetition and the phonetic insistence of sibilants in the first stanza as well as the mirror-like inversions of the second, intimately linking 'he' to 'me'. The speaker's love is not unconditional, nor is it blind: in the fifth stanza she wonders why 'his reflection / already want[s] to wound' her. Knowing that her 'inward broken life' is somehow connected to his, she had not anticipated that her 'soul would be scattered'. The image is crucial as it opposes morality to paramilitary violence: if she condones what, in the seventh stanza, are called his 'miracles of anger', she is in danger of losing her soul. Ironically, 'scattered soul' also denotes the physical consequence of O'Brien's actions. Yet Catholicism – the religious persuasion of both O'Brien and McGuckian – is implicated in republican nationalism: 'I thought first of O'Brien, the carrying of the bomb as precious as a priest with the host. All my/our ambivalence and confusion about the waste of sacrifice.'[189] This explains the proliferation of religious imagery throughout the poem. In the third stanza, for example, the speaker states:

'I, in fact, put in place of *sterile baptismal water*, the
beneficient effects of real water.' Indeed, water is 'the image
of self-consciousness, *the image of the* human *eye ...
the natural mirror of man*.' (xii)

The new and ever newer water,
not the sterile baptismal water,
is the image of his eye, his natural mirror.

That the text borrows from Ludwig Feuerbach's *The Essence of Christianity*[190] (above left, emphasis added) muddies the waters: in the opening three stanzas, is McGuckian intentionally equating O'Brien with God? In one respect the answer is yes: O'Brien becomes a Christlike martyr, sacrificing his life for a higher cause. But the poem is not intended as propaganda and McGuckian's unease with the parallel between Christ (God as man) and IRA volunteer is obvious from her comments. The speaker's rejection of the 'sterile baptismal water' allies her with Feuerbach: both reject orthodox Christian theology in favour of radical subjectivism, a humanism that avoids the 'differencing of God and man' (33). Hence the emphasis on the senses in 'The Pyx Sleeper': for Feuerbach, "'[t]he secret of immediate knowledge is sensuousness" (xii). That the male figure's beliefs do not yet match the speaker's is indicated at the poem's close:

… the world alone obstructs thy soul; it alone is the wall of separation between thee and God, – thy beatified, perfected nature' (109).	… We have a world between us, exactly a world, and the nothing
The nothing, out of which the world came, is nothing without the world. (33)	out of which the world came is nothing without the world.
God as God – as a *purely thinkable* being, an object of the intellect – is thus nothing else than the reason in its utmost intensification become objective to itself. (36)	I take hold of the purely thinkable body with my lips closed, unclosed,
Involuntarily prayer wells forth in sound; the struggling heart bursts the barrier of the *closed lips*. (123–4)	as if there were a rune less divine that could make him mine.

In the original context, Feuerbach is arguing that man's rational view of the world inhibits a true communion with God; in McGuckian's poem, the 'world between us' connotes the ideological differences of the two people.

To read 'The Pyx Sleeper' solely in terms of McGuckian's perception of O'Brien's actions would not only considerably diminish her poetic intentions, it would also fail to recognise the skill with which she uses the palimpsestuous form. One can of course read the 'he' as both O'Brien and (possibly) Feuerbach, but the characteristic sexual imagery of the poem's conclusion ('my lips closed, unclosed') suggests that it has a wider application: the relationship between the poet and her muse. McGuckian has often claimed that there is a sexual dimension to writing: 'I must fix the words into a face that I am loving for the poem,' she says, 'if I can't I might as well go and watch the TV.'[191] The love she feels toward O'Brien in 'The Pyx Sleeper' is the starting point for a meditation upon guilt. As in Feuerbach, the 'he' is God and the speaker struggles to articulate a spiritual love ('the purely thinkable body') which retains a physical dimension:

> But really what is deeply mine is the strangeness *I* feel going to communion as an adult with
> adulterous poems in my head. My own sense that I actually live by and for, my art, as it were,
> is not a Catholic pursuit, as in Hopkins or Herbert, but rooted in psycho-sexuality ... The
> main thing I feel is that *I*, the I in the poem, is a *woman* trying to over-come problems in
> relating to a Godhead or a crucified Christ whose body was presented as the only available
> and desirable nakedness![192]

The closing end-line rhyme of divine/mine achieves a rapprochement of
deity, muse and lover, thereby lessening the intimidation felt by the poet as
a result of the Church's overwhelming patriarchy, and alleviating the poet's
anxiety at not being a priest but a shaman.

McGuckian's encryption of a political subtext into her work by means of
unacknowledged quotations clearly differs from the strategies employed by
both Muldoon and Heaney. The fear which drove her to disguise her political convictions prior to the IRA ceasefires is not in evidence in either of the
male poets' work. Whereas Heaney also uses intertextual allusions when
addressing the theme of poetic responsibility, the references are usually acknowledged in the text itself and are self-explanatory. Muldoon's references
are equally signposted for the reader, but their relation to the Troubles are
not as clear, nor does his work convey Heaney's 'self-doubt and self-
revision'.[193] Muldoon's foregrounding of intertextual relations is intrusive
and sparing in detail, and hence places a heavy burden upon the reader.
Although McGuckian's silence regarding her sources shields the general reader
from the frightening variety of texts consulted during composition, this
reticence very often conceals the poetry's Northern Irish context. It is clear
that the younger poets' recourse to literary and historical traditions is more
complex than Heaney's, and one could surmise that this is due in part to the
criticism which his early poetry attracted because of its more direct approach to the Troubles.[194] However, despite the degree of difficulty posed
by the younger poets' use of quotations, the sincerity with which their work
engages with politics makes it apparent that Iain Sinclair is wrong in his
claim that contemporary Irish poetry is '[p]re-programmed and dead in the
mouth'.[195]

Notes

1 Iain Sinclair, 'Introduction: Infamous and Invisible: A Manifesto for Those Who Do Not
   Believe in Such Things', *Conductors of Chaos: A Poetry Anthology* (London: Picador, 1996) xiii.

2 Sinclair, 'Introduction: Infamous and Invisible', xiii.
3 Sinclair, 'Introduction: Infamous and Invisible', xiii.
4 Stephen Smith, 'Between Omagh and Cookstown', *The Fabulous Relatives* (Newcastle upon Tyne: Bloodaxe, 1993) 42.
5 Peter McDonald, 'Flat Sonnet: The Situation', *Adam's Dream* (Newcastle upon Tyne: Bloodaxe, 1996) 11.
6 Sinclair, 'Introduction: Infamous and Invisible', xiii. See John Kerrigan, 'Solidly Sewn', *Irish Review* 20 (Winter–Spring, 1997) 130–36.
7 Seamus Heaney, 'Calling the Tune', interview by Tom Adair, *Linen Hall Review* 6.2 (Autumn, 1989) 5.
8 Sinclair, 'Introduction: Infamous and Invisible', xiv.
9 Neil Corcoran, *After Yeats and Joyce: Reading Modern Irish Literature* (Oxford: Oxford University Press, 1997) 143.
10 Peter Sirr, 'Troubled by Troubles', *Times Literary Supplement* 20 February 1998, 12.
11 Terence Brown, 'The Eagle and the Truth: Poetry in Ulster', *Lines Review* 52 (May, 1975) 95.
12 Andrew Waterman, 'Ulsterectomy: On the Cushioned Blandness of Northern Ireland's Poetry', *Hibernia* 26 April 1979, 16.
13 See George Watson, 'The Narrow Ground: Northern Poets and the Northern Ireland Crisis', in Masaru Sekine (ed.), *Irish Writers and Society at Large* (Gerrards Cross: Colin Smythe, 1985) 208.
14 Jay Parini, *Some Necessary Angels: Essays on Writing and Politics* (New York: Columbia University Press, 1997) 215.
15 Parini, *Some Necessary Angels* 215–16.
16 Derek Mahon, 'Poetry in Northern Ireland', *Twentieth Century Studies* 4 (1970) 93.
17 Edna Longley, *Poetry in the Wars* 1986 (Newcastle upon Tyne, 1996) 185.
18 Edna Longley, 'Putting on an International Style', *Irish Review* 5 (Autumn, 1988) 77.
19 Edna Longley, 'Including the North', *Text and Context* 3 (Autumn, 1988) 21.
20 Edna Longley, *The Living Stream: Literature and Revisionism in Ireland* (Newcastle upon Tyne: Bloodaxe, 1994) 9.
21 See Edna Longley 'Including the North' 20 and 'Undermining Assumptions: The Irish Poem', *Irish Review* 9 (Autumn, 1990) 56.
22 Seamus Deane, 'Society in the Artist', *Studies* 79.315 (Autumn, 1990) 247.
23 See Neil Corcoran, 'Strange Letters: Reading and Writing in Recent Irish Poetry', in Paul Hyland and Neil Sammells (eds), *Irish Writing: Exile and Subversion* (London: Macmillan, 1991) 234 and Tom Paulin, *Minotaur: Poetry and the Nation State* (London: Faber, 1992) 6–12.
24 Brian McAvera, 'Facing the Photographer: The Photowork', *Directions Out: An Investigation into a Selection of Artists Whose Work Has Been Formed by the Post–1969 Situation in Northern Ireland* (Dublin: Douglas Hyde Gallery, 1987) n.p.
25 Lucy Lippard, 'Activating Activist Art', *Circa* 17 (July-August, 1984) 10–17.
26 Mary Stinson Cosgrove, 'Irishness and Art Criticism', *Circa* 52 (July–August, 1990) 14–23.
27 Joan Fowler, 'Locating the Context: Art and Politics in the Eighties', *A New Tradition: Irish Art of the Eighties* (Dublin: Douglas Hyde Gallery, 1990) 117–29.
28 See Richard Kearney, 'Beyond Art and Politics', *Crane Bag* 1.1 (1977) 13–21 and Edna

Longley, 'Poetry and Politics in Northern Ireland', *Poetry in the Wars* 185–210.

29 Cosgrove, 'Irishness and Art Criticism' 16.
30 Fowler, 'Locating the Context' 118.
31 McAvera, *Art, Politics, and Ireland* (Dublin: Open Air, 1990) 36.
32 McAvera 'Facing the Photographer' n.p.
33 Brendan Kennelly, 'Poetry and Violence', in Joris Duytschaerer and Geert Lernout (eds), *History and Violence in Anglo-Irish Literature* (Amsterdam: Rodopi, 1988) 13.
34 Conor Cruise O'Brien, 'Irishness', *Writers and Politics* (New York: Parthenon, 1955) 98–99.
35 Anthony Bradley, 'Introduction', *Contemporary Irish Poetry: An Anthology* (Berkeley: University of California Press, 1980) 12.
36 Sam Hanna Bell's 'To Chap the Lambeg', *Erin's Orange Lily and Summer Loanen and Other Stories* (Belfast: Blackstaff Press, 1996) is one example of a wholly celebratory account of the marching season. He does not consider the impact upon the Catholic minority of 'the tyrannical thunder of the Lambeg drums' (13).
37 See Liam Kelly, *Thinking Long: Contemporary Art in the North of Ireland* (Kinsale: Gandon Editions, 1996) 79.
38 Longley, *Living Stream* 75.
39 McAvera, *Art, Politics and Ireland* 7.
40 McAvera, *Art, Politics and Ireland* 100.
41 John Roberts, quoted in Kelly, *Thinking Long* 53.
42 See McAvera, *Art, Politics and Ireland* 75.
43 In 'Orangeism as an Irish Institution', *Irish Times* 11 July 1995, Fintan O'Toole pinpoints some of the facts surrounding the setting up of the Orange Order which are not foregrounded: 'What they were up to had little to do with the historical reality of William of Orange or with the Battle of the Boyne a century beforehand. They probably did not know that William was asthmatic and may have been gay, or that he was, by the standards of the time, a remarkably tolerant leader. That many of his troops were Catholic and that he was allied to the Pope and Catholic Austria were hardly, to them, the point. They were not historians alive to the subtleties of the past, but plain people forging a weapon for the present' (11). See also Brian Walker, *Dancing to History's Tune: History, Myth and Politics in Ireland* (Belfast: Blackstaff Press, 1996) 91–92 and Alvin Jackson, 'Irish Unionism', in D. George Boyce and Alan O'Day (eds), *Modern Irish History: Revisionism and the Revisionist Controversy* (London: Routledge, 1996) 120.
44 The 'X' is not only a symbol meaning 'incorrect' but is also used to indicate the candidate of one's choice in UK local and parliamentary elections.
45 Brian McAvera, 'The Limitations of Intelligence and Technique', *Magnetic North: Photoworks by Four Northern Ireland Artists* (Derry: Orchard Gallery, 1987) n.p.
46 McAvera, 'Limitations of Intelligence and Technique', n.p.
47 Seamus Heaney, 'The Marching Season', *Irish Times* 10 July 1998, from the internet. It has since been collected in an amended form in *Electric Light* (London: Faber, 2001) 54.
48 The fact that the British parliament introduced the 1835 Party Processions Act to ban Orange Order parades in Portadown for the next 33 years is conveniently forgotten. See Roy Greensdale, 'Derry Marches towards Replay of the Drumcree Fiasco', *Guardian* 24

July 1996, 4.

49 See Feargal Cochrane, *Unionist Politics and the Politics of Unionism since the Anglo-Irish Agreement* (Cork: Cork University Press, 1997) 337–39.

50 A. T. Q. Stewart, *The Narrow Ground: Aspects of Ulster, 1609–1969* (London: Faber, 1977) 16. 'Irish' appears to be used here as an inclusive label.

51 Stewart, *Narrow Ground* 183–84.

52 See Elmer Andrews, *The Poetry of Seamus Heaney* (Cambridge: Icon Books, 1998) 103.

53 See Seamus Heaney, 'The Diviner', *Death of a Naturalist* (London: Faber, 1966) 36 and *Preoccupations: Selected Prose 1968–1978* (London: Faber, 1980) 48.

54 Seamus Heaney quoting Anna Swir in *The Government of the Tongue* 1988 (London: Faber, 1989) 93.

55 See Deane, 'Society in the Artist', *Studies* 79.315 (Autumn, 1990): 249–50.

56 Seamus Heaney, 'On Irish Expressionist Painting', *Irish Review* 3 (Spring, 1986) 36.

57 Seamus Heaney, 'Place and Displacement: Reflections on Some Recent Poetry from Northern Ireland', in Elmer Andrews (ed.), *Contemporary Irish Poetry*, ed. Elmer Andrews (London: Macmillan, 1992) 130.

58 Heaney, *Preoccupations* 57.

59 See Heaney, *Government* 92 and 96, respectively.

60 See Seamus Heaney *The Redress of Poetry: The Oxford Lectures* (London: Faber, 1995) 5 and 6, respectively.

61 Seamus Heaney, 'Making Strange', *Station Island* (London: Faber, 1984) 32–33.

62 Seamus Heaney, 'Station Island', *Station Island* 93.

63 Seamus Heaney, *The Place of Writing* (Atlanta: The Scholars Press, 1989) 46–47. See also Seamus Heaney, 'Correspondences: Emigrants and Inner Exiles', in Richard Kearney (ed.), *Migrations: The Irish at Home and Abroad* (Dublin: Wolfhound Press, 1990) 22; Heaney, *Redress* 11.

64 Neil Corcoran, *English Poetry since 1940* (London: Longman, 1993) 182. See also Carol Moldaw, 'A Poetic Conscience', *Partisan Review* 62.1 (1995) 144–48; James Woods, 'Scruples', *London Review of Books* 20 June 1996, 3, 6.

65 See, for example, Michael O'Loughlin, 'Mandelstam', *Stalingrad: The Street Directory* (Dublin: Raven Press, 1980) 30; Paul Durcan, 'The Return of Solzhenitsyn', *Going Home to Russia* (Belfast: Blackstaff Press, 1987) 76; Tom Paulin, 'Voronezh', *Fivemiletown* (London: Faber, 1987) 25.

66 See Fintan O'Toole, 'The Lie of the Land', in Christine Redmond (ed.), *The Lie of the Land* (Dublin: Gallery of Photography, 1995) n.p.

67 Heaney, *Government* xx.

68 Seamus Heaney, *North* (London: Faber, 1975) 72–73.

69 See Darcy O'Brien, 'Seamus Heaney and Wordsworth: A Correspondent Breeze', in Robert F. Garratt (ed.), *Critical Essays on Seamus Heaney* (New York: G. K. Hall, 1995) 190.

70 See Neil Corcoran, *Seamus Heaney*, first pub. 1986 (London: Faber, 1990) 124–26.

71 See Nadezhda Mandelstam, *Hope Against Hope*, trans. Max Hayward (London: Collins and Harvill Press, 1971) 172.

72 John Kerrigan, 'Ulster Ovids', in Neil Corcoran (ed.), *The Chosen Ground: Essays on the Contemporary Poetry of Northern Ireland* (Dufour: Seren, 1992) 264.

73 See Seamus Heaney 'The Saturday Interview', interview by Caroline Walsh, *Irish Times* 6 December 1975, 5; 'Two Voices,' *London Review of Books* (20 March 1980) 8; 'Current Unstated Assumptions about Poetry', *Critical Inquiry* (Summer, 1981) 645–51; 'Talking about the Arts in Ireland', *Irish Times* 15 June 1984, Weekend 1–2; 'Envies and Identifications: Dante and the Modern Poet', *Irish University Review* 15.1 (Spring, 1985) 5–19; Heaney, *Government* 71–88.

74 Rand Brandes, 'The Scale of Things', *Irish Literary Supplement* (Fall, 1991) 31. See, for example, Seamus Heaney, 'The Flight Path', *The Spirit Level* (London: Faber, 1995) in which Heaney is 'Up and away. The buzz from duty free. Black velvet. Bourbon. Love letters on high. / The spacewalk of Manhattan. The re-entry' (23).

75 John F. Desmond, 'From Ireland to the World: Seamus Heaney's Journies to Imagined Places', in Toshi Furomoto et al. (eds), *International Aspects of Irish Literature* (Gerrards Cross: Colin Smythe, 1996) 369.

76 Heaney, 'An Open Letter', in Field Day (ed.), *Ireland's Field Day* (Notre Dame: University of Notre Dame Press, 1985) 25.

77 Victor Sloan, *Borne Sulinowo* (Derry: Orchard Gallery, 1995).

78 See Jurgen Schneider, 'Beyond Borne Sulinowo' in Sloan, *Borne Sulinowo* n.p.

79 It is also mildly ironic that, as Kerrigan points out, certain 'significant poets who have experienced totalitarian censorship, such as Brodsky and Milosz, tend to scepticism about the impact of art on politics'. See John Kerrigan, 'From Parable Island to Steel City', *Poetry Durham* 17 (1987) 33.

80 Seamus Heaney, 'Squarings xxxvii,' *Seeing Things* (London: Faber, 1991) 97. See John Wilson Foster, *The Achievement of Seamus Heaney* (Dublin: Lilliput Press, 1995) 52–53.

81 Heaney, 'Away from it All', *Station Island* 16–17.

82 Heaney, 'Away from it All', *Station Island* 16.

83 Heaney, in 'Preface', Richard Kearney and Mark Patrick Hederman (eds), *Crane Bag Book of Irish Studies* (Dublin: Blackwater Press, 1982) i.

84 Heaney, 'Away from it All', *Station Island* 17.

85 Heaney, 'Oysters', *Field Work* (London: Faber, 1979) 11.

86 Blake Morrison, 'Encounters with Familiar Ghosts', *Times Literary Supplement* 19 October 1984, 1191.

87 See also Heaney, *Government*: 'He or she begins to feel that a choice between the two, a once-and-for-all option, would simplify things. Deep down, of course, there is the sure awareness that no such simple solution or dissolution is possible, but the waking mind desires constantly some clarified allegiance, without complication or ambivalence' (xi).

88 See Ciaran Carson's version, 'The Albatross', *First Language* (Meath: Gallery Press, 1993) 70.

89 Corcoran, *English Poetry since 1940* 182.

90 Frances A. Yates, *The Art of Memory* (Routledge and Kegan Paul, 1966).

91 Seamus Heaney, 'Five Derry Glosses', *32 Counties: Photographs of Ireland by Donovan Wylie with New Writing by Thirty-Two Irish Writers* (Secker and Warburg, n.d.) 71.

92 Yates, *The Art of Memory* 157–58. That Heaney is referring to Camillo is confirmed by the poem's theatrical images.

93 Seamus Heaney, 'Squarings xix', *Seeing Things* 75.

94 Yates, *The Art of Memory* 24.

95 Heaney, *North* 35–36.

96 Seamus Heaney, 'Exposure', *North* 73.

97 Seamus Heaney, 'Sandstone Keepsake', *Station Island* 20.

98 See James Albert Scruton, 'A Vocable Ground: The Poetry of Seamus Heaney' (Diss., University of Tennessee, 1988) 191 and Corcoran, *Seamus Heaney* 158.

99 Elmer Andrews, *The Poetry of Seamus Heaney: All the Realms of Whisper* (London: Macmillan, 1989) 187.

100 See Barbara Hardy, 'Meeting the Myth: *Station Island*', in Tony Curtis (ed.), *The Art of Seamus Heaney*, ed. Tony Curtis (Dublin: Wolfhound Press, 1994) 161–63.

101 Seamus Heaney, 'Weighing In', *The Spirit Level* 17–19.

102 Heaney, *Government* 108.

103 Paul Muldoon, 'Getting Round: Notes towards an *Ars Poetica*', *Essays in Criticism* 48.2 (April, 1998) 125.

104 Muldoon, 'Getting Round' 126, 127.

105 See Patricia Craig, 'A Peace in View', *Times Literary Supplement* 19 February 1993, 27; Mark Ford, 'Out of the Blue', *London Review of Books* (10 December 1987) 20; Alan Jenkins, 'The Art of Gentleness', *Times Literary Supplement* 14 November 1980, 1287.

106 John Carey, 'The Stain of Words', *Sunday Times* 21 June 1987, 56.

107 Muldoon took his revenge on Carey in 'Triad', *Times Literary Supplement* 19 May 1995, when he wrote: 'Three things that are hairy and scary: / the curs of Gorey, / the curse of Carey, / the course of Gowrie' (13).

108 Vicki Bertram, 'Postfeminist Poetry?: 'One More Word for Balls', in James Acheson and Romana Huk (eds), *Contemporary British Poetry: Essays in Theory and Criticism* (New York: State University of New York Press, 1996) 283–84.

109 Linda Hutcheon, *A Poetics of Postmodernism: History, Theory and Fiction* (New York: Routledge, 1988) 5.

110 Louis M. Waddell (ed.), *The Papers of Henry Bouquet*, Vol. 6 (Harrisburg: The Pennsylvania Historical and Museum Commission, 1994).

111 Postscript to Jeffrey Amherst's letter to Henry Bouquet, 7 July 1763 (Waddell, *Henry Bouquet* 301.) See also the postscript to Amherst's letter to Bouquet on 16 July 1673 (Waddell, *Henry Bouquet* 315.)

112 Lawrence Shaw Mayo, *Jeffrey Amherst: A Biography* (New York: Longmans, Green and Co., 1916) 235.

113 Mayo, *Jeffrey Amherst* 235.

114 See Bernhard Knollenberg, 'General Amherst and Germ Warfare', *Mississippi Valley Historical Review* 41.3 (December, 1954) 489–94.

115 Muldoon, personal interview at the Yeats Summer School, Sligo, 11 August 1996.

116 Albert Volwiler (ed.), 'William Trent's Journal at Fort Pitt, 1763', *Mississippi Valley Historical Review* 11 (December, 1924) 400. See also Knollenberg, *General Amherst and Germ Warfare* 491.

117 See Waddell, *Henry Bouquet* 8.

118 See Carey, 'The Stain of Words' 56.

119 Seamus Heaney, 'Terminus', *The Haw Lantern* 4–5.

120 Heaney, 'Terminus', *The Haw Lantern* 5.

121 Seamus Heaney, 'Something to Write Home About,' *Princeton University Library Chronicle* 59.3 (Spring, 1998) 629.

122 Heaney, 'Something' 631.

123 See Thomas Moore, 'Preface', *The Poetical Works of Thomas Moore*, Vol. 2 (London: Longman et al., 1840) x–xi.

124 See Henry Adams, *History of the United States of America During the First Administration of Thomas Jefferson*, Vol. 2 (London: G. P. Putnam, 1891) 363–90; Dumas Malone, *Jefferson the President: Second Term 1805–1809*, Vol. 5 (Boston: Little Brown and Co., 1974) 379–82; Henry S. Randall, *The Life of Thomas Jefferson*, Vol. 3 (New York: Derby and Jackson, 1858) 116.

125 Thomas Moore, 'Epistle VII: To Thomas Hume, Esq. M.D.', *Epistles, Odes and Other Poems* (London: James Carpenter, 1806) 209–15.

126 Moore, 'To Thomas Hume, Esq. M.D. from the City of Washington', *The Poetical Works*, Vol. 2, 295–302. See also 'Preface' iii–xxvi.

127 Corcoran, *English Poetry Since 1940* 212.

128 Toni Morrison, *Playing in the Dark: Whiteness and the Literary Imagination* (London: Picador, 1990) xv.

129 Moore, *The Poetical Works*, Vol. 2, note 1, 295.

130 See especially Fawn M. Brodie, *Thomas Jefferson: An Intimate History* (New York, 1974) 226–35. See also John Chester Miller, *The Wolf by the Ears: Thomas Jefferson and Slavery* (New York: The Free Press, 1977) 155–76.

131 See Jefferson to Mazzei, 3 August 1796, in P. Ford (ed.), *Works of Jefferson*, Vol. 8 (New York: Federal Press, 1904) 237–40.

132 Noble E. Cunningham, Jr., *In Pursuit of Reason: The Life of Thomas Jefferson* (Baton Rouge: Louisiana State University Press, 1987) 208.

133 See David Frail, *The Early Politics and Poetics of William Carlos Williams* (Ann Arbor, Michigan: UMI Research Press, 1987) 128.

134 Frail, *William Carlos Williams* 128.

135 Vivien Green Fryd, *Art and Empire: The Politics of Ethnicity in the United States Capitol, 1815–1860* (New Haven, CT: Yale University Press, 1992) 193–94.

136 Charles Cuthbert Southey (ed.), *The Life and Correspondence of Robert Southey*, Vol. 2 (London: Longman et al., 1849–50) 333–34, emphasis added.

137 See Robert Southey, Essays XI (1809), XII (1812) and XIV (1828) in *Essays Moral and Political*, Vol. 2 (London: John Murray, 1832) 279–90, 307–28 and 331–443, respectively.

138 Paulin, *Minotaur* 36.

139 See Jefferson's message to Congress, 18 January 1803 and his letter to Lewis 20 June 1803, in Donald Jackson (ed.), *Letters of the Lewis and Clark Expedition with Related Documents 1783–1854*, 2nd edn. (Urbana: University of Illinois Press, 1978) 11 and 63, respectively.

140 For the prevalence of 'savagism' in America, see Francis Paul Prucha, *The Great Father: The United States Government and the American Indians*, Vol. 1 (Lincoln: University of Nebraska Press, 1984) 8.

141 Neil Corcoran, 'Medbh McGuckian', in Vincent B. Sherry, Jr. (ed.), *Dictionary of Literary Biography*, Vol. 40 (London: Bruccoli Clark, 1985) 353.

142 Rodney Pybus, 'Matters of Ireland: Recent Irish Poetry', *Stand* 22.3 (1981) 78.

143 Frank Ormsby (ed.), *A Rage for Order: Poetry of the Northern Ireland Troubles* (Belfast: Blackstaff Press, 1992) xx.

144 Hugh Haughton, 'An Eye on the Everyday', *Times Literary Supplement* 13 August 1982 876.

145 Ann Beer, 'Medbh McGuckian's Poetry: Maternal Thinking and a Politics of Peace', *Canadian Journal of Irish Studies* 18.1 (1992) 194.

146 Michael Kenneally, 'Preface', in Todd Swift and Martin Mooney (eds), *Map-Maker's Colours: New Poets of Northern Ireland* (Quebec: Nu-Age, 1988) 10.

147 See Joseph Bristow, review of *The Flower Master, Outposts* 136 (Spring, 1983) 29–30.

148 Clair Wills, *Improprieties: Politics and Sexuality in Northern Irish Poetry* (Oxford: Oxford University Press, 1993) 49.

149 Nuala Archer in Nwala Archer and Medbh McGuckian, *Two Women, Two Shores* (Baltimore, MD: Chestnut Hills Press, 1989) 7.

150 McGuckian, 'An Attitude of Compassions', interview by Kathleen McCracken, *Irish Literary Supplement* (Fall, 1990) 21.

151 Ciaran Carson, Edna Longley, Michael Longley and Medbh McGuckian, 'Ceasefire', *Stanza* (BBC 4) 19 August 1995. Interview by Simon Armitage.

152 McGuckian, personal interview, The John Hewitt International Summer School, 28 July 1995.

153 Medbh McGuckian in John O'Mahony, 'Troubles in Mind', *Guardian* 7 July 1993: 4.

154 Medbh McGuckian, personal correspondence, 16 January 1997.

155 Medbh McGuckian, 'Thought for the Day', Radio Ulster, 7 January 1987.

156 Nadezhda Mandelstam, *Hope Abandoned*, trans. Max Hayward (London: Collins and Harvill Press, 1974). Further references are included in text.

157 McGuckian, personal interview, Marine Hotel, Ballycastle, 19 August 1996.

158 This is not unusual in a McGuckian poem. Discussing 'Gigot Sleeves' (*MC* 35–36) and 'A Small Piece of Wood' (*MC* 31–32), McGuckian writes that 'All the three poems are basically incestuous, without intent but I see they are. About women's passions for unsuitable male relatives' (Personal correspondence, 20 January 1998).

159 Her acute sense of vulnerability is made clear in a personal correspondence which states that 'the political element has always had to be kept under wraps and you would need to know but never need to say while I am still alive otherwise my death might be sooner rather than later' (22 January 1997).

160 McGuckian Papers, collection 770, box 21, file 30, Emory University.

161 Medbh McGuckian, personal correspondence, 22 January 1997.

162 McGuckian, personal interview, The John Hewitt International Summer School, 28 July 1995. See also Clair Wills, 'Modes of Redress: The Elegy in Recent Irish Poetry', *Princeton University Library Chronicle* 69.3 (Spring, 1998) 618. Wills, however, clearly has not read either Markham's autobiography (*West with the Night*) or Mary S. Lovell's later biography (*Straight on till Morning*) as her account of the transatlantic flight is inaccurate. See also Medbh McGuckian, '"My Words Are Traps": An Interview with Medbh McGuckian, 1995', interview by John Hobbs, *New Hibernia Review* 2.1 (Spring, 1998) 117–19.

163 McGuckian, personal interview, The John Hewitt International Summer School, 28 July 1995.

164 Dora Sigerson Shorter, 'Sixteen Dead Men', *The Tricolour: Poems of the Irish Revolution* (Cork: C. F. N., 1976) 11.

165 The poet describes how meeting the prisoners was as liberating as watching her father prepare himself for death, and 'was like meeting death and finding him beautiful, finding him good' (personal interview, The John Hewitt International Summer School, 28 July 1995).

166 Steven Matthews, *Irish Poetry: Politics, History, Negotiation: The Evolving Debate, 1969 to the Present* (London: Macmillan, 1997) 3.

167 Peter McDonald, 'The Greeks in Ireland: Irish Poets and Greek Tragedy', *Translation and Literature* 4.2 (1995) 183.

168 Michael Longley, 'Memory and Acknowledgement', *Irish Review* 17–18 (Winter, 1995) 158.

169 Michael Longley, 'Ceasefire', *The Ghost Orchid* (London: Jonathan Cape, 1995) 39.

170 Matthews, *Irish Poetry* 3.

171 Seamus Heaney, 'Mycenae Lookout', *The Spirit Level* (London: Faber, 1996) 29–37.

172 Nicholas Jenkins, 'Walking on Air: Travel and Release in Seamus Heaney', *Times Literary Supplement* 5 July 1996, 11.

173 See Heaney, 'The Art of Poetry LXXV', interview by Henri Cole, *Paris Review* 144 (Fall, 1997) 137.

174 An unpublished poem read by the poet at the John Hewitt International Summer School, 28 July 1995. The poet sent me a copy of the poem on 28 April 1998. The poem was subsequently collected in Medbh McGuckian, *Drawing Ballerinas* (53–54).

175 Carlo Ferdinando Russo, *Aristophanes: An Author for the Stage*, trans. Kevin Wren, 1962 (London: Routledge, 1994). Further references are cited in text.

176 Medbh McGuckian, 'An Invalid in War', *Chattakoochee Review* 16.3 (Spring, 1996) 55.

177 Søren Kierkegaard, *Stages on Life's Way: Studies by Various Persons*, ed. and trans. Howard V. Hong and Edna H. Hong (Princeton: Princeton University Press, 1988). Further references are cited in text.

178 The title itself comes from Kierkegaard: 'How easy it is to admire, and yet Victor has maintained that he will never give expression to his admiration, because a defeat is more terrible than becoming an invalid in war!' (28).

179 See, for example, Seamus Heaney, 'A Migration', 'An Aisling in the Burren', 'Station Island' IX, 'On the Road' in *Station Island* 25–27, 47, 84–86 and 119–21, respectively.

180 Heaney, *The Redress of Poetry* 15.

181 See Heaney, *Redress*. ' ... I want to celebrate the surprise of poetry as well as its reliability; I want to celebrate its given, unforeseeable thereness, the way it enters our field of vision and animates our physical and intelligent being in much the same way as those bird-shapes stencilled on the transparent surfaces of glass or windows must suddenly enter the vision and change the direction of the real birds' flight' (15).

182 Heaney, *Preoccupation: Selected Prose 1968–1978* (London: Faber, 1980) 18.

183 This is also an allusion to a passage in Kierkegaard: 'if with *one single nerve in his eyes* the lover looked at her in the wrong way and admired instead of comprehending the proper expression of being in love, that it was to please him – then he has taken a wrong turn, he is on the way to becoming a connoisseur' (159, emphasis added).

184 Excerpts are quoted in Kierkegaard, *Stages on Life's Way*.

185 Medbh McGuckian, 'A Dialogue with Medbh McGuckian, Winter 1996–1997', interview by Rand Brandes, *Studies in the Literary Imagination* 30.2 (Fall, 1997) 46.

186 Medbh McGuckian, unpublished poem included in personal correspondence, 28 February 1996. The poem was subsequently collected in *Had I a Thousand Lives* (76–77).

187 McGuckian, personal correspondence, 13 October 1997.

188 See *Irish Times* 22 February 1996, 1.

189 McGuckian, personal correspondence, 13 October 1997.

190 Ludwig Feuerbach, *The Essence of Christianity*, trans George Eliot (New York: Harper Torchbooks, 1957).

191 Medbh McGuckian, 'Surfacing: An Interview with Medbh McGuckian', interview by Kimberly S. Bohman, *Irish Review* 16 (Autumn–Winter, 1994) 104.

192 McGuckian, personal correspondence, 13 October 1997.

193 Corcoran, *After Yeats and Joyce* 144.

194 See Corcoran, *After Yeats and Joyce* 145.

195 Sinclair, 'Introduction: Infamous and Invisible' xiii.

4

Writing in the Shit:
The Northern Irish Poet and Authority

This chapter examines the degree to which Northern Irish poets can establish an authorial presence in their texts and how authoritative they feel when, 'mired in attachment',[1] they write about politically sensitive issues. Since a quotation establishes a gap between the quoting text and what is quoted, its effect on the poet's authoritative voice is ambiguous: even if a quotation is used as an embellishment, 'a mere appendage to the main discourse', it is also 'paradoxically privileged, as it appears as a stylistic exemplum'.[2] Similarly, if the citation is used as *auctoritas*, then 'the quoted text is privileged over the text and author quoting' and forces him 'to relinquish temporarily his mastery over his own discourse and to subordinate himself to a more authoritative writer who has expressed what he wants to say in a way he cannot even attempt to equal'.[3] Is literary allusion, therefore, used to invoke the authority of literary exemplars, conferring legitimacy upon a poet's ideas? Does quotation devolve responsibility from the poet to another writer, allowing the former to ventriloquise controversial sentiments through the latter and absolve himself from all consequences? Does this subsume the poet's originality? Is quotation used simply for ludic purposes, a whimsical piece of allusive pomposity? Or does its inclusion self-reflexively call into question the validity of the source text, asserting an essential difference, rather than similarity, between the original and new contexts? This chapter seeks to answer these questions by focusing on how the citation of exemplary figures has been central to the representative discourses – historical, sociological, pictorial and poetic – surrounding the so-called 'dirty protest' and resultant Long Kesh hunger strikes. I have chosen these events in particular because concepts of authority – political legitimacy and the use of quotation – were so central to them.

In an Irish context, the hunger strike as a weapon of redress is afforded a modicum of respectability owing to its historical precedents;[4] indeed, the hunger-striker is often cast in the role of heroic victim once situated within a mythic paradigm. In *Postnationalist Ireland*, Richard Kearney describes how the republican hunger-strikers in the H-Block at Long Kesh (the Maze prison) sought to realign 'their plight with a mythico-religious tradition of *renewal-through-sacrifice*': subscribing to a 'mythic logic', the protesters appealed to 'a "sacred" memory of death and renewal which provided an air of legitimacy for present acts of suffering by grafting them onto paradigms of a recurring past. It thus afforded these acts a timeless and redemptive quality.'[5] Such a conclusion was also reached in David Beresford's *Ten Men Dead*. Whether or not starvation has 'a sublime quality' when taken to the death is a moot point, but Beresford's description of the sense of authority with which the protesters are imbued is, within a warped republican logic, valid: the hunger strike, he says, 'in conjunction with terrorism … offers a consummation of murder and self-sacrifice which in a sense can legitimize the violence which precedes and follows it'.[6] Both Kearney's and Beresford's narratives follow in a long line of similar analyses. Tim Pat Coogan's groundbreaking account of the H-Block crisis, for instance, cites the example of Terence McSwiney, the Sinn Féin Lord Mayor of Cork, who died while on hunger strike in Brixton prison. This protest, in its turn, is explained with reference to practices in medieval Ireland when *Cealachan* (the achievement of justice by starvation) had a place in the Brehon civil code (*Seanchus Mor*).[7] All subsequent protests of this nature recall the earlier deaths in what can be described as a cumulative roll-call of the dead: authority is assured by invoking the ghosts of famous martyrs.

Respectability and legitimacy were also sought by means of the religious symbolism surrounding first the blanketmen, and then the hunger-strikers. As Kearney states, '[w]hile wall-drawings showed battered and emaciated prisoners in Christ-like posture', the wire of Long Kesh was 'transformed into crowns of thorns'.[8] Symbolism of this kind decontextualises contemporary experience by placing it firmly within a religious framework of martyrdom. Just how potent this imagery could be is evident in Richard Hamilton's explanatory remarks concerning 'The Citizen',[9] his oil-painting of a republican prisoner during the 'dirty protest'. The inspiration for this painting came from a Granada Television documentary about conditions in the H-Blocks at Long Kesh. Describing how the prisoners were 'endowed with a mythic power most often associated with art', Hamilton tells us that

An oft declared British view of the IRA as thugs and hooligans did not match the materialization of Christian martyrdom so profoundly contained on film. One became acutely aware of the religious conflict that had resulted in the civil inequalities that gave a platform for IRA activity. The symbols of Christ's agony were there, not only the crucifix on the neck of prisoners and the rosary which confirmed the monastic austerity but the self-inflicted suffering which has marked Christianity from the earliest times.[10]

It is difficult to judge whether Hamilton is responding to the transhistorical symbolism or is adopting it uncritically. His focus on the so-called 'mythic power' of the protest seems to de-historicise the H-Block crisis and aestheticise the IRA's politics of violence. Symbolism initiates a Christian parallel, thereby guaranteeing a modicum of respectability for 'the cause'.

While from a nationalist point of view much of the republican protesters' authority clearly resided in this mythico-religious discourse, recent literature on the 1981 hunger strike pays particular attention to the material conditions of the protest and, in the process, twins corporeality with textuality.[11] The republican battleground emerges in the form of the body-as-text. Joseph Ruane and Jennifer Todd state bluntly that '[t]he struggle between prisoners and warders, republicans and British state, was symbolically fought out on the prisoners' emaciated bodies'.[12] Yet it is important to point out, as Allen Feldman does in his in-depth study of the oral history of the H-Block protests, that while the body may have been the site of conflict, its associated symbolism did not merely have an expressive function; rather, symbolisation came to have 'an affective and determining material performance that reflexively transforms self and social structure'.[13] The refusal to wear prison uniforms, the spreading of faecal matter on cell walls and martyrdom by self-starvation were all practical means by which the republican prisoners could distance themselves from British authority. Their nakedness, for example, instigated a 'countertextualisation' of the body whereby the proposed assimilation of political prisoners into the category of Ordinary Decent Criminal was disrupted. Indeed, Feldman's main thesis contends that material circumstances and practice gave rise to the mythico-religious dimension, and not vice-versa:

The Blanket, 'Dirty', and Hunger Strike protests were informed by the need to eventually recast a collective situation of loss, separation, and social death into emblematic performances that could forge a utopian cultural sensibility. The overwhelming theme of the prison protests was a *future reunification* with rediscovered submerged Republican traditions, with a precolonial Gaelic cultural order, and with the Irish people as a historical/ethical/ linguistic agency to be created. This prospective reunification was tied to the accumulation of paradigmatic acts of resistance that would transform their bodies and thus engender the cultural–historical alterity of the Blanketmen.[14]

Maud Ellmann's *The Hunger Artists* also touches upon this theme, arguing that 'the starving body is itself a text, the living dossier of its discontents, for the injustices of power are encoded in the savage hieroglyphics of its sufferings'.[15] Ellmann regards hunger itself as a form of speech which gives immediate and graphic expression, via the emaciated flesh, to ideologies of religion, nation and gender:

> What is more, the hunger strikes stage-managed by the IRA unsettle chronological accounts of history because they represent what Seamus Heaney calls the 'afterlife' of former protests, former macerations. By hungering, the protestors transform their bodies into the 'quotations' of their forebears and reinscribe the cause of Irish nationalism in the spectacle of starving flesh.[16]

Although the IRA did not, in fact, have full control over the H-Block protests as such, Ellmann is justified in referring to the manipulation of imagery and mythic parallels. The reference to Seamus Heaney's conception of 'afterlife' strives to confirm the supposedly Jungian import of these 'quotations': objects, he says, have an afterlife (or ghost life) which become 'a point of entry into a common emotional ground of memory and belonging'.[17] Common to whom exactly is tactfully left unstated.

What differentiates Ellmann's analysis from those of Kearney, Beresford et al. is her theoretical exploration of the almost self-defeating logic which pertains to hunger-striking. In particular, she discusses the tensions involved when those on hunger strike write their life story. Referring to Bobby Sands, she says that

> his autobiographical endeavors reenact the rigors of the hunger strike itself, insofar as both consist of the evacuation of the self. He writes his life in order to create his own memorial but also to disgorge his mind of history, just as he devoids his body of the fat that represents its frozen past ... In the Kesh, writing and starving both contribute to this disremembering, emptying the mind and body of the burden of the past. In this sense, the autobiographer consumes himself alive, because his flesh is deconstructed by the very words that constitute his afterlife.[18]

It must be admitted that the analogies presented here are suspect: writing does not materially or psychologically 'reenact' ritual starvation. Similarly, Ellmann's assumption that the inscription of stories onto paper 'disgorges' the mind of history in a process of 'disremembering' woefully misrepresents the functions of memory and narrative in order to argue for an abstruse 'poetics of starvation'. Brian Keenan's account of his own writing during his enforced four-and-a-half year incarceration in Beirut suggests two alternative functions: on the one hand, words acted as 'a screen', shielding him from the terrors of his unconscious;[19] on the other hand, they allowed him to become dislocated, a 'Mad Sweeny hiding in his tree of words', one whose 'code of poetry' put his memories, thoughts and reflections into a coherent perspective.[20] However, what remains of interest in Ellmann's thesis is the peculiar tension outlined between the need to redress actual prison conditions and the means by which the prisoners go about this: by constituting an 'afterlife' through quotations (corporeal and textual), the prisoner *embodies* past examples of martydom, thereby gaining authority for his cause. However, this act of quotation is also, literally, *self*-defeating since remembrance of this kind demands that the present text/body slowly cease to exist in order to recall previous texts/bodies.

An equally perplexing double-bind arises when, faced with a republican logic laying emphasis upon the collective and the mythic, Northern Irish poets attempt to examine prison issues and, in particular, the 'dirty protest' and the subsequent hunger strikes. Because of the sensitive socio-political questions involved – a thematics of dissent, tribal affiliation, support or understanding towards an illegal paramilitary organisation – as well as the peculiar representative status accorded to a poet from Northern Ireland,[21] the writers often resort to literary allusion in an effort to garner both a modicum of objecivity and authority for their own poems. This strategy of textual citation is potentially self-defeating in a figurative sense, as it raises suspicions of an abdication of responsibility, a reprehensible aestheticism of conflict and the relinquishment of originality. The poet whose work has been most criticised in these respects is Seamus Heaney.

It might at first appear patently absurd to believe that Heaney – the eminent Nobel Laureate and ex-Professor of Poetry at Oxford – should require literary exemplars to validate his poetic practice, as few contemporaries can match his technical prowess or consistently win the same adulatory critical acclaim. As one reviewer of *Seeing Things* put it, '[f]rom this stage onwards there is no possible rivalry: he must pace himself'.[22] In confirmation, Alan Robinson concludes that '[t]here is a magisterial solemnity, a hushed reverence, about some of the poems, as if Heaney were presiding over his own canonisation' and muses over the increasing emergence of 'Heaneyspeak', 'words or phrases which have distinctive connotations within the poet's idiolect and which, to readers familiar with his other work, can act as a verbal shorthand'.[23] Self-quotation and self-reference are the luxuries (if not the vices) of a poet whose stature secures 'unassailable self-sufficiency'.[24] Yet, as Peter McDonald submits, '[t]he issue of authority has always dogged Heaney's critical thinking, just as it has haunted much of his poetry: the authority of poetry itself, and the authority possessed by the writer of poetry …'.[25] This analysis stems from an earlier paper in which McDonald outlines with perspicacious insight Heaney's need to find precursors who would confirm or implicitly endorse his intuitive poetics. As McDonald says, 'he finds himself participating in literary culture at once suspicious and in search of sources of critical authority'.[26]

Peter McDonald's mindfully antagonistic critique of the Nobel Laureate's stance as regards authority has a fundamental and incisive objection: namely, that the poet's absolute authority stems (unjustly) from poetic form. It is true, as others have shown,[27] that Heaney has a tendency to adopt a judicial lexicon when explicating poetry's characteristic functions. Formulations such as 'the right to govern' and 'the jurisdiction of achieved form'[28] recur throughout Heaney's critical prose. It is also a theme to which McDonald has almost obsessively returned. Questioning a poetics which conveniently puts itself 'beyond discussion for all but the initiated',[29] McDonald notes that Heaney conceives of poetic form as being 'achieved not by dint of the moral and ethical exercise of mind but by the self-validating operations of what we call inspiration'.[30] Similarly, in an article on W. B. Yeats, he finds it necessary to reiterate that Heaney 'insist[s] on the legitimate authority of the perfected forms of the poems themselves'[31] and proceeds to imply that he 'values impersonal authority and artistic inevitability'.[32] Yet McDonald conveniently neglects to alert the reader's attention to an alternative, yet simultaneous dimension of 'governing one's tongue': the 'denial of the tongue's autonomy and permission'.[33] The seemingly decontextualising autonomy guaranteed by Heaney's first definition whereby 'poetic art is credited with an authority of its own'[34] has consistently been offset by the ethical imperatives of Heaney's imagination.

It should be noted, however, that Heaney is constantly impelled to invoke an exemplary writer to bolster his own arguments concerning the authority and jurisdiction of poetic discourse, and it is this same belief in the ethical nature of *poiesis* and the 'configuring act of poetics'[35] which guarantees their place in his personal pantheon. As Neil Corcoran has argued,

Heaney's rhetoric of exemplarity involves a 'self-referential intimacy'[36] which 'deliberately compounds a moral and aesthetic judgement: it implies that the poet's life as well as his work (or the quality of the life, with its gestures and alignments, as it can be read out of the work) is in some sense accountable, available to scrutiny, proposed as pattern and imitation'.[37] The rewards of establishing a personal canon are manifold: not only can the poet subjectively reinterpret the significance of a precursor's oeuvre, he can also subsequently derive poetic authority from it. Heaney has stated that 'when poets turn to the great masters of the past, they turn to an image of their own creation, one which is likely to be a reflection of their own imaginative needs, their own artistic inclinations and procedures'.[38] When he refers to or cites from these 'great masters' it is not simply to demonstrate his own wide-ranging erudition; rather, the poet's empathic (mis)reading and subsequent rewriting of a precursor into his own work procures both status and self-assurance. For example, following Anna Akhmatova, Heaney regards poetry 'as an order "true to the impact of external reality and ... sensitive to the inner laws of the poet's being"'.[39] Stressing the quasi-genetic predisposition of the poet toward poetic form, Heaney invokes Rilke when arguing that a poet possesses a sense of 'a temple inside the hearing, of an undeniable acoustic architecture, of a written vaulting, of the firmness and inplaceness and undislodgeableness of poetic form'.[40] Similarly, emphasising the 'pre-destined contours of the voice',[41] Heaney invokes, in turn, Robert Frost, T. S. Eliot, W. B. Yeats and Sylvia Plath.[42] Finally, in *The Government of the Tongue*, he quotes approvingly from the preface to *Lyrical Ballads* and concurs with the Romantic poet that what counts 'is the quality, intensity and breadth of the poet's concerns between the moments of writing, the gravity and purity of the mind's appetites and applications between moments of inspiration'.[43] Almost paraphrasing Wordsworth's famous dictum concerning the spontaneous overflow of powerful feelings recollected in tranquillity – though in language reminiscent of T. S. Eliot – Heaney states that poetry 'remains free, self-governing, self-seeking, but the worth of the booty it brings back from its raid upon the inarticulate will depend upon the emotional capacity, intellectual resource and general civilization which the articulate poet maintains between the raids'.[44] At each juncture, reference and quotation help bolster and reaffirm his commitment to poetry.

The confidence in exemplarity espoused in Heaney's prose contrasts with the unease with which he discusses such authority in his poetry: instead of assured equipoise there is acute tension. Misunderstanding this crucial distinction, Peter McDonald's review of *The Spirit Level* contains an unwarranted censure of 'The Flight Path':[45]

'The Flight Path' includes a vignette of a kind which by now feels familiar, in which Heaney faces (and faces down) the *J'accuse* of paramilitary republicanism. The elements remain much as they were in the poem 'Station Island' (1984): accusation, dissent ('If I do write something, / Whatever it is, I'll be writing for myself'), and a resolving recourse to Dante ('The red eyes were the eyes of Ciaran Nugent / Like something out of Dante's scurfy hell'). Again, the poetry seems to come from the accustomed level of Heaney's responses and imagination, rather than forcing its way to a different altitude.[46]

It is unclear what exactly Heaney stands accused of. Is his use of Dante perceived as a lapse into unconvincing strategic quietism in the face of a republican call to arms? Is it viewed as a lazy and unimaginative dip into dusty tomes for pithy resolution? McDonald's review is harsh with regard to Heaney's 'authoritative' source: rather than being an easy and overly familiar 'resolving recourse to Dante', the multiple ironies behind the recontextualisation of a passage from *The Inferno* underlines Heaney's own self-reflexive awareness of the dangers attached to allusion. The poem refers back to 1979 when Heaney was upbraided by a Sinn Féin official for not writing poetry on behalf of those on the dirty protest. Commenting on this incident, Heaney states that '[t]he prisoners were living in deplorable conditions. Enduring in order to maintain a principle and a dignity. I could understand the whole thing and recognized the force of the argument. And *force* is indeed the word because what I was being asked to do was lend my name to something that was also an IRA propaganda campaign.'[47] Having summarily dismissed the official's demands 'to write / Something for us' with the declaration that 'If I do write something, / Whatever it is, I'll be writing for myself', Heaney does, in fact, turn to the series of nationalist protests inside Long Kesh:

The gaol walls all those months were smeared with shite.
Out of Long Kesh after his dirty protest
The red eyes were of Ciaran Nugent
Like something out of Dante's scurfy hell,
Drilling their way through the rhymes and images
Where I too walked behind the righteous Virgil,
As safe as houses and translating freely:
When he had said all this, his eyes rolled
And his teeth, like a dog's teeth clamping round a bone,
Bit into the skull and again took hold.[48]

On 14 September 1976, Ciaran Nugent was sent to the Maze where he immediately refused to wear prison-issue uniform in protest at the British government's attempt to do away with the status of 'political prisoner', thereby delegitimizing militant republican nationalism. It is not hard to see how Nugent's stance came to be eulogised in nationalist circles, since it marked the beginning of what became known as the Blanket Protest. The editor of *Magill*, for example, took a dim view of the British authorities' reaction to Nugent's protest: 'Nugent was denied all "privileges" (visits, letters, parcels, newspapers, books, etc.). He was kept in solitary confinement, denied exercise and for every day of his protest he lost a day's remission, which in the circumstances meant that his sentence was doubled.'[49] In light of this (not altogether widespread) journalistic interest in Nugent, it is important to consider whether Heaney's invocation of Dante provides a belated justification of or necessary escape from events inside Long Kesh. Juxtaposed with a disavowal of propagandist intent, the authorial intention in the ten-line stanza is ambivalent. By reimagining Long Kesh in terms of Dante's hell, Heaney could well be accused of an unfortunate aestheticisation of conflict and the invocation of past exemplars to authorise Nugent's actions. 'Scurfy' is ambiguous: one reading celebrates the hardship of the prisoners (contracting skin diseases living in cells 'smeared with shite'), while another condemns Nugent as an irredeemable criminal, a 'scurf'. Heaney's description of how the eyes drill 'their way through the rhymes and images' illustrates the INLA man's contempt for Heaney's aesthetic approach and recalls the ventriloquised self-condemnation in 'Station Island':

> The Protestant who shot me through the head
> I accuse directly, but indirectly, you
> who now atone perhaps upon this bed
> for the way you whitewashed ugliness and drew
> the lovely blinds of the *Purgatorio*
> and saccharined my death with morning dew.[50]

Despite their irreconcilably opposed dispositions, however, Heaney shares Nugent's unease: 'As safe as houses' and 'translating freely' ironically betray the poet's self-regarding disquiet at the implicit contrast between Nugent's trials of imprisonment and his own apparently untrammelled freedom. Understanding Heaney's decision to repeat a tercet from his own translation of the Ugolino episode[51] from Dante's *Inferno* is fundamental to any appreciation of how he copes with this dilemma.

The narrative tells of how Ugolino della Gherardesca, Conte di

Donoratico, came to be arrested by Ruggieri degli Ubaldine, Bishop of Pisa, and imprisoned (for treachery) with his four sons in what subsequently became known as the Torre della Fame, the Hunger Tower. Clearly, as Alan Robinson has shown, in Heaney '[t]he literary source becomes an imaginative resource; its continuing presence down the centuries is one way in which history repeats itself in recurrent structures of feeling'.[52] While it may be true that the 'savage sectarian violence that runs through *Field Work* finds a perfect summation' in Heaney's translation,[53] in retrospect it is chillingly prophetic, and its inclusion in 'The Flight Path' re-contextualises it in light of the 1981 hunger strike. However, the italicised quotation is not propagandist. While the 'he' in 'Ugolino' obviously refers to the Count, in 'The Flight Path' the referent is not so specific. The fiendishly 'red eyes' of Nugent hint that it is he who has bitten 'into the skull and again [taken] hold', but whose skull is being referred to – Virgil's, Heaney's, Ruggieri's or someone else's? It should be noted that by only quoting three lines, Heaney refrains from giving voice to Ugolino's distressing narrative, focusing instead upon his vengeful '*fiero pasto*' (bestial meal). Is Heaney, therefore, calling attention to Dante's lesson that 'we create hell by allowing ourselves to be dominated by these impulses'?[54] Does the poet condemn Nugent and the IRA hunger-strikers for their unrelenting blood feuds and their self-consumption? Whatever way we read the lines, it is clear that Heaney does not regard his recourse to Dante as somehow 'resolving'. He has consistently been self-reflexively attuned to the problematics of quotation when tackling the politically sensitive issue of imprisonment in Northern Ireland and, unlike the hunger strikers' use of quotation, does not uncritically seek the authority which quotation brings.

Although Paul Muldoon is equally attentive to the dangers of quotation, he has been 'accused of formalism, an unfeeling playing around with the tragedies of Ulster'.[55] Ethical probity is supposedly sacrificed to aesthetic considerations as he 'seems drawn to violence for its immediate grotesqueness and what he can make of it verbally'.[56] Yet cultural allusions in his work are neither wholly ludic nor unfeeling; rather, they help create ironic juxtapositions which unsettle the distinctions between art and (political) artefact, avoiding, in the process, the twin dangers of propaganda and uncritical acceptance of a precursor's authority. The oblique manner by which he addresses the dirty protest is a case in point. At the end of 'Gathering Mushrooms' (*Q* 7–9) the speaker is transmuted into 'the head of a horse' that 'speaks with the death-wish seductiveness of dirty protester and hunger-striker':[57]

> If sing you must, let your song
> tell of treading your own dung,
> … … … … … … … . .
> lie down with us now and wrap
> yourself in the soiled grey blanket of Irish rain …
>
>   (Q 9)

Muldoon does subsequently refer to the issue in 'The More a Man Has the More a Man Wants' (Q 40–64), but in no way does he 'lie down' with the republican prisoners:

> He shamelessly
> takes in her lean piglet's
> back, the back
> and boyish hams
> of a girl at stool.
> At last. A tiny goat's-pill.
> A stub of crayon
> with which she has squiggled
> a shamrock, yes,
> but a shamrock after the school
> of Pollock, Jackson Pollock.
>
>   (Q 60)

The scene recalls Heaney's voyeurism in the sixth section of 'Station Island' where the girl's 'honey-skinned / Shoulder-blades and the wheatlands of her back'[58] act as a symbol of nature, and also, perhaps, a famous passage in Beckett's *First Love*: '[w]herever nauseated time has dropped a nice fat turd you will find our patriots, sniffing it up on all fours, their faces on fire'.[59] Yet the sexual element latent in Heaney's poem is fully manifest in the later text and the temptation to equate the girl's body with Ireland (the shamrock) is resisted. Unlike Beckett's negative assessment, the emblematic 'goat's-pill' in Muldoon's poem becomes an example of abstract expressionism 'after the school / of Pollock', estranging the reader from his received perceptions of the iconic 'shamrock'. The reader must consider the multiple metamorphoses of the referent due to the excrement's changes in function: human faeces, writing instrument and patriotic icon. The conjuncture of all three is not fortuitous since excrement became both ink and text during the dirty protest. The prisoners were said to have 'cocooned themselves into their excremental signatures'.[60] The excreta, so Allen Feldman claims, 'went up on the cell wall as a historical record of the conditions of their imprisonment. Like the shaman or sacred clown who ingests polluting menstrual blood, urine, or faeces and transforms these substances into power-laden medicine, the Blanketmen recodified their faeces as the basis for an exclusive cultural identity and a renewable cultural power.'[61] Muldoon alludes to Pollock since the prison walls 'look[ed] like [a] Pollock painting seen in New York'.[62] By equating the prisoner's writing with the Pollock's artwork, Muldoon neither depoliticises nor belittles the prisoner's plight;[63] rather, he gives poignancy to her squiggles and suggests that, although they may be described as an 'unreadable writing',[64] each line and space is 'pure energy, in an art close to being pure abstract, not dependent upon analogues of objects known in the physical world'.[65] Though less crude than Heaney's gaol walls 'smeared with shite', this scene is, for Muldoon, 'a graphic image for the degradation of the situation'.[66] The artistic allusion does not, however, necessarily legitimise the prisoner's cause by conferring upon her the status of a Jackson Pollock, nor does it signal the poet's assent to the dirty protest's aims: 'the school of Pollock' is all (a) cod. ('Cod' here means both the fish [pollock] and codology.) This playful ambivalence between the literal and the figurative is typical of Muldoon, and recurs in *Six Honest Serving Men*. Literalising a cliché, he manages to retain its figurative meaning and, in this way, refuses to resolve the two conflicting responses to the dirty protest:

Taggart: The Chief sure as hell did talk through his ass.
McAnespie: Once you plaster your walls with your own doo
                people start to pay attention to you,
                he did know that.

                        (*SHSM* 21)

While Muldoon relies on brief allusions for an enabling and sufficiently oblique perspective on prison issues, others have felt compelled to write almost entirely from within another's work. Shane Cullen's *Fragmens sur les Institutions Républicaines IV* is one such example. His visual arts installation is comprised of 96 hand-painted panels, inscribed upon which is a series of secret communications (comms)[68] written by Republican prisoners in Long Kesh throughout 1981. The question of authority becomes increasingly abstruse when the spectator realises that Cullen has transcribed the texts exactly as they have been written in David Beresford's *Ten Men Dead*, including all editorial insertions and explanatory meta-texts. Does the absence of authorial interjection from Cullen suggest that he supports the prisoners' arguments? Does he agree with Beresford's own views on the hunger strike? Is Cullen merely a copyist, or, indeed, an author like Pierre Menard, the 'author' of *Don Quixote*, creating a text which would 'coincide – word for word and line for line'[69] with the original? In an appreciative review, Peter Suchin admitted that '[a]round this production of multiple units hovers [not only] the ghost of Warhol's mechanically produced, serial works, but also the 'dumb' copying of the jobbing signwriter'.[70] More seriously, Fintan O'Toole questioned the artist's integrity, claiming that '[b]oth as art and politics' the artwork was 'an act of evasion', that it evaded 'the responsibility of art to transform what it touches'.[71] This criticism is too harsh and fails to comprehend the artwork's memorialising function which bears witness to what John Hutchinson calls 'the mediated spectacle of ten deaths'.[72] By presenting the comms as a collective account of the hunger strike, Cullen suggests that the protesters 'were transformed into potent rhetoric, to the point where … individual humanity is subsumed by the impersonal commemoration of word and symbolic meaning'.[73] In his enlightening catalogue essay, Mike Wilson castigates O'Toole for his failure to consider the exhibition in its proper context by outlining the in-built interpretative strategies of Cullen's artwork: 'his choice of Bodoni typeface with its specific associations of Republican Virtue, the deliberate re-ordering of the typography to conform to the format of a newspaper, the uneven trace of manual touch within the constraints of the chosen mechanical standard, the use of paint, the monumental format and the contemporary art-gallery context'.[74] Crucially, Wilson explains how *Fragmens* conflates the monumental form with that of the news media, the 'columns of text and fragile material (styrofoam) suggest[ing] the throwaway of news print and the unreliable biases of editorialising'.[75] In short, the installation's form focuses attention not only on how the prisoners' words were presented by Beresford, but also on the complexities of media reportage and historical memorialisation.

The misguided criticism of Cullen's appropriative strategies indicate how vital it is for a critic to concentrate on the particularities of a genre and not simply equate quotation with passive acceptance of the original author's ideas. This has specific relevance if one is to perceive Medbh McGuckian as a *bricoleuse*, creating poems out of *objets trouvés* (carefully selected quotations), and not as a failed poet. This congruence of words and waste is not unique. Arguing that originality is illusory and that word usage is fundamentally 'recycling, repetition, quotation',[76] *Finnegans Wake* portrays its 'quashed quotatoes' and 'messes of mottage' as a 'stinksome inkenstink'.[77] McGuckian's slant on this is strikingly different. 'Lime Trees in Winter, Retouched' (*VR* 49), her favourite dirty-protest poem,[78] describes 'the next meconium' as 'my intent and most cherished waste'. The speaker claims the baby's first faeces as her own; faecal matter is equated with poetic product in a manner which is mutually complementary and not degrading. McGuckian's 'writing in the shit', referring both to her method of composition and to the protesters' writing on cell walls, celebrates creativity. I wish to argue that when McGuckian writes about prison issues and the resultant themes of political legitimacy and nationality, she is acutely attentive to her *objets trouvés*, but not in a manner which questions her own originality or authoritative voice.

'The Heiress' (*FM* 50) is a perfect example of how, in her early work, she refers obliquely both to her minority position as a Catholic in Northern Ireland and to the dirty protest. For its first audience (the poet), the poem is 'about contraception and consolation for the lack of a daughter ... But also of course about childbirth and all the blockage, sexual and otherwise, it causes.'[79] However, without having access to the author's intentions or directed analysis, one could feel, like Sarah Fulford, that the reader is being introduced to 'an elusive, allusive and illusive inner voice that although addressing a "you" in the poem seems closed off both from the addressee and the audience of the poem who are allowed to eavesdrop into her inner thoughts.'[80] Fulford's contention (*pace* Clair Wills)[81] that the narrative is overtly concerned with power and dispossession is borne out by a conventional analysis of its image structure.

The opening quatrain outlines two directives imparted to the speaker by an imperious 'other', at once delimiting her activities, disposition and literary subject matter:

> You say I should stay out of the low
> fields; though my hands love dark,
> I should creep till they are heart-shaped,
> like Italian rooms no longer hurt by sun.

The 'I' is constrained by an unwelcome imperative to remain within, as if, due to social and moral considerations, the exterior world is destined to remain beyond her purview ('low' and 'dark' are here not simply physical descriptors, but are moral indicators). Ironically, these imposed restrictions would render the speaker 'low': forced to 'creep' until her hands were 'heart-shaped', she would be physically prostrate and symbolically disempowered. More importantly, this description extends beyond her domestic confinement as the double meaning of 'Italian rooms' (domesticity; stanzaic form) implies a forced disposition towards courtly or romantic verse. The sexual inequality is compounded in the following octet's demarcation of gendered subject positions. The experiential locus is once more the domestic realm, with the speaker lacking agency, looking out at, rather than actively working on, the land: 'When I look at the striped marble of the glen, / I see the husbandry of a good spadesman ...' The poet then feminises the territory, replaying the familiar trope of woman-as-land: 'and my pinched grain, / hanging like a window on the smooth spot / of a mountain exactly ...'. Gendered rhetoric here portrays the speaker as the passive site of colonisation.[82]

Intriguingly, a comparison with Antonia Fraser's acclaimed biography of *Mary Queen of Scots*[83] throws up a more specific narrative concerning a power struggle touching on issues of gender and religion, thus confirming Fulford's contention that the poetic voice is 'allusive'. The penultimate stanza refers to three key moments in the life of Mary Stuart, who became Queen of Scotland on 14 December 1542:

The English queen reacted with her famous outcry, the primitive complaint of the childless woman for a more favoured sister: 'Alack, the Queen of Scots *is lighter of a bonny son*, and I am but of barren stock'. (268) ... *through the slashed sleeves* could be seen *inner sleeves of purple* ... (536) The birth of an heiress generally lead to the swallowing up of the country concerned ... (13)

But I am lighter of a son, through my slashed sleeves the inner sleeves of purple keep remembering the moment exactly, remembering the birth of an heiress means the gobbling of land.
(*FM* 50)

The first excerpt refers to the precarious position of the Virgin Queen after Mary had given birth to a son (James) in 1566. With the death on 17 November 1558 of Mary Tudor, Queen of England, the issue of succession was in much doubt. 'Her throne', Fraser explains, 'was inherited by her half-sister Elizabeth, an unmarried woman of twenty-five. Until such time as Elizabeth herself should marry and beget heirs, Mary was thus the next heiress to the English throne, by virtue of her descent from her great-grandfather Henry VII of England.'[84] With Elizabeth still childless, the birth of James 'duly enhanced Mary's merits as a candidate for the English throne'.[85] This state of affairs contrasts with that described in the third extract which emphasises the apprehension in Scotland surrounding Mary's own birth since '[t]he position of a country with a child heiress at its head was widely regarded as disastrous in the sixteenth century'.[86] McGuckian alludes to the macabre resolution of the conflict between the two Queens in the second excerpt as it refers to the clothes Mary wore on the day of her execution.

'The Heiress' is not, however, simply concerned with the divisive battle for the English throne; rather, the power struggle also centres on sectarian strife, and this has particular relevance to the Protestant–Catholic divide in Northern Ireland. From the outset of her biography, Fraser emphasises the religious quarrels raging in Scotland during the sixteenth century: 'The Scottish national Church, although still officially Catholic for the next seventeen years [from 1542], was already torn between those who wished to reform its manifold abuses from within, and those who wished to follow England's example, by breaking away root and branch from the tree of Rome.'[87] The death of the Catholic Queen is seen as a victory for Protestantism and, with its emphasis on inheritance, the penultimate stanza can be viewed as an analogy for the struggle in Northern Ireland between Catholics and Protestants. Although McGuckian discounts this interpretation, saying firmly, 'I do not think in sectarian ways nor can I really. No power is held here really by either group', nevertheless, she does concede that the poem is 'a Jacobite song'.[88] In actual fact, her use of Fraser's text conceals a more specific instance of (Catholic) grievance: the Republican dirty protest.

The tree image, Fraser's symbol for the Roman Catholic Church, is picked up by McGuckian in the concluding stanza with the speaker walking 'along the beach, unruly' dropping 'among my shrubbery of seaweed' her 'black acorn buttons'. In a personal interview in 1995, McGuckian stated that the poem 'is about the dirty protest' and that the 'black acorns' refer to 'shit', but that she 'would never use a word like shit in a poem'.[89] This explanation was reiterated in a more recent correspondence.[90] The reference is to the Republican prisoners' protest, in the late 1970s and early 1980s, against the British government's attempt at 'normalising' the conflict in Northern Ireland, whereby the special category status granted by William Whitelaw in 1972 to prisoners associated with paramilitary groups was revoked, thus delegitimising the armed struggle.[91] The spreading of faeces on the cell walls was, though prompted by the prevailing material restrictions placed upon the prisoners, a powerfully symbolic attempt to regain political agency. Paddy

Maynes, in his psycho-analytical study of the Republican protests, contends that '[f]or the protesting prisoner the *me*, as represented in the faeces
smeared on all surfaces of the cells, redefined the territory, thereby shifting
the boundaries of the omnipotent self and became the primary means by
which concrete ownership of self and of space could be demonstrated.'[92]
McGuckian transforms Fraser's description of the condemned Mary Stuart
walking to her fate – '[h]er satin dress was all in black, embroidered with
black velvet, and set with *black acorn buttons* of jet trimmed with pearl'[93] –
into an emblem of defiance on the part of Republican prisoners. Although
the quotation is transplanted into a new context, it retains the spirit of the
original: Mary Stuart herself declared, prior to her death, 'I am settled in
the ancient Catholic Roman religion, and mind to spend my blood in defence of it'.[94]

In a perceptive reading of the poem's conclusion, Clair Wills argues that
'the sand is associated with fertility; the speaker finds a place where she can
plant the seed of her authority on the beech – which is without order and
authority in itself, "unruly". The implication is that if the writer/woman is
underrated, her poems/children may have citizenship ...'[95] Recalling the
colloquial term for childbirth ('drop'), McGuckian has the speaker give
birth to 'acorn buttons', thus reactivating an age-old metaphor for
(pro)creativity. As Susan Stanford Friedman argues, in contradistinction to
the pen/penis analogy, 'the childbirth metaphor validates women's artistic
effort by unifying their mental and physical labour into (pro)creativity'.[96] Just
as the prisoner's writing in the shit was an assertion of power, 'cocoon[ing]
themselves in their excremental signatures',[97] the poem's speaker walks on the
margins (on the interstice between land and sea) and composes her 'black
acorn buttons', an act of defiance against being restricted to 'Italian rooms'.

'The Aisling Hat' (*CL* 44–49) is not generally regarded as a hunger-
strike poem, but as a moving elegy on the death of her father, celebrating
the intimate familial relationship as well as a strong sense of his sheer physical presence. The poem's first movement consists of 29 stanzas, during which
the father is portrayed heroically. McGuckian transforms the gritty realism
of a farming life on the River Shesk ('horse-sweat'): the man is an ancient
('Paleolithic'), Romantic ('Promethean head') figure with the personal attributes of courtesy ('handshakes'), cunning ('sliding like a knight's move')
and an intimate connection to the land. Detailing almost in list form his
physical attributes – heart, face, head, arms, lips, eyebrows, thorax, skin, hands,

eyes are all mentioned – her first impulse is to transform him into a bird, thereby affirming his ability to transcend human limitations (his face is 'a cognac eagleskin'). Yet she also, gradually, acknowledges his physical decay:

Twin wings unseverable
were those enormous eyes, legs of the heron
reconciled to their uselessness.
                    (CL 46)

Indeed, in a remarkably concise and evocative image, she conflates the fall of Icarus with her father's coffin entering the ground: 'The earth like some great brown / ceiling came rushing at your head'.

The second movement begins with an enigmatic stanza, at once suggestive of past knowledge and future potential:

Until we remembered that to speak
is to be forever on the road,
listening for the foreigner's footstep.
                    (CL 47)

The lines alert the reader to a particular theme running through the poem, one alluded to in its title, namely the promise offered by the aisling figure of the imminent arrival of a foreign power coming to the aid of a colonised Ireland. That this is not incidental is confirmed by the poem's literary quotations. The entire text is a montage of quotations from Osip Mandelstam's[98] prose by which McGuckian encrypts a nationalist narrative. Consider, for example, the fourteenth stanza:

Your eyebrows arched like a composer's,
an accordion of wrinkles repaired
the fluids of your forehead, then drew apart.
                    (CL 45)

It is noteworthy how the poet fuses together images which are contained in different essays but which complement each other perfectly. In 'Goethe's Youth', Mandelstam tells how Johann Gottfried von Herder, an eighteenth-century German philosopher and literary critic, had 'such a plump mouth, with eyebrows that arch like a composer's' (462). Although McGuckian maintains the musical link in the following line, it is culled from a passage in 'A Journey to Armenia', some one hundred pages prior to the portrayal of von Herder: 'I liked to watch the accordion of Infidel wrinkles on your forehead as they came together and drew apart; it is undoubtedly the most inspired part of your physical appearance' (357). Even more surprisingly,

the two references are related: the 'you' is Boris Sergevich Kuzin, the Curator of the Moscow Zoological Museum who, when in Armenia, encour-
aged Mandelstam to re-read von Herder and other German authors.[99] The
allusion is important thematically since the narrator is striving to establish
the father-figure as one whose work is 'the poetry / of collective breathing',
whose 'urine-colour' has 'the sense of the start of a race': von Herder, as the
notes to Mandelstam's text informs the reader, developed the notion of
Volkgeist (national character or spirit of a people).[100]

It would be surprising if McGuckian were naively to replay the gendered
subject-positions of the aisling genre, especially since there have been so
many corrective readings. For example, Heaney's 'Aisling'[101] is 'a decadent
sweet art', signalling the impending doom for the male (Actaeon); Muldoon's
'Aisling' (*Q* 39) describes the dream-woman as an anorexic patient, suggesting that, as Edna Longley says, 'the Nationalist dream may have declined
into a destructive neurosis';[102] and Rita Duffy's 'Spéirbhean'[103] concretises
the woman's traditional passivity, pinioning her with fortifications and watch-
towers. In fact, McGuckian does not deploy the generic form intact: the father-figure takes on the role of the dream-woman, and is consequently
feminised ('You were intoxicated like a woman'). Yet personal and national
elegies do conjoin: unlike Muldoon's 'Aisling', McGuckian's resurrects the
dying hunger-striker and heralds the simultaneous rebirth of the fatherland.

> October – you took away my biography –
> I am grateful to you, you offer me gifts
> for which I have still no need.
>
>   (*CL* 44)

The three lines are taken from a response Mandelstam made to a question-
naire concerning 'The Soviet Writer and October'. The temporality is not
simply autumnal, connotative of an impending death, but deeply political.
'The October Revolution,' writes Mandelstam, 'could not but influence
my work since it took away my "biography", my sense of individual significance. I am grateful to it, however, for once and for all putting an end to my
spiritual security and to a cultural life supported by unearned cultural in-
come … I feel indebted to the Revolution, but I offer it gifts for which it
still has no need' (275). Although the words remain relatively unchanged
and still maintain their political resonance (albeit deflected towards an Irish
theme with regard to the Aisling form), the alteration of pronouns reworks
them for her own purposes. In a personal interview, McGuckian paraphrased

the opening stanza as follows:

> The first bit was literally what he was doing – he died October 7 – he started to die on a Sunday and died on the Wednesday. It was like the Crucifixion – the three days. I was actually talking to the month – the first week of October was taking my life away and 'thank you'. I meant that not ironically, 'I was grateful to you in the most sincere way for taking that away. That now you offer me gifts for which I have no need. You give me a way of looking at death which I don't need yet, but which I will need'.[104]

Though not obvious in the poem's opening lines, the crucifixion motif is confirmed later on when she describes the dead body in Christlike terms. John Kerrigan picks up on this when he says that 'there is hope in the aisling's last phase, as the father's corpse grows to resemble that of a Republican hunger-striker'.[105] Although Kerrigan has clearly forgotten that the dirty protest was called off during the hunger strikes, a glimpse at the original context of these lines demonstrates the perceptiveness of his analysis, as well as showing how McGuckian yet again encodes a political level into her poetry. While stanzas 42 and 44 are overtly a description of McGuckian's father, the words are taken from a passage in Mandelstam's 'Journey to Armenia' detailing the state of King Arshak's body (377):

1. The body of King Arshak is unwashed and his beard is wild.	His body is unwashed, his beard
2. The King's fingernails are broken, and wood lice crawl over his face.	wild, his fingernails broken,
3. His ears have grown deaf from the silence, but they once appreciated Greek music.	his ears deaf from the silence.
He controls my hair and my fingernails. He grows my beard and swallows my saliva, so accustomed is he to the thought that I am here in the fortress of Anyush.	He controls my hair, my fingernails, he swallows my saliva, so accustomed is he to the thought that I am here.
	(*CL* 48)

By altering little of Mandelstam's text, it is clear that she intends a parallel between her father and a dying prisoner (King Arshak, Osip Mandelstam, a dying hunger-striker). However, by omitting specific details ('King Arshak', 'the fortress of Anyush') she avoids making the politically loaded connection to the hunger strike known to the general reader. Indeed, Nadezhda Mandelstam's account in *Hope Abandoned* provides an insight into how sensitive the image proved during her own time: 'Caesar Volpe, for example, not only published "Journey to Armenia" in *Zvedzda*, but even included the passage, after it had been forbidden by the censorship, about King Arshak, imprisoned by the Assyrian in a dungeon without a ray of light and from which there was no escape.'[106] The parallel between her father

and a republican hero may well be spurious, but it has an emotional value
for McGuckian, allowing her to associate her father with acts of heroic
endurance during illness, hence the description of his 'Promethean head'.

The act of quotation is also crucial for McGuckian's elegy in that it allows her (symbolically) to portray a continuum between the past and the
present. The prisoners are in fact imprisoned by the limitations of mortality, against which she affirms a poetics of presencing, a reassertion that poetry is, in a Heideggerian sense, a form of dwelling:[107]

> Broken sign of the unbroken continuum,
> you fused into a single thread,
> time fed you with lightnings and downpours
>
> so you rained hushing sounds ...
>   (*CL* 45–46)

Although the father's death reduces him, in a physical sense, to a 'broken
sign', McGuckian seeks to recuperate his vitality within the *linguistic* sign.
The first line is taken from a passage in Mandelstam's 'Addenda to "Journey
to Armenia"' in which the Russian poet discusses the ideal conditions under which prose could match reality:

> Reality has the character of a continuum.
> Prose which corresponds to reality, no matter how expressly and minutely, no matter
> how efficiently and faithfully, is always a broken series.
> Only that prose is truly beautiful which is incorporated into the continuum as an entire
> system, although there is no power or method to prove it.
> Thus, a prose tale is nothing more than a broken sign of the broken continuum. (394)

Whilst he laments the temporal constraints of a prose tale, he asserts that
'The ideal description would be reduced to one single all-encompassing
phrase in which all objective reality would be expressed' (394–95). This, as
the note to the text informs us, is a repetition of the doctrine outlined in
'Morning for Acmeism'. There, Mandelstam says, 'To exist is the artist's
greatest pride. He desires no other paradise than existence, and when people
speak to him of reality he only smiles bitterly, for he knows the infinitely
more convincing reality of art' (61). Contrary to the limitations of prose,
he states that 'the poet raises a phenomenon to its tenth power, and the
modest exterior of a work of art deceives us with regard to the monstrously
condensed reality contained within. In poetry this reality is the word as
such' (61). His notion of poetic 'building' (63) is akin to the link forged by
Heidegger between *ich bin* (I am) and *ich baue* (I build)[108] in an ontological
treatise based on the premise that language *says being*.

The wish to form a 'continuum' is not only asserted by the image of the 'single thread', but also by McGuckian's choice of quotation. The image of 'lightnings and downpours' is taken from a passage in which Mandelstam describes how, despite their apparent demise, two linden trees still continued to survive, oblivious to the elements: 'Two barren linden trees, deaf with age, raised their brown forked trunks in the courtyard. Frightening in the rather bureaucratic corpulence of their girth, they heard and understood nothing. Time fed them with flashes of lightning and watered them with downpours; thunder, blunder, it was all the same to them' (352). This storm motif is significantly taken up at the poem's conclusion:

> How cancelled benevolence gains a script
>
> from a departure so in keeping
> with its own structure – his denial
> of history's death, by the birth of his storm. (*CL* 49)

The phrase 'cancelled benevolence' is extracted from a passage in 'Journey to Armenia' in which Mandelstam discusses the relationship between an organism to its environment: the latter is said to 'invite' the organism to grow, and its functions 'are expressed in a certain benevolence which is gradually and continually cancelled out by the severity binding the living body together and rewarding it finally with death' (367). McGuckian's lines contend that this relationship bestows one further benefit to the living being, namely 'a script', a linguistic medium capable of denying 'history's death'. 'History' here refers both to 'his story' (that of McGuckian's father) and the bounds of temporality. The poem symbolically ends with a 'departure' and a 'birth'. The storm represents what Mandelstam calls 'the historical event', a concept which paradoxically encapsulates both a precarious presence as well as emptiness:

> [T]he storm in nature serves as the prototype of the historical event. The movement of the hour hand around the clockface may be considered the prototype of the non-event ... Just as history may be said to have been born, so it may also die; and what, really, is progress, that creation of the twentieth century, if not the denial of history's death in which the spirit of the event disappears? Progress is the movement of the hour hand, and what with its peculiar emptiness, this commonplace represents an enormous danger to the very existence of history. Let us intently heed Tyutchev, that connoisseur of life, in the birth of the storm. (470)

McGuckian's sense of 'departure' bespeaks a transcendence temporality: it is a linguistic application, referring to the conclusion of a poem and her sense that this does not represent an end as such. The quotation from Mandelstam defines 'departure' as follows: 'In poetry, the word "conclusion" (*vyvod*) must be understood literally as a "departure" (*vykhod*) beyond the bounds of everything previously told, a departure naturally in keeping with the force of its own gravity and fortuitously in keeping with its own structure.'

The covert way McGuckian embeds her poem with quotations clearly problematises the issues of exemplarity and authoritative citation. Yet because the presence of quotations in 'The Aisling Hat' has thus far gone unnoticed, she has not been accused, unlike Heaney, of a resolving recourse to Mandelstam, nor has she been censured, like Muldoon, for the wilful obscurity of her quotations, and her wholesale appropriation of text has not, unlike Cullen's, been regarded as unaesthetic. McGuckian avoids what Thomas Docherty terms 'parasitic authority', namely the 'appeal to some prior authority whose function is to invest the present speaker with the weight of history and tradition as vested in prior authority';[109] rather, her poem has a 'nomadicity, as it wanders towards the occupation of a temporary stability (called "understanding"), which the ascription of a proper name as its guiding authority arrests'.[110] However, now that the text's familiar ghost has been identified, is it still 'nomadic'? Does it betray a crisis of authorship? Is McGuckian really the poem's author? Comparing the final text to its primary work sheets[111] – comprising four pages of 223 handwritten phrases – one can see that while her reading of Mandelstam's essays is in chronological order, her subsequent textual recycling is not. Herein lies much of her skill: namely, the way in which she is able to respond imaginatively to a biography or critical essay – to the startling vividness and emotive acoustics of the words themselves – and subsequently dissect and recombine the elements in an original fashion. As McGuckian herself has stated in a personal correspondence[112] 'I did not take from his [Mandelstam's] poems but hoped to impose *my* rhythm on his prose to produce a different and, to my mind, original poetry.'

McGuckian employs the same method of composition when tackling other prison issues such as the authority of the British government to hold Irish prisoners of war or the well-publicised injustices suffered by Irish people at the hands of the British judiciary. In the Spring of 1993, McGuckian conducted a series of poetry workshops for prisoners at the Maze, the experience of which affected her profoundly:

> I found the experience overwhelming and it took my mind off my father to the point where I substituted for him with these men. I had a sort of epiphany with them ... There was one

time when [there] were just three of them, and suddenly I got this overwhelming sense of grief for my father and I burst into tears with these three in the prison and I suddenly realised my father was dead and it was like there was this trinity of three people – it was like all that energy was there for me, they poured all their energy into supporting me and after which they wrote to me and said 'we were your family then'.[113]

In an effort fully to comprehend this totally unexpected substitution of prisoners for her father in the aftermath of his death, she felt it necessary to read books about the experiences other Irish prisoners had in British jails. Gerry Conlon's *Proved Innocent*,[114] for example, provides the vocabulary for 'White Windsor Soap' (*CL* 81). Discussing this poem in an interview with Rand Brandes, she admits, 'I refer to Guiseppe Conlon's [Gerry's father's] illness and death, but this is also to a father who has severe bronchitis and my own father's oxygen mask.'[115] Her subsequent comment that the poem 'is about his dying under the Royal flag'[116] points to a more political reading. Referring obliquely to Conlon's wrongful imprisonment for the Guildford bombings, the poem's title conflates judicial whitewash with Britishness through its reference to the royal family ('Windsor'), and intimates Conlon's (symbolic) refusal to accept such prejudice: 'I wouldn't use the White Windsor soap, because it stank, a foul smell.'[117] However, the poem is not used primarily as a source to rail against a flawed British judiciary. Indeed, she had already done this in 'The Radio Traitor' (*CL* 70), a poem borrowing extensively from Rebecca West's *The Meaning of Treason*,[118] an in-depth analysis of the trial of William Joyce, the infamous Lord Haw Haw:

He had offended, it seems, against the root of the law
against treason ... (9)
At the time of the trial, because of the sealing-off of
the bombed parts, and the heavy black-out, not yet   Because you offended
removed owing to the lack of labour, all the halls and   the root of the law, your halls, stairs, and passages
passages and stairs were in perpetual dusk. (4)   are in perpetual dusk. Because you rejoiced
When we were facing the hazard of D-day,   in the thought of the English dead lying under
he rejoiced in the thought of the English dead   the West Wall, you were always treated
that would soon lie under the West Wall. (3–4)   as British, whether you were or not.
I was in Ireland from 1909 till 1921 when I came to England.   (*CL* 70)
We were always treated as British during the period of my stay
in England whether we were or not. (12)

McGuckian takes issue with West's reading of the Joyce trials, especially those passages pertaining to sovereignty and allegiance. The main issue centred around Joyce's nationality: was the 'radio traitor' (3) British and, if

not, had he actually 'offended ... against the root of the law against treason'
(9)? Although West admits that the trial 'was an Irish drama' (6) and that
he had 'the real Donnybrook air' (7), she still concludes that he owed allegiance to the Crown because he 'had enjoyed the protection of the English
law for some thirty years preceding his departure to Germany' (25).
McGuckian demurs and uses the apparent illogic against West: Joyce was
treated as British, she states, *because* he rejoiced in the thought of 'the English lying dead under / the West Wall'. McGuckian's poem is more subtle
than Muldoon's 'Lord Haw Haw' which simply perpetuates the myth surrounding the enigmatic broadcaster: 'For the English will yield / Before the
corn has yellowed, / Or so one Englishman has argued'.[119] 'The Radio
Traitor' has more in common with Thomas Kilroy's Field Day production,
Double Cross, a play investigating Joyce's complex sense of nationality. Kilroy
has Beaverbrook declare that 'passport or no passport, Britain has acknowledged you British by deciding to execute you for treason. Identity can be a
fiction.'[120] Reclaiming Joyce's Irishness, McGuckian's poem points to the
injustice of his 'dying under the Royal flag'.

'White Windsor Soap' (*CL* 81) is not so caught up with questions of
nationality, but is equally polemical; rather, she uses *Proved Innocent* to write
both an empathic account of imprisonment and an elegy for her father. The
quotations register connections between her own life and events or ideas
discussed in the autobiography. Whereas 'I hear you / being opened up' intimates that the third stanza is a reaction to her father's operation – 'I did hear
him from the room outside being given final surgery'[121] – the selected phrases
from Conlon refer to his isolation in Wakefield Prison's punishment block.
It is not simply a question of reconciling these two readings; rather, one
must bear in mind that her poem is a palimpsest, and that Conlon's experiences interact with McGuckian's rather than cancel them out:

Prison is a world of no strangers. (233)
You can't hug or kiss or anything else, just touch hands
before you sit down. After that, nothing can be exchanged
between the two of you except words. (161)   In a world of no strangers, nothing
The windows had a double-layer of thick perspex with little   can be exchanged except words.
holes drilled in for ventilation ... (157)   From three double-layered one-way
Nazi-type screws opened me up saying, 'Library'. (149)   windows along, I hear you
The exercise yard of the punishment block was at a forty-five being opened up, a source of sounds,
degrees slope. There were wavy lines that went up and down   waving like a snake's back.
the wall of the yard. These were different colours   (*CL* 81)
waving like a snake's back. (157)

McGuckian relates Conlon's desperate sense of aloneness within the penitentiary to her own anxious vigil and agonising separation from her father during his operation. That her appropriative praxis is poetic and not imitative can be seen by how she subtly alters the referent of 'waving like a snake's back': while Conlon describes a shape, her 'waving' is an action, the movements of a rattlesnake about to strike. Hence the 'source of sounds' is not consolatory, but a foreboding of death. Similarly, the final stanza's description of her father's taking-in of oxygen and the unnamed friend's bronchitis ('deep lungfuls') is not directly related to its original context:

The tiles were broken – the first thing that would catch
your eye was the blood, embedded in the tiles on the ceiling
and the wall ... I couldn't help looking at the screws,   I was going to add this blood
thinking am I going to add to this blood. (156)   to the blood embedded in the tiles,
Alarm bells would go off and they'd get me in a headlock,   the headlock of your thoughts
force my arms up my back and frog-march me from the   as you sat there all that time,
main prison to the punishment block. (155)   so scared by deep lungfuls of you.
Someone had been kind to me, the first kindness I'd known since   (*CL* 81)
I was arrested. And it came from a screw ... 'You sat there all that time?' (106)
It was the first time since I'd been at home in Belfast, eight days earlier,
that I'd been able to breathe fresh air. Gratefully I took deep lungfuls of it. (107)

McGuckian's text emphasises the psychological, not the physical: the 'headlock' results not from a punitive measure, but from the incessant circling 'thoughts'; 'lungfuls of you' do not refer to fresh air, but to the patient's frightened self-awareness of his frailty. Yet it cannot be said that McGuckian does not engage with *Proved Innocent*. The 'you' is also Gerry Conlon, agonising over his wrongful imprisonment. It is also his 'blood', but it is significantly *not* added to the tiles. The past tense suggests that reading the autobiography has stemmed McGuckian's initial impulse. As the opening stanza asserts, she has been 'entirely released' through the 'Catholic eyes' not only of her father ('hospital robe'), but also of Conlon ('prison-issue blue'). Though these eyes are enclosed like the prison guards in 'encased bridges' (157), Conlon's narrative, and through it her father's spirit, flows to her 'as fresh air or the lost / sensation of rain'.[122] Conlon's method of reading, in fact, is similar to her own: '[y]ou *read and read the tiny names* scribbled on the walls, *you talk to* those names, have dialogues with them, give them faces ...' (142, emphasis added).

Although it has been clearly established that McGuckian makes the source material her own, does it grant her the authoritative status of the original authors? Are her poems not derivative, at best commentaries at a second

remove? Whereas Gerry Conlon has intimate knowledge of the prison system, McGuckian does not and cannot claim to speak with any great authority about his experiences. What one should bear in mind is that she
is writing as 'Medbh McGuckian' and not as 'Gerry Conlon'. To explore
the complexity of bearing witness to events not experienced at first hand, I
want to conclude with a poem whose focus is not primarily on Northern
Ireland, but on the 1.5-square-mile Jewish ghetto in Lodz, established by
the Nazis in February 1940. After attending a conference in Poland,
McGuckian wrote on 22 January 1998 to say, 'I have had a week of nausea
and shock which would either kill or cure a poet'. This was written on the
back of a postcard picturing the ruins of the Gas Chamber and Cremato-
rium II at Auschwitz-Birkenau. 'Jeszcze Polska', dedicated to the memory
of Dawid Sierakowiak, was written shortly afterwards and included in a
letter saying, 'I wrote a poem for the first time actually acknowledging my
text and addressing it to the writer. Perhaps Auschwitz has chastened me
into a new one-to-oneness with my victims?'[123] 'Victims' betrays a continuing disquietude, an anxiety that her practice of embedded quotation would
be misconstrued as both plagiarism and an exploitative substitution for
originality. Her fears are ungrounded: 'Jeszcze Polska"s borrowings from
The Diary of Dawid Sierakowiak[124] present a diary of her own reading, a
text striving to honour his memory and express solidarity with his unswerv-
ing life-force in the face of incomprehensible cruelty.

In the course of the poem, McGuckian gradually approaches her muse:
she 'almost touches' in the first stanza; she softly touches in the second; in
the third, her 'slow-eyed kiss is thrown from afar'; by the fifth, this kiss has
arrived, a violent (almost sexual) offering of self:

I'm sure the bedbugs drink *half a glass of my blood* every night! (210)   And half-a-glass
The mood of panic is intensifying by the second. All kinds of rumors are   of my blood
repeated *from lips to lips* that we should expect the worst. (216)   from lips to lips
                                                                             down the centre of your throat …

She counters the parasitical feeding of bedbugs by offering up her own
blood, just one stage in the gradual fusion of selves. By the poem's penultimate
stanza, we see her empathising fully with Sierakowiak:

Even so, I'm unable to turn my consciousness away from Mom, and   As though I divide
suddenly, *as though I divide*, I find myself in her mind and body. (226) every bearable passing day
People are already hanging their heads completely because *when July*   when July begins like this
begins like this, then how will we be able to get through the winter? (191) with fields made slippery by mist.

In the original context, 'As though I divide' refers to his grief at the separation from his mother and his feverish thoughts about her impending deportation; here, however, it is McGuckian who finds herself in Sierakowiak's 'mind and body'. This reading is supported visually by the poem's uncharacteristic *mise-en-page*, its double-helix shape suggesting two distinct strands instrinsically linked. It is not coincidental that the poem concludes with his words quoted exactly, voicing their desire in unison to forestall genocide: 'Marne, oh Marne, please happen again ...' (36).

Yet are quotations absolutely necessary in this poem? Does the poet need Sierakowiak's own words, since the subject matter has already been signalled by the dedication? The answer becomes obvious if we ask one further question: how is McGuckian to express her own sense of horror at the holocaust, or, more particularly, at Sierakowiak's fate? Although she feels an ethical compulsion to write, she herself is not an authoritative witness. Indeed, the best testimony lies in the diaries themselves: they painstakingly document the horrors suffered by the Jewish population in Lodz and attest to the inhumane treatment meted out both by the Nazis and the ruling class inside the ghetto. They also record Sierakowiak's gradual demise, his losing struggle with tuberculosis, exhaustion and starvation. McGuckian's poem is caught between two irreconcilable poles: the necessity to express solidarity and the impossibility of fully comprehending systematic oppression. Quotation is certainly used because Sierakowiak is the most credible witness, yet it does not preclude her own sense of authorship. The appropriated extracts are, as ever, juxtaposed in ways inconceivable to the original author. Indeed, the palimpsestic form presents a clash of perspectives, allowing the poet to set up a poignant antithesis between Sierakowiak's viewpoint and her own tragic hindsight. After all, Sierakowiak was, for most of the time, unaware of the Nazis' intentions toward the Jewish population. The clever juxtapositions in the fifth stanza are characteristic of her method:

After dinner the first big air raid on Lodz. *Twelve planes in triangles of three* break through the defense lines and start bombing the city. (32)
The soldiers are not so extraordinary; only their uniforms make them   Twelve planes in triangles
different from Polish soldiers – *steel-green.* (370)   of three, steel-green,
The German medical commission has begun its work.   form a letter whose meaning
All those examined by the commission get an indelible   nobody knows.
Stamp on their chests *a letter whose meaning nobody knows.* (156).

In the original context, the 'letter whose meaning nobody knows' was a marking put on those already examined by German medics to assess a person's aptitude for work; in McGuckian's poem, however, it is the German war-machine which forms an incomprehensible language. The 'Twelve planes in triangles of three' present a sign which no one is able to read, akin to the mysterious appearance in the sky of the letter 'A' in *The Scarlet Letter*, a phenomenon giving rise to multiple interpretations. Although Sierakowiak did not realise it, the 'steel-green' of the German uniforms would give rise to the 'Jewish-yellow' and, ultimately, the '*Davidstern*' that must be worn 'on the right chest, and on the back of the right shoulder' (70). With a post-holocaust sensibility, it is difficult for a poet to express in language how a sign of Sierakowiak's faith came to signify his ultimate fate.

Of the three poets discussed in this chapter, McGuckian's authorative status is the most tenuous, since her appropriative praxis leaves her open to the charge of unoriginality. Paradoxically, however, this means that her work is closest to the original experiences depicted, since she borrows directly from the sociolect of her sources. Although her texts are filled with other peoples' words, it would be difficult to argue that she shares the self-defeating logic pertaining to a hunger-striker's quotations whereby the text/body must slowly cease to exist in order to recall previous texts/bodies. Whereas the hunger-striker's body must fade away to recall other exemplars, McGuckian is present in her texts even when quoting. Like Muldoon and Heaney, she does not sacrifice her own sense of being an author, since the dovetailed quotations enable her to conduct an imaginary dialogue with her precursors.

Notes

1 Seamus Heaney, 'Shelf Life', *Station Island* (London: Faber, 1984) 23.
2 Claudette Sartiliot, *Citation and Modernity: Derrida, Joyce, and Brecht* (Norman: University of Oklahoma Press, 1995) 4.
3 Sartiliot, *Citation and Modernity* 4–5.
4 David Beresford, *Ten Men Dead: The Story of the 1981 Irish Hunger Strike* (London: Grafton Books, 1987) 14–15.
5 Richard Kearney, *Postnationalist Ireland: Politics, Culture, Philosophy* (London: Routledge, 1997) 110.
6 Beresford, *Ten Men Dead* 38–39.
7 Tim Pat Coogan, *On the Blanket: The H-Block Story* (Dublin: Ward River Press, 1980).
8 Kearney, *Postnationalist Ireland* 112.
9 Richard Hamilton, *A Cellular Maze* (Derry: Orchard Gallery, 1983).

10 Hamilton, *A Cellular Maze* n.p.

11 See especially Maud Ellmann, *The Hunger Artists: Starving, Writing and Imprisonment* (London: Virago Press, 1993); Allen Feldman, *Formations of Violence: The Narrative of the Body and Political Terror in Northern Ireland* (Chicago: University of Chicago Press, 1991); Joseph Ruane and Jennifer Todd, *The Dynamics of Conflict in Northern Ireland: Power, Conflict and Emancipation* (Cambridge: Cambridge University Press, 1996) 111.

12 Ruane and Todd, *The Dynamics of Conflict* 111.

13 Feldman, *Formations of Violence* 165.

14 Feldman, *Formations of Violence* 164.

15 Ellmann, *The Hunger Artists* 16–17.

16 Ellmann, *The Hunger Artists* 14.

17 Seamus Heaney, 'The Sense of the Past', *History Ireland* 1.4 (Winter, 1993): 33.

18 Ellmann, *The Hunger Artists* 87–88.

19 Brian Keenan, *An Evil Cradling*, 1992 (London: Vintage, 1993) 65.

20 Keenan, *An Evil Cradling* 81.

21 Poets such as Heaney are frequently cited by figures as diverse as the head of Scotland Yard's anti-terrorist branch and Gerry Adams. See Eoghan Harris, 'Passing the Buck', *Sunday Times* 12 May 1996, Books 3; David McKittrick, 'When the Political Doors Stayed Shut', *Independent* 12 February 1996, 17; Stewart Tendler, 'Prepared for the Worst and Hoping for the Best', *Times* 12 February 1996, 3; Stuart Weir, 'A Freedom to Be Feared', *Guardian* 28 December 1990, 19.

22 See Peter Levi, 'Scythe, Pitchfork and Biretta', *Poetry Review* 81.2 (Summer, 1991) 12–14.

23 Alan Robinson, 'Seamus Heaney's *Seeing Things*: Familiar Compound Ghosts', in Hans Ulrich Seeber and Walter Göbel (eds), *Anglisentag 1992 Stuggart* (Tubingen: Max Niemeyer Verlay, 1993) 47.

24 Peter McDonald, 'The Poet and "The Finished Man": Heaney's Oxford Lectures', *Irish Review* 19 (Spring–Summer, 1996) 98.

25 McDonald, 'The Poet' 99.

26 Peter McDonald, 'Seamus Heaney as Critic', in Michael Kenneally (ed.), *Poetry in Contemporary Irish Literature*, ed. Michael Kenneally (Gerrards Cross: Colin Smythe, 1995) 175.

27 See Henry Hart, 'Seamus Heaney's *The Government of the Tongue*', *Verse* 6.2 (June, 1989) 65–71, and Bernard O'Donoghue, *Seamus Heaney and the Language of Poetry* (New York: Harvester Wheatsheaf, 1994) 141–49.

28 Heaney, *Government* 92.

29 McDonald, 'Heaney as Critic' 178.

30 Heaney, *Government* 92.

31 Peter McDonald, 'Yeats, Form and Northern Irish Poetry', in Warwick Gould and Edna Langley (eds), *That Accusing Eye: Yeats and His Irish Readers* (London: Macmillan, 1996) 226.

32 McDonald, 'Yeats' 227.

33 Heaney, *Government* 96.

34 Heaney, *Government* 92.

35 In *The Poetics of Modernity: Toward a Hermeneutic Imagination* (New Jersey: Humanities Press, 1995), Richard Kearney develops upon what Paul Ricoeur means by the *configuring*

act of poetics: it is an act carried out by the creative imagination 'which presupposes the *prefiguring* act of our everyday temporal experience and culminates in the *refiguring* act whereby textual narratives return us to a world of action. When the story is over we re-enter our lifeworlds transformed, however imperceptibly' (xv).

36 Neil Corcoran, 'Seamus Heaney and the Art of the Exemplary', *The Yearbook of English Studies* 17 (1987) 119.
37 Corcoran, 'Art' 118.
38 Seamus Heaney, 'Envies and Identifications: Dante and the Modern Poet', *Irish University Review* 15.1 (Spring, 1985) 103–04.
39 Seamus Heaney, *Crediting Poetry* (Meath: Gallery Press, 1995) 16.
40 Heaney, *The Place of Writing* (Atlanta: The Scholars' Press, 1989) 32.
41 Heaney, *Government* 148.
42 Heaney, *Government* 148–49.
43 Heaney, *Government* 170.
44 Heaney, *Government* 170.
45 Heaney, 'The Flight Path', *The Spirit Level* (London: Faber, 1996) 22–26.
46 Peter McDonald, 'Levelling Out', *Thumbscrew* 5 (Summer, 1996) 46.
47 Heaney, 'The Art of Poetry LXXV', interview by Henri Cole, *Paris Review* 144 (Fall, 1997) 111.
48 Heaney, 'The Flight Path', *The Spirit Level* 25.
49 Vincent Browne, 'H-Block Crisis: Courage, Lies and Confusion', *Magill* 4.11 (August, 1981) 8.
50 Heaney, 'Station Island', *Station Island* 83.
51 See Heaney, 'Ugolino', *Field Work* (London: Faber, 1979) 63. The episode is taken from Cantos xxxii and xxxiii of Dante's *Inferno*.
52 Robinson, 'Seamus Heaney's *Seeing Things*' 48.
53 David Wallace, 'Dante in English', *The Cambridge Companion to Dante* (Cambridge: Cambridge University Press, 1993) 256.
54 Joan M. Ferrante, *The Political Vision of The Divine Comedy* (Princeton: Princeton University Press, 1984) 193.
55 William Scammell, 'Thumping Along', *London Magazine* 23.9–10 (December 1983–January 1984) 119.
56 John Kerrigan, 'The New Narrative', *London Review of Books* (16 February 1984) 23.
57 Edna Longley, 'Uncovering Deadly Depths', *Fortnight* 200 (December 1983–January 1984) 31.
58 Heaney, 'Station Island' 76.
59 Samuel Beckett, *First Love and Other Stories* (New York: Grove Press, 1970) 30.
60 Ellmann, *The Hunger Artists* 100.
61 Feldman, *Formations of Violence* 181.
62 Paul Muldoon, personal correspondence, 17 February 1998.
63 The prisoner in question is 'Beatrice' who is being held in Armagh jail.
64 Ann Eden Gibson, *Abstract Expressionism: Other Politics* (New Haven, CT: Yale University Press, 1997) 136.
65 Alwynne Mackie, *Art/Talk: Theory and Practice in Abstract Expressionism* (New York: Columbia University Press, 1989) 145.

66 Personal interview with Paul Muldoon on 11 August 1996 at The Yeats Summer School, Sligo.

67 Shane Cullen, *Fragmens sur les Institutions Républicaines IV*, ed. Liam Kelly (Derry: Orchard Gallery, 1997).

68 This is another instance of 'writing in the shit' as the comms were often concealed in the prisoner's rectum.

69 Jorge Luis Borges, *Labyrinths: Selected and Other Writings*, eds. Donald A. Yates and James E. Irby, 1964 (London: Penguin, 1970) 66.

70 Peter Suchin, 'Measured Words: Text and Context in the Work of Shane Cullen', *Circa* 77 (Autumn, 1996) 26.

71 Fintan O'Toole quoted in Mike Wilson, 'Fragments and Responses', *Fragmens*, ed. Kelly, 18.

72 John Hutchinson, *Better than the Brown Earth: On Shane Cullen's Fragmens sur les Institutions Républicaines IV*, (Dublin: Douglas Hyde Gallery, 1996) n.p.

73 Hutchinson, *Better than the Brown Earth* n.p.

74 Wilson, 'Fragments and Responses' 16.

75 Wilson, 'Fragments and Responses' 19.

76 Jennifer Schiffer Levine, 'Originality and Repetition in *Finnegans Wake* and *Ulysses*', *PMLA* 94.1 (January, 1979) 111.

77 James Joyce, *Finnegans Wake*, 1939 (London: Faber, 1975) 183.

78 McGuckian states in a personal correspondence, 12 December 1996, that '[t]he poem I'm most still fond of about the Dirty Protest is the Black poem – "Black is my continuum" – which uses the word "shit" politely in babyspeak at the end. Not a word I could use'.

79 Medbh McGuckian, letter to the author, 16 July 1998.

80 Sarah Fulford, *Gendered Spaces in Contemporary Irish Poetry* (Oxford: Peter Lang, 2002) 176.

81 Fulford, *Gendered Spaces* 176–78. See also Clair Wills, *Improprieties: Politics and Sexuality in Northern Irish Poetry* (Oxford: Clarendon Press, 1993) 71–74.

82 See Sabina Sharkey, *Ireland and the Iconography of Rape: Colonisation, Constraint and Gender* (London: University of North London Press, 1994) 8.

83 Antonia Fraser, *Mary Queen of Scots* (London: Weidenfield and Nicolson, 1969).

84 Fraser, *Mary Queen of Scots* 83. Elizabeth was considered to be illegitimate by Catholics since she was the daughter of Anne Bolcyn.

85 Fraser, *Mary Queen of Scots* 268.

86 Fraser, *Mary Queen of Scots* 13.

87 Fraser, *Mary Queen of Scots* 3.

88 McGuckian, letter to the author, 16 July 1998.

89 McGuckian, personal interview, John Hewitt International Summer School, 28 July 1995.

90 McGuckian, letter to the author, 16 July 1998.

91 See David McKittrick and David McVea, *Making Sense of the Troubles* (Belfast: Blackstaff Press, 2000), 137–41. See also Brian Campbell et al. (eds), *Nor Meekly Serve My Time: The H-Block Struggle 1976–1981* (Belfast: Beyond the Pale, 1994) 104.

92 Paddy Maynes, *Protest and Hunger Strike in the H Block: The Disavowal of Passivity* (London: University of East London, 2000) 13.

93 Fraser, *Mary Queen of Scots* 536, emphasis added.

94 Mary Stuart cited in Fraser, *Mary Queen of Scots* 537.

95 Wills, *Improprieties* 72.

96 Susan Stanford Friedman, 'Creativity and the Childbirth Metaphor: Gender Difference in Literary Discourse', *Feminist Studies* 13.1 (Spring, 1987) 49.

97 Ellmann, *The Hunger Artists* (London: Virago Press, 1993), 100.

98 Osip Mandelstam, *The Collected Prose and Letters*, ed. Jane Gray Harris, trans. Harris and Constance Link 1979 (London: Collins Harvill, 1991). Further references included in text.

99 See Nadezhda Mandelstam, *Hope against Hope: A Memoir*, trans. Max Hayward (London: Harvill and Collins, 1971) 226–28.

100 See notes to Osip Mandelstam, 'Goethe's Youth: Radiodrama', in Mandelstam, *Collected Prose and Letters* 687–88.

101 Heaney, 'Aisling', *North* (London: Faber, 1975) 48.

102 Edna Longley, *From Cathleen to Anorexia: The Breakdown of Irelands* (Dublin: Attic Press, 1990) 3.

103 Rita Duffy, *Banquet* (Belfast: Ormeau Baths Gallery, 1997) n.p.

104 McGuckian, personal interview, Marine Hotel, Ballycastle, 19 August 1996.

105 John Kerrigan, 'Belonging', *London Review of Books* 18 July 1996, 27.

106 Nadezhda Mandelstam, *Hope Abandoned*, trans. Max Hayward (London: Collins and Harvill Press, 1974) 410.

107 See Martin Heidegger, *Poetry, Language, Thought*, trans. Albert Hofstader (New York: Harper and Row, 1971) 74.

108 See Martin Heidegger, 'Building Dwelling Thinking', in David Farrell Krell (ed.), *Basic Writings from Being in Time (1927) to The Task of Thinking (1964)* (London: Routledge, 1978) 344–45.

109 Thomas Docherty, *Alterities: Criticism, History, Representation* (Oxford: Clarendon Press, 1996) 78.

110 Docherty, *Alterities* 78.

111 McGuckian Papers, Emory University, Box 21, folder 29.

112 McGuckian, personal correspondence, 16 January 1997.

113 Personal interview, The John Hewitt International Summer School, 28 July 1995.

114 Gerry Conlon, *Proved Innocent*, first pub. 1990 (London: Penguin, 1991).

115 McGuckian, 'A Dialogue with Medbh McGuckian, Winter 1996–1997', interview by Rand Brandes, *Studies in the Literary Imagination* 30.2 (Fall, 1997) 45.

116 McGuckian, interview by Brandes 45.

117 Conlon, *Proved Innocent* 102. Further references cited in text.

118 Rebecca West, *The Meaning of Treason* (London: Macmillan, 1952). Further references cited in text.

119 Paul Muldoon, 'Lord Haw Haw', *Names and Adresses* (Belfast: Ulsterman Publications, 1978) 9.

120 Thomas Kilroy, *Double Cross* (London: Faber, 1986) 76.

121 McGuckian, interview by Brandes 45.

122 This refers not only to her father's supply of oxygen, but to Guiseppe's own need for 'a flow of fresh air' (190).

123 Personal correspondence, 27 February 1998. The poem was subsequently collected in McGuckian, *Had I a Thousand Lives* (95–96).
124 Dawid Sierakowiak, *Five Notebooks from the Lodz Diaries: The Diary of Dawid Sierakowiak*, ed. Alan Adelson, trans. Kamil Turowski (London: Bloomsbury, 1996). Further references are cited in text.

5

'The eye that scanned it':
The Art of Looking in Northern Irish Poetry

A chapter based upon poets' responses to works of art risks appearing *passé*: from Horace's '*ut pictura poesis*' to J. D. McClatchy's *Poets on Painters*[1] and beyond, the subject has been tackled extensively, if not exhaustively. In relation to Northern Irish poetry, Edna Longley's impressive 'No More Poems about Paintings?'[2] would seem the definitive account. However, this chapter not only corrects certain misconceptions and inaccuracies in Longley's analysis, more importantly it offers a comparative study of 'the gaze' of both Paul Muldoon and Medbh McGuckian. Rather than presenting a study comparing the compositional and technical similarities of poetry and painting, I shall discuss not only the poets' reactions to other people's art but also how the different structures of looking embedded into their poems (scopic drive, voyeurism, zen-like trance, detached gaze, flickering glance) reveal subtle distinctions between their views on politics and gender. This approach does not mean that my focus is on artistic reference rather than intertextual relations; the poets often borrow from biographies and art criticism when composing. Although I intend to contrast the younger poets' obliquity with Seamus Heaney's directness, the greatest difference between them is in their way of looking. I shall argue that Heaney's gaze is singular and self-affirming, engaged as it is in eidetic reduction, the phenomenological search for the Platonic *eidos*. In contrast, the younger poets' points of view problematise this concept, demonstrating that the gaze is neither static nor passive. All three, however, share with Northern Irish visual artists a distrust of the supposedly objective media representations of the Troubles.

Photo-journalistic representations of sectarian conflict in Northern Ireland are renowned for their political *naïveté* and tabloid simplicity; relaying clichéd imagery as a convenient substitute for investigative reportage, photographers have increasingly opted for 'recognition and easy reflexive responses with the manipulative ease of the potboiler'.[3] Ignoring the underlying complexities of the political situation, this unqualified 'retinal reportage'[4] has latched on to one-dimensional imagery, 'massag[ing] the complex into simplistic formulae'.[5] As one commentator has rightly pointed out, by 'trading so unself-critically on the worst stereotypes of the situation, the images themselves have become increasingly bankrupt'.[6] For visual artists, the chronic political instability has curtailed access to a realist aesthetic[7] and they have been forced to subvert the fixed gaze of the camera by foregrounding both mediation and context 'in the form of manipulated images, sequenced images, or combinations of image and text'.[8] Photographs are deliberately marked, toned, layered and edited, undermining the straightforward realism of the documentary image.[9] That this tendency toward self-reflexivity is widespread can be seen from recent exhibitions. Brian McAvera, the curator of the *Parable Island* exhibition held at the Bluecoat Gallery, Liverpool, stressed that for each of the artists involved, '[a] dark and deeply ingrained humour, a sense of irony, and an often angular, oblique and layered attitude to life, colours a perception sieved through the dust motes of mythology, archaeology and the leaf-mould of history'.[10] Similarly, the curators of the *Ceasefire* exhibition noted in their catalogue essay that the artists wished to offer a different type of commentary to 'the familiar visual language of the TV news broadcast or newspaper photograph'.[11]

Willie Doherty,[12] for example, creates phototexts which set up a dialogue between word and image. In *Waiting*, an urban landscape (Rossville Street, Derry) is pictured against a glorious sunset, with the text – *Golden Sunsets/Waiting* – printed across the photograph. Language and image combine to present an ambiguous portrait of a famous landmark in Derry, the 'Free Derry' gable wall: first, the idyllic picture of 'Free Derry' is presented, yet its so-called free status is undermined since the populace is still purportedly 'waiting'; secondly, the work hints that the historical basis of Irish nationalism's 'Brits Out' policy is both fanciful (based on a Golden Age) and on the wane (a sunset, rather than a sunrise). Representation for Doherty is all 'a question of *positioning*: the camera in relation to the object, the text in relation to image, the viewer in relation to the physicality of the photographic installation'.[13] His work, as Dan Cameron has suggested, presents 'a form of parallel discourse to the role played by photographs in the media':[14] although the gable wall had, by the 1980s, become a cliché, Doherty's

phototext has been shot from a different angle, taking in the sky and with-
drawing a considerable distance, using the wall as a background, so that
one is left asking whether the nationalist icon is being approached, or left
behind, and whether its significance has diminished.

This same heightened sense of being watched, combined with uninformed
media-saturation, has also affected poets. In 'Whatever You Say Say Nothing', Seamus Heaney complains about

>   the jottings and analyses
> Of politicians and newspapermen
> Who've scribbled down the long campaign from gas
> And protest to gelignite and sten,
>
> Who proved upon their pulses 'escalate',
> 'Backlash' and 'crack down', 'provisional wing',
> 'Polarization' and 'long-standing hate'.[15]

Complex analysis is the first casualty; quotation marks isolate the already
redundant clichés of journalistic shorthand. Heaney has recently warned
about the dangers of 'channel-surf[ing] over so much live coverage of contemporary savagery',[16] but suggested that poetry has the power to counter-
act the generalising banality of 'those sanctioned, old, elaborate retorts'.[17]
In contrast to the shortcomings of the camera lens, Brian McAvera sees the
innate advantages of poetry:

> It is no accident that the richest, most complex creations of *social reality* have come from
> Northern Irish literature; in particular from poetry. Poetry with its ability to create a succinct
> yet resonant universe, a parallel world to our own ... can provide not just a mirror image – in
> which we recognize ourselves, our landscape, our social relations – but also an informing
> context, be it a moral order, a controlling irony, a dialectic between writer and persons. The
> continual spark of metaphor or the magical manipulations of narrative invest the poem with
> a density of texture (its allusiveness like the warp and woof of the spinner) which is rarely
> present in the photographic image.[18]

It is precisely the 'informing context' and 'allusiveness' of 'The Mud Vision'[19] which make it such an important poem in Heaney's oeuvre. The text
takes as its inspiration Richard Long's *Mud Hand Circles*,[20] displayed during the Rosc exhibition (24 August–17 November 1984). The poem's title
is also derived from the Gaelic word 'Rosc', meaning 'poetry of vision'.[21]
Heaney's idea of 'vision' is not one dictated by party politics; rather, he has
asserted that post-colonial poets 'have long ago been freed to throw away
the cracked looking-glass of the servant and to scan the world instead through
the cunningly arranged and easily manoeuvrable periscope of their

submerged sensibility'.[22] What is remarkable is the manner in which Heaney appropriates the mud circle for his own use. Richard Long, explaining the rationale behind his work, has stated, 'We are water, we have hands; stones are particles of our Earth. Mud is halfway between stone and water. My work is a simple expression of myself in the space and material of the world.'[23] 'The Mud Vision', by contrast, ignores Long's personal history and, more specifically, his Englishness. In an interview with Rand Brandes, Heaney recalls that 'Long had made a huge "flower face" or rose window type of structure entirely by dipping his hand in mud and placing his handprints so as to begin with four handprints in the shape of a cross or compass. [...] But obviously a whole Irish subculture of apparitions and moving statues and such like went into it.'[24] In a more recent lecture, Heaney expanded upon this theme, stating that:

> I began to connect this earthy sign which I'd imagined in the Irish air with de Valera's dream of transforming the local customs with folk catholicism of rural Ireland in the middle of the twentieth century into something more self-conscious and purposeful, his dream of founding a culturally distinct and spiritually resistant Irish republic, a dream which has been gradually abandoned without ever being replaced by any alternative vision of the future.[25]

Heaney's poem does not set up a direct relation with Long's work; rather, he appropriates the 'earthy sign' for his own cultural agenda. Two distinct acts of looking are involved: on the one hand, Heaney's recollected gaze allows him to seize upon an image which will indirectly comment upon '"the new Ireland', the Euro-Ireland of the high-rise offices and expense account lunches, press conferences and image-making';[26] on the other hand, the poem depicts a media-led society which has lost the power of 'vision'.

The poem's opening lines reflect a country which is anything but 'cultur-ally distinct'; rather, it is a country in the throes of future shock, where the medium is the message. The parabolic imagery stems less from the poet's desire for universal relevance, and more from a perception of Irish society as being desacralised. While software programmers, punk rockers, pop stars and popes have each established their own individual niches on the com-munication highway, there is no mention of poets:

> Statues with exposed hearts and barbed-wire crowns
> Still stood in alcoves, hares flitted beneath
> The dozing bellies of jets, our menu-writers
> And punks with aerosol sprays held their own
> With the best of them. Satellite link-ups
> Wafted over us the blessings of popes, heliports

Maintained a charmed circle of idols on tour
And casualties on their stretchers.[27]

This state-of-the-art technology and frenetic message-making induce leth-
argy: the 'charmed circle' has much in common with the lotus-eaters –
more idle than idols. Distinctive cultural traits are dissipated by analysis
and scrutiny: 'We sleepwalked / The line between panic and formulae,
screentested / Our native models and the last of the mummers'.[28] For the
poet, then, the sudden appearance of the 'mud vision' represents hope of a
resacralisation ('Original clay'). The vision's meaning is, however, lost amidst
the media scramble and '*post factum* jabber' indulged by those who fail to
appreciate experience at first hand. 'What might have been origin,' says the
speaker, 'We dissipated in news. The clarified place / Had retrieved neither
us nor itself'.[29] 'The Mud Vision' propounds a despairing thesis similar to
George Steiner's vision of contemporary society: 'The secondary is our nar-
cotic. Like sleepwalkers, we are guarded by the numbing drone of the journalistic, of the theoretical, from the often harsh, imperious radiance of sheer
presence.'[30]

The act of looking in Northern Ireland is not always innocent, especially
when there are socio-political forces involved: the respective gazes of the so-
called colonisers and colonised are not presented as being equivalent. Visual artists like Rita Duffy[31] and Willie Doherty[32] self-reflexively focus upon
the act of looking, analysing the power relations involved. In Duffy's *Banquet, Plantation* and *Outpost*, she juxtaposes images of domesticity with
those of fortification and surveillance. Delineating rigid boundaries between
outside and inside, her oil paintings foreground a mentality in Northern
Ireland of heightened paranoia, whereby all kinds of territory (streets, houses,
nations) must be kept under close watch. The impression that everyone is
scrutinising everyone else is also one which Willie Doherty has striven to
convey in his phototexts. *Last Hours of Daylight*, for example, a black and
white photograph of the Bogside (Derry), taken from an elevated viewpoint,
has the words 'Stifling Surveillance/Last hours of Daylight' printed across it.
The viewer has a privileged vantage point from which s/he can look down at
the houses of Catholics. Counteracting the invasive gaze is an actual
smokescreen, the fumes rising from the chimney pots. The elevated position
contrasted with the poor, crowded housing and (seeming) resistance to being
watched, presents an obvious analogy for the power struggle between the two
communities in Derry. The artist himself explains his work as follows:

Le plus important dans ces photographies est ce qui n'est pas montré, les choses que vous ne pouvez voir ici sont celles qui déterminent le plus votre vie. L'idée que vous êtes épié ou l'idée que cette surveillance est à l'ordre du jour chaque jour. Vous ne pouvez pas photographier ça; ça n'est pas public. Vous ne pouvez seulement photographier que ce qui est physiquement en face de vous, mais vous pouvez suggérer ces idées comme un état psychologique.[33]

While it may be true to suggest that Doherty's work evokes the psychological tensions caused by surveillance, does it really reveal, as Jean Fisher claims, 'the panoptical strategies of regulation and disempowerment' that 'subtly inscribe the fabric of the city'?[34] One work appears at first to justify the claim. *Walls*[35] posits a curious symbiotic relationship between the Catholic and Protestant domains of Derry. While the top half of the photograph is taken up by a panoramic view of the Bogside, the bottom half presents a shadowy view of the city walls. The text mirrors the main division: inscribed in nationalist green across the houses is the phrase 'Always without', while 'Within Forever' is printed in royal blue across the wall. Unlike *Last Hours of Daylight*, the Catholic community is on the same level as the viewer, opening the possibility for counter surveillance. Dan Cameron has analysed this aspect of Doherty's work, showing how the artist generates 'an extraordinary typology of the gaze': 'Beginning with the colonizing look, outwards and downwards, which originates from within the walled city, to the electronic eye of surveillance that engenders mistrust and unease – to be a "subject" in Derry is to have one's freedom to deflect or return the gaze seriously unhindered'.[36] Just as Bentham's conceptual design for his prison intended, according to Michel Foucault, 'to induce in the inmate a state of conscious and permanent visibility that assures the automatic functioning of power', Doherty's work indicates how 'the external look' has become 'an internalized and self-regulating mechanism'.[37] Yet the city is obviously not literally a pantopicon, and it would be incorrect to suggest that Doherty's work simply re-presents a version of Foucault's (reductive) assessment of Bentham's design, outlining 'a technology of power designed to solve the problems of surveillance'.[38] The disruption of perspective by the deliberate conflation of foreground and background creates an ambiguity best summed up by a sentence from Ciaran Carson's 'Intelligence': 'Keeping people out and keeping people in, we are prisoners or officers in Bentham's *Panopticon*, except sorting out who's who is a problem for the naïve user, and some compilers are inclined to choke on the mixed mode – panopticons within panopticons.'[39]

Seamus Heaney's poetry constantly refers to the imperious gaze of the security forces: in 'Triptych' he records 'the helicopter shadowing our march at Newry';[40] in 'Sandstone Keepsake' the speaker is 'staring across at the watch-towers' from his 'free state of image and allusion, / swooped on, then dropped by trained binoculars';[41] and in 'From the Frontier of Writing' the poet writes about 'the marksman training down / out of the sun upon you like a hawk'.[42] In each case, the imagery implies calculated hostility and reveals the speaker's acute vulnerability: 'eyeing with intent / down cradled guns that hold you under cover'.[43] Held under the gaze of the soldiers, the speaker is made aware of his weak position: 'subjugated, yes, and obedient'.[44] For Heaney, the watchtowers, army checkpoints and fortified border crossings are all reminders that Northern Ireland is occupied territory:

> One morning early I met armoured cars
> In convoy, warbling along on powerful tyres,
> All camouflaged with broken alder branches,
> And headphoned soldiers standing up in turrets.
> How long were they approaching down my roads
> As if they owned them?[45]

It is ironic that, for all his understanding of imperial acts of looking, Heaney should be so roundly condemned for his gender-inflected gaze. Patricia Coughlan criticises his work for what she perceives to be a scopophilic drive aimed towards submitting the female personae to a controlling gaze: 'Woman, the primary inhabitor and constituent of the domestic realm, is admiringly observed, centre stage but silent. She is thus constructed by the scopic gaze, her imputed mental inaction and blankness being required to foreground the speaker's naming and placing of her.'[46] Keenly sensitive to 'the scopic spectacle of the girl's utter disempowerment'[47] in 'Punishment',[48] Coughlan laments Heaney's objectification of the Windeby Girl. Yet she does the poet a severe injustice: stating that the poem's speaker 'does to a certain degree interrogate his own position, discerning it as an "artful voyeur"', she misreads his self-condemnation by limiting the word's application to 'his sense of his political ambiguity'.[49]

The very notion of the scopic gaze is itself far from unproblematic. Laura Mulvey's influential 'Visual Pleasure and Narrative Cinema'[50] adapts Freud's analysis of scopophilia and applies it to the structures of looking inherent to filmic pleasure. Her conclusion that cinema constructs the way a woman is to be looked at 'into the spectacle itself' effectively erases the female half of the audience: if the male spectator fixes the female actor in his voyeuristic–scophilic gaze, how exactly is the female spectator regarding the scene – through a filmic construction of the male gaze? Appropriating Mulvey's concept of the scopic gaze, Coughlan also inherits her inverted sexism. Although her feminist mode of analysis is able to discern 'an erotic disrobing narrative' in Heaney's poem 'Bog Queens',[51] can the same be said for 'The Grauballe Man'?[52] Are we to assume that the speaker's scopic gaze is homoerotic? In fact, the poem centres around the act of looking. Staring at the man's 'twisted face / in a photograph', the speaker begins to distrust his initial urge to aestheticise the body:

> but now he lies
> perfected in my memory,
> down to the red horn
> of his nails,
>
> hung in the scales
> with beauty and atrocity:
> with the Dying Gaul
> too strictly compassed
>
> on his shield ... [53]

'The Grauballe Man' is one of those poems which 'challenge the writer's ability to profess a mythic transforming power through language'; rather than embracing a mythic discourse, the speaker adopts both an ethical discourse and 'a self-reflexive discourse of demythification', both of which 'comprehend and question rather than transform'.[54] The lines bespeak an unease at the way memory has 'perfected' the Grauballe Man's image. Relating this falsification ('lies') to art, Heaney, as Helen Vendler points out, 'criticises the sculptor of *The Dying Gaul* because it is too strictly circumscribed by the aesthetic laws the statue was following'; the admonition is aimed as much at his own poetic treatment of 'atrocity' as at the sculptor's. Heaney's way of looking has 'too strictly compassed' his subject.[55]

In *The Poetics of Space*, Gaston Bachelard describes the effect which engravings have upon his mind:

> Primal images, simple engravings are but so many invitations to start imagining again. They give us back areas of being, houses in which the human being's certainty of being is concentrated, and we have the impression that, by living in such images as these, in images that are as stabilizing as these are, we could start a new life, a life that would be our own, that would belong to us in our very depths.[56]

While Heaney would endorse Bachelard's meditation upon 'simple engravings', implying as it does that man's present-day perception straddles both
past memories and possible futures, the poet internalises these images,
changes their fixed material properties and reads into them imaginative
alternatives. In 'Seeing Things',[57] the poet's gaze looks beyond the material
world into the eternal and conjures life from a stone carving. The image of
Christ being baptised by St John in section II of 'Seeing Things' is to be found
as a relief carving on the cathedral at Orvieto. Heaney's use of the 'dry-eyed
Latin word' *claritas* to explain his own reaction to it implicitly invokes Stephen
Dedalus's description of St Thomas Aquinas's use of that word:

> The instant wherein that supreme quality of beauty, the clear radiance of the aesthetic image,
> is apprehended by the mind which has been arrested by its wholeness and fascinated by its
> harmony ... [It] is the luminous silent stasis of esthetic pleasure.[58]

Heaney celebrates here the epiphanic nature of poetic inspiration and attempts to describe the movement beyond the actual. The 'lines / Hard and
thin' are, simultaneously, the sculptural reality and figurative representation; yet these poetic lines can only intimate the nature of poetic inspiration, imploring the reader to accept that 'in that utter visibility / The stone's
alive with what's invisible'. The speaker in Heaney's poetry 'arrests the flux
of phenomena, contemplates the visual field from a vantage-point outside
the mobility of duration, in an eternal moment of disclosed presence'.[59]
Heaney's static gaze attempts to affirm the power of imagination and, like
Wordsworth's invocation of his sister Dorothy as witness in 'Tintern Ab-
bey', the inclusion of his wife lends credence to the experience: 'And the air
we stood up to our eyes in wavered / Like the zig-zag hieroglyph for life
itself'. The text revises an earlier instance of disempowerment, whereby
Heaney stood dumbfounded in front of a stone carving. In 'On the Road'
from *Station Island*, Heaney asserts that

For my book of changes
I would meditate
that stone-faced vigil

until the dumbfounded
spirit broke cover
to raise a dust
in the font of exhaustion.[60]

While the rewards of his zen-like trance[61] are only promissory at this stage,
his concentrated stare in 'Seeing Things' succeeds in translating 'the carved

stone of the water' into 'the zig-zag hieroglyph for life itself'. An equation emerges between the linguistic sign, hieroglyph, and actual carving, suggesting that the word has a living power to take one beyond the actual. Reinvigoration of imaginative power comes about through contemplation of the water sign, part of the actual hieroglyph for life: 'Let rebirth come through water,' he says in 'Squarings xxv', 'I have to cross back through that startled iris'.[62]

What is revealing about the nature of Heaney's gaze is that, as he told me in a personal correspondence (26 February 1996), 'Part II of "Seeing Things" comes from a memory of the carvings on the front of Orvieto Cathedral. We visited there in 1986.' While the first 13 lines intimate that the poet is gazing upon the cathedral façade at the time of writing, the final three lines reveal the event to be a recollection. Yet the juxtaposition of tenses (present simple, present continuous, past simple) suggests that memory helps transform the actual scene. As Catherine Molloy has astutely pointed out, memory in *Seeing Things* does not simply denote recollection; rather, 'the events are transformed from the past even as they capture a moment in time or a remembered thing. By expanding the consciousness of the speaker through discursive emanations and encouraging retrieving and reseeing "things", memory assists the speaker as he uses language to re-view and see "things" from the past as if he is seeing them for the first time.'[63] When the speaker says that 'The stone's alive with what's invisible: Waterweed, stirred sand-grains hurrying off …', the reader is left to puzzle over what time period is being referred to: the past, the present, a replayed or reimagined past?

As is evident from Heaney's meticulous descriptions, the poet's gaze lingers over the physical qualities of *objets d'art*, yet it does not remain preoccupied with the surface minutiae. What attracts the poet is the 'ghost-life' or 'afterlife' that inheres within objects, as if 'a previous time was vestigially alive in them'.[64] The past is not a fixed category for Heaney; instead, it is fluid and accessible. Contrary to the more usual connotation of the past which 'is inscribed upon images that have a definite meaning and implication', what piques Heaney's curiosity is an experiential sensation of the past: 'We read ourselves into a personal past by reading the significant images in our private world. That personal past is not necessarily determined by calendar dates or any clear sense of a time-scale. It is instead a dream-time, a beforehand, a long ago.'[65] Heaney's sense of objects invested with energies (uncertain echoes from the past) bears comparison with Gaston Bachelard's conception of *rêverie*.

> It is on the plane of the daydream and not on that of facts that childhood remains alive and poetically useful within us. Through this permanent childhood, we maintain the poetry of the past. To inhabit oneirically the house we were born in means more than to inhabit it in memory; it means living in this house that is gone, the way we used to dream in it.[66]

Bachelard's phenomenological investigation of inhabited space centres on the effects which household surfaces, shapes and objects have upon the human being; more particularly, it concentrates on a type of *poiesis* (making) whereby the object, memory and imagination all interact. Richard Kearney is correct when he states in his study *Poetics of Imagining* that *rêverie* for Bachelard 'designates imagination as a constant re-creation of reality' whose freedom resides 'at that interstice where being takes leave of itself and launches into becoming'.[67] For Heaney, the experience is an awakening into the reality of the world, one which is far from sentimentality: it happens, he says, 'during the pre-reflective stage of our existence. It has to do with an almost biological need to situate ourselves in our instinctual lives as creatures of the race and of the planet, a need to learn the relationship between what is self and what is not self.'[68]

A more Neo-platonic conception of memory is evident in a recent and impressive poem, 'Here for Good'.[69] Section IV describes Heaney's appreciation of Carolyn Mulholland's 'Chair in Leaf', a sculpture to be found at the junction of Great George's Street and Dame Street in Dublin (a some-time-haven for drug-pushers and late-night drinkers). The opening lines appear literal in their depiction of the sculpture – its straight back does indeed sprout two bronze and twiggy saplings. Yet 'sprouts' and 'twiggy saplings' are not quite accurate: although he qualifies this by saying that they are 'bronze', the organic imagery allows him to state that 'Once out of nature, / They're going to come back in leaf and bloom / And angel step'. Transfiguring a metallic sculpture into leafy bloom, Heaney's description of the imaginative process is not simply elemental but self-consciously abstract in its conception: 'Athenian space, let's call it, less known / Than foreknown, most real when most imagined'. In the revised version, Heaney says 'But for now everything's an ache / Deferred, foreknown, imagined and most real'. Although a similar formulation was used in 'Squarings xlviii', he revises it to emphasise affirmation of (rather than disappointment at) the fleeting nature of the experience: 'That day I'll be in step with what escaped me'.[70] As in 'Seeing Things', the poet's gaze is not simply focused on the artefact, but on an imagined, pre-existent *eidos*.

> I am all foreknowledge.
> Of the poem as a ploughshare that turns time
> Up and over. Of the chair in leaf
> The fairy thorn is entering for the future.
> Of being here for good in every sense.[71]

Heaney explains what is meant by 'foreknowledge' in an essay on the plays of Brian Friel. Memory is described as cathartic, 'that momentary release from confusion which comes from seeing a drama complete itself in accordance with its own inner necessities rather than in accordance with the spectator's wishes'.[72] Once again we have a self-portrait of Heaney as the 'self-enrapturing' Orphic poet.

> [M]emory remains, at any rate, one of the thresholds where the quester for truth undergoes a test. False memory sends the quester into the land of self deception, into the limbo of meaningless invention; but true memory gives access to the dancing place, the point of eternal renewal and confident departure.[73]

The sense of release comes from 'the perception of an order beyond' oneself, which 'nevertheless seems foreknown, as if something forgotten surfaced for a clear moment'.[74]

Whereas Heaney's gaze is usually analogous to that of a painter with his 'eye pealed at the easel',[79] allowing him to scale 'the world at arm's length' giving the 'thumbs up', Paul Muldoon's perspective is not so hopeful. In 'The Sonogram' (*PQ* 21), a picture poem of sorts, we also see a thumb, yet its signification is not so clear-cut. Is Muldoon presenting a political allegory or lyrical effusion for his newly born daughter? The meaning depends on which angle the reader takes. Intimating not only that things differ according to the means and distance from which they are viewed (sonogram or satellite map), the poet also (reasonably) points out the ever-changing flux of experience: the child grows, the country changes (politically, demographically, ecologically). Indeed, in a rather surprising denouement, Muldoon defamiliarises the reader by having the child pass an uncertain judgement 'on the crowd'. Muldoon's picture poems repeatedly foreground these acts of looking and reading by inserting a spectator, a voyeuristic narrator or by implicating the external reader in the process of interpretation. Providing a metacommentary on the work of art, the narrator achieves three objectives: first, experience becomes textualised; secondly, the subjective nature of interpretation undermines our assumptions of objectivity; and thirdly, the identity of place becomes more a matter of culture than of essence.

In contrast to Heaney's mature epiphanies, Muldoon's speakers do not rise above the present moment: his texts refuse closure, circling back on themselves. This is particularly evident in 'Edward Kienholz: *The State Hospital*' (Q 21), a poem which Edna Longley has badly misread. She states that this is a poem about a 'painting', and goes on to say that 'the poem "assumes" details the picture cannot supply'.[80] This account is misleading for two reasons: first, the 'painting' in question is a life-size, three-dimensional, mixed-media installation (first exhibited in 1966); secondly, some of the details which Muldoon is supposed to have imaginatively 'assumed' (the fishbowl, the cartoon bubble) are obvious when looking at the work, and the others (the assumption that an orderly has beaten the patient with a bar of soap and that the bedpan is just out of reach) are documented in Kienholz's blueprint for his creation:

> This is a tableau about an old man who is a patient in a state mental hospital. He is in an arm restraint on a bed in a bare room. (This piece will have to include an actual room consisting of walls, ceiling, barred door, etc.) There will be only a bedpan and a hospital table (just out of reach). The man is naked. He hurts. He has been beaten on the stomach with a bar of soap wrapped in a towel (to hide tell-tale bruises). His head is a lighted fishbowl with water that contains two live black fish, He lies very still on his side. There is no sound in the room.[81]

The first eight lines of Muldoon's poem provide a seemingly objective description of the installation, yet it is highly selective, omitting to provide an account of the exterior (the door, the surrounding white walls and the sign which says *Ward 9*). The second stanza becomes even more subjective: when the narrator states that 'we would never allow ourselves to touch' the head, he is giving a personal response (repulsion) to the figures lying on the bunk beds. The colour of the fish is also speculated upon (black or mauve) and – here Longley would be correct – the narrator conjectures that they are grappling with one bright idea (a pun on the neon-lit cartoon bubble). The crucial moment in the poem, however, is when the narrator addresses to and aligns himself with an implicit spectator or reader:

> Yet the neon-lit, plastic dream-bubble
> he borrowed from a comic strip –
> and which you and I might stretch
> to include Hope, Idaho –
> here takes in only the upper bunk of the bed
> where a naked man, asleep, is strapped.
>   (Q 21)

This is deliberately ambiguous: the narrator seems to wish that the figure's thoughts are in some way linked to 'Hope, Idaho' (the place signifying possibility), but also to the artist (Kienholz created the work when he was based there). The hopelessness of this conclusion, the lack of connection with anyone or anything, is confirmed by Kienholz's description of the installation:

> Above the man in the bed is his exact duplicate, including the bed (the beds will be stacked like bunks). The upper figure will also have the fish bowl head, two black fish, etc. But, additionally, it will be encased in some kind of lucite or plastic bubble (perhaps similar to a cartoon bubble), representing the man's thoughts. His mind can't think for him past the present moment. He is committed there for the rest of his life.[87]

Unlike Heaney's speakers, Muldoon's do not contemplate 'the visual field from a vantage-point outside the mobility of duration, in an eternal moment of disclosed presence';[83] in contrast, their manner of looking manifests what Bryson describes as the 'ungovernable mobility of the glance',[84] problematising the notion of the camera obscura and, consequently, objectivity. The fixity of Muldoon's acts of looking is tempered by multiple points of view and curiously unreliable speakers, an instability that matches contemporary suspicion of 'truth' and 'certainty'. One good example is 'Paul Klee: *They're Biting*' (*MB* 32), a picture-poem whose narrator comments on Klee's work of art. From the start the text is clearly aimed at guiding the reader, describing Paul Klee's picture in precise detail. The qualifying remark ('some kind of') and the use of adjectives ('langorous', 'caricature') present this as a highly subjective reading. When compared to Klee's *They're Biting*, we would also have to question the assumption that the sail-boat is 'an arab dhow' and that the two figures are fishing on a 'lake'. Muldoon plays with our sense of perspective: first, in line 10, he disrupts the seemingly object description with a metacommentary which could apply to his poem, to the narrator's description or to the reader's experience; secondly, by line 11 the reader is aware that Muldoon is playing with our sense of perspective as the description is of a postcard with Klee's picture on it (hence the narrator is not either *in* the picture or in front of it at a gallery).

Three other pieces of text require the reader's attention: the 'I LOVE YOU' message written by the sky-plane, the 'exclamation-mark / at the painting's heart' and the conger mouthing an emphatic 'NO' are read in quick succession by the narrator and hint that the sender of the card has turned him down (a marriage proposal? a declaration of love? a date?); hence he too fell 'hook, line and sinker' for the false hope presented by the sky-writing. If read as a poem about the loss or absence of love, then the attentive reader may notice a possible intertextual reference to Virginia Woolf's *Mrs Dalloway*, in which an aeroplane flies over Regent's Park and writes a message which those on the ground try to interpret.[85] The differing answers given to what is being written echo the narrator's struggle with each different text. Yet Muldoon has played another trick with perspective: the narrator is not necessarily in London at all; what he actually says is that when the card was *sent* the plane was writing the postcard. A political message becomes apparent: the 'NO' is reminiscent of the well-worn Unionist slogan of defiance/intransigence and, if the message of love was sent from London, the conflict of interpretation could indicate the general confusion which prevailed after the Hillsborough Agreement. The poem deliberately refuses the connection promised in line 10, everything remains provisional ('It was as if …').

The first eight lines of the 'Salvador' section of '7, Middagh Street' (*MB* 49–51) mentions three artworks by Salvador Dalí: the infamous *Lobster Telephone* (1936) made for his patron Edward James; *The Enigma of Hitler* (1937); and *Soft Construction with Boiled Beans* (1936). As in his previous picture poems, Muldoon's speaker adopts a neutral tone, describing the artwork's different elements in some detail:

> This lobster's not a lobster but the telephone
> that rang for Neville Chamberlain.
>
> It droops from a bare branch
> above a plate, on which the remains of lunch
>
> include a snapshot of Hitler
> and some boiled beans left over
>
> (*MB* 49)

Yet this depiction of *The Enigma of Hitler* is not merely descriptive. It is crucial to note that the speaker asserts from the beginning that Dalí's painting is not divorced from politics. By alluding to Dalí's own retrospective interpretation, the speaker contextualises the curious telephone image in terms of world politics, namely the Munich Agreement (28 September 1938): 'It constituted a condensed reportage of a series of dreams obviously occasioned by the events in Munich. […] Chamberlain's umbrella appeared in this painting in a sinister aspect, identified with the bat and affected me as extremely anguishing at the very time I was painting it.'[86] The speaker disassociates the painting from Dalí's earlier apolitical work by consciously distinguishing between *The Lobster Telephone*, a surrealist object whose purposelessness discredits 'the ordinary functional objects of the world',[87] and the new image of a decaying telephone with its snapped cord.[88] The speaker further implicates Dalí in Spanish politics by linking *The Enigma of Hitler* with his earlier *Soft Construction with Boiled Beans*. This painting depicts 'a vast human body breaking out into monstrous execrescences of arms and legs tearing at one another in a delirium of auto-strangulation. [...] The soft construction of that great mass of flesh in civil war I embellished with a few boiled beans, for one could not imagine swallowing all that unconscious meat without the presence (however uninspiring) of some mealy and melancholy vegetable.'[89] Although the work was only associated retrospectively by Dalí to the Spanish Civil War, Muldoon takes care to include the poem's subtitle, *The Premonition of Civil War*.[90]

Dalí's *Soft Construction with Boiled Beans* does not, however, treat war naturalistically, nor does it take up a critical position. Rather than siding with the Republican struggle against fascism, he views the war as a biological inevitability and visualises the conflict 'in terms of the warring of basic and instinctual forces'.[91] Similarly, Dalí discounts the political aspects of *The Enigma of Hitler* in favour of personal symbolism: the painting, he says, 'apart from any political intent whatsoever, brought together all the elements of my ecstasy. Breton was outraged. He was unwilling to admit that the master of Nazism was nothing more to me than an object of unconscious delirium, a prodigious self-destructive and cataclysmic force.'[92] Although Dalí's paintings refer to political events, he does not become politcally involved. For him, politics seems 'a cancer on the body poetic'.[93] It is this curious apolitical gaze which Muldoon investigates by having 'Salvador' as a narrator, and it is the major disagreement with André Breton which provides the appropriate setting:

> When Breton
>
> hauled me before his kangaroo-court
> I quoted the Manifesto; we must disregard
>
> moral and aesthetic considerations
> for the integrity of our dream-visions.
>
> What if I dreamed of Hitler as a masochist
> who raises his fist
>
> only to be beaten?
> I might have dreamed of fucking André Breton
>
> he so pooh-poohed my *Enigma of William Tell.*
>   (*MB* 49)

Breton so objected to *The Enigma of William Tell*'s depiction of Lenin as cannibalistic that he convened a meeting of the Surrealists at his studio (42 rue Fontaine). There he demanded that Dalí declare once and for all his Surrealist convictions. Countering each one of Breton's objections, Dalí stated that, for him, 'the dream remained the great vocabulary of Surrealism and delirium the most magnificent means of poetic expression'. Muldoon's poem refers specifically to the manner in which Dalí brought his defence to a close, telling Breton that 'if tonight I dream I am screwing you, tomorrow morning I will paint all of our best fucking positions with the greatest wealth and detail'.[94] Although the passage testifies to Dalí's adherence to Surrealist doctrine, his apolitical stance ran counter to Breton's Marxism. The speaker's reference to Hitler is a case in point. Here Muldoon is alluding to a passage in Dalí's *Unspeakable Confessions* where he describes his utmost admiration for the fascist leader: 'There was no reason for me to stop telling one and all that to me Hitler embodied the perfect image of the great masochist who would unleash a world war solely for the pleasure of losing and burying himself beneath the rubble of an empire: the gratuitous action par excellence that should indeed have warranted the admiration of the Surrealists now that for once we had a truly modern hero!'[95] It is hard to judge whether Muldoon regards this as obscene or simply naive, but redeems Dalí somewhat by having 'Salvador' asks 'Is it that to refer, however obliquely, / is to refer?' (*MB* 50). Although 'Salvador' ends by implying that art is 'an end in itself' (*MB* 51), Muldoon hints that the Catalan painter was not closed off from world politics: 'Which side was I on? / Not one, or both, or none'(*MB* 50).[96]

In 'Madoc – A Mystery' (*MM* 15–261) Muldoon includes an altogether different kind of picture poem: a map. Like many of Willie Doherty's works, he inscribes the coloniser's gaze into his text. Using historical events as a backdrop, Muldoon explores both the assumptions behind and the effects of map-making during the colonial encounter. Whatever its historical veracity, the myth of Prince Madoc was used in the sixteenth century to advance English expansionist policy, most notably by Sir John Dee and Richard Hakluyt.[97] Despite his prior belief in pantisocracy, Robert Southey's version of the story also engages in the promotion of the 'civilising' and 'superior' values of European culture. Madoc's aggression toward those involved in an unchristian religion is described as 'righteous slaughter';[98] power is divinely ordained and manifested in the knowledge, culture and armament of the colonisers. 'Our knowledge is our power', exclaims Madoc, 'and God our strength'.[99] The Welshmen are 'by Heaven / Beloved and favoured more',[100] all of which grants moral justification to 'the conquering arm of Madoc'.[101] Rather than engage in discourses of repression and sub-jugation *per se*, Muldoon's 'Madoc – A Mystery' self-reflexively uses the stratagems by which colonial dominance is inscribed: map-making, heral-dic symbols, place-names and presentational codes.

There are two interlinked instances of map-making in the poem, both of which have latent political implications. The first map was prepared by John Evans, the second by the Lewis and Clark expedition. In '[Smith]', the narrator tells us that Captain Lewis travelled using 'the map drawn up by John Evans / that shows such a vast / unsulliedness the very candle gulps and gutters' (*MM* 124). This rough cartographic representation was drafted during his 1796 expedition and traces the course of the Missouri, plotting a route to the Mandan villages.[102] Evans's overt purpose – the search for the Madogwys, a fabled tribe of Welsh Indians – has to be understood in the context of international politics, namely the battle for supremacy in North America between the four major powers, England, Spain, France and the emerging American nation.[103] Muldoon's poem tells of how Evans 'raised the Spanish ensign / over the Mandan villages' (*MM* 48) on behalf of General Wilkinson who, according to the poem '[Kant],' was '"in the pay of" Spain' (*MM* 125). Rumour, political intrigue and treason turn what is unsullied into 'the slurry-slur' (*MM* 125). The actual search for the Welsh tribe, initi-ated by Iolo Morganwg, was equally politically motivated: as Clair Wills states, Madoc became 'a mainstay of Welsh nationalist arguments for emigration to the new world', a means by which Welsh people could 'claim their demo-cratic heritage free from traditionalist constraints of the British monarchy'.[104]

The use made by Lewis and Clark of Evans's map places the expedition's purpose in context. In fact, one of Jefferson's letters to Lewis states that he should 'inform those through whose country [he] will pass, or whom [he] may meet, that their late fathers the Spaniards have agreed to withdraw all their troops from all their subjects Spanish & French settled there, and all their posts & lands'.[105] The Spanish control established by Evans was now to revert to the Americans. Muldoon does not include in his poem any of the letters between Jefferson and Captain Lewis detailing specific instruc-tions, and the diary entries from the expedition that Muldoon does include all tell of harmless incidents, describe local scenery or talk about searches for food. However, the juxtaposition of two sections (*MM* 121–22) hint that the real significance of the map-making venture was not simply a search for increased knowledge. The description of the 'two Toms, Jefferson and Paine' looking out 'to the illimitabilities of the Louisiana Purchase' (*MM* 121) is loaded with irony. Paine had travelled from France, arriving in Baltimore on 30 October 1802, and was received by Jefferson at Monticello towards the end of the year. That Paine was not received as cordially as expected, owing perhaps both to his unpopularity with Republicans and the untimely nature of his visit (in the midst of the election campaign),[106] is apt since the expansionist aims of the Louisiana Purchase run contrary to the spirit of his egalitarian Jacobinism. In a letter to Senator Breckenbridge (12 August 1803), Jefferson states,

> The inhabited part of Louisiana, from Point Coupeé to the sea, will of course be immediately a territorial government, and soon a State. But above that, the best we can make of the country for some time, will be to give establishments in it to the Indians on the east side of the Mississippi, in exchange for their present country, and open land offices in the last, and thus make this acquisition the means of filling up the eastern side, instead of drawing off its population. When we shall be full on this side, we may lay off a range of States on the western bank from the head to the mouth, and so, range after range, advancing compactly as we multiply.[107]

The aim of building the American nation is achieved in two ways: the appropriation of a greater amount of territory and the enlargement of its commercial concerns. This was, according to Robert Trennert, the precursor to the removal policy and Indian barrier philosophy of the 1820s and 1830s.[108] The fact that the poem which follows, '[Diderot]' (*MM* 122), outlines in brief the preparations for the Lewis and Clark expedition suggests some connection with the Louisiana Purchase. This is confirmed if we look at Jefferson's secret speech to Congress on 18 January 1803, in which he claims that, if successful, the expedition would secure a trade line 'traversing a moderate climate, offering, according to the best accounts, a continued navigation from its source and, possibly, with a single portage from the Western Ocean'.[109] The 'theodolite, quadrant, compass and chain' which are being packed conceal the consequences of the proposed collection of data.

'Unsulliedness' is therefore highly ironic since it conjures up a 'virgin territory', erasing both the indigenous Native American presence and the already-established British control of the Mandan territory. Maps are not objective texts, divorced from politics; rather, they embody the assump-

tions of those who construct them. Erasure was a structural condition for
the imposition of the unificatory desire *E Pluribus Unum*. In his article,
'Inventing America: A Model of Cartographic Semiosis', William Boelhower
also acknowledges the political nature of cartographic discourse and delin-
eates the colonial functions of map-making in the formation of the Euro-
American identity. Boelhower states, crucially, that 'the map preceded the
people and then assumed a normative role in pre-establishing a spatial order for solving the political problem of the one and the many in its territorial and ethnographic forms'.[110] The coloniser's inscription of place-names
and territorial boundaries, therefore, establishes a structural base for socio-
political institutions, thus delegitimising the previous forms of government
and territorial ownership.[111] In this way, the maps themselves legitimate (in
the coloniser's eyes) conquest and empire. The use of three types of maps in
particular – the pictorial map (contact and discovery), the portolan chart (the
activity of colonisation) and the scale map (nation-building) – emphasised
the equation between sight and knowledge.[112] The improvements in survey-
ing, map projections and printing also fostered this scopic regime, engendering a paradigm shift which promoted a visualisation of the land to enable its
conquest, appropriation, subdivision, commodification, and surveillance.[113]
The coloniser's power is manifest, therefore, within the map's graphic nature,
imposing a coordinate geometry and Euclidean syntax upon a territory, erasing the pre-existent Native American boundaries and trap-lines.[114]

The one map printed in 'Madoc' appears, aptly enough, in '[Ptolemy]'
(*MM* 46). As Martin Jay states in his article 'Scopic Regimes of Modernity',
the Ptolemaic grid offers a flat working surface, projecting three dimensions on to two, thereby creating an abstract territory and, far from granting
a perspectival gaze, offers 'a view from nowhere', guaranteeing an omniscient
objectivity.[115] What must be noted, of course, is that the perspective belongs to the settler and not to the Native American. Indeed, as Boelhower
explains at length, inscribed on the map are the differences in perception
between the coloniser and colonised.[116] The scale map in 'Madoc' delin-
eates a border between New York and Pennsylvania, establishing a system of
government alien to the former population. By means of the map, therefore, one can trace 'the West's radical act of removal, the substitution of a
uniform scientific writing in scale for its aboriginal center, the earth'.[117]
Equally new are the place names (Ulster, Athens, New York and Pennsylvania). These have a crucial function since the nomenclature establishes, with

the borders, a structural base for socio-political institutions, all of which
serve to legitimate the newly installed cultural order. This conclusion accords with Harley's findings in 'Rereading the Maps' where he discusses the
ways in which cartographic discourse could be viewed as 'statements of
territorial appropriation, cultural reproduction, or as devices by which a
Native American presence could be silenced'.[118] In terms of nomenclature,
cartography symbolically dispossessed the Native Americans by 'engulfing
them with blank spaces'.[119] Absent from Muldoon's map is any trace of the
former inhabitants, namely the members of the Iroquois Confederacy.[120] It
is important to note that Muldoon begins his poem after these tribes (Sen-
eca, Cayuga, Onondaga, Mohawk, Tuscarora and Oneida) have lost their
lands to the British forces. Hence Coleridge meets Thayendanega [Joseph
Brant] in Canada, not in his former territory near New York.[121] By featuring the map in his poem, Muldoon is not adopting the coloniser's gaze. His
'poetic politics' interrogates the very idea of nationality,[122] showing how it
is often dependent on a colonial gaze and results in violence towards the
native population.[123]

Muldoon's approach to politics in his picture poems is more indirect
than Heaney's. This oblique angle enables his poetry to be, as Ben Howard
states, 'an inclusive but subversive art, where the most sacred cow is both
welcome and subject to demolition'.[124] Such an approach allies him with
Dermot Seymour, a visual artist whose paintings have featured on the cov-
ers of Muldoon's most recent works. Seymour comments on his own art in
a manner that suggests he is as mindful as Muldoon of the conditions of
artistic production:

> I have to find a way of painting that explores rather than just expresses. I haven't any time at
> all for this painterly work, for your big brush-strokes, and your angst-ridden mess. Second
> hand feelings and second hand technique. Now I know I have this painstaking way of putting
> on paint; this has nothing to do with the 'protestant work ethic' and everything to do with
> putting a distance between me and the subject. I have to create a distance before I can see and
> understand. A very meticulous way of painting is a way of objectifying the problem.[125]

It is appropriate, then, that Muldoon's 'Cows' (*AC* 33–35) is dedicated to
Seymour and utilises the techniques of his paintings. The poem centres
around the interpretation of words and symbols, the multiplicity of which
stresses their provisionality.

> Had Hawthorne been a Gael,
> I insist, the scarlet 'A' on Hester Prynne

would have stood for 'Alcohol'.
                    (*AC* 33)

Nathaniel Hawthorne's *The Scarlet Letter* is a novel in which the symbol 'A'
is pinned on to Hester's clothing for sexual transgression (hence the bottle
of *Redbreast*) and subsequently becomes subject to a variety of interpretations by the Puritan community, the Indians, Hester herself and her daughter and illicit lover, all of which change in the course of the narrative. The
narrator of 'Cows', however, does not simply add one more suggestion to
the list (thereby weakening even further the belief in the divine nature of
the sign); his interpretation consciously reinforces an old stereotype, the
drunken Irishman. This has a double purpose: first, Muldoon links this
depiction of the Irish by the British establishment to Hawthorne's exposure
of the power relations behind symbolisation and stereotyping (*the scarlet
woman*), thereby revealing its hidden agenda and demonstrating its inability to foreclose alternative, decolonising interpretations; secondly, the intake of alcohol humorously provides an explanation for the surrealism of
much of the poem.

The narrator similarly pokes fun at a number of sacred cows, namely the
'Devon / cow-coterie' (*AC* 34), 'the metaphysicattle of Japan' (*AC* 34) and
the Irish cattle who trace their ancestry from the time when 'Cuchulainn
tramped Aoife' (*AC* 35). Notions of 'threshold and hearth', 'kith and kine'
are used to unite communities and act as a focus for identity. The narrator,
however, ridicules this essentialist reflex in two ways: first, he undermines
the pretensions to a sacred lineage both through the use of slang ('tramped')
and by invoking an apocryphal account of the birth of Jesus in a manger
(whereby the cattle become symbols for further interpretation); secondly,
reality intrudes in the form of a cattle truck, thus destabilising the cattle's
sense of place and suggesting that, symbol or no symbol, they will be
consumed. The fact that the cattle-trucks may be laden with contraband
goods only heightens the irony: consumerable items do not recognise borders. Muldoon humorously links this idea to the way in which foreign words
are smuggled into the English language.

In the third section, the narrator provides the correct explanation for the
word 'boreen' ('a diminutive form of the Gaelic *bóthar*, "a road"'), as well as
an assertion that this word has entered the English language 'through the
air' / despite the protestations of the *O.E.D*. Muldoon is here commenting
on the translation, transmission, diffusion and reception of language. By

dismissing the *Oxford English Dictionary*'s claim that 'boreen' is 'used only when Irish subjects are referred to', he suggests that purity of race and language are never secure owing to the transmigration and interaction of people. The poem itself is replete with words which have infused into English from outside (cachous, cwms, corries). This point is stressed even further when the narrator proffers several definitions and interpretations of the neologism '*oscaraboscarabinary*': '… a twin, entwined, a tree, a Tuareg; / a double dung-beetle; a plain / and simple hi-firing party; an off-the-back-of-a-lorry drogue?' (*AC* 35). The word is made up of a combination of English, Irish, Italian and Latin words (Oscar, *ab*, arab, scarab, *bosca*, car, *cara*, *carabiniere*, bin, binary), and the definitions provided suggest several others: carabin ('hi-firing party'), abo (possible term of abuse for 'Tuareg') and *crannl arbre* (tree). The poem also refers, however, to another form of interaction between the English and the Irish, one ironically prefigured by the rigorous patrolling of the *Oxford English Dictionary* discussed above: 'Now let us talk of slaughter and the slain, / the helicopter gun-ship, the mighty Kalashnikov: / let's rest for a while in a place where a cow has lain' (*AC* 35).

Kalashnikov, yet another word to have made its way into English from an outside source, signals a menacing exchange. The narrator talks openly about a political meaning behind the poem. The juxtaposition of colonial intrusion and elements of the Irish countryside is the means by which Seymour achieves his aesthetic distance. As one critic reviewing his work states, the Troubles and global pollution appear 'to be the subject of Dermot Seymour's painted landscapes, in which invasion, surveillance, and disaster take place under the baleful stares of domesticated, wild, and exotic animals'.[126] Muldoon self-consciously compares this to his own technique of using oblique literary references ('Enough of Colette and Céline, Céline and Paul Celan'). The fact that the poem ends when he announces his desire to talk openly and in crude form about the political situation which gave rise to the poem/painting suggests that indirection (and commentary on the indirection) is the only feasible approach for art.

A recent picture poem by Muldoon, 'Willem de Kooning: *Clam Diggers*, 1964', begins by following speculation with a statement of fact:

It might be the light over Antwerp, the Antwerp
of Peter Paul Rubens.
Antwerp, Ostende. The light over water and sand
from any of umpteen

dank-dismal skies, any of umpteen dreary-drab
northern European
skies. But this is the light over Long Island Sound,
over Springs, East Hampton ... [127]

We are again in the company of a speaker wishing to control the reader's
view of the picture. The two lively female figures depicted in de Kooning's
Clam Diggers have indeed been compared in the past with Rubens's nudes,[128]
yet the final lines of the first section become progressively speculative and
unsure, viewing the women as 'hoofers' or 'hookers' rather than clam diggers. By describing the painting in terms of a narrative of strip-tease, Muldoon
is reflecting the accepted opinion that the figures are the successors to Picasso's
Demoiselles d'Avignon,[129] yet he concludes in a celebratory tone, depicting
this as a liberation of the female form by which the clam digger truly comes
'into her own / in a flurry of pink and purple puce'. The certainty of tone is,
in its turn, undermined by the two women's multiple identities as well as by
the narrator's admission that 'All's so opaque'. Is Muldoon's speaker a voyeur, objectifying the two women for sexual stimulation? One could argue
that the poem functions as a critique of de Kooning's approach to art: abstract expressionism. As Michael Leja's comprehensive study of the subject explains, it deals in gendered subject positions since the unconscious which the
painter sought to express was thought of in Jungian terms.[130] However, unlike
the certainty in Heaney's picture poems, the reader is unsure whether to read
the poem's conclusion (the removal of 'the body's snare') as ironic or not.

Medbh McGuckian's picture poems share Muldoon's emphasis on refraction, a deliberate interruption of linear reading, a disallowance and frustration of narrative closure. 'Refraction', as Peter Bishop informs us, 'implies a breaking down, a re-fracturing, a fragmenting'; it 'deflects purposive
vision from its desired goal. At the same time it is fragmented to reveal the
colourful display of its constituent parts.'[131] Fracture, in McGuckian's texts,
initiates an investigative and interrogative reflex in the critical reader which
is not just caused by her unconventional syntactical and metaphorical con-
structions. Her narratives are quite simply *dislocated* by (often disguised)
intertextual sources. Like an oil-painting, McGuckian's poems are palimpsests in which 'other surfaces lie concealed beneath the planar display'.[132]
This allows her privately to rewrite or reinterpret the legacy of different
paintings or painters.

It is instructive first to compare an early, uncollected poem by McGuckian
entitled 'Goya'[133] with the poem which it subtly revises, Seamus Heaney's

well-known 'Summer, 1969',[134] in which the poet appears to establish Goya
as an exemplary figure, one who has overcome the dilemma outlined in
Preoccupations. There, the poet states that, with the onslaught of the Troubles,
he 'felt it imperative to discover a field of force in which, without abandon-
ing fidelity to the processes and experience of poetry … it would be possible to encompass the perspectives of a humane reason and at the same
time grant the religious intensity of the violence its deplorable authenticity
and complexity'.[135] Heaney's final two lines, depicting Goya painting 'with
his fists and elbows',[136] encapsulates the commitment of the artist to the
vicissitudes of the socio-political realm, without capitulating to *agitprop* or
propaganda-driven *realpolitik*. However, Heaney's catalogue of Goya's paintings, namely the *Shootings of the Third of May, Saturn Devouring His Children, Duel with Clubs* and *Panic* betray a considerable absence of any historical analysis. The juxtaposition of works ignore or camouflage two essential elements, both of which necessitate a corrective reading: first, all
were created under differing circumstances (for example, while *The Shootings
of the Third of May* was commissioned by the Regency Council in February
1814,[137] *Saturn Devouring His Children* formed part of his 'Black Paintings'
created on the walls of the Quinto del Sordo from 1819–23);[138] secondly,
Heaney appears to endorse the unfounded myth surrounding Goya that he
was an impetuous, impassioned painter eager to reflect the troubles of the
time (a myth dismissed convincingly by Pierre Gassier).[139]

McGuckian's named choice of painting, *Lady with Fan*, could hardly be
more different from Heaney's 'nightmares' and 'Dark cyclones'. So different, indeed, as (wrongly) to tempt one to endorse the myth that McGuckian
is 'merely' a poet of domestic space. All the familiar trappings are in evidence: the house, rooms, silk, darkness and light, the moon. And yet
McGuckian, too, shares with Heaney an unease at her position as poet in a
time of violence: 'Maybe / the trees are more comfortable than any / of us,
obeying their interior sequence / Without a sense of wrong-doing'. One
can see that McGuckian compares reproduction or pregnancy with poetic
creation: the rose room is a womb, the self-fabric suggesting the autobiographical imprint visible in the work of both of them. Unlike Heaney's
narrator, who acts as voyeur in the Prado, McGuckian is more open to
Goya's influence:

> You are the breach
> Through which disorder irrigates me, you're the

Imaginary monument I thought my river
Would preach to deliciously.

This influence is not all one-way. The narrator, in fact, alludes to several of Goya's paintings: rather than naming them, however, she intimates a shared use of imagery. The moon, trees and clouds, for example, appear ominously in Goya's *The Burial of the Sardine*, in which the moon symbolises Death, and little Eros and Psyche appear in his early *Cupid and Eros* painting. Whereas Heaney is drawn towards Goya's darker paintings, McGuckian wishes to bring him 'Into love-play with light'. It is ironic that McGuckian should name the source behind her text, considering her criticism of Eavan Boland's 'From the Painting, *Back from the Market*, by Chardin'.[140] 'The title's naming of the painter', McGuckian claims, 'pays obeisance to his importance. The 'I' is unobtrusive, offered opinion rather than a personal distortion or re-vision.'[141] McGuckian, however, presents an active female gaze, one which seeks to revise (or at least animate) the expressionless *Lady with Fan*.

A poem initiating a full-scale re-vision is 'Road 32, Roof 13–23, Grass 23' (*MC* 42–43). A footnote tells us that '[t]he title derives from the notebooks of the artist Gwen John and signifies the graduated numbers of the spectrum of colours she used' (*MC* 110). It was while at the *Académie Carmen* that John fell under the sway of James McNeill Whistler who taught 'the scientific application of paint and brushes',[142] urging his students to arrange the colours on their palettes in a scientific, orderly fashion. It was through his influence that Gwen John arrived at what her brother Augustus termed 'that methodicity to a point of elaboration undreamt of by her Master'.[143] How she arrived at her system is detailed in a letter to Véra Oumançoff: 'It's a disc with perhaps 85000 numbers. You can turn it and make difficult calculations, the colours and complementary tone of any colour and tone. There are very long lists'.[144] The footnote hints at a hidden narrative: the affinity between Medbh McGuckian and Gwen John, especially through their peculiar use of colour symbolism. I say 'hidden', because the last two lines of the first stanza curiously contain an intertextual reference to John's system: 'The colour of the stem of the wild geranium / And of the little ball holding the snowdrop petals' (*MC* 42). Because the imagery is so unusual and because its deployment instigates a narrative shift in the poem, the reader suspects that the language belongs in another context. In a letter to Ursula Tyrwhitt, John explains that '*Cinabre Clair* was

"the colour of the little ball holding the snowdrop petals," *Rouge Phénicien*
was 'the colour of the stem of the wild geranium'.[145]

The poem becomes clearer once the reader is acquainted with the quotations from Chitty's text which abound in the poem. For instance, the
penultimate verse mentions two texts: the 'letter in her hand' refers both to
Rodin's love letters and to the self-portrait Gwen John did for Rodin picturing the painter pressing a letter to her breast; the letter 'to a woman who
never existed' was to 'Julie', a pet name for Rodin. Similarly, the arrangement of the 'tomato-coloured blooms' in the second stanza refers to the
time at the Slade Academy when she, as a first-year student, 'was banished
downstairs to the Antique Room with a sheet of Ingres paper and a piece of
tomato-coloured chalk to draw the Discobolus and the Venus de Milo for a
year'.[146] The 'picture eased out of her' in which she 'had not wanted her
face' (fourth stanza) is *Lady Reading at a Window*, in which she subsitutes
the face of a Dürer Madonna for her own (she wrote to Ursula Tyrwhitt
explaining that she did not want her own face there). The poem is, in fact,
far more than a narration of the love affair of John and Rodin: it is a palimpsest which, by means of its discursivity, functions as a poetic rewriting of a
particular biography of John, namely Susan Chitty's *Gwen John 1876–1939*.
Except for the first three lines (describing a portrait of John herself) the words
of the text are appropriated from Chitty. Unaware of this, Edna Longley and
Patricia Boyle Haberstroh[147] misread 'Road 32, Roof 13–23, Grass 23':
Longley reads the phrase 'a station of candles' as an allusion to Seamus Heaney;
Haberstroh, though aware of the love affair between Gwen John and the
sculptor Auguste Rodin, is unable to make much sense of the poem:

'Use the other door' – he shut the ever-open
Door behind his doubly-closed face
With the air of a wasted afternoon
Or an occasional gasp that filled
The house, to be scraped off
Afterwards like a point of purple ribbon.
                    (*MC* 42)

The alternating voices of stanza 5 with its rapid shifts of narrative suggest
intertextual reference. Consulting Chitty's biography we find that it is a
conflation of four events in John's life: 'Use the other door' was the command barked by Rodin when he had grown tired of her; his shutting the
door began a cruel period of ostracisation; the 'gasp' which 'filled the house'
refers to Rodin's heavy breathing on his deathbed; and the 'purple ribbon'

was scraped off her painting 'Girl in Profile'. McGuckian's revision occurs when she states that John's 'fear of light began / While his coat still hung over the chair'. In Chitty's account, Gwen John is said to derive comfort from this sight; McGuckian's narrative, in contrast, depicts the debilitating influence of the father/lover figure since, even when dead, John sleeps clutching his letters (a symbol in McGuckian's work for communication with the artists of the past). The images of wood and water, if traced through the poem, suggest a progressive loss of creative ability, culminating in death:

She described her complaint as a 'chill inside' caused by *sitting on her doorstep* to draw a flower. (196) The shed had no door and *the icy rain on her coverlet* woke her in good time, to her satisfaction ... (197)

But sat on her midsummer doorstep Dusted with wood ash like a letter, Or the icy rain, stoked with Fallen boughs, on her coverlet.
(*MC* 43)

Although the concluding stanza refers to the beginning of Gwen John's illness on 3 July 1937 (perhaps abdominal cancer), McGuckian's repeated use of the 'letter' suggests that it was her doomed relationship with Rodin which was the root cause of her untimely demise.

Taking its text from John Elderfield's *The Drawings of Henri Matisse*,[148] 'Drawing Ballerinas'[149] is another poem that reflects upon an artist's life and work; unlike 'Road 32, Roof 13–23, Grass 23', it focuses not on gender politics but on the artist's recourse to aesthetics in a time of violence. That McGuckian intends her poem to be read in relation to both Matisse's artistic *praxis* and the Northern Irish Troubles is confirmed in an article where she states that 'Drawing Ballerinas' sees 'the conflict in terms of the European Holocaust and base[s] itself on Matisse's aesthetic stance which Picasso envied – of continuing to devote himself to the creation of human beauty while his wife agitated against the death-camps'.[150] Like Matisse, McGuckian resolutely upholds the eternal validity and verity of art: 'the pain and outrage continue, and one still feels obliged to draw one's ballerinas against that background'.[151] On one level, the poem exemplifies this principled stance: side-stepping political turmoil, it concerns itself instead with the mechanics of and rationale behind art.

For Matisse, line drawing constituted 'the purest and most direct translation' of his emotion.[152] This response is not to be found in the representation of the model's body but in 'the lines or special values distributed over the whole canvas or paper, which form its complete orchestration, its architecture'.[153] To achieve 'complete orchestration', Matisse emphasised the overriding

importance of visual perception, empathetic analysis and linear simplifica-
tion.[154] Underlying all of this were three basic precepts: 'first, Matisse's virtual
identification of feeling and memory; second, the idea of drawing as the tracing of sensations springing from the model; and third, that this takes place in
a virgin mind emptied of preoccupations'.[155] Selecting key quotations from
Elderfield,[156] McGuckian presents an eloquent metacommentary on Matisse's
theoretical principles of draughtsmanship:

> And the lines' desire is to warp to accommodate
> a body, a lost and emptied memory of a lost
> body, the virgin mind emptied from or of it
> to discover the architecture of pressed-together
> thighs, or lips that half-belong to a face.
> (*DB* 14)

Although one cannot deny that the 'pressed-together thighs' and the 'lips
that half belong to a face' refer to Matisse's *Portrait of Mademoiselle Yvonne
Landsberg* (1914) and *Portrait of Josette Gris* (1915) respectively, the 'lines'
are also McGuckian's poetic lines. Appropriating Matisse's ideas, the stanza
becomes an *ars poetica* espousing not only the importance of remembrance
(as opposed to spontaneity), but also the essential interiority of artistic creation: though the source may be 'accessible to sight', composition relies on
'an image that existed in the artist's mind'.[157] The following stanzas mi-
nutely trace the 'architecture'[158] of one such image:

The figure turns in on itself, becomes an image. (49)
The mutely isolated figure, wrapped in the
womb of sleep, is among Matisse's most haunting   The body turns in, restless, on itself, in
and unsettling images, for all its beauty. (120–21)   a womb of sleep, an image of isolated sleep.
Joining these forms, the branch-like neck and arms –   It turns over, reveals opposing versions of itself,
one broken abruptly at the elbow and wrist, the other   one arm broken abruptly at elbow and wrist,
wrenched downwards by the sheer force of turning   the other wrenched downwards by the force of
and pulling the charcoal back into the body … (63)   the turning

… the movement of a body settling under its own weight. (72)
And yet, Cubism had indeed changed since the time that
Matisse had responded to Picasso's Demoiselles
d'Avignon in certain weighty nudes of 1907. (67)   It settles under its own weight, like some weighty
In one, dated 20 December 1939, the figure   nude. It flattens to the surface on which it lies,
flattens herself to the surface of the table on   a series of fluid, looping rhythms, let loose
which she is resting. (120)   by one last feeling. As if it had obligingly
… a leg so firmly (and unembarrassedly) pulled   arranged its legs, or joined those imprisoning arms.
up toward the head as to create sequences of fluid,
looping rhythms in the centre of the sheet. (119)
Those joined, imprisoning arms we see so often now serve to shade the model's eyes. (88)

In the case of Josette Gris, the oval of the head is a
wire folded in tension by unseen hands ready to
spring back at right angles across the twin
verticals of the neck from which it
has been lifted. (71)
And what he found there renders the 'Cubism'
 which had uncovered it strangely superfluous:
not only a hard, bitter rigidity,
but unnerving sparks of matter that fly around
the nose and the eyes in a miniature storm of emotion. (72)
… those strangely misaligned eyes that keep reappearing in Matisse's portrait drawings. (78)

> The oval of the head is a wire folded
> in tension to spring back at right angles
> across the neck from which it had been lifted.
> And what are those unswerving sparks of matter,
> the astonishingly open, misaligned eyes? (*DB* 14)

Seamlessly juxtaposing phrases from Elderfield, McGuckian presents a composite picture of a model/portrait: stanza 4 takes its corporeal elements from Matisse's *Bonheur de vivre* (1905–6), *The Sleeping Woman* (1940) and *Portrait of Mademoiselle Yvonne Landsberg* (1914); details in stanza 5 come from *Eva Mudocci* (1915), *Young Woman Sleeping in Rumanian Blouse* (1939), *Reclining Nude with Arm behind Head* (1937) and *Reclining Model with Flowered Robe* (c.1923–24); stanza 6 depicts the *Portrait of Josette Gris* (1915). The lines depict a decidedly voyeuristic gaze: the body's actions are described dispassionately (she 'turns in', 'turns over', 'settles', 'flattens to the surface'), the model is given no voice and she is transformed into an artefact ('unnerving sparks of matter', the 'astonishingly open, misaligned eyes'). However, while the speaker's description certainly fragments the body into its constituent parts, her gaze lingering over the model's arm, elbow, wrist, legs, head, neck, and eyes, there is no erotic scopic drive or sexual powerplay involved; rather, the poem foregrounds both the technical virtuosity required for the realisation of an artwork and how the artist reimagines the body 'as a patterned sequence of luminous parts, fabricated from the tonal substance itself'.

According to Matisse, a painter counteracts temporal flux or that 'which constitutes the superficial existence of beings and things' by searching for 'a truer, more essential character, which the artist will seize so that he may give to reality a more lasting interpretation'.[159] His artwork is harmonious and unfragmented and, as his famous manifesto proclaims, what a painter dreams of is 'an art of balance, of purity and serenity, devoid of troubling or depressing subject matter'.[160] In some respects this corresponds to Heaney's gaze, his search for the Platonic *eidos*. Yet the sixth stanza's 'unnerving sparks of matter' and 'misaligned eyes' unsettle this supposed equanimity. Art may not represent troubling social upheavals, but it can refract them or capture their spirit, thereby disturbing the viewer:

Matisse never made again so explicitly a Cubist drawing.
Neither did he make such a disquieting one. (72)
... ranging from transparent, aerated greys to dense
and sooty blacks ... (85)
The design 'bleeds over the whole page' and 'the page
stays light', Matisse said. (104)   That suffer like a camera, and fall asleep
The entirety of the sheets is addressed, whether by   a great deal to subdue the disquieting
invoking them with patterned incident, as in   existence of others – an aerated grey,
the Dahlias, Pomegranates and Palm Trees,   but the page stays light, the paper with ease, at ease,
or by enlarging them with boldly   possesses the entirety of the sheets they occupy.
geometric grids ... (128)   (*DB* 15)
The Reclining Model of c.1919 is one of the more
finished sheets in the group; A Young Girl, with Plumed
Hat, in Profile, of the same date, one of the more quickly drawn studies. They share
an absolute sureness – a sense of having been drawn with ease, at ease ... . (74)

The stanza is extremely difficult to paraphrase: although it contrasts the
'misaligned eyes' that 'suffer like a camera' with the page's 'aerated grey', the
eyes themselves are represented on the page. One can view the lines as pos-
iting distinctions between an artist's possible reactions to social upheaval:
mimetic representation without critical distance (photography); solipsistic
denial of reality (sleep); or painting which has 'a soothing, calming influence on the mind'.[161] The dash in the third line acts as a caesura heralding
a counterpoint, mollifying the growing sense of unease. It is significant that
the lines progress from Matisse's brief experiment with Cubism (*Madame
Matisse*) to the less 'disquieting' *Plumed Hat* series. By the poem's conclusion, the speaker asserts art's organic unity:

... differentiations in the quality of surfaces unified by light. (128)
The Fauve drawings used areas had enriched this method
with broadly drawn lines and spots and scribbles of ink
disposed across open, 'breathing' white grounds. (128)   So that underlaid whiteness is reunified
Whether sent into the water as swimmers or thrown   By light into a breathing white, an undivided
into the air as acrobats, they could finally dance in the Whiteness, a give or take of space
undivided whiteness – that simplest of solutions –   Across or within that same whiteness, that
that Matisse provided for them. (132)   The simplest of solutions, the same whiteness
Showing Aragon one group of the Themes and Variations,   everywhere.
he proudly announced, 'You see, it's the same whiteness
everywhere ... I haven't removed it anywhere ...' (126)

The lines refer to Matisse's *Acrobats* (1952) dancing in 'undivided whiteness' on the walls of the corridor in Matisse's apartment at the Hôtel Le
Régina (Nice). The image expresses, as Elderfield states, 'the ideal of autonomous creativity':[162] the insistence on whiteness, which is 'neither drawing
nor painting, though it partakes of both',[163] means that, like Yeats, we cannot

know the dancer from the dance.

Even though 'Drawing Ballerinas' ventriloquises its sentiments through *The Drawings of Henri Matisse*, McGuckian's picture poems do not advocate a complete avoidance of political subject matter. 'The Dead Are More Alive' (*DB* 12–13), like Heaney's 'Whatever You Say Say Nothing' and 'The Mud Vision', explores the deleterious effects of concentrated media reportage upon a person's consciousness. An inevitable desensitisation and aestheticisation of conflict are what result, or so the poem argues:

> You were shielded against what you saw
> only by never looking away,
> you only broke down what you saw
> by not turning your head,
> as one stares at a map so as never
> to be outside the world.
>
> You seeing did not change you,
> your eyes grew accustomed
> to remaining open, and gathering
> the senselessly scattered things. (*DB* 12)

McGuckian's focus here is neither on paintings nor the lives of painters, but on television pictures. Paradoxically, a willing exposure to media coverage 'shields' one from violent reality. One could argue that the narrative-frames newscasters place around events, even when broadcasting live, allow the viewer to fictionalise what is taking place, thereby maintaining a feeling of at-homeness. Commenting on the poem, McGuckian says that it deals with her son's reaction to news reports of 'the tribal execution of two soldiers who strayed into a funeral procession'.[164] On 19 March 1988, two army corporals were savagely beaten (and later shot) by a mob when they strayed into a West Belfast funeral.[165] 'The events were filmed and relayed almost as they happened', says McGuckian, 'and my second son aged about eight, watched the newsreel as if it had been an American Pulp Fiction. It was the openness to evil of his naked receiving eyes that disturbed me as much as the bloodlust and frenzy of a mob utterly beyond themselves taking animal revenge.'[166]

McGuckian's attention is less on the killings *per se*, and more on how they are perceived. This approach is not unique. Gerald Dawe's 'Mythologies'[167] takes a similar line, tackling 'the instant mythologising' that takes place in Northern Ireland and, in particular, 'the mythologies that lead towards the killing of the two soldiers'.[168] Dawe layers his poem with references to Greek mythology,[169] foregrounding the pernicious role which this type of aggrandisement plays in the Troubles. Although McGuckian's poem shares the graphic intensity of 'Mythologies', it is more oblique and, without her contextualisation, the reader would not interpret it in the light of these particular murders. Nevertheless, it is obvious that the 'senselessly scattered things' refer to violent happenings since, in the second stanza, the speaker talks of how they 'grazed the skin of your mind / with a slashing as if on flesh / by an open blade …'. The speaker contrasts the addressee's reliance on the media to her own strict avoidance of secondary accounts:

> I avoided reading any items
> about them, but I listened to the sounds
> of the day stretching across the city,
> as if everywhere people expected
> bullets to strike again. (*DB* 12–13)

This substitution of looking for listening may well situate her within society. Nevertheless, it is hard not to read it as expressing an attitude of distanced, wise-passiveness. McGuckian is clearly arguing a case for the poet as 'diviner', a conduit for society's collective consciousness – 'The day clashed inside me, till / I felt its blood-filled collapse' – and, like that of Heaney and Muldoon, her gaze upon 'the senselessly scattered things' is thoughtful and measured.

However, discovering the poem's intertext opens up a new, consolatory reading and confirms its status as a 'picture poem'. Taking as its source the second volume of Elias Canetti's autobiography, *The Torch in My Ear*,[170] the opening stanza refers to three different artworks: *The Six Blind Men* and *The Triumph of Death* – both paintings by Breughel – and *The Eternal Countenance*, a book on death masks.

as if these eyes could still open (243)	As if their eyes could still open,
resting from her innocent beauty (241)	were resting from their beauty, still
there is something in them that goes beyond	burning very quietly like candles,
murder (243)	there is something in them that goes beyond
something denied to the eyes (115)	murder, something denied to the eyes,
his large, dark eyes, and he used them for some	the eyes being used for movements
of the movements that were denied his limbs. (341)	denied to the limbs.
	(*DB* 12)

The poem's title refers to Canetti's interpretation of *The Triumph of Death*. On viewing the hundreds of skeletons in amongst the living, he says that 'the dead seem more alive than the living' (115). In contrast to the painting's title, what strikes him is the picture's celebration of life: 'I haven't found anyone *tired* of life in this painting. The dead wrest away from each person something he refuses to surrender voluntarily. The energy of this resistance, in hundreds of variations, flowed into me; and since then, I have often felt as if I were all these people fighting against death' (115). Death is here an occasion for the affirmation of life. Given that the poem was written following the killings on the streets of Belfast in 1988, McGuckian, as in a traditional elegy, brings the dead back to life. The opening line is taken from Canetti's appreciation of *The Eternal Countenance* whereby man is preserved in the face of death: the eyes of the death masks are closed and unchangeable, yet he views them 'as if these eyes could still open, as if nothing irreparable had happened' (243). He sees beyond death – 'there is something in them that goes beyond murder' (243) – and argues that the death masks preserve their subjects' breath: 'Breath is man's most precious possession, most precious of all at the end; and his ultimate breath is preserved in the mask, as an image' (243). The function of art, unlike that of reportage, is not simply to record death, but to bring the victims back to life. The artist, like the fourth figure in Breughel's *The Six Blind Men*, has a more powerful faculty of vision than ordinary mortals and can see 'something denied to the eyes' (115). The second stanza continues this train of thought by asserting that

even if you did not see the fire (249)	Even if you did not see it, nevertheless
grazed the skin of my mind (252)	it grazed the skin of your mind
A slashing as if on flesh (179)	with a slashing as if on flesh
an open knife blade (145)	by an open knife blade, slicing
slicing everything in two (145)	everything in two.
	(*DB* 12)

What 'it' refers to is open to question. It could refer to that 'something' which 'goes beyond murder'. Canetti's biography, however, adds a further referent which echoes McGuckian's immediate point of reference, namely the violent civil unrest on 19 March 1988. Writing about the workers' agitation in Vienna on 15 July 1927, which he witnessed at first hand, Canetti recalls his shock at the burning of the Palace of Justice: 'even if you did not see the fire', he says, 'the sky was red for a great distance …' (249). In a later stanza, McGuckian picks up this narrative thread by citing Canetti's fascination with the reaction of the authorities and the fear that this induced in the crowds:

I avoided reading any newspaper items about them (255) an outspread day, stretching across an entire city (247) as if people expected the bullets to strike here again. (247)	I avoided reading any items about them, but I listened to the sounds of the day, stretching across the city, as if everywhere people expected bullets to strike again. *(DB* 12–13)

The events inspired Canetti's seminal research into the mentality and dynamics of the crowd (*Crowds and Power*), and here McGuckian is linking his findings with the way the mob reacted when the nationalist funeral was interrupted by the arrival of the two undercover army officers. Both Canetti and McGuckian are vigilant, perceptive observers and are undaunted by the awful events. Indeed, the following stanzas reinforce the role of the artist's gaze, citing as they do Canetti's reaction to Grünewald's painting of Christ's crucifixion:

You were shielded against what you saw only by never looking away. You were rescued by *not* turning your head away. (231) by seeing, he *breaks down* what he sees. He looked at the map so as never to be outside the world. (275)	You were shielded against what you saw only by never looking away, you broke down what you saw By not turning your head, as one stares at a map so as never to be outside the world.
the way in which he *sees*, namely in such a way that it doesn't change him. (232) your eyes grew accustomed to remaining open. (299)	Your seeing did not change you, your eyes grew accustomed to remaining open, and gathering the senselessly scattered things. *(DB* 12)

Whereas in real life people turn away from the horror of the violent act, argues Canetti, it can 'still be grasped in the painting' (230). While he was closely studying it in Kolmar, a painter stood in front of it and began copying it. This initiated a complex reaction from Canetti:

> I had to escape the crucifixion, as well as the painting itself [...] I observed him observing me. Is it any surprise that one should notice a real human being in this presence? One needs that person because he is not hanging on the cross. As long as he is busy copying, nothing can happen to him. This was the thought that struck me most. You were shielded against what you saw only by never looking away. You were rescued by *not* turning your head away. It is no cowardly rescue. It is no falsification. But would the copyist be perfection in this salvation? No, for by seeing, he *breaks down* what he sees. He takes refuge in parts, whose connection to the totality is delayed. So long as he paints those parts, they are not part of the totality. They will be part of it once more. But there were times when he absolutely cannot see the totality, since he is absorbed in the detail, which must be accurate. [...] The most unselfconscious thing about him is the way he *sees*, namely in such a way that it doesn't change him. Were it to change him, he could not finish the copy. (231–32)

Neither Canetti nor the artist flee from the horror depicted in the Grünewald. The concentrated, analytical gaze allows both of them a degree of aesthetic detachment, all the better to re-present it accurately. The fact that it 'did not change you' does not, therefore, suggest utter indifference or apathy; rather, it refers to the conditions necessary for the artist to complete his or her work. As with Heaney and Muldoon, therefore, McGuckian's gaze is not voyeuristic, 'mired in attachment'. She will not 'look away' as this would prevent the completion of her work and detract from a keener understanding of the Troubles.

Notes

 1 J. D. McClatchy (ed.), *Poets on Painters: Essays on the Art of Painting by Twentieth-Century Poets* (Berkeley: University of California Press, 1988).
 2 Edna Longley, 'No More Poems about Paintings', in *The Living Stream: Literature and Revisionism in Ireland* (Newcastle upon Tyne: Bloodaxe, 1994) 227–51.
 3 Brian McAvera, review of *Mining the Walls, Creative Camera* 1 (1990) 36.
 4 Declan McGonagle, 'Troubled Land', in *Troubled Land: The Social Landscape of Ireland* (London: Gray Editions, 1987) n.p.
 5 Brian McAvera, 'Marking the North', in *Marking the North: The Work of Victor Sloan* (Dublin: Open Air Press, 1990) 12.
 6 Paul Keen, '"Making Strange": Conversations with the Irish M/Other', *Irish University Review* 26.1 (Spring–Summer, 1996) 83.
 7 See Luke Gibbons, 'L'Art et l'inimaginable: le verbe et l'image dans la culture Irlandaise', in *L'Imaginaire Irlandais* (Paris: Hazan, 1996) 55.
 8 Brian McAvera, *Art, Politics, and Ireland* (Dublin: Open Air Press) 97.
 9 For detailed descriptions and analyses of Victor Sloan's artistic techniques, see James Odling-Smee, 'Victor Sloan', in *Walls* (Derry: Orchard Gallery, 1989) 5–14; McAvera, 'Marking the North' 9–15; Liam Kelly, *Thinking Long: Contemporary Art in the North of Ireland* (Kinsale: Gandon Editions, 1996) 53–55.
10 Brian McAvera, 'Parable Island', *Parable Island* (Liverpool: Blue Coat Gallery, 1991) 14.
11 Brendan Flynn and Lisa Rull, 'Introduction', in *Ceasefire: Reflections of Conflicts by 16 British and Irish Artists* (Wolverhampton: Wolverhampton Art Gallery, 1994) 2.
12 Willie Doherty, *Willie Doherty: Unknown Depths* (Derry: Orchard Gallery, 1990). *Waiting* was included in this exhibition.
13 Jean Fisher, 'Seeing Beyond the Pale: The Photographic Works of Willie Doherty', in Doherty *Unknown Depths* n.p.
14 Dan Cameron, 'Partial View: Transgressive Identity in Willie Doherty's Photographic Installations', in *Willie Doherty* (Dublin: Douglas Hyde Gallery, 1993) n.p.
15 Seamus Heaney, 'Whatever You Say Say Nothing', *North* (London: Faber, 1975) 57.
16 Heaney, *Crediting Poetry* (Meath: Gallery Press, 1995) 27.

17 Heaney, 'Whatever' 57.

18 McAvera, 'The Limitations of Intelligence and Technique', in *Magnetic North: Photoworks by Four Northern Ireland Artists* (Derry: Orchard Gallery, 1987) n.p.

19 Heaney, 'The Mud Vision', *The Haw Lantern* (London: Faber, 1987) 48–49.

20 Richard Long, 'Mud Hand Circles', in *Rosc 4: The Poetry of Vision* (Dublin: Guinness Hop Store, 1984) 36, 96.

21 Kelly, *Thinking Long* 21.

22 Seamus Heaney, 'The Regional Forecast', in R. P. Draper (ed.), *The Literature of Region and Nation*, (London: Macmillan, 1989) 23.

23 Long, 'Mud Hand Circles' 135.

24 Seamus Heaney, interview by Rand Brandes, *Salmagundi* 80 (Fall, 1988) 20.

25 Seamus Heaney, 'The Frontier of Writing', in Jacqueline Genet and Wynne Hellegouarch (eds), *Irish Writers and Their Creative Process*, (Gerrards Cross: Colin Smythe, 1996) 11–12. See also Heaney, 'The Art of Poetry LXXV', interview by Henri Cole, *Paris Review* 144 (Fall, 1997) 118.

26 Heaney, 'Frontier' 10.

27 Heaney, 'Mud Vision' 48.

28 Heaney, 'Mud Vision' 48.

29 Heaney, 'Mud Vision' 49.

30 George Steiner, *Real Presences: Is There Anything in What We Say?* (London: Faber, 1989) 49.

31 Rita Duffy, *Banquet* (Belfast: Ormeau Baths Gallery, 1997). *Banquet*, *Plantation* and *Outpost* were all included in this exhibition.

32 Doherty, *Unknown Depths. Last Hours of Daylight* was included in this exhibition.

33 Doherty in Gibbons, 'L'Art' 57–58.

34 Fisher in Doherty, *Unknown Depths* n.p.

35 *Walls* was included in the Douglas Hyde Gallery exhibition (1993).

36 Cameron, 'Partial View' n.p.

37 Martin Jay, *Downcast Eyes: The Denigration of Vision in Twentieth-Century French Thought* (Berkeley: University of California Press, 1993) 410.

38 Michel Foucault, *Power/Knowledge*, ed. Colin Gordon, trans. Gordon et al. (Brighton: Harvester Press, 1980) 148.

39 Ciaran Carson, 'Intelligence', in *Belfast Confetti* (Meath: Gallery Press, 1989) 79.

40 Seamus Heaney, 'Triptych', *Field Work* (London: Faber, 1979) 12.

41 Seamus Heaney, 'Sandstone Keepsake', *Station Island* (London: Faber, 1984) 20.

42 Seamus Heaney, 'From the Frontier of Writing', *The Haw Lantern* 6.

43 Heaney, 'From the Frontier of Writing', 6.

44 Heaney, 'From the Frontier of Writing' 6.

45 Seamus Heaney, 'The Toome Road', *Field Work* 15.

46 Patricia Coughlan, '"Bog Queens": The Representation of Women in the Poetry of John Montague and Seamus Heaney', in Toni O'Brien Johnson and David Cairns (eds), *Gender and Irish Writing* (Milton Keynes: Open University Press, 1991) 90.

47 Coughlan, 'Bog Queens' 103.

48 Seamus Heaney, 'Punishment', *North* 37–38.

49 Coughlan, 'Bog Queens' 103.

50 Laura Mulvey, 'Visual Pleasure and Narrative Cinema', *Screen* 16.1 (Autumn, 1975): 6–18.
51 Coughlan, 'Bog Queens' 99.
52 Heaney, 'The Grauballe Man', *North* 35–36.
53 Heaney, 'The Grauballe Man', *North* 36.
54 Michael R. Molino, *Questioning Tradition, Language, and Myth: The Poetry of Seamus Heaney* (Washington: Catholic University of America Press, 1994) 87.
55 Helen Vendler, John Kerrigan and Neil Corcoran on Seamus Heaney's *North*, *Centurions*, Radio 3, 1 February 1998.
56 Gaston Bachelard, *The Poetics of Space*, trans. Maria Jolas, repr. (Boston: Beacon Press, 1994) 33.
57 Heaney, 'Seeing Things', *Seeing Things* (London: Faber, 1991) 16–18.
58 James Joyce, *A Portrait of the Artist as a Young Man* (London: Penguin, 1960) 212–13.
59 Norman Bryson, *Vision and Painting: The Logic of the Gaze* (London: Macmillan, 1983) 94.
60 Heaney, 'On the Road', *Station Island* 121.
61 'Book of changes' is a direct translation of *I-Ching*.
62 Seamus Heaney, 'Squarings xxv', *Seeing Things* 83.
63 Catherine Molloy, 'Seamus Heaney's *Seeing Things*: "Retracing the Path Back"', in Catherine Molloy and Phyllis Carey (eds), *Seamus Heaney: The Shaping Spirit* (Newark: University of Delaware Press, 1996) 157–58.
64 See Heaney, 'The Sense of the Past', *History Ireland* 1.4 (Winter, 1993) 34.
65 Heaney, 'Sense' 34.
66 Bachelard, *The Poetics of Space* 16.
67 Richard Kearney, *Poetics of Imagining: From Husserl to Lyotard* (London: Harper Collins Academic, 1991) 93.
68 Heaney, 'Sense' 34.
69 Seamus Heaney, 'Here for Good', *Times Literary Supplement* 22 January 1993 and in *The Spirit Level* as 'Poet's Chair' 46–47. The re-worked version is significantly different and so I will refer to them both.
70 Seamus Heaney, 'Squarings xlviii', *Seeing Things* 108.
71 Seamus Heaney, 'Chair in Leaf', *The Spirit Level* 47.
72 Heaney, 'For Liberation: Brian Friel and the Use of Memory', in Alan Peacock (ed.), *The Achievement of Brian Friel* (Gerrards Cross: Colin Smythe, 1993) 229.
73 Heaney, 'For Liberation' 240.
74 Heaney, 'For Liberation' 229.
75 Frances A. Yates, *The Art of Memory* (London: Routledge and Kegan Paul, 1966).
76 Heaney, 'Five Derry Glosses', *32 Counties: Photographs of Ireland by Donovan Wylie with New Writing by Thirty-Two Irish Writers* (London: Secker and Warburg, n.d.) 71.
77 Yates, *The Art of Memory* 157–58. That Heaney is referring to Camillo is confirmed by the poem's theatrical images.
78 Seamus Heaney, 'Squarings xix', *Seeing Things* 75.
79 Seamus Heaney, 'Squarings xi', *Seeing Things* 65.
80 Longley, 'No More Poems' 240–41.
81 Kienholz in David Scott, *Edward Kienholz: Tableaux 1961–1979* (Dublin: Douglas Hyde Gallery, 1981) 27.

82 Kienholz in Scott, *Edward Kienholz* 27.

83 Bryson, *Vision and Painting* 94.

84 Bryson, *Vision and Painting* 121.

85 Virginia Woolf, *Mrs Dalloway*, repr. (London: Faber, 1989) 20–30.

86 Salvador Dalí, *The Secret Life of Salvador Dalí*, trans. Haakon M. Chevalier (London: Vision, 1968) 371.

87 Dawn Ades, *Salvador Dalí* (London: Thames and Hudson, 1995) 161.

88 Ian Gibson, *The Shameful Life of Salvador Dalí* (London: Faber, 1997) 384.

89 Dalí, *The Secret Life* 357.

90 See Gibson, *The Shameful Life* 359.

91 Ades, *Salvador Dali* 113.

92 Salvador Dalí, *The Unspeakable Confessions of Salvador Dalí: As Told to André Parinuad*, trans. Harold J. Salemson (London: W. H. Allen, 1976) 125.

93 Dalí, *The Unspeakable Confessions* 117.

94 Dalí, *The Unspeakable Confessions* 126.

95 Dalí, *The Unspeakable Confessions* 125.

96 Muldoon is referring to a passage in Dalí's *Secret Life* when he hired an anarchist chauffeur to get him safely out of the country. The driver carried two flags: "'This I will put on the car to get there [France]," and, pulling a Spanish flag out of the other [pocket], he added, "and this will get me back in case they lose their revolution …'" (356).

97 See Clair Wills, *Improprieties: Politics and Sexuality in Northern Irish Poetry* (Oxford: Clarendon Press, 1993) 219 and Tim Kendall, "'Parallel to the Parallel Realm": Paul Muldoon's *Madoc – A Mystery'*, *Irish University Review* 25.2 (Autumn–Winter, 1995) 233. Both take their information from Gwyn A. Williams, *Madoc: The Making of a Myth* (London: Eyre Methuen, 1979) 67. See also Muldoon, interview by Lynn Keller 17.

98 Robert Southey, *Madoc*, first pub. 1805 (London: Henry Zizetelly, 1853) 230.

99 Southey, *Madoc* 49.

100 Southey, *Madoc* 43.

101 Southey, *Madoc* 165.

102 See Richard Deacon, *Madoc and the Discovery of America: Some Light on an Old Controversy* (London: Frederick Muller, 1967) 145.

103 Wills, *Improprieties* 219.

104 Wills, *Improprieties* 219.

105 Thomas Jefferson, *Letters of the Lewis and Clark Expedition and Related Documents 1783–1854*, ed. Donald Jackson, 2nd edn (Urbana: University of Illinois Press, 1978) 165–66.

106 See both Dumas Malone, *Jefferson the President: First Term, 1801–1805*, Vol. 4 (Boston: Little Brown, 1970) 197–98 and John Chester Miller, *The Wolf by the Ears: Thomas Jefferson and Slavery* (New York: The Free Press, 1977) 361.

107 Jefferson in Henry S. Randall, *The Life of Thomas Jefferson*, Vol. 3 (New York: Derby and Jackson, 1858) 69–70.

108 Robert A. Trennert, Jr., *Alternative to Extinction: Federal Indian Policy and the Beginnings of the Reservation System, 1846–51* (Philadelphia: Temple University Press, 1975) 1–3.

109 Jefferson in Richard Dillon, *Meriwether Lewis: A Biography* (New York: Coward-McCann, 1965) 30.

110 William Boelhower, 'Inventing America: A Model of Cartographic Semiosis', *Word and Image* 4.2 (April–June, 1988) 478–79.

111 See J. B. Harley, 'Rereading the Maps of the Columbian Encounter', *Annals of the Association of American Geographers* 82.3 (1993) 522–23.

112 Boelhower, 'Inventing' 480–83.

113 Harley, 'Rereading' 523–24.

114 Harley, 'Maps, Knowledge and Power', in Denis Cosgrove and Stephen Daniels (eds), *The Iconography of Landscape: Essays on the Symbolic Representation, Design and Use of Past Environments* (Cambridge: Cambridge University Press, 1988) 282. For a distinction in the way Native Americans outlined their boundaries and organised their hunting see Hugh Brody, *Maps and Dreams: Indians and the British Columbia Frontier*, first pub. 1981 (London: Faber, 1986) 37. For a detailed analysis of how cartographic representation enacts systematic erasures, see Simon Ryan, *The Cartographic Eye: How Explorers Saw Australia* (Cambridge: Cambridge University Press, 1996) 123.

115 Martin Jay, 'Scopic Regimes of Modernity', in Hal Foster (ed.), *Vision and Visuality* (Seattle: Bay Press, 1988) 13–15.

116 William Boelhower, *Through a Glass Darkly: Ethnic Semiosis in American Literature* (New York: Oxford University Press, 1987) 38.

117 Boelhower, *Through a Glass Darkly* 47.

118 Harley, 'Rereading' 522.

119 Harley, 'Rereading' 531.

120 Jacqueline McCurry, '"S'Crap": Colonialism Indicted in the Poetry of Paul Muldoon', *Éire-Ireland* 27.3 (Autumn, 1992) 101.

121 Albert Britt, *Great Indian Chiefs: A Survey of Indian Leaders in the Two Hundred Year Struggle to Stop the White Advance* (New York: McGraw-Hill, 1938) 84–86.

122 Jacqueline McCurry, 'A Land "Not 'Borrowed' but 'Purloined'": Paul Muldoon's Indians', *New Hibernia Review* 1.3 (Autumn, 1997) 41.

123 See Paul Muldoon, 'Sir Walter', *Out of the Blue* (Belfast: Ulsterman Publications, 1973) 7, 'The Year of the Sloes, for Ishi', (*NSP* 15–18) and 'Promises, Promises' (*WBL* 24). See also Muldoon, interview by Dominique Gauthier, *Études irlandaises* 22.1 (Spring, 1997) 53–63.

124 Ben Howard, 'Histories and Selves', *Poetry* (November, 1994) 101.

125 Dermot Seymour, 'On the Bewilderment and Absurdity of Things: Extracts from a Conversation with Dermot Seymour', *Circa* 26 (January–February, 1986) 13.

126 Jean Fisher, Review of Dermot Seymour's exhibition at the Paula Allen Gallery, *Artforum* (June, 1982): 142.

127 Paul Muldoon, 'Willem de Kooning: *Clam Diggers*, 1964', *Artforum* (November, 1995) 72.

128 See Carter Ratcliff, 'New World Order', *Artforum* (November, 1994): 78; Diane Waldman *Willem de Kooning* (London: Thames and Hudson, 1988) 117.

129 See Donald Kuspit, 'Body of Evidence: Old School Master', *Artforum* (November, 1994) 76–77; David Anfam, *Abstract Expressionism* (London: Thames and Hudson, 1990) calls them 'light floozies' (180).

130 Michael Leja, *Reframing Abstract Expressionism: Subjectivity and Painting in the 1940s* (New Haven, CT: Yale University Press, 1993) 101.

131 Peter Bishop, *An Archetypal Constable: National Identity and the Geography of Nostalgia*

(London: Athlone, 1995) 107.

132 Bryson, *Vision and Painting* 92.

133 Medbh McGuckian, 'Goya', *Outposts* 136 (Spring, 1983) 17.

134 Seamus Heaney, 'Summer, 1969', *North* 69–70.

135 Seamus Heaney, *Preoccupations: Selected Prose 1968–1978* (London: Faber, 1980) 56–57.

136 Heaney, 'Summer, 1969' 70.

137 See Pierre Gassier et al., *Goya: Life and Work*, repr. (Cologne: Evergreen, 1994) 111–12.

138 See Gassier, *Goya* 315.

139 See Gassier, *Goya* 210.

140 Eavan Boland, 'From the Painting, *Back for the Market*, by Chardin', *Collected Poems* (Manchester: Carcanet Press, 1995) 3–4.

141 Medbh McGuckian, 'Birds and Their Masters', *Irish University Review* 23.1 (Spring–Summer, 1993) 31.

142 E. R. Pennell and J. Pennell, *The Life of James McNeill Whistler*, 5th edn (London: William Heinemann, 1911) 377.

143 Augustus John quoted in Cecily Langdale, *Gwen John* (New Haven, CT: Yale University Press, 1987) 21.

144 Gwen John quoted in Ceridwen Lloyd-Morgan, *Gwen John: Papers at the National Library of Wales* (Aberstwyth: The National Library of Wales, 1988) 33.

145 Gwen John quoted in Susan Chitty, *Gwen John 1876–1939* (London: Hodder and Stoughton, 1981) 194–95.

146 Chitty, *Gwen John* 36.

147 See Longley, *Living Stream* 247 and Patricia Boyle Haberstroh, *Women Creating Women: Contemporary Irish Women Poets* (Syracuse, New York: Syracuse University Press, 1996) 155–56.

148 John Elderfield, *The Drawings of Henri Matisse* (London: Thames and Hudson, 1984).

149 Medbh McGuckian, 'Drawing Ballerinas', in Todd Swift and Martin Moorey (eds), *Map-Maker's Colours: New Poets of Northern Ireland* (Montreal: Nu-Age Editions, 1988) 26–27. The poem was subsequently collected in *Drawing Ballerinas* (14–16).

150 Medbh McGuckian, 'Drawing Ballerinas: How Being Irish Has Influenced Me as a Writer', in Lizz Murphy (ed.), *Wee Girls: Women Writing from an Irish Perspective* (Melbourne: Spinifex, 1996) 200.

151 McGuckian, 'How Being Irish' 201.

152 Jack Flam, *Matisse and His Art* (Oxford: Phaidon, 1978) 81.

153 Flam, *Matisse* 82.

154 Elderfield, *Drawings of Henri Matisse* 24–25.

155 Elderfield, *Drawings of Henri Matisse* 27.

156 See Elderfield, *Drawings of Henri Matisse* 25, 27, 63 and 71.

157 Elderfield, *Drawings of Henri Matisse* 28.

158 Elderfield, *Drawings of Henri Matisse* 63.

159 Flam, *Matisse* 37.

160 Flam, *Matisse* 38.

161 Flam, *Matisse* 38.

162 Elderfield, *Drawings of Henri Matisse* 133.

163 Elderfield, *Drawings of Henri Matisse* 132.
164 McGuckian, 'How Being Irish', 200.
165 Tensions were at an all-time high in Belfast as, three days previously, Michael Stone, a member of the UDA, had killed three people attending a funeral at the Milltown Cemetery. The latest funeral was for one of his victims.
166 McGuckian, 'How Being Irish' 200.
167 Gerald Dawe, 'Mythologies', *Heart of Hearts* (Meath: Gallery Press, 1995) 34.
168 Personal interview with Gerald Dawe, 13 August 1995, Trinity College, Dublin.
169 For example, in the first section of the poem, 'Medusa', Michael Stone, the poem's speaker, generates his own myth, stating that 'hatred snaked through my hair' (34).
170 Elias Canetti, *The Torch in My Ear*, trans. Joachim Neugroschel (London: Granta, 1982). Quotations from Canetti are placed to the left of those from McGuckian's text.

6

'Roaming root of multiple meanings': Irish Language and Identity

When it comes to discussing 'Irish identity', critics are inclined to develop an acute sense of place, most notably an indeterminate space tentatively tucked in between inverted commas; indeed, the more seasoned hack will sigh in resignation at having to go and encounter for the millionth time the reality of 'that will-o'-the-wisp which has caused the shedding of so much innocent ink'.[1] One influential writer, Peter McDonald, has recently objected to the intellectually stultifying manner in which identity politics is discussed within Irish studies. However, in his justifiable eagerness to expose the hidden agendas behind the systematic erection of constrictive canonical frames around Louis MacNeice, McDonald is certainly rash in his description of 'Irishness' as being a 'menacing, but ultimately empty, phantom of national "identity"';[2] and although *Misidentities*,[3] his later eloquent disquisition upon the subject, convincingly outlines the political impracticalities of using such an abstract concept to overcome sectarian divisiveness in Northern Ireland, it is impossible to disagree with the counter-assertion that even though 'Irishness' is admittedly an unstable category,[4] often defining itself in opposition to the former colonising power,[5] nevertheless it is an 'anthropological acne' that breaks out no matter what poultice is applied.[6] At the heart of the continuing malaise has been the relegation of Irish to the status of a minority language; in the words of Nuala Ní Dhomhnaill, 'our self-absorbed Irish complex about "Irishness" – so tedious! – would be far less strong if we used our own national language like the Danes, or like Israel, which really did manage to impose Hebrew'.[7] In what follows, I shall explore how Paul Muldoon and Medbh McGuckian cope with the contentious issue of Irishness, and how they use intertextuality to stave off what Thomas Kinsella has diagnosed as the alienated condition of Irish writers – the 'divided mind' – due to the disjunction between English and Irish cultural traditions.[8] As in previous chapters, I shall contrast their indirect strategies with Seamus Heaney's more forthright approach to the politically sensitive issue of composing in the English language.

J. J. Lee has said:

> It may be that there is an Irish emotional reality which is silenced in English. It may be too that many Irish no longer experience that emotional reality, that it has been parched out of them, that a particular stream of Irish consciousness has dried up with the decay of the language.[9]

Although Lee's pronouncement about the Irish language's 'emotional reality' is suppositional, he is thoroughly convinced that 'only the husk of identity is left without the language',[10] a sentiment reiterated by many eminent commentators. Desmond Fennell, for example, claims that without Irish one is left with 'a maimed community'.[11] With equal forcefulness, Thomas Kinsella contests that the effects of losing Irish are all too apparent, 'reducing energies of every kind, undermining individual confidence, lessening the quality of thought'.[12] Perhaps the most eloquent testimony has come from a distinguished contemporary poet writing in Irish, Máire Mhac an tSaoi:

> An old and dear scholar-friend, the late David Greene, endowed with a clearer mind than mine, explained his commitment to the cause of the Irish language like this: 'I came … to accept the reality of an Irish nation … I accepted that this entailed my learning the Irish language so as to take part in the reconstruction of the historic nation, and I took it that this was the duty of every decent citizen'. We can take it, I think, that he speaks for all of us who, against the tide of history, write in Irish, not only because of the magnificent resources of the language, but because we seek to preserve the essential habitat of our country's soul. I do not think the Irish identity would long survive the death of Irish … [13]

To a non-Irish speaker from Cork, with only school training in the language, this essentialism – 'the reality of Ireland', 'the essential habitat of our country's soul' – borders on the offensive and smacks of an outdated Irish Irelandism. Although the advent of *TnaG/T4*, *Foinse* and the increasing prevalence of *gaelscoileanna*[14] are all welcome measures to instil pride in both the national language and culture, those of us who mumble our *cúpla focail* with ever-decreasing proficiency are none the less Irish for that. I tend towards the opposite extreme espoused by Kevin O'Connor who with a severity ill-concealed by humour, says, '[w]e don't want an imposed language at the price of being stopped in O'Connell Street by jackbooted gaelgeóirí and asked to spout Irish at the point of a gun'.[15] Though obviously far-fetched, O'Connor's graphic depiction of linguistic fascism is

pertinent when one considers the degree to which linguistic disinheritance
has become politicised in Northern Ireland.

In her award-winning study *In Search of a State: Catholics in Northern
Ireland*, Fionnuala O'Connor records one young woman's response as to
what, for her, constitutes 'Irishness': 'She listed a love of Irish-speaking
Donegal, Catholicism … and the Irish language. But there had to be "a tie
between the language and the fight here, if you like – not to be treated as
second-class citizens"'.[16] This link between citizenship and language is not
out of the ordinary. After a heated session on 6 January 1998, Belfast City
Council finally recognised the totemic importance of Irish to the nationalist community and agreed to establish a special committee to investigate
how the language could be promoted. The political significance of the language issue can be gauged by the opposition which the measure received,
with one petulant DUP councillor remarking that the decision 'perpetuates
the myth that the Irish language is something of significance in this city, the
myth that people are clamouring to speak Irish. There are more Chinese
speakers in this city.'[17]

As an Irish Catholic writer composing in English, Seamus Heaney would
baulk at such an out-of-hand dismissal of the importance of Irish. In a
menacing throwback to the wily Greeks of 'Whatever You Say, Say Nothing',[18] the poet refers to himself as 'a cultural Trojan horse in the British
citadel'.[19] This unease about English culture can also be seen in comments
made to Caroline Walsh: 'the timbre of the culture is British; Ulster is British, so that the Catholic minority has always conceived of itself as a resistance movement; you affiliated to Ireland as opposed to the notion of Britain'.[20] However, despite his awareness that he is writing in a language with
an imperial legacy, Heaney does not advocate linguistic separatism; instead,
he recognises that the language which he speaks, Hiberno-English, does not
in any way militate against his national identity. In a recent article discussing his translation of *Beowulf*, Heaney declares that we now recognise English 'as a confabulation of Englishes, and in current post-colonial conditions, in a devolving Britain, in an evolving Europe, the more people
realise that their language and their culture are historically amassed pos-
sessions the better'.[21] Focusing upon a plurality of dialects with their own
variations of English, Heaney asserts his own language's national distinc-
tiveness. As his remarks to Harriet Cooke in 1974 make clear, this is not
a new strategy:

In Ireland at the moment I would see the necessity, since I'm involved in the tradition of the English lyric, to take the English lyric and make it eat stuff that it has never eaten before ... like all the messy and, it would seem incomprehensible obsessions in the North and make it still an English lyric. Several people would call that very subversive; in the end, unless Ireland can forge some sense of community, the whole thing's always going to be confused, and I think the writers here have some sort of role here. I think there has to be some act of comprehension and synthesis.[22]

Heaney's early language poems seek this 'comprehension and synthesis' and not, as some myopic critics have asserted, a regression to a mythical past. Discussing 'Anahorish',[23] John Kerrigan cannot see beyond the Celtic mist. Describing the poem as 'a high Romantic urge to empty the scene for sublimity and to authenticate the at-homeness of the speaker by grounding his locale in language', he accuses the poet of ignoring the contingency of sociopolitical networks which inform place-names:

> Yet the poem makes the expressiveness of its vocables subject to the claim that they elaborate a topography enshrined in the name itself in order to suggest that, through the undermusic of *anach fhíor uisce*, we hear a *genius loci* overlaid by colonization. This is to discount what Tim Robinson has brought out in his work on Gaelic place names – that they are contingent, workaday, sometimes obscure, and misunderstood by Irish speakers.[24]

Kerrigan misinterprets the intentions behind Heaney's opening line – 'My "place of clear water"' – contending that its possessiveness is 'elemental and originary' in the sense that it reaches back into 'the Celtic past';[25] rather than grounding the poet in a Heideggerian sense, the place-name actually 'lead[s] past the literary mists of a Celtic twilight into that civilization whose demise was effected by soldiers and administrators'.[26] Heaney intends to uncover the past and signal its colonial history, not simply remain a 'mound-dweller'. After all, he does not reintroduce the 'original' place-name but keeps the English 'Anahorish' with its 'soft gradient / of consonant, vowel-meadow'. As Blake Morrison rightly points out, Heaney's preoccupation with place-names does not constitute a mythological etymology, but 'is a more political etymology' uncovering 'a history of linguistic and territorial dispossession'.[27] Kerrigan also misreads Robinson, contrasting his conclusions with Heaney's reading of landscape. In fact, Robinson's discussion complements 'Anahorish', arguing that place-names are 'the interlock of landscape and language', that they 'make a condensed or elliptic remark about the place, a description, a claim of ownership, a historical anecdote, even a joke or curse on it'.[28] Place-names are, in other words, repositories of history. When Robinson concludes that 'we, personally, cumulatively, communally, create and recreate landscapes – a landscape being not just the terrain but also the human perspectives on it, the land plus its overburden of meanings',[29] he does not dismiss the search for the place-name's history; the intention behind recollection is not to repossess the place's origin, but to understand its past.

Heaney's most evocative account of linguistic colonisation is 'Ocean's Love to Ireland',[30] a poem centred around selected intertextual references:

> Speaking broad Devonshire,
> Ralegh has backed the maid to a tree
> As Ireland is backed to England
>
> And drives inland
> Till all her strands are breathless:
> 'Sweesir, Swatter! Sweesir, Swatter!'[31]

As others have shown, the lines refer to a passage from John Aubrey's *Brief Lives* describing Sir Walter's violent sexual union with his 'first Lady'.[32] That the implied analogy is the colonisation of Ireland is confirmed by a quotation in the poem's second section from Lord Grey's account of the infamous Smerwick massacre (1580).[33] Although Heaney's conflation of woman with landscape – 'The Ground possessed and repossessed'[34] – falls back upon a reprehensibly gendered stereotype,[35] having 'the ruined maid' complain 'in Irish'[36] signals his anger at the enforced decline of Irish language usage ever since the sixteenth century.

The unmistakable rancour shown towards the 'Iambic drums / Of English'[37] dissipates in later collections as he embraces the co-existence of an English language with an Irish undermusic in what can loosely be termed Hiberno-English: 'The British dimension, in other words, while it is something that will be resisted by the minority if it is felt to be coercive, has nevertheless been a given of our history and even of our geography, one of the places where we all live, willy-nilly. It's in the language.'[38] This ability to reconcile a sense of Irishness with a language which is a product of Ireland's colonial history[39] has much to do with the influence of James Joyce, whom he adopts as an exemplar. In 'John Bull's Other Island', Heaney nominates Joyce as both 'a mediator and adjudicator': he has 'one ear cocked to a living speech, and the other tuned to a literary style; and his choice of words, his act of writing is, among other things, an act of reconciliation between these'.[40] Section XII of 'Station Island'[41] features a 'tall man' with a 'fish-cold and bony' hand who welcomes Heaney off the boat from Lough Derg. This figure is Heaney's 'familiar compound ghost / Both intimate and identifi-able'.[42] Whereas T. S. Eliot's 'dead master / Whom I had known, forgotten, half recalled'[43] was Yeats, Heaney chooses Joyce as his tutelary presence.[44]

The final version of the poem contains the lines 'The English language / belongs to us. You are raking at dead fires'.[45] An earlier version of the poem expands on the reference to the 'dead fires', making it more obvious that he is referring to Stephen Dedalus's diary entry for 13 April in *Portrait of the Artist as a Young Man*:

> Old Father, mother's son,
> there is a moment in Stephen's diary
> for April the thirteenth, a revelation
>
> set among my stars – that one entry
> has been a sort of password in my ears,
> the collect of a new epiphany,
>
> the Feast of the Holy Tundish.[46]

Heaney refers to Stephen's diary entry in four articles,[47] focusing specifi-cally on the emblematic significance of the 'tundish'. The Dean's language, English, 'so familiar and so foreign', will always be 'an acquired speech'[48] for Stephen, or so he thought. The 'tundish' initially signifies his exclusion from the English tradition, but later it acquires a new, and liberating sig-nificance: 'Damn the Dean of Studies and his funnel! What did he come here for to teach us his own language or to learn it from us. Damn him one way or the other!'[49] Stephen Dedalus, 'the young Dublin writer and intel-lectual, hypersensitive to the energies and implications of words and ac-cents', recognises that his own mastery of the English language validates his use of language, and he goes on the offensive.[50] However, Elmer Andrews correctly states that the 'deliberate over-writing ... [and] pompous, high-flown rhetoric' of this section 'betrays the speaker's histrionics'.[51] Heaney's supposed identification with Stephen seems almost fanciful.[52] It is impor-tant to note, therefore, that Heaney did not include this part of the poem in his revised version; instead, he indicates an identification with Joyce the father: 'That subject people stuff is a cod's game, / infantile, like this peas-ant pilgrimage'.[53]

Of particular importance to Heaney is Stephen's diary entry for 14 April:

> I like to think of Stephen Dedalus's diary entry for 14 April as emblematic. At the end of *A Portrait of the Artist as a Young Man*, Stephen is preparing to fly in disdain from Ireland, to get out from under the nets of nationality, family and religion. He will express himself by fleeing

his origins, just as others, like John Alphonsus Mulrennan, who is mentioned in the diary entry, seek to find themselves by finding origins.[54]

Stephen Dedalus's diary entry for 14 April recounts John Mulrennan's encounter with an old man: 'I fear him. I fear his red-rimmed horny eyes. It is with him I must struggle all through this night till day come, till he or I lie dead, gripping him by the sinewy throat till ... Till what? Till he yield to me? No, I mean him no harm.'[55] The old man represents a Yeatsian reaction to the fracture in Ireland's history, his attempt to establish 'a tradition with a small t pining for a more inclusive and ample possibility'. Such an attempt is, according to Heaney, 'stay-at-home, inward looking, pious, exclusive and partial'.[56] These dreams of restoration are in many ways congruent with the criticism levelled at Heaney's early language poems, including 'Anahorish'. However, 'Station Island' adopts Stephen's position: 'The cultivated, elaborate and ironical Dedalus will not make a provincial dialect the basis of a style, nor will he finally make the historical wound of a language-shift from Irish to English the basis of a cultural politics.'[57] He refuses to grapple with the old man, as he is free of all that 'subject people stuff':

> The old man represents the claims of the pious archetype on the free spirit. Stephen fears him because his red-rimmed horny eyes are in the end myopic, because that mountain cabin where he lodges is hung with the nets of nationality, religion, family, the arresting abstractions. Yet Stephen will not destroy him. The old man is as much a victim as the writer. His illiterate fidelities are the object of Stephen's scepticism, the substance of what Stephen rejects; and yet they are a part of Stephen himself. Stephen is angry that all his culture can offer him for veneration is this peasant oracle, yet understanding the ruination that he and the old man share, he is not prepared to struggle to the death.[58]

Heaney, like Stephen, will neither fully reject nor accept the old man's beliefs. What the final section of 'Station Island' has shown is that Heaney is willing to review both positions from a critical distance and, like Stephen-Joyce, transmutes the choice *either/or* into *both/and*. Heaney rids himself of his inferiority complex as regards his own language and accepts that he can be adept at his own dialect.[59]

Joyce's notorious linguistic polyvalence has more in common with Paul Muldoon's poetry than Heaney's. Muldoon's leap 'from the "lox" in *Leix*lip to the "schmear" in *Smer*wick' (*KS* 43) recalls Joyce's 'alphybettyformed verbage'.[60] Both writers dismiss thoughts of a pure, indigenous language. Whereas a poet like Maura Dooley can use 'fuchsia' as an emblem for her lost heritage – 'my dreams are hedged with red and purple ... We want the tongue they took such care to lose'[61] – Muldoon is more interested in cross-fertilisation:

> Though it may seem as Irish as Brian Boru
> the fuchsia's blown in here from Chile or Peru,
> its flower a red flare sent up by the crew ... (KS 37)

One can well imagine Muldoon as a Joycean character, stammering up in Peruvian.[62] The etymological derivation of words clearly fascinates Muldoon, yet some critics mistake its parodic intent for something more serious. Comparing his word-play with the macaronic messages of Freud's Wolf Man, Guinn Batten argues that his poetry manifests the 'cryptic speech of melancholia'.[63] This is a wildly inaccurate diagnosis, as any comparison with the Wolf Man's symptoms will confirm.[64] Whether Muldoon is wondering 'how Eglish was itself wedged between / ecclesia and église' (Q 11), or is pondering the 'semantic / quibble' of 'chinook' (MB 9), or is even working out the links between 'beárrthóir' and 'bearradóir', he is always in control. He is perfectly content writing in English and is not afflicted with Kinsella's 'divided mind'. This linguistic confidence manifests itself when poking fun at other people's insatiable quest for origins.

As ever, Muldoon's parody gains its force through ventriloquism. Quoting from Barry Fell's *America BC*, he ridicules the author's discovery of ancient writing by voicing his theories through the mouth of Bucephalus, a syphilitic horse:

> Bucephalus speaks to him in Greek;
>
> 'This is indeed a holy place
> dedicated to the sun god, Bel.'
> Southey can but dimly make out the blaze
> on his poll;
>
> 'Were the secret of the ogam
> script on the edge of this standing stone
> known to the Reverend Samson Occom
> he would hold it in disdain.
>
> Yet his own people, the Mohegan,
> are the seed of the Celtic chieftain, Eoghan.' (MM 65)

In an interview with Lynn Keller, Muldoon admits that much of what Bucephalus utters in 'Madoc – A Mystery' 'comes from, or is not unrelated to, what Barry Fell says – about the Celts coming to North America, how you find a few scratches in a stone somewhere in Massachusetts, and it looks suspiciously like "ogam", and you say, well, obviously the Irish got here'.[65] His first quotation refers to inscriptions found at Mystery Hill, New Hampshire. Convinced that the scratches are not random, Fell claims that '[t]he name of the sun god Bel appears in Ogam script on the lintels of temples dedicated to sun worship'.[66] Muldoon's scepticism seems justified considering the wholly convoluted manner by which Fell arrives at his conclusions:

> As he brushed away the adhering dirt there came into clear view a line of Ogam script that read B-B-L. I could only conclude that this is the same vowelless style as the Punic script and the same as the Portuguese and Spanish Ogam, and the reading was therefore to be taken as *Bi Bel,* that is, 'Dedicated to Bel'. *Bel* is the Celtic sun god, long suspected (but until now never proven) to be the same god as the Phoenician Baal.[67]

Muldoon's second quotation tells of a different set of inscriptions found on the Susquehanna gravestones which match the Irish variety of Ogam script known as 'Edge Ogam'.[68] He mocks Fell's pseudo-analytical style by arbitrarily linking 'Edge Ogam' with Occam's razor and then, through a series of wild etymological guesses, traces the Franciscan philosopher's lineage back to Owen Gwyneth, Madoc's Father (*MM* 220) via the Celtic chieftain Eoghan (*MM* 65).

At the heart of 'Madoc – A Mystery' is the search for traces of Prince Madoc and the mythical Welsh Indians. Crucial to the hypothesis that the Welsh discovered America is the linguistic evidence which has accrued over the years. Richard Deacon is one of many who have accepted this at face value. Quoting Dr Powel, he lists several Welsh words which have been supposedly transplanted to America: 'the island of *Corroceo,* the river *Gwyndor,* and the white rock of *Pengwyn,* which be all British (or Welsh) words, do manifestly show, that it was that countrie Madoc and his people inhabited'.[69] Muldoon, through the mouth of Bucephalus, offers the same etymological proof:

> while Bucephalus goes down on one knee;
> 'Penguin. From the Welsh
>
> *pen* and *gwynn,* meaning "head" and "white"'. (*MM* 147)

Muldoon compounds his parody by having Southey wake in a cold sweat in '[Whitehead]' (*MM* 195) and declare 'penguins don't have white heads'. The passage refers to a key moment in Thomas Stephens's thesis on the

Madoc legend when he concludes that 'the word *pengwyn* proves equally deceptive; for the bird so called has a *black* instead of a *white* head, as also all the birds of that genus; and hence, as an eminent naturalist, our countryman Pennant, pointedly observes, "we must resign every hope founded on this hypothesis, of retrieving the Cambrian race in the new world"'.[70] Much of the humour lies in the comic timing: waiting 48 pages before telling us the obvious, the poet illustrates how easy it is to be deceived by etymology.

The fact that Muldoon has neither launched a scathing polemic against the English language nor eagerly acclaimed Hiberno-English as essential to his work is not solely the result of his facility with words and his suspicion of origins; the fact that he is not afflicted with Kinsella's 'divided mind' is also the result of his ability from an early age to compose in Irish. He even presents a poetic manifesto in the concluding stanza of an early poem, '*Idir*':[71]

Bréag an fhile,
Bréag an tsaoil. Dob'ionann iad.
Is gheofar fírinne an dáin
Idir eatarthu.

The poet's lies and those of the world around him are of the same kind: between them, the poem's truth will emerge. Already in evidence is Muldoon as trickster, writing about life from an oblique angle. The poem also demonstrates his characteristic ingenuity with language, Irish proving no barrier: '*Do chuala mise / Fás an fhéir*' (I heard the grass growing); '*Do chonaic m'éisteacht / Gaoth sa spéir*' (My hearing saw the wind in the sky).

Muldoon's predilection for renovated clichés can be seen in the opening stanza of '*Scoite*':[72]

Ar scáth a chéile
A mhaireas na daoine;
Ar scáth na gcuile
A mhaireas na damhain alla.

The first two lines are a common saying, the Irish equivalent of 'man is a social animal'; the following lines give it a sinister twist by saying that 'spiders live amongst the flies'. Although much of what follows is formulaic ('*Tá mé scriosta anois / Is mo shaol ag sileadh uaim*'), he brings the allegory to a satisfactory conclusion, playing on the phrase '*gréasán an tsaoil*' (the web of life): '*Deirtear go bhfuil téachtadh / sa ghreasán / Ní shníomhann damhan alla damh*' (They say the web is getting thicker, no spider can spin a home).

A final poem, '*Greim*',[73] displays two of Muldoon's most enduring traits: inventive rhymes and a preoccupation with his father. The first eight lines describe a storm over their heads:

Tá spéir os ár gcionn
Mar glaise na dtonn,

Dubh-scammall meisceach
Mar scoil mhór éisc.

Bhí an ceart ag m'athair
Go rabh bailc air,

Sruth mór na fearthainne
Ag bogadh na gcrann.

The downpour is overwhelming: the sky is compared with the colour of waves; the menacing clouds are like a large shoal of fish. In a conventional use of pathetic fallacy, the poet's mood is reflected by the weather. No momentuous decision or revelation is reached. The conclusion is open-ended: '*Toirneach mar gunna mór / Muidinne ár mba faoin aer*' (thunder like a loud blast of a gun, us stuck outside). The poem fails to achieve what the poem's title suggests: '*dul in greim le rud*' means 'to get to grips with something'.

The fact that Medbh McGuckian has published translations of Nuala Ní Dhomhnaill's poetry[74] may at first suggest that she is as comfortable with Irish as Muldoon; however, this is not the case as an analysis of her translations will show. Talking about her translations with Ní Dhomhnaill, McGuckian describes how she alters the original intentions to suit her own outlook. Discussing the line '*An féidir scríobh ar chiúineas?*' from '*Toircheas 1*'/'Ark of the Covenant', McGuckian explains, '[s]o instead of saying, "Is it possible to describe this silence", I say, "How can I begin to explain my quiet to you?" I changed Nuala's words because I bring in an "I" and "you". Whereas she is trusting the quietness, and can do without the personal, I can't. I am not strong enough. I took liberties.'[75] In fact, McGuckian did not have to translate the poems directly from Irish since cribs were provided for her by Ní Dhomhnaill.[76] Word lists included on her worksheets indicate that McGuckian uses both the original and the supplied English version. Looking at the worksheets for 'Daphne and Apollo',[77] one can see that her first impulse is to list synonyms of a word. When translating '*do theichis ar dtúis*', she runs through various options: 'evaded, retreated, absconded, avoided, shunned, went on the run, escaped, fugitive' before arriving at 'your racc from him'. Comparing the crib sheet with McGuckian's own version, one can see the extent to which she alters the original:

When the god leapt towards you	When the arch-poet made a play for you,
with his hot embrace, as eager as a hound	like a bloodhound nosing a hareless scent,
in full chase of a hare on an empty field,	your race from him froze in a skater's pirouette,
at first you ran away, then turned down your heel	a music-box arabesque, a twig that bent.[78]
and put your foot down.[79]	

The changes are startling: 'Hareless scent' suggests the absence of a hare, whereas the original has the hare in full flight; Apollo becomes an 'arch-poet'; 'music-box arabesque' is pure invention and 'the skater's pirouette' improves on the original.

I do not wish to suggest that McGuckian is a poor translator. Indeed, her work for the Dutch and Flemish anthology *Turning Tides*[80] won the admiration of its editor, Peter van de Kamp: writing to McGuckian on 16 February 1992, he said, 'your versions are among the most original ¾ and thus doubly welcome'. That this was not faint praise can be seen if we compare her translation of Mieke Tillema's '*Zo Vroeg*' with both Joan McBreen's version and the crib provided by van de Kamp:

So Soon	So Soon	So Soon
So soon so jaded and	So soon, so tired,	So soon – so without tomorrow –
nothing to view outside	Nothing to see outside	your eye for months together
yourself. Mirrored enough,	yourself. Mirrored enough	sees nothing but roofs.
with scratches and long since	with scratches and long	
weathered. How strange	weathered. How strange	Mirror written to by fog, by rain,
your skin so soon	the spider-webbed skin	by rusty weather – scrap of wallpaper
spider-webbed on your cheek.[81]	on your cheek	scratched by weeks and seasons.
	so soon.[82]	
		How pure child
		your Tuesday skin,
		now Friday is in your cheeks.[83]

McBreen sticks rigidly to the crib and her concluding lines are clumsy. By contrast, McGuckian's translation avoids clichéd descriptions of wrinkles by saying 'now Friday is in your cheeks'. Her version also solves a problem raised by van de Kamp: writing to McGuckian, he says, '"het weer erin" has the same colloquial tone as, for instance, "there's heat in this sun"; literally "the weather in it", it denotes that the mirror has rusty patches. *Is* there an English equivalent? Musty?' Taking her cue from van de Kamp, she not only uses the image of the mirror as 'rusty', but also takes the weather indoors (and by extension, inside the person's mind) and states that the 'scrap of wallpaper' is 'scratched by weeks and seasons' (hence 'musty'). The editor thanked her on 16 January 1992 for her versions and said, 'I was quite chuffed that you transformed my old mirror into a poem (wow, I didn't know my lake could be so deep!). This is just what the anthology needed: a poet who doesn't slavishly adhere to the original.'

The manner in which McGuckian compiles wordlists and relies on cribs for translations is analogous to her method when composing in English. She in fact treats English as a foreign language. Unlike Heaney and Muldoon, her anxiety about colonial inheritance is inscribed into the very core of her language. In recent interviews she has consistently emphasised her antipathy to English: 'I am more and more aware of English as being a foreign medium';[84] '[a]ll of the English language repels me';[85] 'it's an imposed language, you see, and although it's my mother tongue and my only way of communication, I'm fighting with it all the time';[86] 'I resist and I'm angry – we're always angry, because every time we open our mouths we're slaves'.[87] For McGuckian, the psychological discord arising from her mother tongue is not a recent phenomenon, as is evident from thoughts recorded in her 1968/69 diary: 'English is very sour upon the tongue ... I keep finding fault with English these days, like a mother with her child.' What is particularly noteworthy is her desire to redress the situation: 'John says English here is sterile – maybe I will inseminate it.'[88] Taking up the theme again in a letter to a researcher, Stacia Bensyl (8 February 1989), McGuckian writes:

> About English: I feel languageless, I feel my soul tongue-tied, but many of the other Irish poets do also, the male ones, if you read what they say about Irish and their disassociation from it. You feel odd writing and speaking a language which you know was imposed historically recently, the place-names being still Gaelic in tone.... I think when I write the poetry I solve the problem, I develop a specialized language of my own, fairly private, which is not English, less than, more than English, which subverts, deconstructs, kills it, makes it the dream-language I have lost. At least – this I think is the motivation.[89]

How is McGuckian to use English without reinforcing her own sense of dispossession? Unlike Muldoon, whose historical consciousness is less narrowly focused on the era when 'Irish' people spoke Irish, McGuckian sets up the language as essential to her identity; like Heaney's psyche, hers flits 'like a capable bat between the light of a practical idiom and the twilight of a remembered place, alert as any linguistic philosopher both to the arbitrariness of signs and the ache of the unspoken'.[90] It is not that she longs to speak Irish,[91] but, convinced that English has been 'imposed' on the Irish people, she cannot be 'fully at home' using it.[92] Her decolonisation of the mind does not take the usual approach of actively appropriating English or foregrounding Hiberno-English;[93] instead her work deterritorialises the English language, subjecting it to a radical displacement. It is what Deleuze and Guattari call 'a minor literature'.[94] Her deterritorialisation attempts to disrupt its structures: 'I feel perhaps in poetry a meta-language where English and Irish could meet might be possible, and disturbing the grammar or messing about like Hopkins is one method of achieving this.'[95] But her poetry is nothing like that of Hopkins. Her 'leaping, glistening, splashed / And scattered alphabet' forms 'double-stranded words' (BB 57), altered quotations stitched together to form her 'dream language'. Her palimpsestuous texts do not bespeak an anxiety of influence; they manifest a deliberate estrangement from the English language. McGuckian does not compose, she appropriates; the words are not hers, but are used by her.

In the revised edition of On Ballycastle Beach, 'Harem Trousers' (RBB 40–41) appears to signal an engagement with Irish by its dedication to Nuala Ní Dhomhnaill, one of the most celebrated contemporary poets composing in the language. Asked in a personal interview about the relevance of the poem's title, McGuckian replied that 'it was dedicated to Nuala Ní Dhomhnaill, so I think that's the Turkish thing in the title, Nuala being married to a Turk … Her trousers were a very feminine kind of trousers. I wanted to suggest that Nuala was very masculine in her art but very feminine in her nature.'[96] While this may undoubtedly be true, the title itself proposes the presence of another poet, namely Marina Tsvetaeva. The words 'harem trousers' refer to the clothing worn by the mother of the Russian poet, Maximilian Voloshin. On arrival at the poet's home at Koktebel on 5 May 1911, Tsvetaeva was introduced to his mother, the account of which is recorded as follows:

> 'And now I will introduce you to Mama. Elena Ottobaldovna Voloshna – Marina Ivanovna Tsvetaeva.'
>
> Mama: grey hair swept back, an aquiline profile with a blue eye, a long white caftan, sewn with silver, blue, ankle-length harem trousers, Kazan-style boots. Transferring a smoking cigarette from right to left: 'Hello!'[97]

When evidence of the Tsvetaevan intertext was presented to McGuckian, she confirmed the affinity she perceived between the two writers: 'Yes, because Nuala had been translating her and because Nuala is very similar in many ways.' When pressed further about the speaker's identity, she said, '[t]he I is me. I suppose that I was saying that I was the one in the revolutionary world but that Nuala was the one who had the resources to deal with it in the language which I admired in her – only [she] had the Tsvetaevan serious language – so if we could have united those things in a borderless union of self.'[98] The inference here is that the poet writing in Irish is somehow able to transcend the conscious (and colonial) discourse. This was touched upon during a previous interview when, replying to a question about the deliberate confusion of the narrative speaker in many of her poems, she replied (in her wonderfully enigmatic fashion), 'if you were talking to Nuala Ní Dhomhnaill she would talk about the 'ego-grinder', … how poetry, in order to resolve them, … we are normally very cut off in our own private world … and also it is a way at hammering at English – it's not like Irish where the noun comes first, where the pronoun is in the verb, isn't it? Certainly with the 'I' part. I get really annoyed, I hope I get subconsciously annoyed, at the placing of the pronoun.'[99]

The fact that linguistic disinheritance and dislocation preoccupies McGuckian is confirmed in a review she did of *Art in the Light of Conscience* in which, significantly, the three poets are again conjoined:

> The experience of the community in the North of Ireland since 1969, while the emigration was not of the same kind or under the same pressures, nevertheless in its relentlessness, its day to day despair, has influenced the artists affected by it in many of the ways that 1917 shaped Tsvetaeva. One bereavement Marina with her trilingual upbringing did not suffer was the substitution of a people's language, literature, culture, and religion by those of the colonising neighbours ¾ so deeply destructive a displacement, we are scarcely aware of the damage. And it is not in any of *my* poems that Marina's voice echoes defiantly, but in the still-Gaelic verses of Nuala ní nDhomhnáill [sic] (I search for a 'fada' on the keyboard).[100]

Apart from the self-deprecating position adopted by McGuckian with respect to her own verse, one should note that Ní Dhomhnaill's presence can be said to have the symbolic and political valency of having a primal connection to uncolonised territory. While McGuckian feels she does not have access to this 'resource', her 'borderless union of self' in 'Harem Trousers' is a way of dislodging the logic of English within her own poetry; indeed, the unacknowledged sources[101] and multiple personae, as well as her unique use of imagery and syntax, are all part of her declared aim of 'repudiating the anglicisation of myself'.[102]

Asleep on the coast I dream of the city.
A poem dreams of being written
Without the pronoun 'I'.

The poem's opening lines intimate a wish for circumstances to be other than they are at present. In particular, the speaker desires the dissolution of subjectivity: rejecting the symbolic order (English), she wishes to regress back to the imaginary and reverse the fall into language. The lines are taken from Karlinsky's renowned biography of Tsvetaeva. Describing a reading given by Tsvetaeva at the Polytechnic Museum in Moscow, 11 December 1920, he says that, upon listening to Briusov's introductory lecture regarding the inability of women poets to write on any topic other than love and passion, Tsvetaeva read out to the assembled audience of Red Army soldiers and revolutionary students a poem expressing 'her right to shout "Hurrah!" for the Tsar 'the way the street urchins shout it in all the squares of the world"'.[103] Her reasoning behind such a bold move is revealing:

'This was obvious insanity,' she later commented, 'but I was guided by two, no three, four aims: (1) seven poems by a woman without the word 'love' and without the pronoun 'I'; (2) proof that poetry makes no sense to the audience; (3) a dialogue with some one particular person who *understood* (perhaps a student); (4) and the principal one: fulfilling here, in the Moscow of 1921, an obligation of honor. And beyond any aims, aimlessly, stronger than aims, a simple and extreme feeling of: what if I do?'[104]

Aims 2 and 3 are notable in their implications for McGuckian's poetry, as they point both to the relative obscurity of the embedded quotations and to the existence of a primary audience for her verse. The desire to write a poem 'without the pronoun "I"' involves a peculiar tension in its original context: though Tsvetaeva seeks to resist conventional expressions of love by submerging her personality, the final sentiment seemingly contradicts this by declaring the strength of her individualism. Within McGuckian's poem, however, the tension is deflected, the 'I' being shared by three individuals ('this one, or that one, or a third'). The lines themselves recall sentiments expressed in Tsvetaeva's *Art in the Light of Conscience* entitled 'Poets with History and Poets without History':

What is the 'I' of a poet? It is – to all appearances – the human 'I' expressed in poetic speech. But only to appearances, for often poems give us something that had been hidden, obscured, even quite stifled, something the person hadn't known was in him, and would never have recognised had it not been for poetry, the poetic gift. Action of forces which are unknown to the one who acts, and which he only becomes conscious of in the instant of action. An almost complete analogy to dreaming. If it were possible to direct one's own dreams – and for some it is, especially children – the analogy would be complete. That which is hidden and buried in you is revealed and exposed in your poems: this is the poetic 'I' of your dream-self.[105]

According to Tsvetaeva, the poet's identity is made up of distinct selves, one irrational, the other conscious, expressed through language: 'The poet's self is a dream-self and a language-self; it is the "I" of a dreamer awakened by inspired speech and realised only in speech.'[106] Here Tsvetaeva's thoughts on poetic conception are in harmony with those of McGuckian: while the initial promptings of a poem are external to the poet's conscious self, they reveal something which lies dormant within her own being. McGuckian, when discussing in an interview with Margaret Wright how the Russian writers transmute experience into poetry, states that 'Dream is probably the best analogy I can use to talk about art. It is said that ninety-five per cent of the mind is subconscious, only five per cent being conscious. If that is the kind of balance, then dream is much more important than we imagine.'[107] This dream-language represents for McGuckian the means of writing poetry without being conscious of writing in a foreign language. However, 'Harem Trousers' does not simply restate Tsvetaevean poetics; rather, while McGuckian ultimately agrees with the necessity of making that final transition from unconscious prompting to linguistic creation, she uses the quotations to register her own fundamental unease that this involves a stage of utter passivity (thus questioning by extension Eliot's notion of 'continual self-sacrifice'). Indeed, during our interview in Ballycastle she stated, still referring to Ní Dhomhnaill, 'Nuala would want to lose all sense of the ego, I don't know if I would.'

The poem has a dual focus: first, it attempts to enact the movement from unconscious prompting to the emergence of the 'dream self' into language; secondly, it comments briefly upon the relationship between the creative artist and the public world. From the outset, inspiration resists the impulse towards language and wishes to exist outside all grammatical structure ('Without the pronoun "I"'). This is a condition which the poem describes as 'innocence', the movement beyond figuring in terms of injury and violence ('anything / That is being hurt overflows its innocence'). Yet if we go to *Art in the Light of Conscience*, this is described in terms of a 'birth' (synonymous in McGuckian with poetic creation), one which is welcomed and wished for. The difference in perception is compounded in stanza 3 where the narrative of how 'it' arrives into the public realm is related negatively by McGuckian, yet positively by Tsvetaeva. Much of the reader's confusion surrounding the uncertain referent to 'it' is allayed when one reads in Tsvetaeva that '[t]he condition of creation is a condition of entrancement.

Till you begin – *obsession*; till you finish – *possession*. Something, someone, lodges in you; your hand is the fulfiller not of you but of *it*. Who is *it*? That which through you wants to be.'[108] Discounting the possibility of a mere coincidental textual parallel, and confirming a conscious comparison on McGuckian's part, is the inclusion of a more explicit quotation from the same essay:

> Things always chose me by the mark of my power, and often I wrote them almost against my will. All my Russian works are of this sort. Certain things of Russia wanted to be expressed, they chose me. And how did they persuade, seduce me? By my own power: only you! Yes, only I. And having given in – sometimes seeingly, sometimes blindly – I would obey, seek out with my ear some assigned aural lesson. And it was not I who, out of a hundred words (not rhymes! but in the middle of a line), would choose the hundred and first, but *it* (the thing), resisting all the hundred epithets: that isn't *my* name.[109]

Whereas Tsvetaeva accepts and celebrates the intuitive processes involved in the choice of the hundred-and-first word, McGuckian's image is one of traumatic dislocation from the initial dreamworld:

> It holds the hundred and first word
> In its fingers and tears it apart,
>
> So the openness within the sound
> Is forced to break, dislodging
> Its already dove-grey music.
> An extreme and simple feeling
> Of 'What if I do enter? –

The unique nature of the dreamstate is shattered, its 'dove-grey music' is dislodged. Yet this is also an implicit commentary upon the often negative impact of society upon a writer: the 'it' is clearly 'timid and incongruous' among the harsh realities of the community ('roadblocks and breadlines').

The final two stanzas project antithetical selves, an 'I' and a 'you'; whereas the former exists in a free and abandoned state ('Unkempt'), the latter represents the formal, refined condition of the English language ('A stem, a verb, a rhyme'). It is at this point that McGuckian returns to a more faithful rendering of Tsvetaeva's ideas about the volatile, unstable nature of writing poetry: the rational attempt verbally to embody the unpredictable rhythms of the unconscious risks expulsion back into what is 'involuntary'. The concluding lines are a neat paraphrase of the following passage (with the prior reservation concerning annihilation):

> Genius: the highest degree of subjection to the visitation – one; control of the visitation – two. The highest degree of being mentally pulled to pieces, and the highest of being – collected. The highest of passivity, and the highest of activity.

> To let oneself be annihilated right down to some last atom, from the survival (resistance)
> of which will grow – a world.[110]

McGuckian's poetic texts are not only intertextual in the sense of using literary sources, but also in the more specialised Kristevan sense of transposition which 'specifies that the passage from one signifying system to another demands a new articulation of the thetic – of enunciative and denotative positionality'.[111] McGuckian's use of quotations translated from the Russian produces 'a semiotic polyvalence'[112] which works against the grammatical rationale of the English language. Her resistance to the English language and her desire to articulate the inexpressible are best described in 'Elegy for an Irish Speaker' (*CL* 42–43), an elegy whose five stanzas comprise forty quotations taken from 21 essays by Osip Mandelstam.[113] The tortured syntax and uncertain referents of the opening stanza are an example of the semiotic emerging through the symbolic order:

> Numbered day,
> night only just beginning,
> be born very slowly, stay
> with me, impossible to name.

It is difficult to tell when the 'Numbered day' ends and the 'night' begins. By juxtaposing the two, McGuckian again links birth with death, but reverses the usual chronology by having the former follow on from the latter. The male persona (a fusion between her own father and Mandelstam) is said to 'fertilize' death and make a new level of communication possible. This partly explains the ambivalence surrounding the phrase 'impossible to name'. While it seems to signify McGuckian's inability to name death through the medium of language, the original context suggests that this is far from negative: 'How dreadful that man (the eternal philologist) has found a word for this: "death". Is it really possible to name it? Does it warrant a name? A name is a definition, a "something we already know". So Rozanov defined the essence of his nominalism in a most personal manner: the eternal cognitive movement, the eternal cracking of the nut which comes to nothing because there is no way to gnaw through it.'[114] McGuckian's use of language is neither static nor monological, but metamorphic and dialogical, and it facilitates her assumption of a priest-like role:

> Today a kind of speaking in tongues is taking place. In sacred frenzy poets speak the language
> of all times, all cultures. Nothing is impossible. As *the room of a dying man is open to everyone*,
> so the door of the old world is flung wide open before the crowd. Suddenly everything

becomes public property. Come and take your pick. Everything is accessible: all labyrinths, all secret recesses, all forbidden paths. The word has become not a seven-stop but a thousand-stop flute, brought to life all at once by the breathing of ages. The most striking thing about speaking in tongues is that the speaker does not know the language he is speaking.[115]

The passage from which McGuckian takes her quotation emphasises the inspired and unconscious manner in which a poet writes. Here she is reiterating the earlier thematics of 'Harem Trousers' which contrasted the conscious use of language with what she called the 'involuntary window'. It is on this level that communication can take place with her father/Mandelstam:

He breaks away from your womb
to talk to me,
he speaks so with my consciousness
and not with words, he's in danger
of becoming a poetess.

The father/Mandelstam are said to be reborn when celebrated in McGuckian's poetry, and a fusion occurs between all three. The fact that the dead do not use 'words' confirms the unconscious nature of the exchange. McGuckian deliberately reads Mandelstam's text against the grain and uses her quotation to modify the poles of his word/consciousness binary opposition:

But too often we fail to see that the poet raises a phenomenon to its tenth power, and the modest exterior of a work of art often deceives us with regard to the monstrously condensed reality contained within. In poetry this reality is the word as such. Right now, for instance, in expressing my thoughts as precisely as possible, but certainly not in a poetic manner, *I am essentially speaking with my consciousness, not with the word.*[116]

For Mandelstam, speaking with one's 'consciousness' is not poetic and contrasts with the inspired use of 'the word', the religious overtones of which re-emphasise the poet's 'speaking in tongues'. McGuckian subtly alters the quotation by pluralising 'the word' (thereby secularising it) and by emphasising the spiritual nature of her communication with the dead. Whereas Mandelstam uses 'poetess' as a term of abuse for Mayakovsky,[117] McGuckian's use is wholly positive.

Most foreign and cherished reader,
I cannot live without
your trans-sense language,
the living furrow of your spoken words
that plough up time.

Two of her quotations are from passages which she has already referred to in earlier poems. In '"Constable's 'Haywain'" (*CL* 36), McGuckian describes the father's coffin as if it were a funerary ship and she repeats the image here: 'How can one equip this ship for its distant voyage, without furnishing it with all the necessities for *so foreign and cherished a reader*?'[118] In 'The Dream Language of Fergus' (*OBB* 57), the poet uses a religous register of language when distinguishing the poetic from the non-poetic use of language: 'Not the rudiment / Of half a vanquished sound, / The excommunicated shadow of a name ...'. Repeating the reference, she reaffirms her commitment to what is poetic: '*I cannot live without language*, I cannot survive excommunication from the word. Such, approximately, was Rozanov's spiritual state. The anarchistic, nihilistic spirit recognized only one authority: the magic of language, the power of the word ...'[119] While it is obvious from the context that the audience at whom her poetry is addressed is her father/Mandelstam, the poem's title offers an alternative reading of what she might mean by 'foreign'. McGuckian extends the meaning of 'trans-sense language' to include not only 'those transitional forms which succeeded in not being covered by the semantic crust created by the properly and correctly devloping language',[120] but also the unconscious/uncolonised traces of the Irish language which reside in McGuckian's father (he did not actually speak Irish). This is emphasised by the connection she establishes between land and language: while not quite 'racy of the soil', the 'trans-sense language' is a form of earth writing, creating 'the living furrow of your spoken words / that plough up time'. She has need of this language for a deeper understanding of the past. When she states, 'Instead of the real past / with its deep roots, / I have yesterday ...', she is quoting Mandelstam's belief that one should study the literature of the past and present in order to get a fuller understanding of both: 'whoever fails to comprehend the new has no sense of the old, while whoever understands the old is bound to understand the new. Nevertheless, it is our great misfortune when, instead of *the real past with its deep roots*, we understand the past merely as "yesterday"'.[121]

Notes

1 Brian Fallon, 'A Field Day for Anthology Addicts', *Irish Times* 20 November 1991, Arts 12.
2 Peter McDonald, *Louis MacNeice: The Poet in His Contexts* (Oxford: Clarendon Press, 1991) 1.
3 McDonald, *Mistaken Identities: Poetry and Northern Ireland* (Oxford: Clarendon Press, 1997).

4 See Seamus Deane, 'Heroic Styles', in *Field Day* (ed.), *Ireland's Field Day* (Notre Dame, IN: University of Notre Dame Press, 1986) 57–58; Edna Longley, 'Anglo-Irish Resurrection', *Honest Ulsterman* 82 (Winter, 1986): 106; Roy F. Foster, 'Varieties of Irishness', in Maurna Crozier (ed.), *Cultural Traditions in Northern Ireland: Varieties of Irishness* (Belfast: Institute of Irish Studies, 1989) 5–24; Edna Longley, *From Cathleen to Anorexia: The Breakdown of Irelands* (Dublin: Attic Press, 1990) 6–7 and 'Opening up: A New Pluralism', in Robert Johnson, Robin Wilson and Robert Bell (eds), *Troubled Times: Fortnight Magazine and the Troubles in Northern Ireland 1970–91* (Belfast: Blackstaff, 1991) 142; and David Trimble and Edna Longley, in Crozier (ed.), *Varieties of Irishness* 45–46 and 56–57, respectively.

5 Colin Graham, in '"Liminal States": Post-Colonial Theories and Irish Culture', *Irish Review* 16 (Autumn–Winter, 1994), states that 'the very idea of nationality which was used by decolonising peoples to coalesce themselves into a coherent political force was itself transferred to the colonies by imperialist ideology' (37). See David Cairns and Shaun Richards, *Writing Ireland: Colonialism, Nationalism and Culture* (Manchester: Manchester University Press, 1988) 1–21; Seamus Deane 'Civilians and Barbarians', *Ireland's Field Day* 45–58 and 'The Production of Cultural Space in Irish Writing', *Boundary 2* 21.3 (Fall, 1994) 117–44; Terry Eagleton, 'Nationalism: Irony and Commitment', in Seamus Deane (ed.), *Nationalism, Colonialism, and Literature* (Minneapolis: University of Minnesota Press, 1990) 23–39; and David Lloyd, *Anomalous States: Irish Writing and the Post-Colonial Moment* (Dublin: Lilliput Press, 1993) 88–89, 112.

6 Medb Ruane, 'Opinion', *Irish Times* 30 March 1998, from the internet.

7 Nuala Ní Dhomhnaill in John Ardagh, *Ireland and the Irish: Portrait of a Changing Society* (London: Penguin, 1995) 300.

8 See Richard Kearney, *Transitions: Narratives in Modern Irish Culture* (Dublin: Wolfhound Press, 1988) 9; Robert F. Garratt, *Modern Irish Poetry: Tradition and Continuity from Yeats to Heaney* (Berkely, CA: University of California Press, 1986) 261; Thomas Kinsella, 'The Divided Mind', in Sean Lucy (ed.), *Irish Poets in English: The Thomas Davis Lectures on Anglo-Irish Poetry* (Cork: Mercier Press, 1973) 208–19.

9 J. J. Lee, *Ireland 1912–1985: Politics and Society* 1989 (Cambridge: Cambridge University Press, 1990) 668.

10 Lee, *Ireland 1912–1985* 662.

11 Desmond Fennell, *Heresy: The Battle of Ideas in Modern Ireland* (Belfast: Blackstaff Press,1993) 249.

12 Thomas Kinsella, *The Dual Tradition: An Essay on Poetry and Politics in Ireland* (Manchester: Carcanet, 1995) 87.

13 Máire Mhac an tSaoi, 'Writing in Modern Irish: A Benign Anachronism?' *Southern Review* 31.3 (July, 1995) 431.

14 Anonymous, 'All-Irish Schools Are "in Demand"', *Irish Times* 6 April 1998, from the internet.

15 Kevin O'Connor, 'Ireland: A Nation Caught in the Middle of an Identity Crisis', *Irish Independent* 20 July 1985, from the internet.

16 Fionnuala O'Connor, *In Search of a State: Catholics in Northern Ireland* 1993 (Belfast: Blackstaff Press, 1995) 348.

17 Gerry Moriarty, 'Opinion', *Irish Times* 7 January 1998, from the internet.

18 Seamus Heaney, 'Whatever You Say Say Nothing', *North* (London: Faber, 1975) 60.
19 Seamus Heaney, 'Calling the Tune', interview by Tom Adair, *Linen Hall Review* 6.2 (Autumn, 1989) 5.
20 Seamus Heaney, interview by Caroline Walsh, *Irish Times* 6 December 1975: 5.
21 Seamus Heaney, 'Beowulf', *Sunday Times* 26 August 1998: Books 6.
22 Seamus Heaney, interview by Harriet Cooke, *Irish Times* 28 December 1973: 8.
23 Seamus Heaney, 'Anahorish', *Wintering Out* (London: Faber, 1972) 16.
24 John Kerrigan, 'Earth Writing: Seamus Heaney and Ciaran Carson', *Essays in Criticism* 48.2 (April, 1998): 147 and 148, respectively.
25 Kerrigan, *Earth Writing* 148.
26 Seamus Heaney, *Preoccupations: Selected Prose 1968–1978* (London: Faber, 1980) 36.
27 Blake Morrison, *Seamus Heaney*, first pub. 1982 (London: Methuen, 1983) 41.
28 Tim Robinson, 'Listening to the Landscape', *Irish Review* 14 (Summer, 1993) 24 and 25, respectively.
29 Robinson, *Listening to the Landscape* 30.
30 Seamus Heaney, 'Ocean's Love to Ireland', *North* (London: Faber, 1975) 46–47.
31 Heaney, 'Ocean's Love to Ireland', *North* 46.
32 See Morrison, *Seamus Heaney* 64–65 and Neil Corcoran, *Seamus Heaney* 1986 (London: Faber, 1990) 120–21.
33 See Corcoran, *Seamus Heaney* 121.
34 Heaney, 'Ocean's Love to Ireland', *North* 47.
35 For Heaney's clumsiness with the 'landscape = body = sex = language' equation, see Edna Longley, '*North*: "Inner Emigré" or "Artful Voyeur"?' in Tony Curtis (ed.), *The Art of Seamus Heaney* (Dublin: Wolfhound, 1994) 80–81.
36 Heaney, 'Ocean's Love to Ireland', *North* 47.
37 Heaney, 'Ocean's Love to Ireland', *North* 47.
38 Heaney, *The Redress of Poetry*, first pub. 1990 (Oxford: Clarendon Press) 202.
39 Heaney, in the following comments to Tom Adair, has come to adopt a moderate position in relation to the whole question of 'identity': 'I could neither go unambiguously with the name "British", nor would I wish to be in the position of espousing cultural tariff barriers – all that kind of bigoted, parochial "Little Irelander" stuff. You can't have that either' (5).
40 Seamus Heaney, 'John Bull's Other Island', *Listener* 29 September 1977, 397.
41 Heaney, Section XII, 'Station Island', *Station Island* (London: Faber, 1984) 92–94.
42 T. S. Eliot 'Little Gidding', *T.S. Eliot' Complete Poems 1909–1962* (London: Faber, 1963) rept. 1986, 217. Heaney tells us in the notes to *Station Island* that the title poem is 'a sequence of dream encounters with familiar ghosts' (122). Also, the first version of section XII had the working-title of 'A Familiar Ghost' published in *Irish Times* Supplement, 2 February 1982, 2.
43 Eliot, 'Little Gidding' 217.
44 Heaney's reference to 'Old father' recalls Stephen Dedalus's final entry in his diary: 'Old father, old artificer, stand me now and ever in good stead' (James Joyce, *A Portrait of the Artist as a Young Man* (London: Penguin, 1960) 253. The line 'His voice eddying with the vowels of all rivers' also recalls Anna Livia Plurabelle from *Finnegans Wake*. Peter Meares in '"Ah Poet, Lucky Poet"', *Agenda* 22.3–4 (1985–1986) managed to see Patrick Kavanagh as

Heaney's final ghost (92).

45 Heaney, 'Station Island', *New Selected Poems 1966–1987* (London: Faber, 1990) 193.

46 Heaney, 'A Familiar Ghost' 2.

47 Seamus Heaney, 'John Bull's Other Island', *Listener* 29 September 1977 397–99; 'The Interesting Case of John Alphonsus Mulrennan', *Planet* January 1978, 34–40; 'A Tale of Two Islands: Reflections on the Irish Literary Revival', in P. J. Drudy (ed.), *Irish Studies* (Cambridge: Cambridge University Press, 1980) 1–20; *Among Schoolchildren: A John Malone Memorial Lecture* (Belfast: John Malone Memorial Committee, 1983) 10–11.

48 Joyce, *A Portrait of the Artist as a Young Man* 189.

49 Joyce, *A Portrait of the Artist as a Young Man* 251.

50 Heaney, 'Interesting Case' 35 and 39, respectively. See Heaney, *Among Schoolchildren*: 'What had seemed disabling and provincial is suddenly found to be corroborating and fundamental and potentially universal. To belong to Ireland, to speak its dialect, is not necessarily to be cut off from the world's banquet because that banquet is eaten at the table of one's own life, savoured by the tongue one speaks. Stephen now trusts what he calls 'our own language' and in that trust he will go to encounter what he calls 'the reality of experience'' (10–11).

51 Elmer Andrews, *The Poetry of Seamus Heaney: All the Realms of Whisper* (London: Macmillan, 1989) 173.

52 Heaney's birthday falls on 13 April.

53 Heaney, 'Station Island', *Station Island* 94.

54 Heaney, 'John Bull's Other Island' 397.

55 Joyce, *A Portrait of the Artist as a Young Man* 243.

56 Heaney, 'Interesting Case' 39.

57 Heaney, 'John Bull's Other Island' 397.

58 Heaney, 'A Tale' 17.

59 See Kieran Quinlan, 'Under Northern Lights: Re-visioning Yeats and the Revival', in Leonard Orr (ed.), *Yeats and Postmodernism* (Syracuse: Syracuse University Press, 1991) 71.

60 James Joyce, *Finnegans Wake* 1939 (London: Faber, 1975) 183.

61 Maura Dooley, *Explaining Magnetism* (Newcastle upon Tyne: Bloodaxe, 1991) 30.

62 Joyce, *Finnegans Wake* 252.

63 See Guinn Batten, '"He Could Barely Tell One from the Other": The Borderline Disorders of Paul Muldoon's Poetry', *South Atlantic Quarterly* 95.1 (Winter, 1996) 171–204.

64 See Nicolas Abraham and Maria Took, *The Wolf Man's Magic Word: A Cryptonomy*, trans. Nicholas Rand (Minneapolis: University of Minnesota Press, 1986).

65 Paul Muldoon, interview by Lynn Keller, *Contemporary Poetry* 35.1 (Spring, 1994) 18.

66 Barry Fell, *America BC: Ancient Settlers in the New World* (London: Wildewood House, 1978) 54.

67 Fell, *America BC* 90–91.

68 Fell, *America BC* 54.

69 Richard Deacon, *Madoc and the Discovery of America: Some Light on an Old Controversy* (London: Frederick Muller, 1967) 64–65.

70 Thomas Stephens, *Madoc: An Essay on the Discovery of America by Madoc Ap Owen Gwynedd in the Twelfth Century* (London: Longmans, Green and Co., 1893) 158.

71 Paul Muldoon, '*Idir*', Gaelic Language Manuscripts: Early Poems, Muldoon Papers, Spe-

cial Collections, Emory University, Atlanta.

72 Paul Muldoon, '*Scoité*', *Imreanna le Pol Ó Maolduin*, Gaelic Language Manuscripts: Early Poems, Muldoon Papers.

73 Paul Muldoon, '*Greim*', *Imreanna le Pol Ó Maolduin*, Gaelic Language Manuscripts: Early Poems, Muldoon Papers.

74 Medbh McGuckian, 'The Bond', 'Ark of Covenant', 'Gate of Heaven', 'Night Fishing', and Nine Little Goats' in Nuala Ní Dhomhnaill, *Pharoah's Daughter* (Meath: Gallery Press, 1990), and 'Daphne and Apollo,' 'The Marianne Faithfull Hairdo,' 'The Mermaid in the Labour Ward,' and 'The Merfolk and the Written Word' in *Southern Review* 31.3 (July, 1995) 433–43.

75 Medbh McGuckian, '*Comhrá*', *Southern Review* 31.3 (July, 1995) 600.

76 See cribs, Box 26, File 8, McGuckian Papers, Emory University.

77 Box 26, File 7, McGuckian Papers, Emory University.

78 McGuckian, 'Daphne and Apollo', *Southern Review* 31.3 (July, 1995) 433.

79 Nuala Ní Dhomhnaill, crib of 'Daphne and Apollo', Box 26, File 7, McGuckian Papers, Emory University.

80 Peter van de Kamp, ed., *Turning Tides: An Anthology of Dutch Poetry in English Versions by Irish Poets* (Brownsville: Story Line Press, 1994).

81 Crib supplied to McGuckian by Peter van de Kamp, Box 26, McGuckian Papers, Emory University.

82 Version by Joan McBreen, van de Kamp, *Turning Tides* 345.

83 Version by McGuckian, van de Kamp, *Turning Tides* 345.

84 Medbh McGuckian, interview by Rand Brandes, *Chattahoochee Review* 16.3 (Spring, 1996): 60.

85 McGuckian, 'Surfacing: An Interview with Medbh McGuckian', interview by Kimberly S. Bohman, *Irish Review* 16 (Autumn–Winter, 1994) 98.

86 McGuckian, 'Comhrá' *Southern Review* 31.3 (July, 1995) 605–6.

87 McGuckian, '"My Words Are Traps": An Interview with Medbh McGuckian', interview by John Hobbs, *New Hibernia Review* 2.1 (Spring, 1998) 114.

88 McGuckian, 'Rescuers and White Cloaks: Diary 1968–69'. This was sent to me by McGuckian.

89 McGuckian in Stacia L. Bensyl, '"To Populate New Ground"': Fertility Imagery in the Poetry of Medbh McGuckian' (Diss., University College Dublin, 1989) 193.

90 Heaney, 'Correspondences: Emigrants and Inner Exiles', in Richard Kearney (ed.), *Migrations: The Irish at Home and Abroad* (Dublin: Wolfhound Press, 1990) 26.

91 McGuckian, 'An Attitude of Compassion', interview by Kathleen McCracken, *Irish Literary Supplement* (Fall, 1990) 21.

92 McGuckian, interview by Hobbs 114.

93 Toni O'Brien Johnson, 'Making Strange to See Afresh: Re-visionary Techniques in Some Contemporary Irish Poetry', in Margaret Bridges (ed.), *On Strangeness* (Guntar Narr Verlag Tubingen, 1990) 134.

94 See Gilles Deleuze and Félix Guattari, *Kafka: Toward a Minor Literature*, trans. Dana Polon (Minneapolis: University of Minnesota Press, 1986) 16–27.

95 McGuckian, interview by Brandes 61.

96 McGuckian, personal interview, Marine Hotel, Ballycastle, 19 August 1996.

97 Marina Tsvetaeva, *A Captive Spirit: Selected Prose*, ed. J. Marin King (Michigan: Ardis, 1980) 53.

98 McGuckian, personal interview, Marine Hotel, Ballycastle, 19 August 1996.

99 Personal interview with Medbh McGuckian at the John Hewitt International Summer School, 28 July 1995.

100 Medbh McGuckian, 'How Precious Are Thy Thoughts Unto Me', review of *Art in the Light of Conscience* by Tsvetaeva, *Common Knowledge* 2.1 (Spring, 1993) 135.

101 McGuckian's mainly borrows from Simon Karlinsky's *Marina Tsvetaeva: The Woman. Her World and Her Poetry* (Cambridge: Cambridge University Press, 1985), but also quotes passages from Tsvetaeva's *Captive Spirit* and *Art in the Light of Conscience: Eight Essays on Poetry by Marina Tsvetaeva*, trans. Angela Livingstone (London: Bristol Classical Press, 1992).

102 McGuckian, interview by Rebecca E. Wilson, in Gillean Somerville-Arjat and Rebecca E. Wilson (eds), *Sleeping with Monsters: Conversations with Scottish and Irish Women Poets* (Edinburgh: Polygon, 1990) 6.

103 Karlinsky, *Marina Tsvetaeva* 97.

104 McGuckian in Karlinsky, *Marina Tsvetaeva* 97–98.

105 Tsvetaeva, *Art in the Light of Conscience* 136.

106 Tsvetaeva, *Art in the Light of Conscience* 136.

107 McGuckian, 'Poetry from Northern Ireland', Interview by Margaret Wright. See McGuckian Papers, Emory University, Box 26, folder 16.

108 Tsvetaeva, *Art in the Light of Conscience* 172.

109 Tsvetaeva, *Art in the Light of Conscience* 173.

110 Tsvetaeva, *Art in the Light of Conscience* 152.

111 Kristeva, *Revolution in Poetic Language*, trans. Margaret Waller (New York: Columbia University Press, 1984) 60.

112 Julia Kristeva, *Revolution* 60.

113 The essays are contained in Osip Mandelstam, *The Collected Prose and Letters*, trans. Jane Gray Harris and Constance Link, ed. Harris, first pub. 1979 (London: Collins Harvill, 1991).

114 Mandelstam, *Collected Prose and Letters* 124.

115 Mandelstam 116, *Collected Prose and Letters*, emphasis added.

116 Mandelstam, *Collected Prose and Letters* 61, emphasis added.

117 See Mandelstam, *Collected Prose and Letters* 147.

118 Mandelstam, *Collected Prose and Letters* 132, emphasis added.

119 Mandelstam, *Collected Prose and Letters* 123, emphasis added.

120 Mandelstam, *Collected Prose and Letters* 168.

121 Mandelstam, *Collected Prose and Letters* 176, emphasis added.

Conclusion

Throughout this monograph I have argued that for a comprehensive appreciation of Paul Muldoon and Medbh McGuckian's poetry the reader must unearth labyrinthine networks of intertextual relations. While Muldoon's intrusive literary allusions demand the reader's attention, his poetry would remain opaque and open to the charge of pretentiousness if their functions and effects were not properly understood. The same is not true of McGuckian's poetry: unaware of its true dialogism, the reader is likely to detect only disembodied voices. This work has not only introduced the reader to the capacious intellectual resources in which their poetry is grounded, it has also demonstrated the subtlety with which they employ their familiar ghosts and has attempted to show why both poets initiate intertextual relations: parodically to rewrite or comment upon a precursor's work; to approach politically sensitive themes from an oblique angle; to assert an authoritative presence as an Irish poet writing in the English language. Throughout this book Seamus Heaney's work has been used as a contrastive foil to that of the two younger poet: while his use of intertextuality is more direct and more reader-friendly, it is also more self-conscious and angst-ridden given his unease at using literary allusions with respect to the Troubles. The reader may well feel that the work required to comprehend the younger poets' respective oeuvres is inordinate: although Muldoon provides a thread, his labyrinth is myriadfold; McGuckian does not even supply the thread. The directness of Heaney's poetry with its ostensible transparency seems a more manageable proposition: his intertextual references are, by and large, self-explanatory and provide the reader with the solution to his own particular maze. Yet because of changing historical circumstances and their very different perception of the poet's representative status, the younger poets cannot be expected to reproduce Heaney's characteristically self-conscious style; in Muldoon's case, this is something which is actively

opposed. While Heaney's poetry continues to muse upon its intersection
with politics in almost prosaic clarity, the younger poets have moved on,
bringing other voices and contexts into the equation. In many respects they
have learned from the critics' reaction to the older poet's tortured equivocation about his recourse to literary allusion: Muldoon brazenly wears his
knowledge on his sleeve, McGuckian hides hers in the seams.

Muldoon's poetry is certainly difficult: it both delights and alienates critics in equal measure due to its urge towards 'the cryptic, the encoded, the
runic, the virtually unintelligible' – a quality he finds in much Irish literature since Amergin.[1] A fascination with the ideas of liminality and
narthecality – and all things in-between – results in a 'tendency towards the
amalgam, the tendency for one event to blur and bleed into another'. Inconclusive, indeterminate, and hybrid: Muldoon's poems 'delight to tread
upon the brink / of meaning' (*H* 3). Is the author dead, then, in the
Barthesian sense, and does the reader now assume the role of arbiter? (Or
for 'arbiter' should we read 'arbitrary'?) At its least successful, his poetry can
appear unforthcoming and self-delighting, criticisms which he anticipates
in *The Prince of the Quotidian* when he has the horse-head berate him as
follows: '"Who gives a shit about the dreck / of your life? Who gives a toss
/ about your tossing off?"' (*PQ* 40). While it is true, as Jeffrey Wainwright
has argued, that '[t]he first wonder of poetry lies in the immediate effects of
language' and that what 'constitutes the primary pleasure and amazement
of verse' is the way words 'are drawn from the myriad, their particular sounds
heard and then associated by rhythm, and sometimes their visual appearance'.[2] Nevertheless, there are times when the reader needs guidance so as
to avoid utter frustration at Muldoon's excessive gnomic tendencies:

> I ought to begin with Evelyn Waugh's
> 'How old's that noise?'
>
> when you wander arbi-
> trarily into *Le Déjeuner sur l'herbe*.[3]

While there is nothing arbitrary about the third line's felicitous enjambment,
without Tim Kendall's useful gloss on the poem the reader would be at a
complete loss to understand its meaning.[4] (For 'excess' do not read 'access'.)

However, Muldoon is always alive to the dangers of 'the slip and slop of
language' and rarely shows a 'disregard for the line between sense and nonsense'.[5] Indeed, in 'Pineapples and Pomegranates', a sonnet first published
on 29 October 2000 in the *Observer* and subsequently collected in *Moy*

Sand and Gravel (2002), the poetic speaker muses upon the (far from fruit-
ful) indeterminacy stemming from both incorrect etymological attribution
and multiple signification:

> To think that, as a boy of thirteen, I would grapple
> with my first pineapple,
> its exposed breast
> setting itself as another test
> of my will power, knowing in my bones
> that it stood for something other than itself alone
> while having absolutely no sense
> of its being a worldwide symbol of munificence.
> *Munificence* – right? Not munitions, if you understand
> where I'm coming from. As if the open hand
> might, for once, put paid
> to the hand grenade
> in one corner of the planet.
> I'm talking about pineapples – right? – not pomegranates.
>
> (*MSG* 25)

Dedicated to the memory of the Israeli poet Yehuda Amichai who died in
2000, the text meditates upon the difficulties a poet has when writing about
political conflict and the necessity to be as responsible and precise as possible
when choosing one's words. The speaker struggles with the pineapple's two
different referents: it is the exotic and enticing, juicy, edible fruit of the *Ananassa
sativa*; yet it is also the destructive hand grenade, or light trench mortar. As a
universal symbol, the pineapple represents friendship, hospitality and, as the
poem would have it, 'munificence'. Yet the text indicates an instability at the
heart of *that* word since, although it stems from the Middle French *munificence* ('generosity'), there is also an erroneous etymological derivation – after
the classical Latin *munire*, 'to fortify' – that links it to 'munitions'. Further
destabilising polysemy stemming from linguistic misprision is signalled towards the end of the poem where the reader is reminded that it speaks of
'pineapples' and not 'pomegranates': while the latter refers to the fruit of the
Punica Granatum, the *Oxford English Dictionary* suggests that, due to the
common element of *granate*, the word is also linked to 'grenade'. The text
nods towards section 19 of *Speech! Speech!* by Geoffrey Hill, a contemporary
of Muldoon, whose work is equally characterised by 'ethical gravity, painstak-
ing probity and intensely registered moral scruple':[6]

> For stately archaic detail ½ tag Dürer's
> LORD MORLEY with POMEGRANATE: self-shielding,
> Facet-compacted, its glitter-hearted scarce-
> Broken ½ FIDUCIA. Go easy: think GRENADE.[7]

Like Muldoon's poem, the thematic focus of this text centres on the responsibility of the writer and the moral imperative to be precise when choosing
one's words. Just as there is a slip between 'pomegranate' and 'grenade', Hill's
text ironically asserts that 'Semiotics / rule ½ semi-automatics'. Yet 'such rule
does not govern weapons, save in the field where words respond to words'.[8]
Hence, the poet must guard against the tongue's atrocities (improper clichés,
unintentional ambiguities, the unwarranted glamour of grammar) and ensure that atrocity does not 'get flattened down into the casually "atrocious"' or
'get fattened up into that debased form of imagination which is prurience'.[9]
By self-reflexively commenting on lexical misprision, both Muldoon and Hill
signal their awareness that, while they may speak about atrocities, they must
not speak atrociously.

Does the discovery of a poet's 'sympathetic ink' mean that Muldoon's poetry will be treated more or less sympathetically? The answer is likely to be in
the affirmative since an analysis demonstrating the logic behind his intertextual
references renders his work more accessible, rebuts accusations of elitism and
demonstrates the precision of his word choice. The answer is less clear-cut in
McGuckian's case. While I have been called a 'sympathetic critic' for engag-
ing in 'critical sleuthery' by Leontia Flynn in her recent study of McGuckian's
relationship with her critics,[10] Flynn voices a concern with my approach:

> One of the ironies of Shane Murphy's study is that in studying the poet's personal worksheets
> and manuscripts, he is directed elsewhere – not simply to literary figures, Tsvetaeva or Brontë,
> but to what Olga Ivinskaya has written about Tsvetaeva or Winifred Gérin about Brontë; that
> is, in a circular move, to other author-based studies and not to the authors themselves.

Because of this circularity, 'attempts by critics to explicate [McGuckian's
work] with reference to the author's life (or intentions) ... ring hollow'.[11]
This is not necessarily the case. Interviews with poets are illuminating and
can provide invaluable context to their poetic texts; the detection of intertexts
does little to invalidate the author's stated intentions. However, literary commentators should not cleave to the biographical information provided by
an author, nor should they uncritically accept their explicatory pronounce-
ments. Part of the rationale behind *Sympathetic Ink* is to provide a way in to
seemingly hermetic texts and to explore the poets' complicating, oblique
approach to issues of identity and politics. As an interpretative strategy for
McGuckian's poetry, source-hunting can be enlightening and it usefully
attempts to resolve a problem adverted to by Rachel Buxton in her review
of another of my articles:

> Although direct quotation might be one of the most explicit ways of signalling a poet's presence, it can also be risky: these fragments and phrases from other poems, if they are not easily identifiable as such, can cause confusion, and the allusions might well fall flat.[12]

All I have attempted to do in relation to McGuckian's work is to uncover sources and provide my own readings based on these findings, none of which is intended to be either complete or definitive.

Although there are times, of course, when I find my approach to be limited and limiting, failing to take me closer to a satisfactory reading of a poem, the scholarly work of uncovering sources can at least shed some light on a poetic text and enable readers to use the findings for their own interpretations in the future. Take, for example, 'Shaferi', a text which has received little comment to date (*MC* 29–30). While it begins with the admission of 'Ten simple mistakes', the reader is none the wiser as to what exactly these are, or why (and how) they impact upon the poet. One of the 'mistakes' is perhaps a failure of memory: the inability to discern between 'a song thrush' and a 'mistle thrush'; the wrong attribution of a season to the time she is attempting to recall. From her present-day perspective, the moment being recollected by the speaker seems somewhat colder, less comforting: 'Perhaps it was late / Summer and I remembered the burning / Brown of its polished trees as autumn'. Yet what is the reader to make of 'All those letters / About handkerchiefs (meaning passports)' and 'All those code-names for towns beginning / With cooler initials'? Such details, along with the situating place-names – the 'ominous address' at the corner of 'Gendarme and Prison Street' – all imply a loco-specific context. A narrative is being recounted, yet the reader struggles to discern its meaning. The author's veiled secrecy, the refusal to be more open, perhaps corresponds with the enforced covertness of the speaker's own activity: she must take care when plucking the letters 'Out of the network of the war-time mail' as she inhabits 'the most closely-watched place / In the Empire'. However, the reader still asks whether or not the text is a lyric poem suffused with autobiographical subject matter, or whether it is a dramatic monologue, with the poet adopting a mask and empathising with the life experiences of an exemplar. Perhaps because of its enigmatic character, the literary detective has a role to play in shedding light on this text. The worksheets provide a clue to one of the sources, as they make reference to 'The Union of Struggle' and name-check Lenin. Because my earlier research demonstrated that the surrounding poems in the collection take as their sources the writings of (or about) strong, exemplary women – Tsvetaeva, Ivinskaya, Brontë, Tatyana Tolstoy, amongst others – it did not take long to discover that 107 of the phrases used in the worksheets derive from Robert McNeal's biography of Lenin and Krupskaya, his wife.[13]

<table>
<tr><td>

All those letters about handkerchiefs (meaning passports) … all those code-names for towns beginning with the same letter as the town itself … all the substituting of women's names for men's … (99)
the Police had to pluck these letters out of the mails in Russia (100)
Tskarkoe Selo … was probably the most closely watched place in the Empire (37)
an aged retainer of the Romanovs who reverently turned the plates so that the double-headed eagle on the crest faced the diner. (186)

</td><td>

All those letters
About handkerchiefs (meaning passports);
All those code-names for towns beginning
With cooler initials; all the substituting
Of women's lives for men's; I plucked them
Out of the network of the war-time mail
To the most closely-watched place
In the Empire, and turned them
As he turned the plates so the double-headed
Eagle faced the diner.

</td></tr>
</table>

Much work has still to be done to tease out the possible connections between McGuckian's use of McNeal's text and the (as yet) unidentified second source that is used for the poem's opening lines. Nevertheless, the reader can see how, by 'plucking' the above quotations from the out-of-print source text, McGuckian pays homage to Krupskaya's ingenuity and indefatigable courage. The nostalgic turning of the plates by the Romanov's aged retainer is likened to, yet simultaneously countered by, Krupskaya's more revolutionary turn against the State powers. Reworking the text, the then 'most closely watched place in the Empire', Tskarkoe Selo, is linked to that of the present: Northern Ireland. While political circumstances dictate Krupskaya's mode of subterfuge, aesthetic concerns motivate McGuckian's: her 'turn' is to take what is ostensibly a story of conjugal love and political struggle, one that foregrounds the agency and equal status of the wife within the marital partnership, and to use the narrative to celebrate a free expression of desire and female authority:

> It wasn't true when he said it,
> 'Love is of the body'; it *became* true
> Later on, one winding and the other
> Unwinding, when it became unspoken,
> As my copper ring, fatigued, tightened
> In my baggy pocket into a book-shaped
> Brooch.

Citing Mr Emerson's advice to Lucy from *A Room with a View* that 'Love is of the body', a liberating counsel which, on the one hand, stresses a necessary balance between emotion and intellect and, on the other, discourages the repression of the heart's desire, McGuckian reads McNeal's account of Krupskaya's union with Lenin as analogous to her own adoption of the female pen. The 'copper ring' worn by the couple at the marriage ceremony 'to satisfy the rotten capitalists' (66) is transmuted, over time, into the 'hand-made brooch inscribed "Karl Marx"' (81). McGuckian's juxtaposition of the two items of jewellery marks the divestment by Krupskaya of all things linked to capitalism, and stresses her total commitment to her husband's Marxist philosophy. Yet by altering the quotation – the brooch becomes 'book-shaped' – the poet self-reflexively refers to her own progression as a writer. While both Krupskaya and McGuckian may well be depicted as inhabiting a domestic space and undertaking traditionally feminine tasks ('sewing gold stars / Into a skirt'), none the less both are authors who have succeeded in escaping from 'the many-faceted glass coffins of the patriar-chal texts whose properties male authors insisted that they are'.[14]

Will such a reading help or hinder McGuckian's reputation? It may be that, as reviewers become aware of the extent of her palimpsestuous method, readers will, when unable to locate the source of a particular poem, feel even more excluded by her writing than has been the case so far. Though regrettable, this should be no barrier to the ultimate recognition of her great achievement. Her method is certainly not unique. Describing the lengths to which one has to go in order to decipher Ezra Pound's Canto XXXIII, William Chace states that '[t]here is a considerable disequilibrium involved between Pound's opaque brevity and the prosaic lengths to which one must go in penetrating that opacity. Yet going to such lengths seems inevitable if one is to gain anything more than a transparently impression-istic sense of the poem.'[15] This has particular relevance for McGuckian's poetry since Pound's Canto XXXIII is a cento, made up entirely of quota-tions from letters to and from Thomas Jefferson. Though regarded initially as inaccessible, the canto became less so over time. Indeed, one could com-pare McGuckian's work with that of Marianne Moore who, as Elizabeth Gregory has demonstrated, includes unacknowledged quotations from 'such little-regarded sources as conversations overheard, park monuments, and books of the sort we generally consider "secondary material", such as biog-raphies, religious commentaries, and natural-history texts'.[16] By quoting 'secondary material', both Moore and McGuckian reflect their 'paradoxical position as [poets] who both [aspire] to authority and [question] the hierarchical terms on which authority circulates'.[17] As Gregory outlines, women poets often encounter the difficulty in establishing voices for themselves 'within a tradition that has been composed almost entirely of men', a tradition which 'operates on an understanding that the feminine is properly the object of poetic description, and is therefore of secondary importance, while the describer – the poet – is defined as masculine and primary through the opposition'.[18] By revealing McGuckian's engagement with exemplary figures like Brontë, Dickinson and Tsvetaeva, and by providing an informed reading of her sympathetic ink, the critic is able to facilitate an understanding of her struggle for authority.

It would be wrong, however, to regard Heaney, Muldoon and McGuckian as exceptional cases with regard to the use made of intertextuality by Northern Irish poets. A more comprehensive and exhaustive study would include examples from the work of Ciaran Carson, Gerald Dawe, John Hughes, Joan Newmann, Michael Longley, Derek Mahon, Frank Ormsby, Tom Paulin and James Simmons, amongst others. By way of a conclusion to this current study, I wish to explore briefly the use made of intertextuality by just one of these poets: Tom Paulin.

Paulin, the G. M. Young Lecturer in English Literature at Hertford College, Oxford, is a poet, dramatist, literary critic and editor, and has been a highly regarded television pundit on the BBC's *Late Review*. Yet he does not come across as an establishment figure; rather, he is a pugnacious dissenter, a 'lit-crit troublemaker'.[19] Paulin is, in Valentine Cunningham's words, 'a one-man literary awkward squad, the sort that doesn't compromise'.[20] While reviewers and academics have been quick to allude to his 'incisive tetchiness' and 'his irrepressibly maverick aggression'[21] – indeed, one critic goes so far as to claim that he 'seems disarmingly keen to sound mad … as if acting out some counter-stereotype of the graceless Ulster Prod'[22] – it would be wholly incorrect to dismiss his directly political writing as the product of some gauche antic disposition.

At times, of course, Paulin has been uncomfortably forthright and personal in his criticism, referring to Anthony Thwaite, the editor of Philip Larkin's *Selected Letters*, as 'a little balsawood minor man of letters who is of no consequence at all'.[23] Such vituperation, however, is an index not only of his passionate intensity, but also of his determination to break silence and seek redress. (In this instance, Thwaite was accused of being duplicitous in his editing of Larkin's letters, withholding passages which might have reflected badly on the poet.)[24] 'There are times in criticism', Paulin argues, 'when you just want confrontation and blood on the walls in order to break through all that civility and facetious protocol.'[25] In the introduction to *Writing to the Moment*, Paulin expresses a keen fascination for writing which is 'instant, excited, spontaneous, concentrated' and for journalistic texts that are 'provisional, off-hand, spontaneous, risky in this volatile mindset'.[26] In his fifth collection, *Walking a Line*, his lines acquire just such an austere brevity, avoiding iambic pentameter and punctuation; his lines of thought become less rigid. '51 Sans Souci Park' effectively presents his poetic manifesto:

> and a voice thrashing in the wilderness
> an unstill enormous
> is offering me this wisdom
> action's a solid bash
> narrative a straight line
> try writing to the moment
> as it wimples like a burn
> *baby it's NOW!*[27]

When applied to poetry, such a style can risk appearing impetuous, unfinished and off-the-cuff. In 'Chaos Theory', for example, Paulin denigrates the rationale behind François Mitterand's intervention in the Balkan conflict – he paid a six-hour visit to Sarajevo on 28 June 1992 to hasten the shipment of humanitarian relief by demonstrating that the airport was secure – as simply a publicity stunt by 'a little old man / corrupt near death'.[28]

Yet his polemical verse becomes far more successful when he adopts intertextual allusions as a shorthand, a form of writing to the moment that is briefly descriptive and that connects to wider debates. In 'Marc Chagall, *Over the Town*' he begins by describing the painting referred to in the title, reading the artistic text biographically: Chagall and his wife Bella are identified as the two figures 'flying happily over Vitebsk'. Although as an artist Chagall is 'above war revolutions pogroms', Paulin implies that this artistic exemplar is unafraid of representing the real socio-political conditions of his time, albeit obliquely (the painting was produced during the first winter of the Russian revolution). In *Over the Town*, there is 'a lout / squatting on the mud' and, like a figure from a Pieter Brueghel canvas, 'he's laying a turd'. What concerns Paulin is the way in which this is elided in modern reproductions – 'many a reproduction / mars this famous painting / by omitting not just his arse / but the entire squatting lout' – and he reads this as symptomatic of the way in which contemporary commentators attempt to separate art from politics. As he argued in his preface to *The Faber Book of Political Verse*, he does not believe 'that poems exist in a timeless vacuum or a soundproof museum, and that poets are gifted with an ability to hold themselves above history, rather like skylarks or weather satellites'.[29] He utterly disavows any crude distinction between the private and public realms, stating, 'what I'm agonizing about is how the public life – which is cruel and involves seeing people as statistics or mass aggregates – subsidizes certain people who are able to escape it, to get beneath their duvets and supposedly relate to each other'. As a poet, he rejects what he terms 'the cult of the intimate', arguing that 'the privatization of life' involves a deplorable 'retreat from any commitment to the public world'.[30] In 'Marc Chagall, *Over the Town*', he reiterates this argument by conjoining the censorship of the Russian Jew's painting with the literary establishment's silence over T. S. Eliot's supposed anti-Semitism:

> how quite a few
> critics of T. S. Eliot
> choose
> either to forgive or forget
> those bits of verse
> and one piece
> of coldly sinister prose
> that're about
> his fear and hatred of all Jews[31]

These jagged, colloquial lines act as a poetic gloss on his own favourable review of Anthony Julius's *Anti-Semitism and Literary Form* in which Paulin rails against 'those critics like Denis Donoghue, whose indifference to Eliot's anti-semitism makes them complicit in it'.[32] Rhyming 'few', 'choose' and 'Jews' reminds the reader not just of the Jews as 'the chosen few', but also of the choices made by critics to overlook the anti-Semitic strain in poems such as 'Dirge', 'A Cooking Egg', 'Gerontian' and 'Sweeney among the Nightingales'.[33]

The ramifying potential of intertextuality for Paulin can be seen if we look at a poem such as 'An Ulster Unionist Walks the Streets of London',[34] which focuses on the signing of the Anglo-Irish Agreement by the British and Irish governments at Hillsborough, Co. Down on 15 November 1985. In an early typescript draft the text appeared as follows:

> For six hours ~~yesterday~~
> there was no flag ~~flying~~

[over] on the Governor's mansion.
Neither tricolour
nor the union flag
could let itself go
among rook-crawk and wind-rip.
I stood in the sealed square
knowing the world of signs
sighed for an absence
like that ordinary moment
when you forgot to hold your breath.[35]

At this stage, the poem is a first-person lyric, with the protagonist identifiable as the poet himself who registers a sense of loss, enclosure, disenfranchisement and alienation. The deletions are all amendatory, ridding the text of superfluous detail and rendering it more immediate (there is no longer a temporal distance from the day of signing). In the finished text Paulin incorporates key intertexts – both included by him, as editor, in his section on 'Northern Irish Oratory' in the third volume of *The Field Day Anthology of Irish Writing* – that crucially alter the poem's scope and focus, and allows for a rare empathy with the Unionist position in Northern Ireland:

All that Friday
there was no flag –
no Union Jack,
no tricolour –
on the governor's mansion.
I waited outside the gate-lodge,
waited like a dog
in my own province
till a policeman brought me
a signed paper.

The phrase 'waited like a dog / in my own province' is taken from a speech made by the then deputy leader of the Official Unionist Party, Harold J. McCusker, in the House of Commons on 27 November 1985, on the subject of the Agreement. Excluded from the talks prior to the Agreement and forced to wait 'like a dog' outside Hillsborough Castle while the signing ceremony was taking place, he felt that the British government had 'sold [his] birthright'. Following the Agreement, what constitutes 'my own province' and 'my own people' is left uncertain for the disaffected Unionist. In his speech, McCusker argued that his own children now had the status of 'some sort of semi-British citizen'. Extending the poem and comparing the

speaker's position with that of the three Hebrew children from the Book of
Daniel (Shadrach, Meshech and Abednego), refusing to bow down before a
foreign power, Paulin quotes from a second speech, this time made by the
leader of the Democratic Unionist Party, Ian Paisley, on 14 November, de-
nouncing the Agreement: 'Like the three Hebrew children, we will not budge,
we will not bend and we will not burn. This simple sum you will have to
learn the hard way – six into 26 will never go'.[36]

The way in which Paulin includes quotations in the above poems is akin
to Muldoon's use of intertextuality: he references the names of artists and
historical figures to guide the reader. However, in other poems he seems
closer to McGuckian's method of citation. In 'Trotsky in Finland',[37] for
example, Paulin touches upon the poetry–politics dialectic by appropriating quotations from a single text. The poem's subtitle informs the reader
that the poem centres upon 'an incident' (SM 29) from the Russian
revolutionary's memoirs. Juxtaposing the poem with an extract from My
Life,[38] we can fully appreciate the extent to which Paulin imports text from
Trotsky's autobiography:[39]

	The pension is very quiet. It is called Rauha, meaning 'peace' in Finnish. The air is transparent, perfecting The pine trees and lakes. … … … … … … … . .
The environment in which I lived in Finland, with its hills, *pine-trees and lakes, its transparent autumn air,* and its peace, was scarcely a reminder of a permanent revolution. At the end of September I moved still farther into the Finnish interior and took up my quarters in the woods on the shore of a lake, in an isolated pension, *'Rauha'. This name in Finnish* *means 'peace'.* The huge *pension* was almost empty in the *autumn.* A *Swedish writer* was staying there during these *last days* with an English actress, and they left without paying their bill. The *proprietor rushed after them to Helsingfors.* His wife was very ill; they could only *keep her heart beating* *by means of champagne.* I never saw her. She died while the proprietor was still away. Her body was in a room above me. (*ML* 173–74, emphasis added)	The last days of autumn. The Swedish writer Adds another sonnet to his cycle. His English mistress drifts through the garden. An actress, she admires her face Bloomed in the smooth lake. At night her giggles and frills dismay The strictness of minor art. They leave without paying their bill. The owner chases them to Helsingfors. His invisible wife is lying in the room Above – they must give her champagne To keep her heart beating, but she dies While her husband screams for money. The head-waiter sets out to find him.

Yet the poetic speaker is no Pangloss, uttering only quotations; rather, he
selects material related to one particular period in Trotsky's life and

embellishes upon the pregiven narrative. Paulin chooses to concentrate upon Trotsky's peaceful interim in Finland prior to his return to Russia in 1905. Presented as a hiatus between events of historical importance, Trotsky's stay at the Finnish pension – 'Rauha' – allows the poet to indulge in imaginative speculation:

> It might be somewhere Swiss,
> The wooden cuckoos calling to an uneventful
> Absence, their polyglot puns
> Melting in Trieste or Zürich.

'Uneventful' is ironic since quite a lot happens: the Swedish writer and his mistress flee without paying their bill; the pension's owner chases them to Helsingfors; his wife dies of heart failure. This period is associated with art and stasis: the writer produces 'minor art'; the actress indulges in 'giggles and frills'. In contrast to this 'bourgeois moment', the arrival of the 'St Petersburg papers' precipitates the plunge 'from stillness into history' (*SM*, 30), namely his famous speech to the assembled masses 'in the great hall of the Polytechnic Institute in St Petersburg' (*ML* 174). However, the poem does not frame its argument within a strict binary opposition between artistic creation and political action. Although Paulin refers to the stay in Finland as 'a kind of Chekovian flimsiness', the literariness of Trotsky's prose at this juncture[40] complicates matters. In fact, Paulin rewrites a section from Trotsky's autobiography as a poem and portrays the revolutionary as a poet: "'If this were a fiction, it would be Byron / Riding out of the Tivoli Gardens, his rank / And name set aside. Forced by more than himself" (*SM* 30). Commitment to art does not preclude political engagement. Paulin himself views his own act of appropriation as a means of transforming history, 'translating it into imaginative terms'.[41] Clearly, bricolage can be a transformative praxis as opposed to a medley of spare parts, and the originality lies in the ingenuity of the connections.

Paulin's poetry has become increasingly more allusive, incorporating snippets of remembered phrases and quotations to form centos. Writing about this form, particularly with regard to William Hazlitt's prose which he describes as 'a version of Milton's poetic centos',[42] he states that the cento's function is to provide old ideas with 'a redemptive life'. In Hazlitt's prose, for example, he argues that there is 'a new quickening spirit which melts down or decomposes quotations, sources, and subjects in order to recompose'.[43] In his introduction to the recent Penguin edition of Hazlitt's writings,

Paulin expands upon this theme: 'If the critic is an epic compiler of centos, a Cellini melting down prefabricated materials, he is also an actor, someone who imaginatively participates in the works he evaluates.'[44] The writer who creates centos is not equated with the lowly jobbing copyist; rather, he is a creative artist, one who all the while performing the task of iteration is also carrying out one of evaluation. The collage of quotations is, therefore, not like the 'stinksome inkenstink', the 'alphybettyformed verbage' of *Finnegans Wake* in which the 'quashed quotatoes' emphasise unoriginality and detritus.[45] Although Paulin has previously used the image of faeces to suggest the impossibility of originality through language in both 'The New Year' ('my own language / where each word / strains to utter itself / like a mallety wooden turd') and 'Middle Age' ('that sunny little turdshrine / called *My Personal Wisdom*'),[46] here the derivative nature of the quotations is celebrated, stressing the vibrancy of their sounds. Indeed, in his most recent collection, *The Invasion Handbook*, he rehabilitates the image to describe the art of Kurt Schwitters:

> where what to me is Schmiere
> is grease
> to you's *a kind*
> *of faecal smearing*
> just pure shite
> no stainedglass saint
> glowing inside a church
> where these bits – little bits and pieces
> call them des bribes et des morceaux en
> plein air – I mean plain air
> are fixed with glue
> and yet they're preserved
> - well like faeces –
> is to miss the way each series
> of matched jerks
> ....
> asserts the necessary the found beauty
> I have called Merz[47]

Schwitters created assemblages, transforming *objets trouvés* by establishing relationships between the materials through an intuitive logic. His was not the disposable anti-art of Dadaism; rather, as he argued, 'whereas Dadaism merely poses antitheses, Merz reconciles antitheses by assigning relative values to every element in the work of art. Pure Merz is art, pure Dadaism is anti-art; in both cases deliberately so'.[48] Writing centos has, in some respects, become an artistic principle for Paulin, just as it has for McGuckian. By joining together citations and remembered quotations, he incorporates the writing styles of others in his own text, often offering either a critique or analysis of the author in the process. For example, in 'The Four', a prose text based on the Versailles Treaty negotiations, from his latest collection *The Invasion Handbook*, he creates an assemblage from sections taken from John Maynard Keynes's *The Economic Consequences of Peace*, inserting occasional lines of his own to augment the vitriolic attack on the policies dictated by the presiding heads of state (Clemenceau, Wilson, Lloyd George). By adopting the cento form, Paulin not only succeeds in presenting a condensed version of Keynes's treatise, he also deflects the earlier criticism concerning his verbal truculence: not only are his arguments a matter of ventriloquism, he presents the antithetical arguments in the very next poem, 'Mantoux', based on Étienne Mantoux's rejection of Keynesian economics in *The Carthaginian Peace*.

Notes

1   Paul Muldoon, *To Ireland, I* (Oxford: Oxford University Press, 2000) 5.
2   Jeffrey Wainwright, *Acceptable Words: Essays on the Poetry of Geoffrey Hill* (Manchester: Manchester University Press, 2005) 1.
3   Paul Muldoon, 'Bears', *The Wishbone* (Dublin: Gallery Press, 1984) 11.
4   See Tim Kendall, *Paul Muldoon* (Brigend: Seren, 1996) 120–1.
5   Muldoon, *To Ireland, I* 107.
6   Stephen James, 'Geoffrey Hill and the Rhetoric of Violence', *Essays in Criticism* 53.1 (2003) 33.
7   Geoffrey Hill, *Speech! Speech!* (Washington, DC: Counterpoint, 2000) 10.
8   Wainwright, *Acceptable Words* 100.
9   Christopher Ricks, *The Force of Poetry* (Oxford: Clarendon Press, 1984) 285.
10 Leontia Flynn, 'The Life of the Author: Medbh McGuckian and Her Critics', in Fionnuala Dillane and Ronan Kelly (eds), *New Voices in Irish Criticism 4* (Dublin: Four Courts Press, 2003) 162.
11 Flynn, 'The Wife of the Author' 166.
12 Rachel Buxton, *Robert Frost and Northern Irish Poetry* (Oxford: Clarendon Press, 2004), 13.
13 Robert H. McNeal, *Bride of the Revolution: Krupskaya and Lenin* (London: Victor Gollancz, 1973). Further references are cited in text.
14 Sandra M. Gilbert and Susan Gubar, *The Madwoman in the Attic: The Woman Writer and the Nineteenth-Century Literary Imagination* (2nd edn) (New Haven, CT: Yale University Press, 2000) 43.
15 William M. Chace, 'The Canto as Cento: A Reading of Canto XXXIII', *Paideuma* 1.1

(Spring-Summer, 1972) 100.

16   Elizabeth Gregory, *Quotation and Modern American Poetry* (Houston: Rice University Press, 1996) 129.

17   Gregory, *Quotation* 130.

18   Gregory, *Quotation* 131.

19   Graham Wood, 'The Perils of Paulin', *Times Magazine* 17 April (1993) 14.

20   Valentine Cunningham, 'The Civil War is Still Going On', *Observer* 12 January 1992, 45.

21   Keith Silver, 'Going Somewhere', *PN Review* 105 (September–October, 1995) 70.

22   Edna Longley, *Poetry and Posterity* (Northumberland: Bloodaxe, 2000) 224.

23   Paulin, cited in Wood, 'The Perils of Paulin' 15.

24   See the exchange of letters between Paulin and Thwaite in the *Times Literary Supplement* 6 November–4 December 1992.

25   Paulin, cited in Wood, 'The Perils of Paulin' 15.

26   Tom Paulin, 'Introduction', in Paulin, *Writing to the Moment: Selected Critical Essays, 1980–1996* (London: Faber, 1996) xii.

27   Tom Paulin, '51 Sans Souci Park', in Paulin, *Walking a Line* (London: Faber, 1994), 33–4.

28   Tom Paulin, 'Chaos Theory', in Paulin, *The Invasion Handbook* (London: Faber, 2002), 136.

29   Tom Paulin, 'Introduction', in Paulin (ed.), *The Faber Book of Political Verse* (London: Faber, 1986) 17.

30   Paulin in John Haffenden, *Viewpoint: Poets in Conversation* (London: Faber, 1981) 164–65.

31   Tom Paulin, 'Marc Chagall, *Over the Town*', in Paulin, *The Wind Dog* (London: Faber, 1999) 19–20.

32   Tom Paulin, 'T. S. Eliot and Anti-Semitism', in Paulin, *Writing to the Moment* 151.

33   The piece of 'coldly sinister prose' is a review of *The Yellow Spot: The Outlawing of Half a Million Human Beings* (1936) published in Eliot's *Criterion*. Paulin subsequently admitted that he was wrong in identifying Eliot as the author of the piece.

34   Tom Paulin, 'An Ulster Unionist Walks the Streets of London', in Paulin, *Fivemiletown* (London: Faber, 1987) 42–3.

35   Paulin, 'The Hillsborough Treaty', TS draft in Box 20 Folder 5, MSS 880 Tom Paulin Papers, Special Collections, Robert W. Woodruff Library, Emory University.

36   The phrase '6 into 26 will never go' refers to the Unionist slogan rejecting any move to bring the six counties that make up Northern Ireland into a united Ireland (32 counties). '6 into 26' was also the title of an early version of 'The Defenestration of Hillsborough' which was published alongside 'An Ulsterman Walks the Streets of London' in the *Irish Times* on 21 June, 1986.

37   Tom Paulin, 'Trotsky in Finland', *The Strange Museum* (Faber, 1980), 29–30. Hereafter referred to in text as *SM*.

38   Leon Trotsky, *My Life* (London: Peter Smith, 1970). Hereafter referred to in text as *ML*.

39   In an interview with John Haffenden, Paulin says that he has 'pinched' the poem from Trotsky's memoir. See John Haffenden, *Viewpoints: Poets in Conversation with John Haffenden* (London: Faber, 1981), 168.

40   Paulin in interview with Haffenden, 168.

41   Paulin in interview with Haffenden, 168.

42 Tom Paulin, *The Day-Star of Liberty: William Hazlitt's Radical Style* (London: Faber, 1998) 95.

43 Paulin, *Day-Star* 95.

44 Paulin, 'Introduction', in *William Hazlitt: The Fight and Other Writings* (London: Penguin, 2000) xii.

45 James Joyce, *Finnegans Wake*, first pub. 1939 (London: Faber, 1975) 183. See Jennifer Schiffer Levine, 'Originality and Repetition in *Finnegans Wake* and *Ulysses*' *PMLA* 94.1 (January, 1979) 106–20.

46 Paulin, *Walking a Line* 9, 15.

47 Paulin, 'Merz', *The Invasion Handbook* (London: Faber, 2002) 33.

48 Kurt Schwitters cited in John Elderfield, *Kurt Schwitters* (London: Thames and Hudson, 1985) 67.

Select Bibliography

SEAMUS HEANEY

Primary Sources

Collected Poems

Death of a Naturalist. London: Faber, 1966.
Door into the Dark. London: Faber, 1969.
Wintering Out. London: Faber, 1972.
North. London: Faber, 1975.
Field Work. London: Faber, 1979.
Sweeney Astray. London: Faber, 1983.
Station Island. London: Faber, 1984.
The Haw Lantern. London: Faber, 1987.
New Selected Poems 1966–1987. London: Faber, 1990.
Seeing Things. London: Faber, 1991.
The Spirit Level. London: Faber, 1996.
Electric Light. London: Faber, 2001.

Prose

'John Bull's Other Island'. *Listener* 29 September 1977, 397–99.
'The Interesting Case of John Alphonsus Mulrennan'. *Planet* (January, 1978) 34–40.
'Two Voices'. *London Review of Books* 20 March 1980, 8.
'A Tale of Two Islands: Reflections on the Irish Literary Revival', in P. J. Drudy, *Irish Studies.* Cambridge: Cambridge University Press, 1980, 1–20.
Preoccupations: Selected Prose 1968–1978. London: Faber, 1980.
'Current Unstated Assumptions About Poetry'. *Critical Inquiry* (Summer, 1981) 645–51.
'Osip and Nadezhda Mandelstam'. *London Review of Books* 2 September 1981, 3–6.
'The Nerves in Leaf'. *Ireland of the Welcomes* 31.2 (March–April, 1982) 19–20.
Preface, in Richard Kearney and Mark Patrick Hederman (eds), *Crane Bag Books of Irish Studies.* Gerrard's Cross: Colin Smythe, 1983, i–ii.
Among Schoolchildren: A John Malone Memorial Lecture. Belfast: John Malone Memo-

rial Committee, 1983.

'Envies and Identifications: Dante and the Modern Poet'. *Irish University Review* 15.1 (Spring, 1985) 5–19.

'"Place and Displacement": Recent Poetry from Northern Ireland'. *Wordsworth Circle* 16.2 (Spring, 1985) 48–56. Repr. in Andrews (ed.), *Contemporary Irish Poetry* 124–44.

The Government of the Tongue: The T. S. Eliot Memorial Lectures and Other Critical Writing. London: Faber, 1988.

The Place of Writing. Atlanta: Scholars Press, 1989.

'Learning from Eliot'. *Agenda* 27.1 (Spring, 1989) 17–31.

'The Regional Forecast', in R. P. Draper (ed.), *The Literature of Region and Nation.* London: Macmillan, 1989, 10–23.

'Above the Brim: On Robert Frost'. *Salmagundi* (Fall, 1990) 275–94.

'Correspondence: Emigrants and Exiles'. Richard Kearney (ed.), *Migrations: The Irish at Home and Abroad.* Dublin: Wolfhound Press, 1990, 21–31.

'The Sense of the Past'. *History Ireland* 1.4 (Winter, 1993) 33–37.

The Redress of Poetry: Oxford Lectures. London: Faber, 1995.

'The Frontier of Writing', in Jacqueline Genet and Wynne Hellegouarch (eds), *Irish Writers and Their Creative Process.* Gerrards Cross: Colin Smythe, 1996, 3–16.

Interviews

Interview by Harriet Cooke. *Irish Times* 28 December 1973, 8.

Interview by Caroline Walsh. *Irish Times* 6 December 1975, 5.

'Unhappy and at Home'. Interview by Seamus Deane. *Crane Bag* 1.1 (1977) 61–67.

Interview by James Randall. *Ploughshares* 5.3 (1979) 7–22.

'Artists on Art: An Interview with Seamus Heaney'. Interview by Frank Kinahan. *Critical Inquiry* 8.3 (Spring, 1982) 404–15.

Interview by June Beisch. *Literary Review* 29.2 (Winter, 1986) 161–69.

Interview by Rand Brandes. *Salmagundi* 80 (Fall, 1988) 4–21.

'Calling the Tune'. Interview by Tom Adair. *The Linen Hall Review* 6.2 (Autumn, 1989) 5–8.

'Seamus Famous: Time to Be Dazzled'. Interview by Blake Morrison. *The Independent on Sunday* 19 May 1991, 26–27.

'Between North and South'. Interview by Richard Kearney, in Kearney (ed.), *Visions of Europe: Conversations on the Legacy and Future of Europe.* Dublin: Wolfhound Press, 1992, 81–89.

'The Art of Poetry LXXV'. Interview by Henri Cole. *Paris Review* 144 (Fall, 1997) 89–138.

Secondary Sources

Allen, Michael. 'The Parish and the Dream: Heaney and America, 1969–1987', in Patten (ed.*)*, *Returning to Ourselves: Second Volume of Papers from the John Hewitt Summer School.* Belfast: Lagan Press, 1995, 227–39.

Allison, Jonathan. 'Acts of Union: Seamus Heaney's Tropes of Sex and Marriage'. *Éire–Ireland* 27.4 (1992) 106–21.

Anderson, Nathalie F. 'Queasy Proximity: Seamus Heaney's Mythical Method'. *Éire–Ireland* 23.4 (1988) 103–113.

Andrews, Elmer. *The Poetry of Seamus Heaney: All the Realms of Whisper.* London: Macmillan, 1988.

— (ed.). *Seamus Heaney: A Collection of Critical Essays.* London: Macmillan, 1992.

— (ed.). *The Poetry of Seamus Heaney.* Cambridge: Icon Books, 1998.

Annwyn, David. '"The Distance Within": Nationalism in the Poetry of Seamus Heaney.' *Poetry Wales* 23.2–3 (1988) 46–50.

Atfield, J. R. 'Creative Tensions in the Poetry of Seamus Heaney'. *Critical Survey* 3.1 (1991) 80–87.

Brown, Richard. 'Bog Poems and Bog Books: Doubleness, Self-Translation and Pun in Seamus Heaney and Paul Muldoon'. Corcoran (ed.), *Chosen Ground* 153–67.

Browne, Vincent. 'Violent Prophecies: The Writer and Northern Ireland'. *Éire–Ireland* 10.2 (1975) 109–19.

Cahill, Eileen. 'A Silent Voice: Seamus Heaney and Ulster Politics'. *Critical Quarterly* 29.3 (1987) 54–70.

Corcoran, Neil. *Seamus Heaney.* London: Faber, 1986.

Cosgrove, Brian. 'Inner Freedom and Political Obligation: Seamus Heaney and the Claims of Irish Nationalism.' *Studies* 79 (1990) 268–80.

Coughlan, Patricia. '"Bog Queens": The Representation of Women in the Poetry of John Montague and Seamus Heaney', in Toni O'Brien Johnson and David Cairns, *Gender in Irish Writing.* Milton Keynes: Open University Press, 1991, 89–111.

Cullingford, Elizabeth Butler. 'Thinking of Her … as … Ireland: Yeats, Pearse, and Heaney'. *Textual Practice* 4.1 (Spring, 1990) 1–21.

Curtis, Tony (ed.). *The Art of Seamus Heaney* (3rd edn). Dublin: Wolfhound Press, 1994.

Deane, Seamus. 'The Timorous and the Bold'. *Celtic Revivals.* London: Faber, 1985, 174–86.

Fennell, Desmond. *Why Seamus Heaney is No. 1.* Dublin: ELO Publications, 1991.

Foster, John Wilson. *The Achievement of Seamus Heaney.* Dublin: Lilliput Press, 1995.

Foster, Thomas C. *Seamus Heaney.* Dublin: O'Brien Press, 1989.

Garratt, Robert F. (ed.). *Critical Essays on Seamus Heaney.* New York: G. K. Hall, 1995.

Haberstroh, Patricia. 'Poet, Poetry, Painting and Artist in Seamus Heaney's *North*'. *Éire–Ireland* 23.4 (1988) 103–13.

Hart, Henry. *Seamus Heaney: Poet of Contrary Progressions.* New York: Syracuse University Press, 1992.

Hederman, Mark Patrick. 'Seamus Heaney: The Reluctant Poet'. *Crane Bag* 3.2 (1979) 61–70.

Horton, Patricia. '"Time that Was Extra, Unforeseen and Free": Representations of Childhood in the Poetry of Seamus Heaney', in Patten (ed.), *Returning to Ourselves* 287–96.

Jenkins, Nicholas. 'Walking on Air'. *Times Literary Supplement* 5 July 1996, 10–12.

John, Brian. 'Contemporary Irish Poetry and the Matter of Ireland: Thomas Kinsella, John Montague and Seamus Heaney', in Richard Wall (ed.), *Medieval and Modern Ireland.* New Jersey: Barnes and Noble, 1988, 34–59.

Kerrigan, John. 'Earth Writing: Seamus Heaney and Ciaran Carson'. *Essays in Criticism* 48.2 (April, 1998) 144–68.

Kiberd, Declan. 'Culture and Babarism: Heaney's Poetry and its Recent Critics'. *Poetry Ireland Review* 27 (1989) 29–37.

Kinzie, Mary. 'Deeper than Declared: On Seamus Heaney'. *Salmagundi* (Fall, 1988) 22–57.

Longley, Edna. '"Inner Émigré" or "Artful Voyeur"?: Seamus Heaney's *North*', in Curtis (ed.), *The Art of Seamus Heaney* 65–95.

Malloy, Catherine and Phyllis Carey (eds). *Seamus Heaney: The Shaping Spirit.* Newark: University of Delaware Press, 1996.

Molino, Michael. *Questioning Tradition, Language, and Myth: The Poetry of Seamus Heaney.* Washington: Catholic University of America Press, 1994.

Morrison, Blake. *Seamus Heaney.* London: Methuen, 1982.

— 'Encounters with Familiar Ghosts'. *Times Literary Supplement* 19 October 1984, 1191–92.

O'Brien, Conor Cruise. 'A Slow North-East Wind'. *Listener* 25 September 1975, 404–5.

— 'An Unhealthy Intersection'. *New Review* 2.16 (July, 1975) 3–8.

O'Brien, Darcy. 'Piety and Modernism: Seamus Heaney's "Station Island"'. *James Joyce Quarterly* 26.1 (Fall, 1988) 51–65.

O'Donoghue, Bernard. *Seamus Heaney and the Language of Poetry.* London: Harvester Wheatsheaf, 1994.

Parker, Michael. *Seamus Heaney: The Making of a Poet.* Dublin: Gill and Macmillan, 1993.

Sailer, Susan Shaw. 'Time Against Time: Myth in the Poetry of Yeats and Heaney'. *Canadian Journal of Irish Studies* 17.2 (1991) 54–63.

Sharpe, Tony. 'Politics and Art: Forms of Engagement in Poems by Marvell, Yeats, and Heaney'. *Durham University Journal* 51.1 (1990) 19–28.

Smith, Stan. 'The Distance Between: Seamus Heaney', in Corcoran (ed.), *Chosen Ground* 35–61.

Stanfield, Paul Scott. 'Facing *North* Again: Polyphony, Contention'. *Éire–Ireland* 23.4 (1988) 133–44.

MEDBH MCGUCKIAN

Primary Sources

Collected Poems

Portrait of Joanna. Belfast: Ulsterman Publications, 1980.
Single Ladies. Devon: Interim Press, 1980.
Trio Poetry 2. Belfast: Blackstaff Press, 1981.
Poetry Introduction 5. London: Faber, 1982.
The Flower Master. Oxford: Oxford University Press, 1982.
Venus and The Rain. Oxford: Oxford University Press, 1984.
On Ballycastle Beach. Oxford: Oxford University Press, 1988.
Two Women, Two Shores: Blue Farm. Maryland: Chestnut Hills Press, 1989.
Marconi's Cottage. Meath: Gallery Press, 1991.
The Flower Master and Other Poems. Meath: Gallery Press, 1993.
Captain Lavender. Meath: Gallery Press, 1994.
On Ballycastle Beach (revised edn). Meath: Gallery Press, 1995.
Shelmalier. Meath: Gallery Press, 1998.
Drawing Ballerinas. Meath: Gallery Press, 2001.
The Face of the Earth. Meath: Gallery Press, 2002.
The Soldiers of Year II. North Carolina: Wake Forest Press, 2003.
Had I a Thousand Lives. Meath: Gallery Press, 2003.
The Book of the Angel. Meath: Gallery Press, 2005.

Interviews

Interview by Rebecca E. Wilson, in Gillean Somerville-Arjat and Rebecca E. Wilson (eds), *Sleeping with Monsters: Conversations with Scottish and Irish Women Poets*. Edinburgh: Polygon, 1990, 1–7.
'An Attitude of Compassion'. Interview by Kathleen McCracken. *Irish Literary Supplement* (Fall, 1990) 20–21.
'Medbh McGuckian: Imagery Wrought to its Uttermost'. Interview by Cecile Gray, in Fleming, *Learning the Trade* 165–77.
'An Interview with Medbh McGuckian'. Interview by Susan Sailer Shaw. *Michigan Quarterly Review* 32.1 (1993) 111–27.
'Surfacing: An Interview with Medbh McGuckian'. Interview by Kimberly S. Bohman. *Irish Review* 16 (Autumn–Winter, 1994) 95–108.

'A Hinge into Something Larger: Meetings with Medbh McGuckian'. Interview by Helen Kidd. *Oxford Poetry* 8.2 (Winter, 1994–1995) 53–57.

Interview by Rand Brandes. *Chattahoochee Review* 16.3 (Spring, 1996) 56–65.

'The Resolution of Opposites: Part Two'. Interview by Sarah Broom. *Poetry and Audience* 37.2 (Summer, 1996) 10–17.

'A Dialogue with Medbh McGuckian'. Interview by Rand Brandes. *Studies in the Literary Imagination* 30.2 (Fall, 1997) 37–47.

'"My Words Are Traps": An Interview with Medbh McGuckian'. Interview by John Hobbs. *New Hibernia Review* 2.1 (Spring, 1998): 111–20.

'*Comhrá*.' Interview by Laura O'Connor. *Southern Review* 31.3 (Summer, 1995) 581–614.

'I Am Listening in Black and White to What Speaks to Me in Blue'. Interview by Helen Blakeman. *Irish Studies Review*. 11.1 (April, 2003) 61–69.

Secondary Sources

Allen, Michael. 'The Poetry of Medbh McGuckian'. Elmer Andrews (ed.), *Contemporary Irish Poetry*. 286–309.

Beer, Ann. 'Medbh McGuckian's Poetry: Maternal Thinking and a Politics of Peace'. *Canadian Journal of Irish Studies* 18.1 (July, 1992) 192–203.

Bendall, Molly. 'Flower Logic: The Poems of Medbh McGuckian'. *Antioch Review* 48.3 (Summer, 1990) 367–71.

Byron, Catherine. 'A House of One's Own: Three Contemporary Irish Women Poets'. *Women's Review* 19 (May, 1987) 32–33.

— 'The Room is a Kind of Travel Also: An Appreciation of the Poetry of Medbh McGuckian'. *Linen Hall Review* 5.1 (Spring, 1988) 16–17.

— '"Such Declarations May Be Routine Enough in the McGuckian Household"'. *Honest Ulsterman* 88 (1989) 87–88.

Cahill, Eileen. '"Because I Never Garden": Medbh McGuckian's Solitary Way'. *Irish University Review* 24.2 (Autumn–Winter, 1994) 264–71.

Docherty, Thomas. 'Initiations, Tempers, Seductions: Postmodern McGuckian', in Corcoran (ed.), *Chosen Ground* 191–210.

Fogarty, Anne. '"A Noise of Myth": Speaking (as) Woman in the Poetry of Eavan Boland and Medbh McGuckian'. *Paragraph* 17.1 (March, 1994) 92–103.

Fulford, Sarah. *Gendered Spaces in Contemporary Irish Poetry*. Oxford: Peter Lang, 2002.

Grant, Patrick. *Rhetoric and Violence in Northern Ireland, 1968–1998: Hardened to Death*. Basingstoke: Palgrave, 2001.

Maron, Meva. 'The Stamps Had Squirrels on Them'. *Honest Ulsterman* 88 (1989) 33–34.

McGuinness, Arthur E. 'Hearth and History: Poetry by Contemporary Irish Women', in Michael Kennealy (ed.), *Cultural Contexts and Literary Idioms in Contemporary Irish Literature*. Gerrards Cross: Colin Smythe, 1988, 197–220.

O'Brien, Peggy. 'Reading Medbh McGuckian: Admiring What We Cannot Understand'. *Colby Quarterly* 28.4 (December, 1992) 239–50.

Robinson, Alan. *Instabilities in Contemporary British Poetry*. London: Macmillan, 1988, 202–208.

Wills, Clair. 'Voices from the Nursery: Medbh McGuckian's Plantation', in Kennealy (ed.), *Poetry in Contemporary Irish Literature* 373–99.

PAUL MULDOON

Primary Sources

Collected Poems

Knowing My Place. Belfast: Ulsterman Publications, 1971.
New Weather. London: Faber, 1973.
Spirit Of Dawn. Belfast: Ulsterman Publications, 1975.
Mules. London: Faber, 1977.
Names and Addresses. Belfast: Ulsterman Publications, 1978.
The O-O's Party, New Year's Eve. Dublin: Gallery Press, 1980.
Why Brownlee Left. London: Faber, 1980.
Quoof. London: Faber, 1983.
The Wishbone. Dublin: Gallery Press, 1984.
Meeting the British. London: Faber, 1987.
Madoc: A Mystery. London: Faber, 1990.
The Prince of the Quotidian. Meath: Gallery Press, 1994.
The Annals of Chile. London: Faber, 1994.
The Last Thesaurus. London: Faber, 1995.
New Selected Poems 1968–1994. London: Faber, 1996.
The Noctuary of Narcissus Batt. London: Faber, 1997.
Hay. London: Faber, 1998.
Moy Sand and Gravel. London: Faber, 2002.
Medley for Morin Khur. London: Enitharmon Press, 2005.

Play and Opera

Shining Brow. London: Faber, 1993.
Six Honest Serving Men. Meath: Gallery Press, 1995.

Prose

'Paul Muldoon Writes'. *Poetry Book Society Bulletin* 106 (Autumn, 1980) 1.
'Paul Muldoon Writes'. *Poetry Society Bulletin* 118 (Autumn, 1983) 1.
'A Tight Wee Place in Armagh'. *Fortnight* 206 (July-August, 1984) 19, 23.
'Getting Round: Notes towards an *Ars Poetica*'. *Essays in Criticism* 48.2 (April, 1998) 107–28.
'The Point of Poetry'. *Princeton University Library Chronicle* 59.3 (Spring, 1998) 503–16.
To Ireland, I. London: Faber, 2000.

Interviews

'Paul Muldoon'. Interview by John Haffenden. *Viewpoints: Poets in Conversation.* London: Faber, 1981, 130–42.
'A Conversation with Paul Muldoon'. Interview by Michael Donaghy. *Chicago Review* 35.1 (1985) 76–85.
'An Interview with Paul Muldoon'. Interview by Clair Wills et al. *Oxford Poetry* 3.1 (Winter, 1986–87) 14–20.
'Q. & A.: Paul Muldoon'. Interview by Kevin Barry. *Irish Literary Supplement* 6.2 (Fall, 1987) 36–37.
'Lunch with Pancho Villa'. Interview by Kevin Smith. *Rhinoceros* 4 (1990) 75–94.
'An Interview with Paul Muldoon'. Interview by Lynn Keller. *Contemporary Poetry* 35.1 (Spring, 1994) 1–29.
'Smelling of Elderflowers'. Interview by Patrick Barron. *Fortnight* 332 (October, 1994) 42–44.
Interview by Edward Brunner et al. *Crab Orchard Review* 1.2 (1996) 13–23.
Interview by John Redmond. *Thumbscrew* 1.4 (Spring, 1996) 2–18.
'It's Always the Right Word: An Interview with Paul Muldoon'. Interview by Stephen Magee. *Honest Ulsterman* 102 (Autumn, 1996) 109–15.
'An Interview with Paul Muldoon'. Interview by Dominique Gauthier. *Études Irlandaises* 22.1 (Spring, 1997) 53–70.
'The Invention of the I: A Conversation with Paul Muldoon'. Interview by Earl G. Ingersoll and Stan Sanvel Rubin. *Michigan Quarterly Review* 37.1 (1998) 63–73.

Secondary Sources

Allison, Jonathan. 'Questioning Yeats: Paul Muldoon's '7, Middagh Street', in Fleming, *Learning the Trade* 3–20.
—'"Everything Provisional": Fictive Possibility and the Poetry of Paul Muldoon and Ciaran Carson'. *Études Irlandaises* 20.2 (Autumn, 1995) 87–93.
Andrews, Elmer (ed.). *Contemporary Irish Poetry: A Collection of Critical Essays.* London: Macmillan, 1992.

Batten, Guinn. '"He Could Barely Tell One from the Other": The Borderline Disorders of Paul Muldoon's Poetry'. *South Atlantic Quarterly* 95.1 (Winter, 1996) 171–204.

Brown, Richard. 'Bog Poems and Book Poems: Doubleness, Self-Translations and Pun in Seamus Heaney and Paul Muldoon', in Corcoran (ed.), *Chosen Ground* 153–67.

Brown, Terence. 'Telling Tales: Kennelly's *Cromwell*, Muldoon's "The More a Man Has the More a Man Wants"', in Kenneally (ed.), *Poetry in Contemporary Irish Literature* 144–57.

Buchanan, Barbara. 'Paul Muldoon: Who's to Know What's Knowable?', in Andrews (ed.), *Contemporary Irish Poetry* 310–27.

Connor, Lester I. 'Paul Muldoon', in Vincent B. Sherry, Jr. (ed.), *Dictionary of Literary Biography. Vol. 40: Poets of Great Britain and Ireland since 1960*. London: Bruccoli Clark, 1985, 400–4.

Copplestone, Fenella. 'Paul Muldoon and the Exploding Sestina'. *PN Review* 106 (November–December, 1995) 33–36.

—'Strange Letters: Reading and Writing in Recent Irish Poetry', in Paul Hyland and Neil Sammels (eds), *Irish Writing: Exile and Subversion. Insights*. London: Macmillan, 1991, 240–42.

Corcoran, Neil (ed.). *The Chosen Ground: Essays on the Contemporary Poetry of Northern Ireland*. Dufour: Seren Books, 1992.

Engle, John. 'A Modest Refusal: Yeats, MacNeice, and Irish Poetry', in Fleming, *Learning the Trade* 71–85.

Feinstein, Elaine. 'The Judges' Report'. *Poetry Book Society Bulletin* 164 (Spring, 1995) 8–9.

Fleming, Deborah (ed.), *Learning the Trade: Essays on W. B. Yeats and Contemporary Poetry*. Locust Hill Literary Studies 11. West Cornwall: Locust Hill Press, 1993.

Frazier, Adrian. 'Juniper Otherwise Known: Poems by Paulin and Muldoon'. *Éire–Ireland*. 19.1 (Spring, 1984) 123–33.

Garratt, Robert F. 'The Poetic State of Ireland'. *Concerning Poetry* 20 (1987) 158–64.

Gauthier, Dominique. '*Meeting the British* de Paul Muldoon. Brève Rencontres, Libres Parcours.' *Études Irlandaises* 15.1 (June, 1990) 97–110.

Goodby, John. '"Armageddon, Armagh-geddon": Language and Crisis in the Poetry of Paul Muldoon', in Brigit Bramsback and Martin Croghan (eds), *Proceedings of the Ninth International Congress of the International Association for the Study of Anglo-Irish Literature*. Vol. 1. Uppsala: Almqvist and Wiksell, 1988, 229–41.

—'Hermeneutic Hermeticism: Paul Muldoon and the Northern Irish Poetic', in C. C. Barfoot (ed.), *In Black and Gold: Contiguous Traditions in Post-War British and Irish Poetry*. Studies in Literature 13. Amsterdam: Rodopi, 1994, 137–68.

—'"The Narrow Road to the Deep North": Paul Muldoon, the Sonnet, and the Politics of Poetic Form'. *Swansea Review* 14 (1995) 26–35.

Hancock, Tim. 'Identity Problems in Paul Muldoon's "The More a Man Has the More a Man Wants"'. *Honest Ulsterman* 97 (Spring, 1994) 57–64.

Hufstader, Jonathan. *Tongue of Water, Teeth of Stones: Northern Irish Poetry and Social Violence.* Kentucky: The University Press of Kentucky, 1999.

Johnston, Dillon. 'Poetic Discoveries and Inventions of America'. *Colby Quarterly* 28.4 (December, 1992) 202–15.

Kenneally, Michael (ed.). *Poetry in Contemporary Irish Literature.* Irish Literary Studies 35. Gerrards Cross: Colin Smythe, 1992.

Kendall, Tim. 'Paul Muldoon and the Art of Allusion'. *Verse* 11.1 (Spring, 1994) 78–83.

— '"Parallel to the Parallel Realm": Muldoon's *Madoc – A Mystery*'. *Irish University Review* 25.2 (Autumn–Winter, 1995) 232–241.

— *Paul Muldoon.* Brigend: Seren, 1996.

Kendall, Tim and Peter McDonald (eds). *Paul Muldoon: Critical Essays.* Liverpool: Liverpool University Press, 2003.

Kirkland, Richard. 'Paul Muldoon's "Immram" and "Immrama": Writing for a Sense of Displacement'. *Essays in Poetics* 17.1 (April, 1992) 35–43.

Marken, Ronald. 'Paul Muldoon's "Juggling a Red Hot Brick in an Old Sock"'. *Éire–Ireland* 24.1 (Spring, 1989) 79–91.

Maxwell, D. E. S. 'Imagining the North: Violence and the Writers'. *Éire–Ireland* 8.2 (Summer, 1973) 91–107.

— 'Contemporary Poetry in the North of Ireland', in Douglas Dunn (ed.), *Two Decades of Writing.* Cheshire: Carcanet, 1975, 166–85.

McCracken, Kathleen. 'A Northern Perspective: Dual Vision in the Poetry of Paul Muldoon'. *Canadian Journal of Irish Studies* 26.2 (December, 1990) 92–103.

McCurry, J. '"S'Crap": Colonialism Indicted in the Poetry of Paul Muldoon'. *Éire–Ireland* 27.3 (Fall, 1992) 92–109.

— 'A Land "Not Borrowed but Purloined": Paul Muldoon's Indians'. *New Hibernia Review* 1.3 (Autumn, 1997) 40–51.

McDonald, Peter. *Mistaken Identities: Poetry and Northern Ireland.* Oxford: Clarendon Press, 1997.

Midzunoe, Yuichi. 'A Quest for Identity in Modern Irish Poets: Hewitt, Kennelly, Heaney and Muldoon', in Tjebbe A. Westendorp and Jane Mallinson (eds), *Politics and the Rhetoric of Poetry: Perspectives on Modern Anglo-Irish Poetry.* Amsterdam: Rodopi, 1995, 57–63.

O'Neill, Charles L. 'Paul Muldoon's *Madoc: A Mystery* and the Romantic Poets'. *Wordsworth Circle.* 24.1 (Winter, 1993) 54–56.

O' Séaghdha, Barra. 'The Tasks of the Translator'. *Irish Review* 14 (Autumn, 1993) 143–47.

Rácz, István D. 'Mask Lyrics in the Poetry of Paul Muldoon and Modern Irish Poetry', in Donald E. Morse, Csilla Bertha and István Pálffy (eds), *A Small Nation's*

Contribution to the World: Essays on Anglo-Irish Literature and Language. Gerrards Cross: Colin Smythe, 1993, 107–18.

Stabler, Jane. 'Alive in the Midst of Questions: A Survey of the Poetry of Paul Muldoon'. *Verse* 8.2 (Summer, 1991) 52–61.

Stanfield, Paul Scott. 'Another Side of Paul Muldoon'. *North Dakota Quarterly.* 57.1 (Winter, 1989) 129–43.

Tell, Carol. 'Utopia in the New World: Paul Muldoon's America'. *Bullán* 2.2 (Winter–Spring, 1996) 67–82.

Wills, Clair. *Improprieties: Politics and Sexuality in Northern Irish Poetry.* Oxford: Clarendon Press, 1993.

Wilson, William A. 'Paul Muldoon and the Poetics of Sexual Difference'. *Contemporary Literature.* 28.3 (Fall, 1987) 317–31.

— 'The Grotesqueries of Paul Muldoon, "Immram" to *Madoc*'. *Éire–Ireland* 28.4 (Winter, 1993) 115–132.

— 'Yeats, Muldoon, and Heroic History', in Fleming, *Learning the Trade* 21–38.

Zinnes, Harriet. 'Paul Muldoon: "Time-Switched to the Trough"'. *Hollins Critic* 38.1 (February, 1996) 1–12.

Index